The
TEXAS HILL COUNTRY
Book
A Complete Guide

Eleanor S. Morris

THE
TEXAS HILL
COUNTRY

A Complete Guide

INCLUDING AUSTIN AND SAN ANTONIO

SECOND EDITION

ELEANOR S. MORRIS

Berkshire House Publishers
Lee, Massachusetts

On the Cover and Frontispiece
Front Cover: *Bluebonnets on Willow City Loop Road near Fredericksburg, Texas.* Photo © Dick
    Dietrich/Dietrich Photography.
Frontispiece: Photo by Eleanor S. Morris
Back cover: Author photo by Herman Morris.

The Texas Hill Country Book: A Complete Guide
Copyright © 1997, 2000 by Berkshire House Publishers
Cover and interior photographs © 1997, 2000 by credited sources
Maps by Ron Toelke Associates.

Library of Congress Cataloging-in-Publication Data

Folwell, Morris, 1944-
    The Texas Hill Country book : a complete guide ; including Austin and San Antonio /
Eleanor S. Morris.—2nd ed.
        p. cm. — (Great destinations series, ISSN 1056-7968)
    Includes bibliographical references and index.
    ISBN 1-58157-017-1
        1. Texas Hill Country (Tex.)—Guidebooks. I. Title. II. Series.

    F392.T47 M67 2000
    917.64'30463—dc21
                                                        99-057103

ISBN: 1-58157-017-1
ISSN: 1056-7968 (series)

Managing Editor: Philip Rich. Design and composition: Dianne Pinkowitz. Cover design
and composition: Jane McWhorter. Maps: Ron Toelke Associates. Index: Diane Brenner.

Berkshire House books are available at substantial discounts for bulk purchases by corpora-
tions and other organizations for promotions and premiums. Special personalized editions
can also be produced in large quantities. For more information, contact:

Berkshire House Publishers
480 Pleasant St., Suite 5; Lee, Massachusetts 01238
800-321-8526

Manufactured in the United States of America
First printing 2000
10 9 8 7 6 5 4 3 2 1

No complimentary meals or lodgings were accepted by the author or reviewers in gathering
information for this work.

Berkshire House Publishers'
Great Destinations™ travel guidebook series

Right on the money.

— THE NEW YORK TIMES

. . . a crisp and critical approach, for travelers who want to live like locals.

— USA TODAY

Great Destinations™ guidebooks are known for their comprehensive, critical coverage of regions of extraordinary cultural interest and natural beauty. The authors in this series are professional travel writers who have lived for many years in the regions they describe. Each title in this series is continuously updated with each printing, in order to insure accurate and timely information. All of the books contain over 100 photographs and maps.

Neither the publisher, the authors, the reviewers, nor other contributors accept complimentary lodgings, meals, or any other consideration (such as advertising) while gathering information for any book in this series.

Current titles available:
The Adirondack Book
The Berkshire Book
The Charleston, Savannah & Coastal Islands Book
The Chesapeake Bay Book
The Coast of Maine Book
The Hamptons Book
The Monterey Bay, Big Sur & Gold Coast Wine Country Book
The Nantucket Book
The Newport & Narragansett Bay Book
The Napa & Sonoma Book
The Santa Fe & Taos Book
The Sarasota, Sanibel Island & Naples Book
The Texas Hill Country Book
Wineries of the Eastern States

If you are traveling to, moving to, residing in, or just interested in any (or all!) of these enchanting regions, a **Great Destinations**™ guidebook is a superior companion. Honest and painstakingly critical, full of information only a local can provide, **Great Destinations**™ guidebooks give you all the practical knowledge you need to enjoy the best of each region. Why not own them all?

Acknowledgments

A bit of the magic of the Texas Hill Country is found in the attitude of the the friendly, open folks who inhabit the region. There are too many to name them all here, but I'd like to thank everyone I spoke with along the many miles I covered while writing the guide, as well as those of the local Convention and Visitors Bureaus and Chambers of Commerce who were so helpful in providing information and their county and town. Special thanks to Gwen Spain, Director of the Austin Visitors Bureau; Ernest J. Loeffler, Jr., and his helpful staff at the San Antonio Convention and Visitors Bureau; and Patricia Moore of the Bandera County Convention & Visitors Bureau. These people were very busy but always ready to help.

Thanks, too, to the folks at Berkshire House — Dale Gelfand, editor; Jean Rousseau, publisher; Carol Bosco Baumann, marketing and sales director; Mary Osak, office manager; and Philip Rich, managing editor. They helped me put everything together.

Contents

CHAPTER ONE
A Land Worth Fighting for
HISTORY
1

CHAPTER TWO
On the Trail
TRANSPORTATION
12

CHAPTER THREE
The Violet Crown
AUSTIN AND TRAVIS COUNTY
21

CHAPTER FOUR
Out In the Territory
HILL COUNTRY WEST AND SOUTH OF AUSTIN
BLANCO, BURNET, GILLESPIE, HAYS, KIMBLE, LLANO, & MASON COUNTIES
79

CHAPTER FIVE
Along the River
SAN ANTONIO AND BEXAR COUNTY
163

CHAPTER SIX
Old West and Old Country
**THE HILL COUNTRY WEST AND
NORTH OF SAN ANTONIO**
BANDERA, COMAL, KENDALL, KERR, MEDINA, REAL, & UVALDE COUNTIES
200

CHAPTER SEVEN
Hill Country Help
INFORMATION
281

Introduction

Welcome to the second edition of this guide to the Texas Hill Country.

Since the first edition, Austin and San Antonio have continued to grow at a fast pace, nevertheless retaining their charm. These two vibrant metroplexes offer an astounding array of places to see and things to do, mixing and merging the traditional and the contemporary and a variety of cultural influences. The two cities also serve as gateways to a lesser-known but deeply treasured gift of nature and history: the Texas Hill Country.

The Hill Country has been slower to change — a good thing. To many, the Hill Country is a magical place — the view is wider, the air fresher, rivers clearer, people friendlier. Part of the charm is the Old Country *gemütlichkeit* of towns like Fredericksburg and Boerne. The there's the authentic cowboy ambience of Banders, the serenity of Utopia, and the beauty of the Lost Maples at Leakey. And best of all, it's true; it's not the imagination of a bewitched few. In the Hill Country the horizon is farther, the views greater, the air is clearer, the rivers and streams are cleaner, the people are friendlier — and the road is all yours.

You'll find neither traffic or crime; what you will find is that Nature has smiled on the Hill Country with rivers, lakes, deep caverns, and, of course, the hills. Hills high and low, hills undulating and steep, hills and valleys with panoramic views as far as the eye can see (and in Texas that can be pretty far). Small valleys contain scattered farms and ranches where fat cattle or sheep graze among the rocks and cedar. Many farmhouses and other buildings are built of the limestone, rocks pride from the soil and blocks quarried from the hills. Oak and mesquite line the roads, and every once in a while cactus, either yucca or prickly pear, appears in the underbrush amid the rocks.

Drive for miles and miles, and you won't see a billboard or sign of any kind. In fact, if you ignore the telephone and power lines along the way there'd be nothing except the wooded hills, broad ranchlands, and wide vistas. Good rural roads take you winding through the hills and valleys, down to the low-water crossings (read the gauges: flash floods can occur), over wild roller-coaster roads, and up and away to the highest, most picturesque spots. In between, small towns welcome you with their history, art, regional foods, crafts, and festivals. Some towns have several motels and inns, others may have only one, but Texas Hill Country hospitality is everywhere.

When the Texas Department of Commerce queries out-of-state visitors on what impresses them most about Texas, the number one answer is "the friendliness of the people."

Where is the Hill Country? The geographical boundaries of the Hill Country are rather hard to describe, but loosely the region encompasses the area of spring-fed streams and hills along the southern edge of the Balcones Escarpment south of the Edwards Plateau and east to the boundaries of Travis and Bexar counties along Interstate 35.

The Balcones Escarpment is a lower extension of the Great Plains stretching from the High Plains of northwest Texas at the foot of the Rocky Mountains southward to the Rio Grande. The escarpment, which angles across the state from south to north, causes heavy warm air from the Gulf of Mexico to release most of its moisture on the lower eastern portion of the state, saving the Hill Country from the arid climate of the western part of the state.

The Burnet-Llano Basin lies at the junction of the Colorado and Llano rivers in Burnet and Llano counties on the northern reaches of the Hill Country. Minerals were found in abundance here; the town of Llano was once known as the Pittsburgh of the South.

The Highland Lakes north from Austin to Burnet and Llano counties offer some of the finest fishing in the entire state, were formed by a series of dams impounded along the Colorado River, beginning with Lake Buchanan to the north. This large reservoir, and the one to the south, Lake Travis in the western part of Travis County, form the boundaries of the Highland Lakes. In between, from north to south, there are three small reservoirs: Inks Lake, Lyndon B. Johnson (originally called Granite Shoals), and Marble Falls. Lake Austin is just north of the city of Austin, and Town Lake flows through the city, making pleasant and possible the outdoor activities that add so much to the Austin experience.

So you might say that the Hill country is mound after mound of undulating hills all the way to the Edwards Plateau south of Staked Plains — the *Llano Estacado*. The farther west you go, the higher the hills become, until they almost seem like small mountains before they drop down to the Badlands, the desert where outlaws like John King Fisher lurked in the old days.

Amid the rocky soil and undulating hills there is water, water, everywhere. Ten rivers (counting Onion Creek) flow through the Hill Country, providing fishing, swimming, rafting, and canoeing much of the year; the Colorado, Frio, Guadalupe, Llano, Medina, Nueces, Pedernales, Sabinal, San Antonio, and San Marcos, to take them alphabetically. Cool, even cold, and especially popular in the hot Texas summer, are the springs along the eastern rim of the Hill Country: Barton Springs at Austin, San Marcos Springs at San Marcos, Comal Springs in New Braunfels, and several in San Antonio.

Eleanor S. Morris
Austin, Texas

THE WAY THIS BOOK WORKS

The Hill Country of Texas covers a large area in the center of the state and is composed of an assortment of counties and towns, each of them prizing their separate identities, as well as being part of a whole entity, also prized:

the "Hill Country." The sixteen counties covered by this book have been divided into four main regions:

The gateways to the Hill County:
  Austin and Travis County
  San Antonio and Bexar County
The remaining counties of the Hill Country:
  The seven Hill Country counties west and south of Austin:
  Blanco, Burnet, Gillespie, Hays, Kimble, Llano, and Mason.
The seven Hill Country counties west and north of San Antonio:
  Bandera, Comal, Kendall, Kerr, Medina, Real, and Uvalde

While we have divided the Hill Country in this way to make such a large area manageable, we also want to make clear that the Hill Country is one homogeneous area, both geographically and culturally — although, of course, each county treasures its particular history and the unique features of its landscape. However, except for a small sign by the side of the road naming which county you are entering, you'll generally find that it is indistinguishable from the one you are leaving as you cross the county line.

Within these geographical groupings, listings are arranged alphabetically — first by town or topic, and then by establishment names. Some entries, such as those in the "Shopping" sections, are usually arranged by category; hence, all the craft shops appear together.

Factual information was researched at the latest possible time before publication, but be advised that many of these "facts" are subject to change. Chefs and innkeepers come and go, hours change, shops appear and disappear. When in doubt, phone ahead.

Specific information (such as addresses and location, telephone numbers, hours of business, and a summary of special features or restrictions) is presented in the left-hand column or at the beginning of a listing.

Because actual prices for lodgings and restaurants are constantly changing, we have noted price ranges instead, explained below:

Lodging prices are given for a per-room rate, double occupancy. It's a good idea to phone ahead for any price changes or other information and for reservations:

Lodging Rates:

Inexpensive	Up to $65
Moderate	$65 to $100
Expensive	$100 to $175
Very Expensive:	Over $175

These rates do not include room taxes or service charges. (Note: EP, or European Plan, means that breakfast is included.)

Restaurant prices indicate the cost of an individual's meal, which includes appetizer, entrée, and dessert, but does not include cocktails, wine, tax, or tip. Restaurants with a prix-fixe menu are noted accordingly.

Dining Rates:

In Austin and San Antonio:

Inexpensive	Up to $20
Moderate	$20 to $30
Expensive	$30 to $50
Very Expensive:	Over $50

Out in the Counties

Inexpensive	Up to $10
Moderate	$10 to $20
Expensive	$20 to $35
Very Expensive:	Over $35

Meals are abbreviated as follows:
    B: Breakfast
    L: Lunch
    D: Dinner
    SB: Sunday Brunch

Credit cards are abbreviated as follows:
    AE: American Express
    CB: Carte Blanche
    D: Discover
    DC: Diner's Club
    MC: MasterCard
    V: Visa

The
TEXAS HILL COUNTRY
Book
A Complete Guide

CHAPTER ONE
A Land Worth Fighting Over
HISTORY

Eleanor S. Morris

The massive dome of Precambrian pink granite for which Enchanted Rock State Natural Area in Gillespie County is named.

From the beginning, Texas has been a place coveted by all who passed this way, and the Hill Country fought over practically to the present day. First came the Paleo-Americans, then the fierce Plains Indians. Then the French came, seeking land for France; and then the Spanish, seeking gold, silver, and souls for Spain. Their colonists — Mexican-Indians, and the Anglos enticed there with promises of land — also strove to claim the territory as their own.

Why did they want this land, this hilly, rocky, thin-soiled ground covered with cacti and mesquite, unsuitable for farming? The Anglo settlers who finally tamed the Hill Country with their settlements became ranchers, raising herds of cattle, sheep, and goats. Here they could take advantage of the Hill Country's clear and plentiful spring water, magnificent rivers, and invigorating air and enjoy the beauty of the open space.

These days, of course, it's friendliness, not fighting, that is found throughout the Hill Country, from the sophisticated mix of cultures and creativity of Austin and San Antonio to the down-home informality out in the surrounding counties.

NATURAL HISTORY

HILL COUNTRY GEOGRAPHY

To begin to understand the Hill Country geologically, it helps to divide the region into three areas. The larger area to the north of the Hill Country is the Llano Estacado (Staked Plains), itself divided into the North and South Plains. The Edwards Plateau, forming more than half of the lower regions of the Llano Estacado, extends eastward toward the Balcones Escarpment or fault, a rugged, flat limestone table that extends from the Rio Grande at Del Rio eastward to San Antonio and north to Austin on the Colorado River. The Balcones Escarpment, rising to heights of 300 to 1,000 feet, provides a clear break between the High Plains/Edwards Plateau and the coastal plains.

The area of the Edwards Plateau that lies on the edge of the Balcones fault is divided into two sections: the Hill Country, the popular name for this land of hills and spring-fed streams, and the Burnet-Llano Basin lying at the junction of the Colorado and Llano Rivers in Burnet and Llano Counties. For our purposes the latter is also included in the Hill Country.

Geologically, the hilly central Texas basin is in an intermediate stage of erosion between the youth of the Edwards Plateau and the old age of the central lowlands. Separated from the coastal plains by the fault zone, the Hill Country rises with low, wooded areas along the uplifted side of the limestone fracture.

ROCKS AND WATER EVERYWHERE

A shallow sea covered much of Texas during the Cretaceous Period, about 100 million years ago. The land was part of a reef system inhabited by shelled sea creatures. As these creatures died and their shells decomposed over the millennia, thick beds of limestone were formed that make up the Edwards Plateau.

For millions of years, layer after layer built up over the Edwards until powerful earthquakes uplifted the land, forming hills and shearing the rock, exposing sections of the limestone formations. Water filtered through the cracks, dissolving millions of holes in the porous limestone, forming both large caves and tiny honeycomblike holes in the rock.

If you peeled away the tops of many of the hills of the Hill Country, you'd find lots of these holes, carved over the millions of years by underground rivers and streams. Many are still filled with water today; others, relatively dry, form networks of caves that have become tourist attractions. Others are home to creatures that have adapted to life in the underground: Scientists have discovered dozens of rare species, such as a blind cave millipede and a harvestman (a relative of the spider), which have evolved over hundreds of thousands or millions of years, totally isolated underground.

With only a thin layer of topsoil, barely covering the limestone bedrock, the Hill Country is not conducive to agriculture, even with its wealth of water. Barton Creek, for instance, rises from limestone strata in the Balcones Fault formed millions of years ago when the area west of Austin uplifted to create the Edwards Plateau. The thin limestone-based soil does support cedar, mesquite, post oak, and live oak in abundance, along with laurel, sumac, prickly pear cactus, and range grass. And parts of the Hill Country, those near reliable water sources, are famous for their peaches: Stonewall and Fredericksburg, in particular, lay claim to exceptionally tasty fruit.

GOATS, SHEEP, CATTLE — AND ARMADILLOS

The land of the Hill Country is more suited for the grazing of cattle, sheep, and goats, and rural residents are usually ranchers rather than farmers. There is grass for the cattle, weeds for sheep, and tree foliage for goats — the region is the nation's leading producer of angora and mohair as well as one of the country's leading sheep and wool areas. Angora goats from Turkey were introduced to the Hill Country in 1849. Just about all the angora goats in the United States live on ranches between Uvalde in the Hill Country and San Angelo to the west; Texas produces 97 percent of all U.S. mohair.

White-tailed deer, jackrabbits, possums, raccoons, and wild turkeys all inhabit the brush, and the roads are strewn with the bodies of one of nature's most interesting animals, the armadillo — so many that the nine-banded armadillo (*Dasypus novemcinctus*) is a Texas joke as well as a Texas symbol.

In 1981 a resolution that the armadillo be declared officially the "state mammal" — joining the bluebonnet, the mockingbird, the longhorn, the pecan tree, and chili as a state symbol — was presented to the legislature. The House of Representatives OK'd it, but the Senate balked when adversaries substituted the opossum, buffalo, and even the unicorn in opposition. So that was the end of the "official" armadillo.

SOCIAL HISTORY

THE FIRST TEXANS

Historians believe that tens of thousands of years before recorded history, the first humans to take possession of Texas soil were people who crossed the narrow land bridge that rose after the Ice Age to connect Asia with Alaska.

Archaeologists named these original Texans Paleo-Americans. Hunters and scavengers, they roamed across the High Plains, leaving behind them nothing more than traces of their tools and bones all the way from Clovis, New Mexico, through Abilene, Texas. Walking from cactus to mesquite in search of food,

A portrait of Mirabeau Buonaparte Lamar. As president of the Republic of Texas, he was instrumental in establishing Austin as the Texas capital.

Courtesy of Austin History Center, Austin Public Library: #C00197

these early Texans evidently had learned to make fire, perhaps to protect themselves with basic clothing, and to make simple tools of bone and stone.

Moving eastward, they came to the Llano Estacado, hunting the mastodon and the massive forerunner of today's buffalo, until they came to the banks of the Hill Country's Pedernales River, just above the Balcones Escarpment.

Then they disappeared, to be replaced by newer arrivals across the land bridge. Europeans later gave these newcomers the name of Indian. While many of them went south into Mexico and Central and South America, others scattered across the High Plains of Texas into the central plateaus, chasing the bison across the arid land. These groups of "Llano Man," as anthropologists named them, are identified by their hunting tool, a primitive flint spear called the Clovis fluted point.

Those who penetrated farther into the Hill Country, to the spectacular scenery formed by ancient limestone above the Balcones Escarpment, discovered they could live on deer and smaller game, until they, too, vanished, leaving evidence of some form of ritual cannibalism from this Archaic Age.

NATIVE AMERICANS

Next, a series of Indians appeared in various areas of Texas: the Karankawas in the coastal bend; the Caddos in the piney woods of East Texas; the Coahuiltecans, who came the closest to the Hill Country; and the Tonkawas, who roamed over the Balcones Escarpment, ranging from the Edwards Plateau east to the Brazos Valley.

A far fiercer tribe held sway over the richest hunting grounds of the Pleistocene Age, the High Plains above the central Texas plateau with its millions of bison, antelope, deer, and elk: the Apache. Distinct from the Western Apache (the Navaho, San Carlos, Chiricahua, and Mescalero, who settled in Arizona and New Mexico), these Eastern Apache (Lipan, Palomas, Carlanas, and Jicarillos) made themselves masters of the High Plains, learning to live off buffalo and warring with the Tonkawas.

THE SPANISH IN TEXAS

In 1540 Texas was invaded from the south by a new contender. Alvar Nuñez Cabeza de Vaca, from Spain, had already made landfall, shipwrecked on the Gulf Coast in 1528; his records were the first written mention of the land. Along came Francisco Vásquez de Coronado, annoyed but undaunted by his failure to find the famed cities of gold in Arizona or New Mexico. (What he expected to be the fabled city of Cibola turned out to be a dusty Zuni pueblo.) With his retinue of three hundred Spanish, Mexican Indians, and priests determined to convert the natives to Christianity, Coronado pursued his dream of fabulous New Spain gold and silver into what was to become Texas. Refusing to return to Spain as a failure, he and his horde sowed the seeds of their own destruction.

For the Spanish brought horses, something unknown in the Southwest at the time. Freely helping themselves to the animals, mounted Apaches successfully harried and discouraged the Spanish for the next 200 years. Swooping down from the plains on horseback, they burned the missions and *presidios* (forts) in San Antonio and elsewhere that the Spanish were desperately trying to establish.

Meanwhile, the horse had filtered northward, and by the early 1700s a group of fierce Plains Indians called Comanche by the Spanish also found a natural affinity for horseback hunting and warfare: Mounted, they believed themselves invincible. Historians have compared them to the mounted hordes of Genghis Kahn as they came thundering south to the Llano Estacado and the Balcones Escarpment to plunder a far richer concentration of bison than anything seen on their barren plains.

They learned to ride for thousands of miles, to strike and turn back, and they attacked the Lipan Apache, driving them south. One hundred fifty years before the white settlers of Texas learned to dread the "Comanche Moon," the Apache first and then the Spanish knew that on nights when the moon was bright enough to see by and the grass tall and fresh to feed their horses, the Comanches were sure to strike.

THE FRENCH THREAT

At the same time as the Spanish were establishing their missions, the French, spilling over from Louisiana, were attempting to establish a foothold in this part of the New World, too. Robert Cavelier de La Salle (who

Eleanor S. Morris

Now a museum, the French Legation was built in 1841 by Alphonse Dubois de Saligny, French chargé d'affaires to the Republic of Texas.

came to a bad end in East Texas at the hands of either Karankawas or his own men; nobody knows for sure) and others of his ilk are important to the Texas story mainly because they were perceived as a threat by the Spanish.

Failing to settle colonists north of the Rio Grande through the missions, even as the French were spreading into Texas from the east, the Spanish attempted at least to establish the "rancheros" that were successful in New Spain (northern Mexico), ranches that gave rise to the *vaquero* (cowboy) and other icons of today's Western culture. But the Indian peril never stopped: Apaches still struck from the west, and from the north Comanches never ceased their moonlight raids in spring and fall.

The combination of hostile Indians, the failure of widespread conversion of the less warlike Indians to Christianity, and the decline of Spanish colonies above the Rio Grande contributed to the end of the Spanish attempt to gain dominion over Texas at this time. By the beginning of the 18th century, all was abandoned as they finally retreated south, leaving behind them only the ruins of one or two missions and lean and longhorn cattle.

For the three centuries following Cabeza de Vaca and Coronado, the missions, and the encounters with the French, Texas remained virtually unoccupied by Europeans — except for three small settlements that the Spanish, in response to the French threat, had established by 1800: San Antonio on the southern edge of the Hill Country, Goliad south toward the border, and

Nacogdoches in East Texas. (It would not be until the 20th century that Hispanic influence of any weight would be felt in Texas as a whole; in the Hill Country this would be mainly in San Antonio.) Attempting to ensure their continued presence in this part of Texas, the Spanish devised a novel plan to populate the area — although it was one that proved to be their undoing. This was the "empresario system," whereby they offered huge grants of land to those who would undertake to bring in large groups of settlers.

EARLY ANGLO SETTLERS

Around the time of the American Revolution, hardy Anglo frontiersmen had pushed their way from the Atlantic seaboard to the banks of the Mississippi. Several thousand new American citizens emigrated west to Missouri and Upper Louisiana, and they prospered. Why not invite these hardened pioneers to settle Texas? the Spanish reasoned. But the land still belonged to Spain; to alleviate the danger of an Anglo takeover, two conditions were imposed: The settlers had to swear allegiance to the king of Spain and embrace Catholicism.

Having little or no connection with the revolution that had raged behind their backs as they forged westward, frontiersmen such as Daniel Boone, William Morgan, and their fellows had no compunction against the first condition; as for the second, so long as they agreed to become Roman Catholics, they were assured officially that their religious practices would not be scrutinized. Under these circumstances, how could they refuse the title of *empresario,* which came with enormous acreages of free land?

But while the Spanish sought to attract these Anglos to Texas and ensure their loyalty to Spain, they overlooked those few Mexicans who had earlier taken advantage of the empresario system. The Mexican-born Spanish colonists and Mexican-Indian mestizos became impatient with Spanish rule. Their rebellion in 1810 led to the Mexican War of Independence, and Mexico became a sovereign nation.

One American who had taken advantage of the Spanish land offer, swearing allegiance to Spain, was Moses Austin; in 1821 he was granted permission to settle 300 colonists on his land. But he died 6 months later, leaving it to his son, Stephen Fuller Austin, to take over, forming the first Anglo colony in Texas.

Every Texas schoolchild knows the story of Stephen F. Austin's "First Colony" of 300: After the elder Austin's death, Mexico at first refused to honor the land grant. A year's worth of protest by Stephen Austin finally convinced the Mexican government to recognize the claim, but it was only on the condition that Mexican law prevail among the settlers.

Soon other Anglo colonists followed. By the mid-1830s around 30,000 were living in Texas, outnumbering the Mexicans by about four to one and rejecting the Spanish language and Spanish-Mexican culture in favor of their own. The Mexican government viewed their growing numbers with alarm, but attempts to discipline and disarm them failed.

THE TEXAS WAR OF INDEPENDENCE

Fighting erupted at the Anglo settlement of Gonzales on October 2, 1835, when the Mexicans demanded the town's cannon from the colonists. Told to "Come and get it!" the Mexicans not only lost the first battle of the Texas Revolution, but the taunt also has served as the Gonzales motto ever since.

In December colonists captured San Antonio, held by Mexicans, who then agreed to withdraw to Mexico. But on March 2, when Texans were meeting at Washington-on-the-Brazos to declare their independence by establishing the Republic of Texas, General Antonio López de Santa Anna arrived to recapture San Antonio.

There followed the famous Battle of the Alamo. The Mexicans began a siege of the presidio on February 24. The fort was defended by 155 men, including Davy Crockett, James Bowie, and Colonel William Travis. "We consider death preferable to disgrace. . . . For God's sake and the sake of the country, send us reinforcements," Travis wrote, threatened by more than five thousand Mexicans. Refusing to surrender to Santa Anna, all the Texans perished in hand-to-hand fighting.

After the Alamo fell, Colonel James Fannin, commanding 100 men at Goliad, was ordered to retreat; but before he could do so, he was overtaken by the Mexicans. Again greatly outnumbered, he surrendered after a hopeless battle. Imprisoned in Goliad, the entire force was slaughtered in cold blood by order of Santa Anna.

This outrage gave the Texans a double battle cry: "Remember the Alamo! Remember Goliad!" The two forces met for the last time at San Jacinto near today's city of Houston. In a surprise attack during the Mexicans' siesta, General Sam Houston prevailed over the larger force, and Santa Anna, caught unawares, was captured. (He was later freed.)

THE REPUBLIC OF TEXAS

The republic endured for ten years, with Sam Houston elected president on July 23, 1836. However, it was a straggling frontier community with hardly more than 40,000 people, and recognition, if not annexation, by the United States, became a sought-after solution to the problems of a republic with no economy and no money, no banks, no improved roads, no schools, and, worse, with a territory still occupied by hostile Indians, especially in the Hill Country, the High Plains, and the Panhandle.

A resolution for statehood fared badly in both the Senate and the House. Northerners, ignorant of Texas geography, were afraid that adding Texas to the United States would expand slavery throughout the Southwest (even though slavery had come as far as it could go — the narrow belt of cotton plantations along the Brazos).

The Texas solution to this impasse was to pretend to be indifferent to its fate as part of the Union. Stephen Austin leaked the information that if the United States was not prepared to extend aid and recognition, Texas might have to look elsewhere — England, for example. Neither Austin nor Houston seriously considered becoming involved with Great Britain, but the idea of a new British colony in the middle of America finally made an impression on the antiexpansionists of the Northeast. Andrew Jackson was able to cap his career as president by recognizing Texas. And finally, in 1845, still fearing Britain's motives, the United States Congress narrowly approved the annexation of Texas.

Houston was elected to the Senate soon after, spending nearly fourteen years in office, until 1859. He was then elected governor of Texas but was deposed when his pleas for national unity were repulsed by the people of Texas, who voted to secede from the Union during the Civil War.

Although Texas participation in the War Between the States was limited to supplying men, material, and services, it cost her dearly. Ninth state in the union in wealth per capita in 1860, Texas was thirty-sixth when Reconstruction ended in 1880. Texas also was one of the last Confederate states to be readmitted to the Union — not until 1870.

SETTLING THE HILL COUNTRY

Back in the days of the republic, Texas was still working on the problem of underpopulation. Just as the Spanish and Mexicans had before, the new government employed the empresario system to populate the empty frontier. German-born Henry Fisher had acquired a huge land grant north and west of Austin, in country still held by the Comanche. He was commissioned by Sam Houston to represent the republic to the German states of the Rhine to attract colonists to the Hill Country. The timing was perfect: Life was hard in the Rhineland in the 1840s, with crop failure and economic depression. Twenty-five altruistic noblemen had formed an organization to support emigration and to encourage the Germans, once in Texas, to stay together. This was the Adelsverein, a Society for the Protection of German Immigrants to Texas.

Under the leadership of Prince Carl of Solms-Braunfels, the Adelsverein raised $80,000 to purchase land and settle German pioneers. Enter Fisher, who in June of 1844 convinced the gullible Prince Carl to spend $9,000 on the purchase of 4,000,000 of his own acres. Misrepresenting the land, he claimed that it was accessible, fertile, and perfectly suited for coastal commerce; never mind that it was Comanche territory. The first contingent of immigrants was to arrive in December, and Prince Carl sailed to the new land to prepare for their arrival.

Once there, he saw how he had been taken. There was nothing to be done but to make other arrangements, and he looked for a second site where his people could settle and organize their resources before expanding into Indian country. He found 9,000 acres on the Guadalupe River thirty miles northeast of San Antonio, and there at the foot of the Balcones Escarpment he laid out a town that he called — what else? — New Braunfels.

Austin's Congress Avenue in the late 19th century, viewed from the river to the Capitol.

This done, he sailed for home to retrieve his bride, Princess Sophie. But the princess balked at the idea of adventure in a raw, uncivilized new land, and Prince Carl never returned to Texas. When in Galveston to board the ship home, however, he had met the man who replaced him. This was another nobleman but, unlike the prince, one who renounced his title. Baron von Meuesbach became plain John O. Meuesbach, citizen of Texas, fated to become the salvation of the town of Fredericksburg.

The history of the German settlers in the Hill Country is told in greater detail in the stories of their counties later on in this guide. Suffice it to say that many of the customs, crafts, and traditions of the "old country" have been carefully preserved by the descendants of these hardy pioneers.

But the story of Hill Country settlement is not exclusively about the German immigrants, although they have contributed much to the culture of the area, outranking Mexicans as the second most numerous ethnic group in Texas. Other Hill Country settlers came from the east and southeast United States and from other places in Europe — Danes, Dutch, Belgians, French, Norwegians, Slavs, and Swedes purchased land from the holders of Spanish or Mexican land grants. Like the Germans, they began communities that have retained their distinctive ethnic qualities.

Henri Castro, the Texas consul general in Paris in 1839–42, was also a successful colonizer, bringing several hundred Alsatian colonists to the Medina River south of San Antonio in the early 1840s. There they began a thriving community that retained the Alsace-Lorraine ethnic culture and cuisine that are an important part of the Hill Country to this day.

Sturdy, thick houses of hand-quarried limestone bear witness to the determination of the settlers to endure with some comfort Hill Country weather, with extremes from 100-degree summer temperatures to below-20 degrees of a winter "blue norther" blowing down from the far northern reaches of Canada. The new residents of the Hill Country held the land dearly, building by hand miles of stone fences outlining fields and pastures.

THE HILL COUNTRY TODAY

Hill Country people strongly identify with their cultural heritage and are eager to share these many and diverse blessings with all comers. The land once fought over is today a land of friendly hospitality, delighting visitors with the rich variety of Hill Country traditions and attractions, new and old.

Courtesy of Austin History Center, Austin Public Libray: #C01090

The Driskill Hotel in Austin, established in 1886, brought grandeur to the Texas frontier.

CHAPTER TWO
On the Trail
TRANSPORTATION

A barge meanders along San Antonio's River Walk.

Folks came here first on horseback and in covered wagons; the first supplies for building Austin came by mule train. The San Antonio story offers a little more glamour: Here was the beginning of the Chisholm Trail, route of the cattlemen driving their herds north to the stockyards of Kansas City. The Old Spanish Trail from Laredo cut across the southeast corner of the territory that would become the city; the stagecoach route to El Paso passed straight through San Antonio from east to west — a century or two of steady traffic that shows no sign of letting up.

Today U.S. Highway 90 follows the same east-west trail through San Antonio that the stagecoach once plied — but it's a safe bet those passengers wouldn't recognize the route now. Both Austin and San Antonio are centers of growth and therefore traffic, with congestion possible throughout the day and into the early evening. Drivers here are urged to be "Texas friendly" in all their comings and goings. (There is talk of constructing an additional highway parallel to and east of Interstate 35, the north-south corridor between Austin and San Antonio.)

However, on the way out to the Hill Country, you'll find quieter, slower,

TEXAS HILL COUNTRY ACCESS

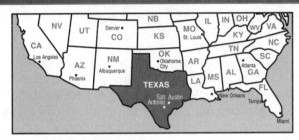

Approximate distances from outside Texas

From	To Austin	To San Antonio
Albuquerque	890 miles	818
Atlanta	917	993
Chicago	1245	1320
Denver	1067	945
Los Angeles	1428	1356
New Orleans	527	560
New York	1762	1838
Oklahoma City	390	466
Phoenix	1059	990
Washington, DC	1525	1600

Approximate distances within Texas

From	To Austin	To San Antonio
Austin	—	78
Brownsville	329	283
Dallas	201	279
El Paso	590	582
Houston	163	201
San Antonio	78	—
Texarkana	352	430

and wonderfully scenic routes — the Farm to Market Road and the Ranch Road. Leaving Austin and San Antonio behind via these smaller and less traveled roads, you'll feel as though the clock has been turned back and that you're seeing the same inspiring views that lured the Spanish, the cowboys, and the pioneers to these parts in the first place.

This chapter lists the many ways — plane, car, train, and bus — that you can arrive at the Hill Country's two gateway cities, Austin and San Antonio. It also details the modes of transportation available to you within these two cities: airport transit, taxi, limousine, local bus, rental car (and your own car). When you are ready to sally forth into the hills, you'll see several ways to get to and around the Hill Country — by bus or by car (your own or a rental).

GETTING TO THE HILL COUNTRY GATEWAY CITIES

Austin

GETTING TO AUSTIN BY AIR

Since Austin is both the capital of the state of Texas and the site of the main campus of the University of Texas (with a student enrollment that swells the population of the city by some 50,000 every year), most major airlines have frequent flights to the city from anywhere in the U.S.

Austin-Bergstrom International Airport (512-530-ABIA; www.ci.austin. tx.us./newairport; 3600 Presidential Blvd., Austin, TX 78719) is Austin's new airport (replacing Robert Mueller Municipal Airport), located at the site of the former Bergstrom Air Force Base. It is planned to meet Austin's air traffic needs far into the 21st century. The airport opened in the spring of 1999 with potential for international passenger service, which Mueller Airport did not have. The 45,000-square-foot terminal building is the result of years of work by airport planners, in order to meet the growing demand for expanded airport facilities. For reservations and information on flights, call:

America West	800-235-9292
American	800-433-7300
Continental	800-525-0280
Delta	800-221-1212
Northwest	800-225-2525
Southwest	800-435-9792
TWA Domestic	512-454-8900
TWA International	800-892-4141
United	800-241-6522
USAir	800-428-4322

Airport Transit Service
Gray Line Tours   800-950-8285

Taxicab Service
Metered service, set by city ordinance, is based on $1.50 for pickup and $1.50 per mile. Average fare from the airport to downtown is about $9 or $10.

American Yellow Checker Cab Company   512-452-9999
Austin Cab Company   512-478-2222
Roy's Taxis   512-482-0000

The Hill Country covers a lot of territory and is best experienced by car. However, if you're with a group — or want to pamper yourself — more than a dozen companies offer limousines, sedans, vans, "whatever is needed." Here are several:

Limousine Service
Austin Area Limousines   512-386-8600
                                       or 800-767-4090
Capitol City Limousines   512-474-2733
Lone Star Limousines   512-990-8482
Texas Limousine   512-335-6655

GETTING TO AUSTIN BY BUS

Gray Line Tours   800-950-8285   512-345-6789
Greyhound Bus Lines   800-231-2222   512-458-3823
Kerrville Bus Company   512-389-0319

GETTING TO AUSTIN BY TRAIN

Amtrak Station (800-872-7245; 250 N. Lamar Blvd. and W. Cesar Chavez St.) The Amtrak Eagle, a two-level passenger train, provides daily direct service to major U.S. hubs. On Monday, Wednesday, and Saturday, trains depart for San Antonio, New Orleans, and Los Angeles; on Sunday, Tuesday, and Thursday, trains leave for Chicago. Reservations are required.

GETTING TO AUSTIN BY CAR

Austin has one major interstate freeway leading into the city from north and south: **Interstate 35** between Laredo, TX–San Antonio–Austin–Duluth, MN. As in any other large city, it's a good idea to avoid the 7 to 9am and 5 to 7pm rush hour traffic if possible.

San Antonio

GETTING TO SAN ANTONIO BY AIR

San Antonio International Airport (210-207-3450; www.ci.sat.tx.us/aviation; 9800 Airport Blvd., San Antonio, TX 78216) is 13 miles from the Downtown River Walk and is directly linked via the McAllister Freeway (U.S. 281) to Broadway, which will take you straight to the Alamo in the heart of downtown San Antonio.

Terminal One:

Aerolitoral	800-237-6639
Delta	800-221-1212
Mexicana	800-531-7921
Northwest	800-225-2525
Southwest	800-435-9792
United	800-241-6522

Terminal Two:

Aeromexico	800-237-6639
America West	800-292-2274
American	800-433-7300
Continental	800-525-0280
Trans World Airlines	800-221-2000

Airport Transit Service
SATRANS: For reservations and fares, call 210-281-9900.

Taxicab Service
Metered service based on $2.10 for the first mile and $1.10 for each additional mile. Time to central business district is approximately 15 minutes, with the average fare being $15 plus tip. Four ride for the price of one; fare is subject to change.

GETTING TO SAN ANTONIO BY BUS

Greyhound Bus Lines/Trailways	800-231-2222
Kerrville Bus Company	210-227-5669

GETTING TO SAN ANTONIO BY TRAIN

Amtrak has service to San Antonio via Austin, Ft. Worth, Dallas, Little Rock, St. Louis, Springfield, and Chicago. Call 210-223-3226; toll-free reservations: 800-872-7245.

GETTING TO SAN ANTONIO BY CAR

San Antonio has four major interstate freeways (Interstates 10, 35, and 37 and Interstate 410, a loop around the city) and four U.S. highways (U.S. 90, 181, 87, 281) leading into it from every direction. All highways lead into the central business district (or to connections to this district), which is linked directly to the airport by the McAllister Freeway (U.S. 281). As in Austin, the morning and afternoon rush hour traffic is best avoided.

Interstate Highways
I-35: Laredo, TX–San Antonio–Duluth, MN
I-10: Jacksonville, FL–San Antonio–Los Angeles, CA
I-37: Corpus Christi, TX–San Antonio
I-410: Circumferential Loop around San Antonio

GETTING AROUND AUSTIN AND SAN ANTONIO

Street parking in bustling Austin and San Antonio is both limited and metered; the meters offer various time options and are regularly checked. However, both cities have open parking lots and covered parking garages (for a fee). Visitors to both cities can walk comfortably and safely around the downtown areas and can use public and tourist transportation (described below), some of it for free.

Austin

Public transportation within and around the city of Austin offers visitors and residents some convenient choices:

In the capitol area, the **"Dillo Express"** is "free for the taking" (512-474-1200). You can park free at two Park & Ride lots, one at the City Coliseum (Barton Springs and Bouldin) and the other at Austin High School (MoPac Expressway and West 1st St.), and the Dillo will take you to downtown, the UT campus, the state office complex, and restaurants and clubs along 6th Street. In the rest of town, **Capital Metro** offers forty-eight routes downtown and around town (512-474-1200).

The Austin Downtown Rangers are also at your service, on the alert for lost or displaced tourists. It's easy to spot their distinctive uniforms: a white polo shirt and bike helmet with a red star, plus black cycling shorts with a red stripe. Armed with maps of the city and two-way communication equipment, they provide assistance to visitors, answering questions and reporting problems to city agencies.

Renting a Car in the Hill Country

Even with the abundance of car rental agencies in Austin and San Antonio (and at the two airports), it's a good idea to reserve ahead.

Austin

Ace		512-474-2091
Advantage	800-777-5500	512-388-3377
Alamo	800-327-9633	
Avis	800-831-2847	512-476-6137
Budget	800-527-0700	512-478-6437
Capps Van and Car Rental		512-323-0003
Dollar		512-322-9881
Enterprise	800-325-8007	
Hertz	800-654-3131	512-478-9321
National	800-227-7368	512-476-6189
Payless	800-729-5377	
Thrifty	800-367-2277	512-474-2985

San Antonio

A&P Recreational Vehicles Rentals		210-667-1838
Advantage	800-777-5500	210-341-8211
Alamo	800-327-9633	210-828-7967
American Auto Rental		210-922-9464
Avis	800-831-2847	210-826-6332
Budget	800-527-0700	210-828-8888
Capps Van and Car Rental		210-822-8655
Dollar		210-524-3250
Enterprise	800-325-8007	210-224-6363
Hertz	800-654-3131	210-225-3676
National	800-227-7368	210-824-1841
National Car Rental	800-227-7368	210-342-8545
Rent-A-Van		210-340-8267
Thrifty	800-367-2277	210-341-4677

San Antonio

Public transportation in San Antonio also offers choices:

Metropolitan Transit Service (210-362-2000) is the city bus company.

Via Transit (210-362-5050) for the disabled.

Via Information (210-362-2020).

San Antonio streetcars run on five downtown routes, taking you to the Alamo, Spanish Governor's Palace, La Villita, Institute of Texan Cultures, and the King William Historic District. Fare: 50¢; 25¢ for children.

Austin's Capitol and trolley.

Eleanor S. Morris

GETTING TO AND AROUND
THE HILL COUNTRY

A car (your own or a rental) is your best bet for traveling through the Hill Country beyond the major cities. First of all you'll want a map. To get a free travel guide and map by mail, write to the Texas Department of Transportation, Travel and Information Division, 112 East 11th St., Austin TX 78701, or call 800-452-9292. Or you can buy a road map at any gas station in the state.

From Austin

Depending upon your destination, you have a choice of four major highways out of Austin: **U.S. Highway 183** goes northwest through Travis County to Burnet County; **State Highway 71** goes northwest through Travis County to Llano County; **U.S. Highway 290** goes west through Travis County to Hays, Blanco, Gillespie, and Kimble Counties; and **I-35 South** skirts the eastern boundaries of Travis, Hays, and Comal Counties. Once you've headed west, U.S. Highway 83, stretching north and south between I-10 and U.S. Highway 90, goes through Kimble, Kerr, Real, and Uvalde Counties.

Eleanor S. Morris

The Hill Country Flyer excursion steam train travels from Cedar Park (just west of Austin) to this station in Burnet, where there's an Old West gunfight reenactment.

From San Antonio

Depending on your destination in the Hill Country, you have a choice of five major highways out of San Antonio: **U.S. Highway 90** goes west to Medina and Uvalde Counties; **State Highway 16** goes northwest through Bexar County to Bandera, Kerr, Gillespie, and Llano Counties; **I-10** goes northwest through Bexar County to Kendall, Kerr, and Kimble Counties; **U.S. Highway 281** goes north through Bexar Country to Comal, Kendall, Blanco, and Burnet Counties; **U.S. Highway 87** goes northwest through Bexar County to Kendall, Kerr, Gillespie, and Mason Counties. I-35 skirts the eastern boundaries of Comal, Hays, and Travis Counties. Once you've headed west, U.S. Highway 83, stretching north and south between I-10 and U.S. Highway 90, goes through Kimble, Kerr, Real, and Uvalde Counties.

Farm to Market Roads and Ranch Roads: To get away from it all, once outside of Austin or San Antonio, take the numerous good but small roads between the larger highways to experience even more of the Hill Country (identified as FM and RR on your Texas highway map). Instead of traffic, you'll see scenic hills, the foliage of oak, mesquite, and cactus, and maybe a deer or armadillo sharing your road.

CHAPTER THREE
The Violet Crown
AUSTIN AND TRAVIS COUNTY

Eleanor S. Morris

The Governor's Mansion on Colorado Street, diagonally across from the Capitol.

For all its rapid growth, Austin, the capital of Texas, remains a city that is very much a part of the landscape. Even in its most bustling commercial areas, you never feel cut off from the natural beauty of the Texas Hill Country. The surrounding county, Travis, is the gateway west to the Hill Country.

To make it easy to navigate around both city and county, this chapter explores Austin first, discussing the city's history, its lodgings, restaurants, and food purveyors; its culture, recreational opportunities, and places to shop. Then Travis County's offerings are described.

Downtown Austin

1. Recreation Center
2. Travis Co. Court House
3. Post Office
4. O. Henry Home and Museum
5. Austin Convention Center

AUSTIN HISTORY

The imagination of even the romantic will not be disappointed on viewing the Valley of the Colorado, and the fertile and gracefully undulating woodlands and luxuriant prairies at a distance from it.
   — Mirabeau B. Lamar, vice president of the Republic of Texas, 1838

Austin was named for Texas hero Stephen F. Austin, but it wasn't easy. In 1835 the trader Joseph Harrell established a small settlement along the mouths of three streams: Waller, Shoal, and Barton Creeks, all draining into the Colorado River, and he called it Waterloo. In 1838 his friend Mirabeau B. Lamar, vice president of the Texas republic, came visiting to hunt buffalo. Camping on the banks of the Colorado, Lamar was greatly impressed with the beauty of the area. In the following years he battled with Sam Houston — elected president of the republic in 1836 — not only for political power but also over the choice of a site for the state capital, then Washington-on-the-Brazos, where Texas had originally declared its independence.

When Lamar succeeded Sam Houston as president in 1838, he quickly sent his agent to Waterloo to build a new capital city for the republic. It was to be named for Stephen F. Austin, father of Texas.   That spring 200 workmen arrived in oxcarts. Lots were sold at auction (for about $120) and grand 120-foot-wide Congress Avenue became lined with not-so-very-grand log cabins and plank houses.

But then Houston was re-elected president in 1842. The first thing he did was to move the capital seat to Houston, and then he moved it back to Washington-on-the-Brazos. All, that is, but the General Land Office, the repository of the republic's archives. In this he was thwarted by the heroic efforts of one Angelina Eberly, doyenne of a nearby boardinghouse.

Fervently believing that the archives belonged in Austin, Eberly set off the cannon usually employed to warn of Indian raids. The people came to the rescue, routing Houston's men who had come to take away the archives and sending them back empty-handed. The archives remained safely stashed away in the Eberly boardinghouse, and this little contretemps has gone down in local history as the "Archives War."

In 1844 new president Anson Jones moved the capital back to join the archives in Austin. When Texas joined the United States in 1845, Austin remained as the capital, albeit shakily; the issue wasn't settled until it passed two statewide voter referendums, one in 1850 and another in 1852.

The city flourished, growing from 856 people in 1840 to 3,494 in 1860. A limestone capitol was built in 1853, but it was gutted by fire. The new building, of fossilized red granite from Hill Country quarries, was built in 1888. This engendered a Texas boast that the dome is 7 feet higher than the national one in Washington, D.C. The Governor's Mansion was built in 1856, and the oldest surviving office building in Texas, the general land office, was built around 1857. In the 1890s short-story writer William Sydney Porter (known by his pseudonym O. Henry), who lived for a while in Austin, was so taken with the surrounding hills that he described the city as set in the hills like a "Violet Crown."

In 1938 the Lower Colorado River Authority began building the series of dams that gave the Austin area and the Hill Country the Highland Lakes. It has been said that the lower lakes — Lake Austin and Lake Travis — added still more jewels to Austin's "Violet Crown," a crown now set over the heads of more than half a million inhabitants and still growing.

But Austin has remained as laid back as it ever was, an open-minded, down-home kind of place that, in spite of its growth from a low-tech sleepy town to a high-tech bustling city, not only tolerates but also likes and respects people who are different. During a recent high-tension football game here between the Fighting Irish of Notre Dame and the valiant Longhorns of the University of Texas, the local paper printed this advice: "In Rome do as the Romans do; in South Bend do as the Irish do; in Austin do whatever the heck you wanna do!"

It's the mix of country, hills, and clear-water lakes with an educated, philosophical population comfortable with different cultures and ethnicities that makes Austin the community everyone loves to love. You're apt to see a fellow in a Gucci suit sporting a ponytail as well as ponytailed workers doing street repairs. And drive 10 or 15 minutes in any direction and you're out under the stars in quiet, calm, unspoiled country of hills and wide horizons.

AUSTIN LODGING

A s the seat of state government and a major university town, Austin has an abundance and a variety of places to stay. Visitors should note that the highest demands for lodging tend to fall in March, for major basketball games and other popular events, and in May, when the University of Texas and other colleges around town hold commencement exercises. For comprehensive listings of places to stay, visit the web site: austin.citysearch.com.

HOTELS

L ike any large city, Austin has its share of large national-chain hotels, such as Doubletree (800-222-8733), **Embassy Suites** (800-362-2779), **Hilton** (800-445-8667), **Hyatt** (800-233-1234), **Radisson** (800-333-3333), **Renaissance** (800-468-3571), **Marriott** (512-478-1111), and **Westin** (800-228-3000). Uniquely Austin, however, are **The Driskill** for its history and architecture, and the **Four Seasons** for its location on Austin's glory, Town Lake.

The historic Driskill Hotel, built in 1886 for $400,000. That's a bust of Col. Jess Driskill on top.

Eleanor S. Morris

THE DRISKILL
Manager: Jeffrey Trigger.
512-474-5911, 800-252-9367.
austin.citysearch.com
  Search: The Driskill.
604 Brazos St., Austin, TX
  78701.
Price: Expensive.
Credit Cards: AE, CB, D,
  DC, MC, V.
Handicap Access: Yes.
Special Features: Walking
  tours of the historic
  property.

The Driskill is an Austin treasure, opened in 1886 with a grandeur that was a rarity on the Texas frontier. Having recently undergone yet another of its many transformations, the emphasis is on restoration, not renovation, returning the hotel to its original turn-of-the-century Victoriana.

The four-story L-shaped building had three grand entrances, arched windows, balconies, columns, corbels, gargoyles, and more. The hotel welcomes dignitaries, heads of state, legislators, and lobbyists. The hotel has 177 luxuriously appointed rooms and twelve suites, a full-service restaurant, lobby piano lounge, 24-hour room service, gift shop, concierge desk, valet parking — and it's right on the corner of Brazos and 6th Street, Austin's famed entertainment district. (Rooms on the east side have an entertaining view right down 6th Street.)

The recent additional work has polished up the hotel to even greater heights, opening a rooftop swimming pool and a health club in the near future.

FOUR SEASONS HOTEL
Manager: Edward Searle.
512-478-4500, 800-332-3442.

The hotel prides itself on pampering guests in the manner of fine European hotels, amidst a Southwest decor that somehow manages to be ele-

austin.citysearch.com
  Search: Four Seasons
  Hotel.
98 San Jacinto Blvd.,
  Austin, TX 78701.
Price: Very Expensive.
Credit Cards: AE, CB, DC,
  MC, V.
Handicap Access: Yes.

gant even though a rugged crystal and iron chandelier hangs over the lobby. There are sofas upholstered in brown-and-white steerhide, tables of genuine mission doors with ox-yoke legs, and an elk head mounted over the fireplace. Half of the 292 guest rooms are rooms with a view over Town Lake, and there's an outdoor pool on the lake, too. (Nobody swims in the lake.) Special are the Sunday Brunch and dinners in the hotel restaurant, the Café at Four Seasons.

OMNI HOTEL
Manager: Leslie Reynolds.
512-476-3700,
  800-THE-OMNI.
austin.citysearch.com
  Search: Omni Austin
  Hotel.
700 San Jacinto Blvd.,
  Austin, TX 78701.
Price: Expensive.
Credit Cards: AE, D, DC,
  MC, V.
Handicap Access: Yes.

Located downtown at 8th Street, just a few blocks from the Convention Center and the State Capitol and a mile from the University of Texas, the hotel is also steps away from lively 6th Street entertainment. With 375 guest rooms, the hotel also has a penthouse health club, sauna, heated outdoor pool, hot tub, and massage therapy as well as Ancho's restaurant and a lobby bar featuring live entertainment along with cocktails and light fare.

The hotel recently remodeled its condos into suites.

BED & BREAKFASTS

For those who want a more intimate, less anonymous place to spend the night, the good news is that the bed & breakfast idea has caught on in the Southwest. There is no B&B association (as yet!), but here are listed a selection of romantic, historic, convenient, and sociable inns that will pamper you and help you find your way around town and out of it.

FAIRVIEW
Innkeepers: Nancy and
  Duke Waggoner.
512-444-4746, 800-310-4746.
austin.citysearch.com
  Search: Fairview.
1304 Newning Ave., Austin,
  TX 78704.
One mile south of the
  Congress Ave. bridge
  over Town Lake.
Price: Expensive.
Credit Cards: AE, CB, D,
  DC, MC, V.
Handicap Access: No.

It's quite a surprise to find this Texas Colonial Revival mansion barely a mile from busy downtown. It was built in 1910 and is set in spacious landscaped grounds well off the street and shaded by large old oak trees. The lovingly restored home carries an Austin Landmark designation and a 1993 Austin Heritage Award for historic preservation. This neighborhood near the center of town is known as Travis Heights, and it's safe enough to walk the streets at night. "You'll meet our neighbors out walking their dogs as late as 10:30 in the evening," Duke says. Best of all, Nancy can tell you tales of famous Texans who were entertained in the mansion in the past — names, she says, that she learned about in seventh-grade Texas history.

All the rooms are Texas-sized: There are four guest rooms in the big house and two suites in the carriage house in the rear, all with private bath. Breakfast features Texas goodies such as Texas peach-pecan syrup served with the Belgian waffles and Texas-shaped corn chips with black bean salsa dip.

McCALLUM HOUSE
Innkeepers: Nancy and
    Roger Danley.
512-451-6744.
austin.citysearch.com
    Search: McCallum
    House.
613 W. 32nd St., Austin, TX
    78705.
Six blocks north of the
    University of Texas.
Price: Moderate.
Credit Cards: D, MC, V.
Handicap Access: No.

This B&B, built in 1907, was the home of an early 20th-century suffragette, Jane Y. McCallum. Being close to the University of Texas, it's a comfortable home-away-from-home for many visiting professors, which makes for lively breakfast conversation. The five guest rooms and suites all have a private bath, kitchen, and even their own private porches. In fact, it's a house of porches, including a screened one running around the whole side of the house, with inviting white wicker furniture.

Both Nancy and Roger cook, and you'll get a delicious breakfast from either one. Nancy's specialty is a scrambled egg dish; Roger's is a crunchy shredded-potato-crusted quiche.

THE MILLER-
    CROCKETT HOUSE
Innkeeper: Kathleen
    Mooney.
512-441-1600, 888-441-1641.
www.millercrockett.com.
112 Academy Dr., Austin,
    TX 78704.
Price: Moderate to
    Expensive.
Credit Cards: AE, MC, V.
Handicap Access: Yes, in
    the cottages.

Just two blocks from downtown, with a spectacular view of Austin's skyline, this bed & breakfast has three guest rooms, each with bath and balcony, and two private cottages.

The 1888 building "just got a historical marker," Kathleen says happily.

For breakfast you might be fed delicious huevos rancheros along with sausage or bacon and Texas Ruby Red grapefruit with strawberries, kiwi, and crystallized ginger — very tasty.

WOODBURN HOUSE
Innkeepers: Sandra and
    Herb Dickson.
512-458-4335.
austin.citysearch.com
    Search: Woodburn House.
4401 Avenue D, Austin, TX
    78751.
In historic Hyde Park just
    north of downtown.
Price: Moderate, EP.

Here's a chance to stay in Austin's Hyde Park neighborhood, one of the areas the Austin Visitor Center suggests for touring for its lovely old homes. This bed & breakfast, an Austin Landmark, is named for a former occupant, Bessie Hamilton Woodburn, the daughter of a Texas provisional governor after the Civil War. The spacious mansion has porches both upstairs and down and five guest rooms, all with private bath and lace curtains at the long windows.

Named for the daughter of a Texas provisional governor, Woodburn House is now a bed & breakfast inn.

Eleanor S. Morris

Credit Cards: AE, MC, V.
Handicap Access: No.

Breakfast is often Mexican — "real Mexican, not Tex-Mex," says Sandra, whose family hails from Guadalajara. She grows her own Mexican spices and makes her own salsa. But not to be scorned are the Belgian waffles, French toast, and quiches that Herb serves.

Nearby is the very informal all-American eatery, the Hyde Park Grill — another plus.

AUSTIN RESTAURANTS AND FOOD PURVEYORS

According to those who know such things, Austinites eat out more than the denizens of any other city in Texas. Perhaps part of the attraction for dining out is explained by yet another fact from the same sources: Austin also has the highest number of restaurants per capita of any other American city. Which leads to a vast number of cuisine choices, from chicken-fried steak and cream gravy to grilled tenderloin of ostrich with sauce porcini; from pit-cooked brisket barbecue to curried lamb with basmati rice; from enchiladas in salsa verde to chipotle shrimp over mushroom and rice pilaf.

To open a restaurant anywhere is cited as a tricky business venture at best. Faced with such an array of competitive establishments, Austin restaurants tend to come and go. One advantage of this form of natural selection is that there is absolutely no room for a bad restaurant; they just don't make it. So in almost any eating emporium in Austin you're pretty sure to be served excellent cuisine in any category: American, Western, Southwestern, Mexican, French, Italian, Spanish, Chinese, Japanese, Taiwan, Korean, Indian, Greek, Indonesian, Indian, Middle Eastern. . . .

As for decor, this, too, goes from one extreme to another, from barbecue-stand informality to French café coziness, from limestone walls to romantic candlelight, from Mexican cliche to Victorian gentility.

What to wear? Austin is informal; many restaurants subscribe to the City Grill's definition and dress code: "Classy and refined, yet casual enough to wear your jeans." Or as they say at Jean Pierre's, "Feel free to leave your coat and tie at home." Just don't get so laid-back that you flout the health code: shirt and shoes worn at all times.

All of Austin's restaurants are nonsmoking. This caused quite a flap when it was instituted, but things have settled down considerably, and folks seem to eat out as often as before. Following is the result of a considered selection from all the many good restaurants in Austin, along with some of Austin's food purveyors, specialty shops reflecting the area's German and Spanish traditions, and the eclectic interests of an increasingly sophisticated clientele. Check the restaurant's web page for more information, or visit the Austin web site: austin.citysearch.com.

BRIO VISTA
512-342-2642.
www.briovista.com.
9400-B Arboretum Blvd.,
   Austin, TX 78759.
Next to Renaissance Hotel.
Price: Moderate to
   Expensive.
Cuisine: Continental,
   Asian.
Serving: D.
Credit Cards: AE, CB, D,
   DC, MC, V.
Reservations: Not
   necessary but
   recommended.
Handicap Access: Yes.
Special Features:
   Complimentary valet
   parking.

This restaurant on up-and-coming West 6th Street is one of the newer ones in town, offering what they like to call "spirited dining." Both the artistic presentation and the vigorous seasoning live up to it, although it might be a smidgen too spicy for some palates. For starters we had shredded duck rolled into scallion crêpes with shredded cucumber, Napa celery, and bean sprouts and spiced with a Thai sauce. The spinach salad with Gorgonzola/goat cheese crusted with walnuts was crisp and refreshing. Pesto angel-hair pasta came with miniature carrots, zucchini, red peppers, and tiny nuggets of yellow squash, but it was a little disappointing. More sauce, or a tastier one, would have improved it; in comparison to the other dishes, it was pretty bland. For dessert, chocolate Brio trio — chocolate truffle layered between rich chocolate cake — came a close second to the pear tart stuffed with chunks of pear and walnut and topped with shredded pear and vanilla ice cream.

CHUY'S
512-474-4452.
austin.citysearch.com
   Search: Chuy's.
1728 Barton Springs Rd.,
   Austin, TX 78704.
Just south of downtown.
Price: Inexpensive.

Funky Chuy's is Austin at its most whimsical. A thousand wooden fish dangle from the ceiling of the bar, and hubcaps cover the ceiling of the dining room. The result is hilarious. Walls are Mexican pink and green, piñatas dangle invitingly, asking to be smacked (but never are — too messy), and a memorial altar to Elvis is by the

Diners enjoying mild winter weather at a café on Barton Springs Road.

Eleanor S. Morris

Cuisine: Tex-Mex.
Serving: L, D.
Credit Cards: AE, D, MC, V.
Reservations: No.
Handicap Access: Yes.

front door. The crowd most nights testifies to the great taste of the Tex-Mex fare. The menu may be limited, but regulars favor the taco salad, the blue corn tortillas, the barbecued chicken tacos, and the chips and salsa.

CITY GRILL
512-479-0817.
austin.citysearch.com
    Search: City Grill.
401 Sabine St., Austin, TX
    78701.
One block west of I-35
    between 4th and 5th
    Sts.
Price: Moderate.
Cuisine: Mesquite Grill.
Serving: D.
Credit Cards: AE, CB, D,
    DC, MC, V.
Handicap Access: Yes.

The City Grill, specializing in mesquite-grilled steaks and seafood, is in a refurbished 1890s warehouse. The old wood floors and beamed ceilings contrast with the elegance of the candles and the linen tablecloths, all of which lives up to the restaurant motto: "classy and refined, yet casual enough to wear your jeans."

We found the beef tender and the grilled fish moist and tasty, all in line with the restaurant's popular reputation.

COUNTY LINE ON THE LAKE
512-346-3664.
austin.citysearch.com
    Search: County Line on
    the Lake.
5204 FM 2222, Austin, TX
    78731.
0.25 mile east of Loop 360.
Price: Moderate.
Cuisine: Barbecue.
Serving: L, D.

Always popular, so you may have to wait, but the beautiful Hill Country view makes that easy. Continue to enjoy it by eating outdoors if the weather is nice (which is most of the time in the Hill Country!), and enjoy the view from the hill while digging into the big meaty ribs, lean brisket, and special sausage the County Line is famous for throughout the Southwest. The atmosphere here is upscale roadhouse. From the Longneck Bar we downed ice-cold beer and frozen margaritas as we watched the view of Bull

Credit Cards: AE, CB, D, DC, MC, V.
Reservations: Only for 10 or more.
Handicap Access: Yes.

Creek as it runs into Lake Austin. For dessert, the Kahlúa pecan brownie is a must.

CAFÉ JOSIE
512-322-9226.
austin.citysearch.com
  Search: Café Josie.
1200-B W. 6th St., Austin, TX 78703.
Price: Moderate.
Cuisine: American Tropics.
Serving: L, D (no lunch Sat., closed Sun.).
Credit Cards: AE, DC, MC, V.
Reservations: No.
Handicap Access: No.

If you find yourself hungry for spicy, innovative, and artistically served food, head for Café Josie. The cafe is sort of hidden at the rear of an antiques shop in Pecan Square, but you can spot it from the shiny cover over the dining patio in front; the indoor dining room is beyond the patio.

Consider beginning with blue crab quesadillas or pistachio-encrusted goat cheese. For an entrée, try sesame-crusted salmon or mesquite-grilled yellow-fin tuna. And all are served almost too attractively to eat.

ELLA'S
512-458-2148.
austin.citysearch.com
  Search: Ella's.
One Jefferson Sq., Austin, TX 78731.
Price: Expensive.
Cuisine: Eclectic Texas.
Serving: L, D daily, Sun. Buffet.
Credit Cards: AE, D, DC, MC, V.
Reservations: Yes.
Handicap Access: Yes.

Ella's is elegant, even for lunch, with white linen tablecloths and (large) napkins, tasteful pictures on the walls, a handsome bar area, and bright windows looking out toward the square. Besides a soup of the day, the menu offers yellow tomato gazpacho with lump crabmeat and cucumber salsa. For a main course, try hot and crunchy chicken or trout with mango chutney or duck quesadillas served with seasonal slaw, field greens and pico de gallo.

For vegetarians there is a vegetable tower of sautéed vegetables, stuffed tomato, braised greens caramelized onions, portabella mushrooms, all heaped on your choice of mashed potatoes or rice.

Salads are rich and hearty as are the sandwiches on the lunch menu. All dishes are beautifully presented by friendly servers.

GREEN MESQUITE
512-479-0485.
austin.citysearch.com
  Search: Green Mesquite.
1400 Barton Springs Rd., Austin, TX 78704.
Corner of South Lamar.
Price: Inexpensive.
Cuisine: Barbecue, Tex-Mex, Cajun.

This rustic and homey Austin tradition serves up music from local bands on weekends, along with the food: chicken-fried steak, catfish, jambalaya, and "bubba tacos" — soft flour tortillas stuffed with your choice of barbecued beef, turkey, or chicken and topped to the gills with lettuce, tomato, and shredded cheddar cheese, served with a homemade salsa and a choice of two "sides." The

Serving: L, D.
Credit Cards: AE, D, DC,
  MC, V.
Reservations: No.
Handicap Access: Yes.
Special Features: Bluegrass,
  blues, and country-
  western music live on
  Fri., Sat., and Sun. nights.

GREEN PASTURES
512-444-4747.
austin.citysearch.com
  Search: Green Pastures.
811 W. Live Oak, Austin,
  TX 78704.
Live Oak is about 1.5 miles
  south of downtown; turn
  right off Congress for 9
  blocks.
Price: Expensive.
Cuisine: Southern,
  Continental.
Serving: L, D, SB.
Credit Cards: AE, D, MC, V.
Reservations: Yes.
Handicap Access: Yes.

HULA HUT
512-476-4852.
austin.citysearch.com
  Search: Hula Hut.
3826 Lake Austin Blvd.,
  Austin, TX 78703.
On Lake Austin.
Price: Moderate.
Cuisine: Polynesian
  Mexican.
Serving: L, D.
Credit Cards: AE, D, DC,
  MC, V.
Reservations: No.
Handicap Access: Yes.

HYDE PARK BAR &
  GRILL
512-458-3168.

beans were a little too sweet, the Cajun rice a little oily, but the big chunky coleslaw was seasoned just right, and the favorite potato salad was mellow. The po' boy sandwiches are as authentic as any you'll get in New Orleans, and of course all the pies are homemade. Owners Tom and Liz Davis are carrying on the welcoming tradition of this little old shack on an important corner (right on South Lamar) since before Harry Truman was president.

Shades of the Old South! This white mansion, surrounded by manicured grounds and strutting peacocks, is instant Scarlet O'Hara–Rhett Butler ambiance. Retro Southern gentility and the best Sunday brunch in Texas make this an Austin classic. Everybody likes not only the good taste of the food but also the sheer abundance of the spread — a large assortment of cheeses and fruits, shrimp, salads, maybe a choice between prime rib and grilled blue marlin tampico (tomato, green pepper, onion sauce), three or four vegetables, and at least four desserts. The peach and plum strudel and the Green Pastures bread pudding are recommended.

The mix may sound weird, but once you try it, you're hooked. You can dine inside or out over the lake, where boaters tie their craft up by the giant fish guarding the pier bar. We began with the Huli Huli Luau Platter of BBQ ribs and chicken tacos, grilled chicken nachos, chicken flautas, little garlic roasted potatoes, and chili con queso. Then we went on to Hawaiian grilled chicken: a grilled breast topped with fresh poblano chilies, grilled pineapple slices, jack cheese, and crispy smoked bacon.

The tacos and enchiladas have to be the largest ever seen; the taco stuffed with char-grilled mahi mahi, red cabbage, cilantro, and jalapeño lime sauce was pretty peppy.

Hyde Park Bar & Grill's super lentil soup is on the menu daily, and there's also a soup of the day if you want a change. We like their stir-fry and

austin.citysearch.com Search: Hyde Park Bar & Grill.
4206 Duval St., Austin, TX 78705.
Historic Hyde Park neighborhood north of downtown.
Price: Inexpensive.
Cuisine: American.
Serving: L, D, Sat. & Sun. Brunch.
Credit Cards: AE, D, DC, MC, V.
Reservations: No.
Handicap Access: Yes.

the spicy chicken salad, but the spinach salad is delicious, too, in this very informal all-American eatery.

IRON WORKS BARBECUE
512-478-4855.
austin.citysearch.com Search: Iron Works Barbecue.
100 Red River, Austin, TX 78701.
East edge of downtown.
Price: Moderate.
Cuisine: Barbecue.
Serving: L, D.
Credit Cards: AE, MC, V.
Reservations: No.
Handicap Access: Yes.

Delicious brisket, chicken, sausage, and ribs are to be had in this rustic tin shed, for years the home of Weigl Iron Works, near the Convention Center. The classic barbecue plate comes with a choice of two out of three side dishes: beans, salad, or coleslaw. Top this off with a slice of pecan, apple, or cherry pie or peach cobbler while you enjoy deciphering the dozens of brands burned into the wooden walls.

JEAN PIERRE'S UPSTAIRS
512-454-4811.
www.austin360.com Search: Jean Pierre's.
3500 Jefferson St., #201, Austin, TX 78731.
Off 35th St. on the second level.
Price: Moderate.
Cuisine: Continental, Southwest.
Serving: L Mon.–Fri., D Mon.–Sat.
Credit Cards: AE, DC, MC, V.
Reservations: Recommended.
Handicap Access: Yes.
Special Features: Covered parking.

Feel free to leave your coat and tie at home," is what they say at Jean Pierre's, soft lighting and linen tablecloths notwithstanding. They're famous for their dessert soufflés (Grand Marnier is a favorite), the only restaurant so far in town to serve them, so be sure to save room. But that's not too easy to do if you order the grilled salmon wrapped in apple-smoked bacon and served with a Key lime port sauce or the tequila beef tenderloin with a burgundy peppercorn sauce, all with tender julienne vegetables.

JEFFREY'S
512-477-5584.
www.virtualrestaurants.
com/jeffreys.
1204 West Lynn, Austin, TX
78703.
Bet. 6th St. and Enfield Rd.
just west of downtown.
Price: Very Expensive.
Cuisine: New Texan,
Continental.
Serving: D daily.
Credit Cards: AE, D, DC,
MC, V.
Reservations:
Recommended.
Handicap Access: Yes.

Talk about adventurous cuisine — this fine dining establishment in the historic Clarksville neighborhood takes high honors indeed. Chef David Garrido, recently acclaimed by the James Beard Foundation, makes magic with an amazing array of flavors. For starters, how about shredded goose on a small blue corn taco sauced with fresh mango puree? Or crispy oysters on root chips (sea sprouts) with habañero honey aïoli? Or skookum oysters with caviar and chervil lemon mignonette? "I've tried leaving oysters off the menu," Chef David says, "but our patrons raised the roof." He's publishing a cookbook, *Nuevo Tex-Mex*, with recipes using all the flavors that he says "make a good marriage."

The portabella mushroom with Brie on pureed maple sweet potato garnished with baby bok choy was yet another delicious starter. Sturgeon, pecan-wood smoked for sweetness and served in an orange champagne sauce, was accompanied by a black Oregon truffle in a wine-butter-shallot sauce; elk was served with hazelnut wild rice and huckleberry thyme sauce; lamb was flavored with roasted shallot custard, ginger, honey, and saffron.

Orange saffron crème brûlée, hazelnut mascarpone cheesecake with plum compote, and apple spice cake with macadamia and rum raisin sauce raised dessert to the heights. The menu varies, but a must, like the oysters, is chocolate intemperance, a dense bittersweet chocolate mousse with a brownie crust covered with melted chocolate.

KATZ'S DELI & BAR
512-476-3354.
www.katzneverkloses.com.
618 W. 6th St., Austin, TX
78701.
Downtown, west of
Congress Ave.
Price: Inexpensive to
Moderate.
Cuisine: New York Deli.
Serving: B, L, D.
Credit Cards: AE, D, DC,
MC, V (no checks).
Reservations: No.
Handicap Access: Yes.
Special Features: Open 24
hours a day.

We Never Klose" is the boast of this establishment, which has been providing Austinites with their kosher-style deli fix since 1979, introducing "bagel" and "deli" into the Texas vocabulary. Bagels abound, of course, from the basic $1.95 toasted with butter to the legendary $8.95 cream-cheese-slathered roll thick with lox and lettuce, tomato, and purple onion. The chicken-in-a-pot contains award-winning consommé, both noodles and matzo balls, vegetables, and a whole quarter chicken; the homemade cheese blintzes come with a choice of apple, blueberry, or hot fudge topping. There's Lexington Avenue egg cream and New York–style cheesecake. Capping the Katz's experience is Top of the Marc (see "Nightlife") with music and dancing nightly: jazz, rock, and blues.

This isn't San Francisco's Top of the Mark; the "Marc" here is Marc Katz, who followed his father, Meyer Katz, as restaurateur par excellence. (Now next-generation Culinary-Institute-of-America-trained Barry is the boss.) With Times Square and Nathan's posters all over the walls, the busy and intimate ambiance makes you feel part of what's happening.

KERBEY LANE CAFE
512-445-4451.
austin.citysearch.com
  Search: Kerbey Lane
  Cafe.
2700 S. Lamar Blvd.,
  Austin, TX 78704.
South of downtown.
Price: Inexpensive.
Cuisine: American, Tex-
  Mex.
Serving: B, L, D.
Credit Cards: AE, D, DC,
  MC, V.
Reservations: No.
Handicap Access: Yes.
Special Features: Open 24
  hours a day.

It's true what they say: Austin couldn't get along without its supply of wholesome food available any hour of the day or night, and this homegrown restaurant is the place for it. Breakfast, lunch, and dinner all feature fresh locally grown produce, and are served round the clock every day. Lots of green vinyl and light wood and a bucolic mural of hills and fields set the tone; the waitstaff wear whatever they're comfortably casual in, and the service is friendly and snappy. Legendary among the healthy and wholesome offerings are Kerbey Lane's pancakes, sandwiches, crisp salads, and all sorts of imaginative specials. The migas (eggs scrambled with crispy tortilla bits) with spicy red sauce are recommended.

OLD PECAN STREET
  CAFE
512-478-2491.
austin.citysearch.com
  Search: Old Pecan Street
  Cafe.
310 E. 6th St., Austin, TX
  78701.
At Trinity and San Jacinto.
Price: Moderate.
Cuisine: Texas-Style
  American.
Serving: L, D, Sat. & SB.
Credit Cards: AE, D, DC,
  MC, V.
Reservations: No.
Handicap Access: Partial.

The menu here doesn't change from week to week, so when you find something you really like, you can count on its being there (although there are certain favorites for each night, too). Like the Old Pecan Street chicken, a chicken breast, flattened, spread with pesto, rolled up and simmered in brandy. That the pecan pie is a perennial favorite goes without saying. The building is the historic Platt-Simpson, in 1871 part of a livery stable, in 1901 a hardware store. Inside are stone walls and wooden floors; outside you'll find a historic plaque on the red brick, and bright blue awnings shade the restaurant windows.

SHORELINE BAR &
  GRILL
512-477-3300.
www.shorelinegrill.com.
98 San Jacinto Blvd.,
  Austin, TX 78701.
On Town Lake at 1st St.
Price: Expensive.

This is *the* place for watching the Austin bats at sunset (see the "Nature" section in this chapter) while overlooking Town Lake and enjoying a memorable seafood or prime rib meal. We had the grilled prime rib and the grilled shrimp and crab cake entrée, both served with a fresh vegetable medley of green and wax beans, squash, and bell

Cuisine: Seafood.
Serving: L, D.
Credit Cards: AE, D, MC, V.
Reservations: Recommended.
Handicap Access: Yes.

peppers. We topped it off with the Shoreline special of crème brûlée and chocolate "intensive," a triple chocolate confection that becomes more decadent with each bite.

THREADGILL'S
512-472-9304.
www.threadgills.com.
310 Riverside Dr., Austin, TX 78704.
South of Town Lake at Barton Springs Rd.
Price: Moderate.
Cuisine: Southern.
Serving: L, D.
Credit Cards: MC, V.
Reservations: No.
Handicap Access: Yes.

Here's the same good old Threadgill's, now opened just south of downtown — called their "world headquarters" — so there's no need to go to the original one up at 6416 North Lamar. But you'll have to do without the musical memories of the original Threadgill's up north, where Janis Joplin used to sing in this Austin institution. But this is still the place for tried-and-true chicken-fried steak and cream gravy on homemade biscuits. There are plenty of neon signs and old beer clocks on the walls to transport you back in time while you chow down on pork roast and liver and chicken and dumplings with black-eyed peas and okra. He-man portions, great vegetables, and fresh home cooking make this Austin landmark a winner. As for that chicken-fried steak, lots of our friends say it's the best in town.

WEST LYNN CAFE
512-482-0950.
austin.citysearch.com
   Search: West Lynn Cafe.
1110 West Lynn, Austin, TX 78703.
Bet. 6th St. and Enfield Rd. just west of downtown.
Price: Inexpensive.
Cuisine: Vegetarian.
Serving: L, D, Sat. & SB.
Credit Cards: AE, D, DC, MC, V.
Reservations: No.
Handicap Access: Yes.

The scent of food is so delicious as you enter the café, it makes you want to become a vegetarian if you aren't already. The zucchini poblano —a casserole of fresh zucchini, corn, and poblano peppers — is baked in a fresh tomato sauce with New Mexico spices and a hint of fresh cilantro, topped with melted jack cheese.

The innovative menu includes such dishes as spanakopita, a classic Greek dish of flaky filo dough layered with spinach, eggs, sliced almonds, fresh dill, and oregano, with ricotta and feta cheeses. A Caribbean stir-fry is a mélange of fresh vegetables and tofu with cashews and tropical fruit in a ginger sauce, served with black beans. And dishes on the menu that are starred can be prepared zero cholesterol/nondairy if you wish.

Sandwiches, salads, smoothies, fresh juices, and natural sodas are on the menu in this attractive café, where you can eat outdoors under an arbor or indoors under a slanted ceiling decorated with stars and squares and a changeable art show exhibited on the walls.

Eleanor S. Morris

Z Tejas Grill, a popular eating spot on West 6th Street serving innovative Southwestern fare, outdoors or in.

Z TEJAS GRILL
512-478-5355.
1110 W. 6th St., Austin, TX
    78703.
West edge of downtown.
Price: Moderate.
Cuisine: Southwestern.
Serving: B, L, D, Sat. & SB.
Credit Cards: AE, CB, D,
    DC, MC, V.
Reservations: No.
Handicap Access: No.
Special Features:
    Complimentary valet
    parking in evening.

There's a climb here, up the front steps to the restaurant's outdoor and indoor dining, but the exertion is worth it. The crunchy catfish beignets served with jalapeño tartar sauce and the chicken and sausage gumbo ya-ya got us off to a great start. Voodoo tuna was served with black peppercorn vinaigrette and soy mustard sauce, and the Z'green salad was mixed greens with roma tomatoes and colored peppers with a sun-dried tomato-basil dressing. Another specialty is the pork tenderloin, stuffed with chorizo, jack cheese, grilled onions, and poblano peppers in a roasted garlic cream sauce.

AUSTIN FOOD PURVEYORS

BAKERIES

Old Bakery and Emporium (512-477-5961; www.austin360.com Search: Old Bakery and Emporium; 106 Congress Ave., Austin, TX 78701; year-round

Mon.–Fri. 9am–4pm, Dec., prior to Christmas, Sat. 10am–2 pm) Dating from 1876 and built by Swedish immigrant Charles Lundberg, the bakery now sells baked goods and handicrafts made by Austin senior citizens.

Sweetish Hill Bakery (512-472-1347; austin.citysearch.com Search: Sweetish Hill Bakery; 1120 W. 6th St., Austin, TX 78703; Mon.–Sat. 6:30am–7pm, Sun. 6:30am–5pm) There's also a small sidewalk café at 922 Congress, but here's where all the baking is done and where the main action is, especially on a Saturday morning. Celebrating their 25th anniversary in 2000, the bakery boasts of being Austin's first "from-scratch" bakery, using real butter and fresh eggs for such goodies as sticky buns and Cyprus horns, a delicious cinnamon and almond croissant. They offer gourmet lunches, such as ham and Brie on a baguette, plus other sandwiches and hot dishes, too. The coffee is Anderson's, a fresh-roasted blend made especially for Sweetish Hill. "We use only local stuff," is a bakery byword.

Texas French Bread (512-499-0544; austin.citysearch.com Search: Texas French Bread; 2900 Rio Grande, Austin, TX 78705; Mon.–Fri. 7am–7pm, Sat. 7am–6pm, Sun. 7am–5pm) Here's a true Texas success story: early in the 1980s Judy Willcott began baking out of her house for friends and a few restaurants. Today there are Texas French Bread establishments all over Austin — but the one on Rio Grande is where most of the culinary work is done. It's also where you can enjoy outdoor Austin: There are café tables in front and picnic tables under the big tree alongside the garden that grows all the herbs used in the bakery.

There's hardly a party in Austin where the food doesn't include a Texas French Bread French bread. But also popular are the sourdough bread, the baguettes, and the bollos (crusty rolls). The Hyde Park chocolate cake is a marvel, but so are all the other cakes in the display case plus scones, croissants, muffins, and Texas-shaped cookies in butter, ginger, and chocolate. You can get coffee, tea, and lunch here, as well — one of the best-liked specials is the TFP, a vegetarian salad bursting at the seams.

COFFEE SHOPS

Joe's Bakery and Coffee Shop (512-472-0017; austin.citysearch.com Search: Joe's Bakery; 2305 7th St., Austin, TX 78702; daily 7am–3pm) Joe says he's now more of a restaurant than a coffee shop, "That's what I named it when I opened," he says. But you can still get great coffee, along with fresh, made-on-the-premises Mexican pastries like empanadas and pan dulce, "from my own recipes," Joe promises.

Quack's 43rd Street Bakery (512-453-3399; 411 E. 43rd St., Austin, TX 78751; Mon.–Fri. 6:30am–11pm, Sat. & Sun. 8am–11pm) You can get your coffee fix here just about any time of the day or night. A bakery and a coffee shop, "half and half," so you can be sure of delicious pastries to go along with your coffee.

The Ruta Maya Coffee Company, with a colorful mural along the wall below.

Ruta Maya Coffee Co. (512-472-9637; austin.citysearch.com Search: Ruta Maya Coffee; 218 W. 4th St., Austin, TX 78701; Sun.–Thurs. 7am–1am, Fri. & Sat. 7am–2am) You can't miss this wild place whether you walk or drive down 4th Street: The cement triangle facing the street (and concealing the steps on either side) is painted with a pseudo-Mayan fresco, the shouting colors an introduction to all the Mayan art inside. About four or five tables sit outside on the elevated entrance, and indoors the cavernous room is redolent of the delicious coffee beans roasted just inside the entrance. Bags of coffee beans are everywhere in this funky establishment where all sorts of coffee, chocolate, and fruit drinks are served along with various sandwiches (prepackaged), pie, sweet rolls, and empanadas stuffed with pumpkin, spinach, apricot, etc. The clientele is a mix of nightlifers, students, and, as our waitress told us, "the bar crowd and general freaks." There is a connection with the Ruta Maya Coffee Company in El Salvador, and group tours to the homeland are sometimes offered.

FARM, ORCHARD, AND PRODUCE MARKETS

Central Market (512-206-1000, 800-360-2552; austin.citysearch.com Search: Central Market; 4001 N. Lamar Blvd., Austin, TX 78756; daily 9am–9pm) The sheer magnitude of this indoor market has caused it to become a tourist attraction, one of the first things locals love to show off to visitors. "Have you seen Central Market yet?" is the cry, and it's off to what must be one of the largest selections of comestibles most anywhere. How about 7 kinds of bananas, 10 varieties of potatoes and 11 of mushrooms, 18 kinds of apples, 19 styles of olives, 20 choices of sushi, 25 kinds of salad greens, 37 varieties of coffee beans, 2,500 different wines — you get the idea.

And you can get your fill of samples as you wander thorough all 68,000 square feet of food, on any given day sampling a tasty sharp cheese in the cheese department, bite-size bits of amandine tart in the bakery, Mom's spaghetti sauce on a bit of pasta, and Mamo's garlic sauce for chicken and fish in the sauce department, Oka's dressing for salad and dip on both a tortilla chip and in a tiny cupful of lettuce, or albino salmon hot in coconut sauce in the fish department. There's almost no need to adjourn to the Central Market Café, although the food there, indoors or out on the covered patio (with fans for cooling), is an adventure, as well, especially the Texas-size breakfast tortilla served daily until 11am.

Specializing in high-quality food free from chemicals, the market offers more than 500 organic products throughout the store, including produce, olive oil, wine, and dairy products. Regularly scheduled cooking courses are also offered, such as the fancy hors d'oeuvre class taught by the chef of a local catering service.

And now you can duplicate the Central Market experience on the south side of town at 4477 S. Lamar Blvd. (512-899-4300), with the same fresh produce, exotic specialties, café, and tempting samples as the original.

Travis County Farmers' Market (512-454-1002; austin.citysearch.com Search: Travis County Farmers' Market; 6701 Burnet Rd., Austin, TX 78757; Daily 8am–6pm) There's a lot going on under the roofs of this open-air market. Among the produce are such Texas specialties as the 1015 onion (which wins over even the Vidalia in sweetness and size), chili peppers, and fabulous Hill Country peaches. Sweetie Pie's Bakery makes mouthwatering lemon meringue pie (and other varieties) and cinnamon rolls; Rinehart's Barbecue brags about its real Texas barbecue; Celia's Tacos is a Mexican restaurant offering great beef and chicken fajitas, and the Farmers' Market Trading Company is big on Texas antiques, with lots of primitive armoires and cabinets. The cabinets are stocked with local products made by farmers, such as salsa, chilies, and spices.

HEALTH AND NATURAL FOODS

Sun Harvest Farms (512-444-3079; austin.citysearch.com Search: Sun Harvest Farms; 4006 S. Lamar Blvd., Austin, TX 78703; daily 8am–10pm) This specialist in all-natural foods offers a farmers market of organic produce, meats untreated with antibiotics, vegan (no animal products) baked goods, gourmet organic cheeses, homeopathic vitamins, herbs, and remedies, and a café and juice bar.

Whole Foods Market (512-476-1206; austin.citysearch.com Search: Whole Foods Market; 601 N. Lamar Blvd., Austin, TX 78703; daily 8am–11pm) Whole Foods considers itself alone in the entire nation for a quality standard prohibiting artificial color, flavors, additives, preservatives, chemicals, and growth hormones in any Whole Foods products. Food that has been irradiated or grains and grain products that have been bleached or bromated are not sold.

AUSTIN CULTURE

The modern main branch of the Austin Public Library, downtown on Guadalupe Street.

Austin natives and visitors alike enjoy the rich bounty of cultural opportunities here that reflect not only the area's history and traditions but also the latest trends in the arts and entertainment.

ARCHITECTURE

Austin has some wonderful old buildings to view on foot or by car. First and foremost, the red granite Texas State Capitol, downtown at 11th and Congress Ave., has always been deep in the heart of Texas. Built in 1888, it was declared a National Historic Landmark in 1986 and was recently renovated. It's constructed of native granite eons old — if you get up close you can see fossils imbedded in the stone. The dome, crowned by a statue of woman holding aloft a star, is 7 feet higher than the Capitol dome in Washington, D.C.

The dome is special for more than its height. Travelers to Paris, Florence, and Rome marvel at three of the four examples in all the world of a "floating dome," while the fourth is right here in Austin. (A floating dome is an inner one constructed within an outer one.) The Texas floating dome can be viewed from the fourth balcony display area, where you can look down from a dizzy-

Historic downtown homes with a backdrop of modern structures.

Eleanor S. Morris

ing height to the beautiful mosaic floor of the rotunda below, or up to the bronze star and the letters TEXAS on the ceiling.

Tours start every 15 minutes Mon.–Fri. 8:30am–4:30pm, Sat. & Sun. 9:30am–4:15pm, beginning next to the Information Desk left of the front entrance on the first floor.

Also in Austin's **downtown area** are elegant business houses, dating from 1850 to 1940, along Congress Avenue and 6th Street. In the **Bremond Block,** view fashionable Victorian-era residences. **Hyde Park,** just north of downtown, is a still-viable neighborhood of Victorian and Craftsman homes. The **Texas State Cemetery** is the final resting place of many Texas patriots, including Stephen F. Austin.

Detailed brochures with maps are available at the **Austin Convention and Visitors Bureau, Visitor Information Center** (512-478-0098, 800-926-2282; www.austin360.com/acvb; 201 E. 2nd St., Austin, TX 78701; Mon.–Fri. 8:30am–5pm, Sat. 9am–5pm, Sun. noon–5pm).

Three free **guided walking tours** depart promptly from the south entrance of the State Capitol (weather permitting). The 60-minute Capitol grounds tour leaves at 2pm on Sat. The 90-minute Bremond Block tour leaves at 11am on Sat. and Sun. The Congress Avenue and E. 6th Street tour, another 90-minute tour, departs at 9am on Thurs., Fri., Sat.; 2pm on Sun.

Free visitors parking lots are at 15th and Congress, and 12th and San Jacinto. For information, call 512-478-0098 during the day or 800-926-ACVB, ext. 4577, to leave a message, at any time.

DANCE

Austin's Annual Festival of Dance, "a celebration of the human spirit," featuring national dance companies, takes place every March. Recent festivals have included Ballet Austin, San Francisco Ballet, Sharir Dance Company, Dallas Black Dance Company, and others.

Ballet Austin (512-476-2163; www.balletaustin.org; 300 Guadalupe St., Austin, TX 78705) Austin's first professional ballet company is known for both classical and contemporary works presented during the fall to spring season. An annual offering is *The Nutcracker* every December.

Sharir + Bustamante Danceworks (512-458-8158; www.internetv.com/sharir; PO Box 339, Austin, TX 78767) Organized in 1982, this professional dance company in residence at the College of Fine Arts at the University of Texas is considered the leading modern dance company in Texas. Led by award-winning choreographers Yacov Sharir and Jose Luis Bustamante, the company mounts three to four home season productions in addition to touring nationally and internationally.

University of Texas (512-471-1444, 800-687-6010; www.utexas.edu/cofa/theatre; Department of Theatre and Dance, University of Texas at Austin, Austin, TX 78712; box office: Bass Concert Hall, 23rd St. and E. Campus Dr.) The Department of Theater and Dance offers performances regularly.

Tapestry Dance Company (512-474-9846; www.tapestry.org; TDC Studios, 507-B Pressler, Austin, TX 78703) A professional multiform dance organization, Tapestry performs often at Austin's Paramount Theater, as well as holding classes in the Tapestry Dance Academy, located on Pressler near 5th Street.

GALLERIES

Take a walk along 6th Street — and 3rd and 4th, too — for some interesting galleries.

ACA Gallery (512-474-7799; www.austin360.com Search: ACA Gallery; 1705 Guadalupe St., Austin, TX 78701; Mon., Tues., Wed., Fri. 10am–6pm, Thurs. noon–9pm, Sat. noon–6pm) The Artists' Coalition of Austin features work by members. There's a changing exhibit every month, and you might find paintings, sculpture, wood constructions, or mixed media. The next-door space is for rent to local artists who want to have their own show, so there's always plenty of interest at both galleries.

Clarksville Pottery and Gallery (See "Shopping.")

Fire Island Hot Glass Studio (512-389-1100; austin.citysearch.com Search: Fire Island Hot Glass; 3401 E. 4th St., Austin, TX 78202; Mon.–Fri. 9am–5pm, Sat. 9am–noon) All sorts of handblown glass is for sale here: paperweights, vases, perfume bottles, oil lamps, drinking glasses, Christmas ornaments, glass bead jewelry, fish, even refrigerator magnets. You can watch it being blown, too. Demos take place Sat. 9am–noon from Sept.–Jan. and Mar.–May.

Flatbed Galleries (512-477-9328; www.flatbedpress.com; 2832 E. Martin Luther King Jr. Blvd., Austin, TX 78702; Tues.–Sat. 10am–5pm, otherwise by appointment) Master printers Katherine Brimberry and Gerald Manson specialize in intaglio, relief, and monotype prints in this print gallery and publishing workshop. But paintings, drawings, photographs, and sculpture are also on view for purchase.

Galería Sin Fronteras (512-478-9448; www.io.com/~gsf; 1701 Guadalupe St., Austin, TX 78701; Tues.–Sat. 11am–6pm) Contemporary Latino art: paintings, prints, photographs, and other media. The works of local artists are the primary focus in this gallery "without borders."

Spirit Echoes Art Gallery (512-320-1492; www.spiritechoes.com; 701 Brazos St., Suite 120, Austin, TX 78701; Mon.–Fri. 9:30am–5pm, Sat. 10am–5pm) Located in the lobby of the Omni hotel, this gallery features a wide selection of paintings, monotypes, collage, prints from realistic gardens of florals to native American images.

Wally Workman Gallery (512-472-7428; 1202 W. 6th St., Austin, TX 78703; Tues.–Sat. 10am–5pm) Specializing in excellent fine art, the gallery features original works by many Austin artists.

HISTORIC HOMES

In addition to the historic homes you can see in Austin's Bremond Block and Hyde Park neighborhood (see "Architecture") are these mansions open to the public.

GOVERNOR'S MANSION OF TEXAS
512-463-5518.
www.governor.state.tx.us/ mansion.
1010 Colorado St., Austin, TX 78701.
Open: Tours every 20 minutes Mon.–Fri. 10–11:40am.
Admission: Free.

Master builder Abner Cook built this Greek Revival mansion in 1856, and every Texas governor since then has called it home. Outside, the two-story fluted columns were built of Bastrop pine, and inside its brick walls were plastered by an African-American slave. Governor Elisha Pease was the first occupant, and he was pleased to be able to view the Capitol Fourth of July fireworks from the balcony.

THE NEILL-COCHRAN MUSEUM HOUSE
512-478-2335.
austin.citysearch.com
Search: Neill-Cochran Museum.
2310 San Gabriel St., Austin, TX 78705.
Open: Wed.–Sun. 2–5pm.
Admission: $2.

A blend of Greek Revival architecture and native Texas materials makes this mansion a unique Austin landmark. Abner Cook, the master builder who also built the Governor's Mansion, used native limestone and pine from Bastrop to construct this home in 1855 for Washington L. Hill. It was home to a succession of owners (during the Civil War, Federal soldiers were hospitalized here, and some are buried near the house) until purchased in 1958 by the Colonial Dames of America.

LIBRARIES

The Austin History Center, an Art Deco rendering of Renaissance Revival architecture.

Eleanor S. Morris

AUSTIN HISTORY CENTER
512-499-7480.
www.ci.austin.tx.us/
    library/lbahc.htm.
810 Guadalupe St., PO Box
    2287, Austin, TX 78768.
Open: Mon.–Thurs.
    9am–9pm, Fri. & Sat.
    9am–6pm, Sun.
    noon–6pm.
Admission: Free.

CENTER FOR AMERICAN HISTORY AT THE UNIVERSITY OF TEXAS AT AUSTIN
512-495-4515.
www.lib.utexas.edu/Libs/
    CAH.
2.101 Sid Richardson Hall,
    Austin, TX 78712.
University of Texas campus
    on Red River next to the
    LBJ Library.
Open: Mon.–Sat. 9am–5pm.
Admission: Free.

JOHN HENRY FAULK CENTRAL LIBRARY
512-499-7301.

The history center is housed in another of Austin's historic buildings, this one an Art Deco interpretation of Renaissance Revival style. It was built in 1933 as the Austin Public Library and is still fondly referred to as "Old Main." (The new building, ultramodern glass and cement, is right next door.) Everything ever printed or recorded about Austin and Travis County is zealously collected and protected within its walls, and the library is run by a very helpful and friendly staff.

If you're looking for Texas history, you'll find it here, with 120,000 volumes of Texana. Stephen F. Austin's papers and those of his father Moses Austin are here as are the Bexar Archives, the Barker Texas History Collections, and other important historical materials dealing with the settling of the state. A closed-stack library, it's open for research to anyone abiding by the rules.

This four-story main branch of the Austin library system offers business information as well as books, children's as well as consumer ser-

The University of Texas displays Santa Rita No. 1 oil rig. The gusher from this well was the first to provide revenues for the university.

Eleanor S. Morris

austin.citysearch.com
    Search: John Henry Faulk
    Central Library.
800 Guadalupe St., Austin,
    TX 78705.
Open: Mon.–Thurs. 9–9,
    Fri.–Sat. 9–6, Sun. 12–6.
Admission: Free

vices plus periodicals dating back to the 1800s. Out in front one of the city's Art in Public Places is Eagle II, by David L. Deming, made of Cor-Ten steel.

**LORENZO DE ZAVALA
STATE TEXAS
ARCHIVES AND
LIBRARY**
512-936-INFO.
www.tsl.state.tx.us.
1201 Brazos St., PO Box
    12927, Austin, TX 78711.
Open: Mon.–Fri. 8am–5pm;
    Genealogy Dept.
    Tues.–Sat. 8am–5pm.
Admission: Free.

Some of Texas's most important historical documents and collections are housed here in the Texas state library, including genealogy records. In the lobby of the building — named for an elected interim vice-president of the Texas republic — a 13 by 45.5-foot mural, painted by Peter Rogers in collaboration with Peter Hurd, depicts events and personages of the republic. Also in the lobby are exhibits displaying artifacts of the Texas republic, and on the second floor is a colorful display of every flag that played a part in Texas history. A large statue of Sam Houston stands at the entrance to the building.

**LYNDON BAINES
JOHNSON LIBRARY
AND MUSEUM**
512-916-5137.
www.lbjlib.utexas.edu.
2313 Red River St., Austin,
    TX 78705.
Open: Daily except
    Christmas 9am–5pm.
Admission: Free.

The presidential library houses forty million pages from the entire public career of Lyndon Baines Johnson and also those of close associates (used primarily by scholars). Year-round exhibits for public viewing of the permanent historical and cultural collections include gifts from foreign heads of state, a moon rock, and a replica of the Oval Office. Visitors' remarks suggest the library's scope and impact: "I don't know when I've seen a place so educational, so beautiful, or emotional in my life," and "This is what a presidential library should be like."

Don't miss the First Lady's Room, a comprehensive exhibit of Lady Bird Johnson's life and times.

MUSEUMS

A ustin museums reflect the history of both the city and state, as well as the sometimes esoteric interests of its residents.

THE AUSTIN MUSEUM OF ART AT LAGUNA GLORIA
512-458-8191.
austin.citysearch.com
  Search: Austin Museum
  of Art at Laguna Gloria.
3809 W. 35th St., Austin, TX
  78703.
Open: Tues.–Sat. 10am–
  5pm, Thurs. 10am–8pm,
  Sun. noon–5pm.
Admission: Adults $2,
  student $1, children 12
  and under free.

Set on 12 green acres of lovely grounds once owned by Stephen F. Austin, who purchased the land in 1832 but died before he could build on it, the museum is nationally known for its art exhibits, sculpture gardens, and educational programs. The museum building was once the home of Clara Driskill Servier, considered a heroine for her work in preserving the Alamo for posterity, and was deeded to the Texas Fine Arts Commission in 1943. The grounds, in the middle of the city, are secluded, shady, and spacious, with wandering walks, sunken sculpture gardens, and rock terraces down to the shores of Lake Austin.

The museum specializes in American art since 1900 and is a showcase for modern painters, sculptors, photographers, and architects. A museum shop is downtown (see "Shopping").

JACK S. BLANTON MUSEUM OF ART
(formerly Huntington Art
  Gallery)
512-471-7324.
www.utexas.edu/cofa/hag.
Two locations at the
  University of Texas: Art
  Building at 23rd and San
  Jacinto; Harry Ransom
  Resource Center at 21st
  and Guadalupe Sts.
Mail: Blanton Museum of
  Art, 23rd and San Jacinto
  Sts., Austin, TX 78712.
Open: Mon., Tues., Wed.,
  Fri. 9am–5pm; Thurs.
  9am–9pm; Sat. & Sun.
  1pm–5pm.
Admission: Free.

These galleries are home to 20th-century artwork of both North and Latin America as well as the Michener Collection of art deeded to the university by novelist James A. Michener and his wife. You can also see a Gutenburg Bible printed in 1455 plus exhibits of photography and the theater arts. The museum has acquired the Suida-Manning Collection, one of the most important collections of Old Masters in private hands.

Eleanor S. Morris

The parlor of the French Legation, Austin's oldest building, displays furniture of the period. The portrait is of Louis Philippe, king of France at the time.

THE FRENCH LEGATION MUSEUM
512-472-8180.
www.french-legation.mus.tx.us.
802 San Marcos St., Austin, TX 78702.
Open: Tours Tues.–Sun. 1–4:30pm.
Admission: adults $3, seniors $2, children under 18 $1.

This Greek Revival bayou-style mansion, built in 1841, is Austin's oldest standing building. Preserved by the Daughters of the Republic of Texas, it was built by Alphonse Dubois de Saligny, named chargé d'affaires to the Republic of Texas when Louis Philippe of France recognized the republic in 1839. But the French nobleman never occupied the legation; he left in a huff because of the "Pig War." The pigs on a neighboring site ate Saligny's corn, and perhaps even worse, chewed on some table linens that he had purchased in New Orleans on his way to this outpost of civilization. His servant shot the pigs, the animals' owner beat the servant, and the "war" was on.

The legation's kitchen is the only authentic reproduction of an early Creole kitchen in the United States. There's a bang-up Bastille Day celebration every July 14th.

O. HENRY HOME AND MUSEUM
512-472-1903.

Austin is proud to boast that William Sidney Porter, otherwise known as short story master O. Henry, once lived in Austin — from 1893 to 1895

www.ci.austin.tx.us/parks
  /ohenry.htm.
409 E. 5th St., Austin, TX
  78701.
Open: Wed.–Sun.
  noon–5pm.
Admission: Free.

— and his 1886 Queen Anne–style cottage contains his desk, writing materials, and other period furnishings. The first weekend in May the museum sponsors the O. Henry Pun Off competition. Open to the public, it's held in the backyard, where both a book fair and a country-western band are going on at the same time. All three trophies — first, second, and third — are of "the rear end of a horse."

ELISABET NEY MUSEUM
512-458-2255.
www.austin360.com
  Search: Elisabet Ney
  Museum.
304 E. 44th St., Austin, TX
  78751.
Open: Wed.–Sat.
  10am–5pm, Sun.
  noon–5pm, closed Mon.
  & Tues.
Admission: Free.

Elisabet Ney was Texas's first sculptor, and she was famous well before she settled in Austin in 1892. Born in Münster, Germany, in 1833 she was the first woman to be accepted into the Munich Art Academy. She sculpted such notables as Bismarck, Garibaldi, and Ludwig II of Bavaria, whose life-sized likenesses may be seen in the restored former home and studio today. She and her Scottish husband, Dr. Edmund Montgomery, moved to the United States to avoid the Franco-Prussian War. After a 20-year hiatus, she resumed her career in 1892 when she received commissions to model Sam Houston and Stephen F. Austin for the Columbian Exposition in Chicago.

Today these marbles are in the Texas State Capitol, but the plaster models are in the museum. A plaster model of Lady Macbeth, which Ney considered her masterpiece, stands in the full light of the large studio window. Sculpted between 1902 and 1905, the marble statue has been in the collections of the Smithsonian in Washington, D.C., since 1916.

**TEXAS MEMORIAL
  MUSEUM**
512-471-1604.
www.utexas.edu/depts
  /tmm.
2400 Trinity St., Austin, TX
  78705.
Open: Mon.–Fri. 9am–5pm,
  Sat. 10am–5pm, Sun.
  1–5pm.
Admission: Free.

An eclectic mix of Texas's cultural and natural history, with dinosaur fossils, antique firearms, wildlife dioramas, native American artifacts, rare gems and minerals, and the original Goddess of Liberty statue removed from the Capitol dome during a recent restoration. Gift shop.

**UMLAUF SCULPTURE
  GARDEN AND
  MUSEUM**
512-445-5582.
www.io.com/~tam/
  umlauf.

In 1985 Charles and Angeline Umlauf gave their home, studio, and work to the city of Austin. The museum was built with private funds and contains more than 200 sculptures by Charles Umlauf, internationally known sculptor. The works are displayed by rotation in 6 acres of gardens. The set-

605 Robert E. Lee Rd., Austin, TX 78704.
Open: Wed.–Fri. 10am–4:30pm, Sat. & Sun. 1–4:30pm.
Admission: Adults $3, seniors $2, students $1, children 6 and under free.

ting is lovely, with a waterfall, streams, and ponds under tall cedars and oaks. The works are executed in diverse materials, from exotic woods to terra cotta, bronze to alabaster, and range from detailed realism to lyrical abstractions. A 10-minute video shows the late artist telling about his work and philosophy and describing his methods.

MUSIC AND NIGHTLIFE

Austin celebrates music all year long, indoors and out. The SXSW (South By Southwest) Festival brings thousands of musicians and listeners from all over the world, some as far away as Australia. Free outdoor concerts draw aficionados to Auditorium Shores on Town Lake in the spring; Blues on the Green attracts droves of blues fans to the Arboretum Lawn each summer.

Here music and nightlife are synonymous: Austin lays claim to the title of "Live Music Capital of the World," and there's certainly enough going on all over town — all the time — to merit the title. Through the years Austin has been a magnet for creative souls, giving rise to a live music culture where many popular rock 'n' roll, blues, jazz, and country-western singers like Willie Nelson got their start. The legacy of Stevie Ray Vaughan and Janis Joplin, Jerry Jeff Walker, the Fabulous Thunderbirds, and others have made Austin a music mecca. Famous for its club scene, Austin's line both sides of East 6th Street (once Old Pecan Street).

You can pick up a walking map of six-block-long 6th Street, listing clubs, restaurants, and shops, at the **Austin Convention and Visitors Bureau, Visitor Information Center** (512-474-5171, 800-926-2282; www.austin360.com/acvb; 201 E. 2nd St., Austin TX 78701). Here nightspots pack in patrons with high-energy levels for music live and lively, other entertainment, and food. Look for well-known Austin music venues like **Babe's**, with maybe country on one stage and heavy metal on the other; **Maggie Mae's** for pop and rock; **Bob Popular** for current dance tracks, oldies, and hip Texas music as well as twisting rockabilly sound. Especially famous is **Antones** for the blues. Hit **Top of the Marc** at **Katz's** on West 6th Street to kick back to some great jazz. Then wander down to Congress Avenue to the **Elephant Room** for more of the same. For country-western music along with dance, the **Broken Spoke** on South Congress is a classic Texas dance hall; Willie Nelson got his start here.

What makes Texas music in particular so varied, so rich? Those in the know credit the intermingling of so many cultures — Hispanic and Spanish, German, Black, Czech, and Anglo — all celebrated in the "Live Music Capital of the World."

And it's not only blues, jazz, rock 'n' roll, and country that moves musical Austin — Austinites have a vibrant interest in classical music, as well. The Austin Symphony Orchestra, for instance, has a dedicated following: More than 200,000 people attend the orchestra's performances each year.

Austin Symphony (512-476-6064; www.austinsymphony.org; 1101 Red River St., Austin, TX 78701) The oldest symphony orchestra in Texas is under the leadership of Maestro Sung Kwak, former assistant conductor of the Cleveland Orchestra. With its high level of musicianship, the orchestra delights Austin music lovers. Performances are at Bass Hall at the University of Texas, at Palmer Auditorium, Riverside Dr. and S. 1st St., and other venues around town.

University of Texas Performing Arts Center (512-471-1444, 800-687-6010; www.utpac.org; PO Box 7818, Austin, TX 78713) The center includes Bass Concert Hall, Bates Recital Hall, McCullough Theater, and B. Iden Payne Theater, and hosts music, dance, Broadway, and comedy performances regularly, with major stars, great diversity, artistic integrity, and just plain fun. The center is a flagship institution in the state of Texas; when the English National Opera's production of Prokofiev's *War and Peace* came to the United States, it played in only two venues — the Metropolitan Opera and UT's Bass Concert Hall, where the facilities, audiences, and amenities are first class. Call for more information.

THEATER

In Austin, the theater arts are thriving, with a host of offerings noted for both creativity and professionalism. Ticket services include **Austin Circle of Theaters Hotline** (512-320-7168), a service provided by Austin's theaters. Updated every Monday and Thursday morning, it gives theater listings, ticket availability, information on box offices, and half-price tickets where available. Another ticket service is **Austix** (512-397-1450), giving information on half-price "day of performance" tickets and full-service theater tickets.

Esther's Follies (512-320-0553; www.esthersfollies.com; 525 E. 6th St., Austin, TX 78701; Thurs. 8pm, Fri. & Sat. 8 and 10pm) One of Texas's premier musical and comedy troupes, performing hilarious original and topical satire and musical parody. Both revered and feared for its biting wit, the Follies are a centerpiece of the 6th Street entertainment strip. The large store window on the street behind the stage reveals passersby, who stop in wonder at what's going on inside, all of which adds to the fun.

Hyde Park Theatre (512-452-6688; austin.citysearch.com Search: Hyde Park Theatre; 511 W. 43rd St., Austin, TX 78751) Productions range from comedy to tragedy and everything in between in this theater on the northern edge of the city's Hyde Park Historical District, performed by a variety of groups.

Paramount Theatre (512-472-5470; www.theparamount.org; 713 Congress Ave., Austin, TX 78701) Classic movies on a big screen and local and national touring artists are on the bill in this restored movie palace. Built in 1915, one of those opulent beauties that drew crowds in vaudeville and early movie days, the Paramount has been beautifully restored and is considered one of the country's most richly detailed historic theaters.

State Theater Company (512-472-5143; www.statetheatrecompany.com; 719 Congress Ave., Austin, TX 78701) The theater performs new, innovative productions as well as traditional theater pieces. Performances are usually year-round, from October to the following September.

Zachary Scott Theatre (512-476-0541; www.zachscott.com; 1510 Toomey Rd., Austin, TX 78704) Named for the Austin native turned movie star, this organization is actually two theaters in one: the main stage in the larger building and the Arena Stage around the corner, a theater-in-the round. The long season runs virtually year-round, so interested visitors ought to be able to catch something. Productions in this regional theater (using both local and national talent) include musicals, contemporary comedy, and drama.

SEASONAL EVENTS

There's something — often more than one something — happening every month of the year in Austin. The **Austin Convention and Visitors Bureau, Visitor Information Center** (512-474-0098, 800-926-2282; www.austin360.com /acvb; 201 E. 2nd St., Austin, TX 78701) has a complete list.

In JANUARY, **Dancefest** features 500 dancers showcasing multidisciplinary and cross-cultural artistic dance (512-454-TIKS for tickets and/or performance information; www.austindancefest.com).

FEBRUARY brings forth Mardi Gras, feasting, partying, and parading on 6th Street before Lent (512-499-0980).

MARCH is time for the annual **Austin-Travis County Livestock Show and Rodeo**, with more than 150,000 turning out for twelve different rodeos, not to mention loads of family fun. Cattle auctions, square dancing, continuous country music, and carnival rides (512-467-9811; austin.citysearch.com, Search: Austin-Travis County Livestock Show).

March also brings **Jerry Jeff Walker's Birthday Celebration**. More than 5,000 fans turn out for the 3-day birthday bash honoring the legendary country-western songwriter. Included in part of the excitement of this party are 5K runs, golf tournaments, rodeos, and dances, culminating in a Saturday night performance in Austin's historic Paramount Theatre downtown (512-477-0036).

South by Southwest (SXSW) is a massive gathering each year of local and national critics, who come to judge musicians from all over the world hoping to make their mark — Austin isn't called "The Music Capital of the World" for nothing. Workshops, panel discussions, and hundreds of concerts performed at more than twenty-five city venues bring 15,000 music aficionados to the streets and clubs of Austin (512-467-7979; www.SXSW.com). (See "Music and Nightlife" above for more information.)

As for APRIL, for the athletes among us there's the renowned **Capitol 10,000,** an event that puts thousands of runners on the downtown streets. Part of the show: the unique costumes that appear among the racers (512-445-3598).

For the more sophisticated crowd, the annual **Texas Hill Country Wine and Food Festival** gathers together the state's chefs, food consultants, food writers, and the gourmets among us all. A highlight is the Hill Country wine auction (512-329-0770; www.main.org/txwinefood).

MAY brings the **O. Henry Pun-Off** (see "Museums" for more information; 512-472-1903; www.ci.austin.tx.us/parks/ohenry). And the **Old Pecan Street Spring Arts and Crafts Festival** turns East 6th Street (known in the mid-1880s as Pecan Street) into a pedestrian mall filled with more than 400 art, crafts, and food booths, with live music (512-441-9015; www.roadstarproductions.com).

There are more of the same festivities at **Austin Fine Arts Festival**, set on the grounds of the Austin Museum of Art at Laguna Gloria on the shores of Lake Austin (see "Museums"). Begun in 1956, the fiesta's outdoor booths draw more than 30,000 visitors for art, food, and drink, and the event now ranks as one of the country's top ten art shows (512-458-6073; austin.citysearch.com Search: Austin Fine Arts Festival).

JUNE brings the **Hyde Park Historic Homes Tours**, showcasing Austin's first planned residential suburb, founded in 1891 and now practically a part of downtown, since the city has grown so. Victorian and early 20th-century homes are opened to the public in what remains a pleasant old-fashioned neighborhood (512-452-4139; www.hydepark-na.org).

JULY is ushered in with one of Austin's most popular traditions — 50,000 Austinites usually turn out to Zilker Park for the **Freedom Festival and Fireworks** on the Fourth of July. Top entertainers perform, there are food and beer booths and activities for the kids, and it all ends with a bang with the Austin Symphony playing the *1812 Overture* on the Auditorium Shores outdoor stage as a fantastic fireworks show explodes over Town Lake.

Bastille Day at the French Legation also celebrates independence, on July 14th, French Independence Day. Once the headquarters of the French chargé d'affaires to the Republic of Texas (see "Museums"), the legation is the site of festivities with gourmet wines and pastries, French fashions, French singers, and even fencing duels (512-472-8180).

AUGUST brings the **Austin Fiery Foods Show** to Palmer Auditorium, with everything to do with hot foods as well as cookbook signings and a 5K race (512-977-0501).

In SEPTEMBER. the **Austin Jazz and Arts Festival,** formerly the Clarksville Jazz Festival, celebrates jazz with performances, exhibitions, workshops, and kids' activities (512-477-9438).

There's more jazz in September, with the **Zilker Park Fall Jazz Festival,** when the best of Austin's night owl jazz is played outdoors at the Zilker

Hillside Theater stage. The free two-day music festival attracts some 10,000 jazz lovers each year (512-440-1414).

Also in September and into OCTOBER: Shakespeare Under the Stars, an annual festival celebrating the Bard, with plays performed on the Hillside Theater in Zilker Park (512-454-BARD; www.members.aol.com/asf).

Be forewarned that **Halloween on 6th Street** brings some 60,000 costumed revelers to fill the barricaded seven blocks of Austin's best-known entertainment area (512-478-0098).

NOVEMBER pays homage to its Hispanic population with an eerie parade down Congress Avenue to celebrate **Día de los Muertos**, the Day of the Dead. The Halloween-like celebration brings parade floats of skeletons and ceremonial altars (512-480-9373).

Victorian Christmas on 6th Street transforms Austin's entertainment district into 19th-century London so that Thanksgiving weekend shoppers can get a head start on their Christmas shopping. Booths are filled with holiday craft and gift items (512-441-9015; www.roadstarprodutions.com).

DECEMBER is ushered in with one of Austin's best-loved holiday traditions. Every year a **165-foot Christmas tree** lights up the sky, to be seen from miles away. Surrounding the tree is a mile-long trail of lights, an extensive and impressive display of holiday figures and winter scenes (512-397-1468).

The **Armadillo Christmas Bazaar** is a uniquely Austin holiday market, with renowned Southwest artists selling their handiwork. In keeping with the Southwest theme, you can nibble on tasty Tex-Mex food and move to the ubiquitous live Austin music while you shop (512-447-1605; www.armadillobazaar.com).

AUSTIN RECREATION

A ustin prides itself on being in tune with nature. The city lives and breathes within a beautiful natural environment, embracing a total of 191 parks, and is a leading innovator in environmental issues in the nation.

BOATING AND WATER SPORTS

Emma Long Metropolitan Park (512-346-1831; austin.citysearch.com Search: Emma Long Metropolitan Park; 1600 City Park Rd., FM 2222 west of Loop 360) With boat ramps and camping facilities here at Austin's largest park, the public can launch boats on Lake Austin all year long.

Town Lake, the section of the Colorado River that bisects north and south Austin, is a year-round training spot for many U.S. collegiate rowing teams, clubs, and amateurs just out to enjoy the water, the weather, and the scenery. **Austin Canoe and Kayak** (512-719-4386; austin.citysearch.com

Search: Austin Canoe and Kayak) and **Zilker Park Canoe Rental** (512-478-3852) are handy if you haven't brought your own canoe.

CAMPING

Given Austin's usually mild weather, the camping season is year-round, with August to October the most popular time at both public parks and private RV parks, plus March, an event-filled month. Reserving for these times at least a month in advance is recommended.

Crestview RV Park (512-295-2308; www.gocampingamerica.com/crestview; S. IH-35; PO Box 1028, Buda, TX 78610) 80 sites with full hookup, 100 sites total.

Emma Long Metropolitan Park (512-346-1831, 1600 City Park Rd., FM 2222 west of Loop 360) Austin's largest park, with two boat ramps, fishing, water-skiing, and swimming; 20 utility campsites with electricity, 50 tent sites. Entry fee $5 per car, $6 per night.

Lone Star RV Resort (512-444-6322, 800-562-26686; www.gocampingamerica. com/lonestar; 7009 S. IH-35, Austin, TX 78744) This nationally award-winning park has log cabins, full hookups for RVs, tent camping areas, a pool, and the Hitchin' Post shop offering gifts with a Texas flair. On IH-35 barely 5 miles southeast of the state capitol.

Pecan Grove RV Park (512-472-1067; 1518 Barton Springs Rd., Austin, TX 78704) 13 three-way hookups, self-contained RVs only.

Royal Palms RV Park (512-385-2211; www.gocampingamerica.com/royal-palms; 7901 E. Ben White Blvd., Austin, TX 78741) 64 sites with full hookups, group facilities, no tents.

Shady Grove RV Park (512-499-8432; 1600 Barton Springs Rd., Austin, TX 78704) 32 sites with three-way hookups.

FAMILY FUN

Families with children will find plenty of activities in the Austin area. The free brochure *101 Things for Kids to Do in Austin* is available at the **Austin Convention and Visitors Bureau, Visitor Information Center** (512-474-0098; 800-926-2282; www.austin360.com/acvb; 201 E. 2nd St., Austin, TX 78701.

AUSTIN CHILDREN'S MUSEUM
512-472-2499.
www.austinkids.org.
201 Colorado St., Austin, TX 78701.
Open: Tues.–Sat. 10am–5pm, Sun. noon–5pm; open Wed. till 8pm.

This museum's philosophy is that learning is fun — exhibits and programs are designed to appeal to children's interest in science and technology, how people live, and creative expression. Popular permanent exhibits are the Whole Foods Market, where children learn about nutrition while "playing store"; the Music Room, where they can

Admission: $4.50, children under 2 free; free admission Wed. 5pm–8pm and Sun. 4pm–5pm.

AUSTIN NATURE AND SCIENCE CENTER
512-327-8180.
www.ci.austin.tx.us/nature -science.
301 Nature Center Dr., Austin, TX 78746.
Located in Zilker Park off Stratford Dr.
Open: Mon.–Sat. 9am–5pm, Sun. noon–5pm.
Admission: Free.

OURDAN-BACHMAN PIONEER FARM
512-837-1215.
www.pioneerfarm.org.
11418 Sprinkle Cut-Off Rd., Austin, TX 78754.
Open: Year-round, Sun. 1pm–5pm; June–Aug., Mon.–Thurs. 9:30am–1pm; Sept.–May, Mon.–Wed. 9:30am–1pm.
Admission: Adults $4, children 3–12 $3, under 3 free.

play simple instruments and dance; and the Sound Track Studio, equipped with keyboard and microphone.

The center offers hands-on education programs about ecology and offers exhibits about science, natural history, and botany. The Nature Center is on 80 acres of canyons, meadows, and trails just west of Zilker Park.

This living-history museum tells the story of life as it was lived in the 1850s on a 2,000-acre cotton farm. Docents in costume demonstrate the work of those days. Depending on the day and time of year, youngsters can watch cows being milked or horses shod by a blacksmith, or food cooking on an old wood-burning stove. Children can also help plant or pick cotton, watch it being spun into yarn, and they can plan on scrubbing clothes on a washboard anytime.

STEAM TRAINS

Austin Steam Train Association (512-477-8468; www.main.org/flyer/asta) operates three separate excursions on the 143-ton Southern Pacific Locomotive 786, built in 1916: Hill Country Flyer, River City Flyer, and Twilight Flyer. The locomotive pulls 1920s Pennsylvania day coaches and post–World War II streamlined lounge and parlor-sleeper cars.

Hill Country Flyer: Runs year-round from Cedar Park to Burnet and back again, 68 scenic miles each way, the 5-hour excursion starts at the station behind Cedar Park City Hall (north of Austin on U.S. 183 near RR 1431), and there's a short layover in small-town Burnet for some entertainment (an enactment of a Wild West shoot-out) before the train heads back. Check their Web site (www.main.org/flyer) for their current schedule.

River City Flyer: Runs June through November, with 90-minute round-trips every Saturday and Sunday from Cedar Park to Austin, with a 2.5 hour layover downtown for shopping and dining. Check their Web site (www.main. org/flyer) for their current schedule.

Twilight Flyer: Seasonal celebrations or theme entertainment on selected Saturday and holiday evenings, round-trip from Cedar Park. Check their Web site (www.main.org/flyer) for their current schedule.

WATER EXCURSIONS

Lone Star Riverboat (512-327-1388; austin.citysearch.com   Search: Lone Star Riverboat; south shore of Town Lake between the Congress and First St. Bridges) A real old-fashioned paddle wheeler, the *Lone Star* takes sailors for a 90-minute scenic cruise on the Town Lake. Hours: Mar.–May, Sat. & Sun. 3pm; June–Aug., Wed., Sat., Sun. 5:30pm and Fri. moonlight cruise at 10:30pm; Sept. & Oct., Sat. & Sun. 3pm. Also additional bat-watching Sunset Tours Mar.–Oct.

Austin Duck Adventure (512-477-5274; www.austinducks.com; 1605 W. 5th St., Austin, TX 78703) Tour Austin's historic and scenic streets, then splash into Lake Austin for a spin on the water in a unique amphibious vehicle.

Capital Cruises (512-480-9264; www.capitalcruises.com; Hyatt-Regency Boat Dock, Town Lake) Bat-watching excursions, nightly 1-hour cruise departing 20 to 30 minutes before sunset. Also, hourly boat rentals of canoes, pedal boats, kayaks, and electric boats.

GOLF

Eleanor S. Morris

Golfers ponder their strategy at the Lions' course.

Austin lays claim to one of the country's premier golf locations. Proof is in the huge number of courses: twenty public ones and eighteen large country clubs in the area. Listed below are half a dozen. For more information, contact the **Austin Convention and Visitors Bureau, Visitor Information Center** (512-474-0098, 800-926-2282; www.austin360.com/acvb; 201 E. 2nd St., Austin, TX 78701) or check out www.lonestar.texas.net~/timbaby for a comprehensive review of public golf in and around Austin.

Bluebonnet Hill Golf Course (512-272-4228; 9100 Decker Ln., Austin, TX 78724) Greens fees: $15 weekdays, $24 weekends.

Butler Park Pitch & Putt (512-477-9025; www.mygolf.com/golf/courses/ 14666; 201 Lee Barton Dr., Austin, TX 78704) $4 for 9 holes.

Circle C Golf Club (512-288-4297; www.golfsw.com/tx/circlec/cchp; 7401 Hwy. 45, Austin, TX 78739) Greens fees (includes cart): Mon.–Thurs. $50, Fri.–Sun. $65, holidays $51.

Hancock Austin Municipal Golf Course (512-453-0276; austin.citysearch.com Search: Hancock Municipal Golf; 811 E. 41st St., Austin, TX 78751) Established in 1899, this is the oldest golf course in Texas. It's for walkers. Greens fees: $8 for 9 holes on weekdays, $9 weekends; $13.50 for 18 holes on weekdays, $15 weekends; seniors $7.25 for 9 or 18 holes weekdays or weekends; juniors (under 18) $6.25 for 9 or 18 holes weekdays or weekends.

Lago Vista Golf Club (512-267-1179; 4616 Rimrock Dr., Lago Vista, TX 78645) Greens fees: $25 weekdays, $35 weekends.

Lions' Municipal Golf Course (512-477-6963; austin.citysearch.com Search: Lions Municipal Golf; 2901 Enfield Rd., Austin, TX 78703) Greens fees: $13.50 weekdays, $15 weekends and holidays.

Morris-Williams Public Golf Course (512-926-1298; austin.citysearch.com Search: Morris-Williams Golf; 4305 Manor Rd., Austin, TX 78723) Greens fees: $13.50 weekdays, $15 weekends.

HIKING, BIKING, AND RUNNING

Austin offers an excellent 30-mile network of trails, 18 of them on well-surfaced scenic paths following natural greenbelts into all areas of the city. An additional 14 miles of trails are natural surface. No motor vehicles are allowed at any time, and all trails have a 10pm–5am curfew. Dogs must be controlled; Austin has a leash law enforced by the Austin Park Police (Rangers). For maps of the seven **Hike and Bike Trails of Austin**, contact the **Austin Parks and Recreation Department** (512-499-6700; Mon.–Fri. 8am–5pm; www.ci.austin.tx/parks).

Barton Creek Greenbelt: Some runners and bikers prefer paths that follow picturesque creeks. Here you'll find 7.5 miles of natural surface both east and west of MoPac Expressway (Loop 1).

Town Lake Greenbelt: A host of joggers and bikers enjoy Town Lake Trail because of the visual beauty of its 10-plus miles of granite gravel and con-

Cyclists on the 10-mile Hike and Bike Trail around Town Lake.

Eleanor S. Morris

crete. Loop A, from MoPac Bridge to Lamar Boulevard is 2.9 miles; Loop B, Mo-Pac Bridge to South 1st Street is 4.1 miles.

The Veloway: This 3.1-mile paved asphalt loop wanders through creeks and meadows on more than 100 acres of parkway. Catch it on south Loop 1 or from Bowie High School (512-414-5247, 4103 Slaughter Ln.). Open from dawn to dusk.

Waller Creek Walkway: Just east of the main downtown area, Waller Creek Walkway follows the creek from 15th Street down where it flows into Town Lake, 0.75 mile of granite gravel, concrete, and brick surface. The Waterloo Park area, 15th Street south to 10th Street, is 0.25 mile. Lower Waller Creek Development, 10th Street south to Town Lake, is 0.5 mile.

    Bike rentals are available at **University Schwinn Cyclery** (512-474-6696; austin.citysearch.com Search: University Schwinn Cyclery; 2901 N. Lamar Blvd., Austin, TX 78705) and **Bicycle Sport Shop** (512-477-3472; www.bicy clesportshop.com; 1426 Toomey Rd. or 512-345-7460; 10947 Research Blvd., Austin, TX 78759).

NATURE AND NATURE PRESERVES

A ustin's greenbelts are parks that follow rivers, creeks, and scenic ravines. These areas of scenic beauty are designed to accommodate walking, hiking, jogging, running, bicycling, and even rock climbing in some places. Another special feature of Austin's many natural attractions is its bat colony.

A natural phenomenon unique to Austin is, of all things, its bat colony. Just after sunset between March and November the largest urban colony of Mexican freetail bats in North America (about 1.5 million at last count) fly out from under Town Lake's Congress Avenue bridge. Clouds of them blot out the sky as they zoom out on their nightly quest for dinner fare: insects — about 10,000 to 30,000 pounds a night, for which Austin is mighty grateful.

AUSTIN'S BATS
Bat Conservation International (512-327-9721; www.batcon.org) or *Austin American Statesman* (512-416-5700, ext. 3636).
Congress Avenue Bridge.
Open: Daily at sunset Mar.–Nov.
Admission: Free.

*K*arst originally referred to a limestone plateau in Germany, but the word now means any area with limestone rocks, deep fractures, and caves that feed rainwater directly into underground lakes and streams. This 10-acre preserve over the Edwards Aquifer Recharge Zone features caves, sinkholes, and honeycomb outcroppings along the 1/3-mile trail, a pleasant winding walk of about 20 minutes (including stops for bird watching and inspecting the caves and sinkholes).

KARST NATURE PRESERVE
512-327-8181.
austin.citysearch.com Search: Karst Nature Preserve.
3900 Deer Ln., Austin, TX 78749.
Open: Dawn to dusk.

*F*ormerly the National Wildflower Research Center, this nonprofit educational organization is unique in its focus on native plants, resource conservation, and ecologically sensitive design. Created by Lady Bird Johnson in 1982 as part of a national beautification project, the center will give you an eyeful of natural beauty — this is the only institution in the nation dedicated exclusively to conserving and promoting the use of plants native to North America, including 75 species of wild-flowers. The 42-acre site includes numerous research display gardens, landscaped areas, theme gardens, preserved woodlands, and natural grassland. The gift shop is open Tues.–Sat. 9am–5:30pm, Sun. 1pm–4pm; the Wildflower Café is open Tues.–Sat. 9am–4pm, Sun. 11am–4pm.

LADY BIRD JOHNSON WILDFLOWER CENTER
512-292-4100.
www.wildflower.org.
4801 La Cross Ave., Austin, TX 78739.
Open: Grounds Tues.–Sun. 9am–5:30pm.; visitors gallery Tues.–Sat. 9am–4pm, Sun. 1–4pm.

*T*hese 227 acres of beautiful Hill Country were set aside in the mid-1970s to preserve the land through active management, nature education, and research. Operated with the help of trained volunteers, about 2.5 miles of trails pass through woodland, grassland, and streamside habitats. (Part of a pedestrian-only trail is wheelchair accessible.) Wild Basin is home to some threatened and endangered species of plants, animals, and birds, such as the golden-cheeked warbler and the black-capped

Admission: Adults $4, students and seniors $2.50, children 4 years and under free.

WILD BASIN WILDERNESS PRESERVE
512-327-7622.
www.wildbasin.org.
805 N. Capital of Texas Hwy., Austin, TX 78746.
Open: Daily from sunrise to sunset.
Admission: Voluntary $2 adults, $1 students and children, $6 maximum per family.

vireo, as well as hundreds of both common and unique species. The office and gift shop are open Mon.–Fri. 9am–4:30pm, Sat. & Sun. 8am–3pm.

On the west end of Zilker Park, this 60-acre pre-serve with 2 miles of trails features a creek bed (sometimes there's water there, sometimes not) edged with meadows and high cliffs with shallow caves. Foot trails begin under the Loop One (MoPac)Bridge and lead up to the dry areas that are endemic to the Edwards Plateau, abundant with mountain laurel, myrtle croton, and croton bush. A rock-walled ramada (an open, covered shelter) overlooks both the preserve and the Austin skyline.

PARKS

ZILKER NATURE PRESERVE
512-480-3060.
www.ci.austin.tx.us/ preserves/zilker.
302 Nature Center Dr., west of Loop One(MoPac); park on Barton Springs Rd.
Mail: Austin Parks & Recreation Dept., 200 S. Lamar Blvd., Austin, TX 78704.
Open: Dawn to dusk.

Austin enjoys 320 beautiful days a year, so when visitors want to be outdoors, they can be sure to find Austinites already there, taking advantage of the city's 191 parks. Austinites are outdoor people and no matter how large the city is getting, there are parks aplenty for fun, fitness, and relaxation for everyone. It's a rare neighborhood that doesn't have its own park — and rarer still to see one empty. Austin has the distinction of being cited as one of the four best cities in the nation for parks.

Emma Long Metropolitan Park (512-346-1831; austin.citysearch.com Search: Emma Long Metropolitan Park; FM 2222 west of Loop 360) is Austin's largest park, with 1,147 acres. The public can launch boats on Lake Austin year-round as well as camp, fish, water ski, and barbecue.

Mayfield Park and Preserve (512-480-3060; www.ci.austin.tx.us/preserves; 3505 W. 35th St.) is also a preserve; its 22 acres are on Barrow Brook Cove at Lake Austin. On the grounds are lily ponds, peacocks and hens, and trails meandering through woods and over creek bridges and foot stones. On display is a home representative of suburban lake cottage retreats during the late 1800s. Open daily 8am–5pm.

McKinney Falls State Park (512-243-1643, 800-792-1112; www.tpwd.state. tx.us/prk/mckinney; 5808 McKinney Falls Pkwy.) is a 744.4-acre state park just 13 miles southeast of the state capitol. The park offers 3.5 miles of hiking and biking trails for viewing such wildlife as birds, white-tailed deer, raccoons, squirrels, and armadillos as well as fishing, picnicking, and camping. Open year-round. Entrance fee $1 per person 13 and over.

Mount Bonnell Park (austin.citysearch.com Search: Mount Bonnell; 3800 Mt. Bonnell Dr.) is Austin's most romantic park, famed throughout town history (it was established in the 1850s) for trysts at sunrise and sunset. It's the highest scenic spot (you'll climb ninety-nine steps) for viewing Austin and the surrounding Hill Country. The mountaintop park is 775 feet above sea level, and there's a shade structure and picnic tables on the bluff overlooking Lake Austin. The park is open from 5am–10pm.

Pease District Park (austin.citysearch.com Search: Pease Park; 1100 Kingsbury St., on Shoal Creek along Lamar Blvd.) was the first city park, dedicated in 1876 by Governor Pease himself. One of the city parks with a picnic area for large groups, it also has a wading pool and children's playground, and it's popular for informal volleyball and softball games.

Symphony Square (also downtown, at Red River and 11th Sts.) was given to the city by the state in 1982. Waller Creek runs underneath the street, separating the theater and four restored 100-year-old buildings open for touring. The Jeremiah Hamilton home is the only original one — the other three were moved here from other locations. Jeremiah Hamilton had been the slave of A. J. Hamilton, a governor during Reconstruction. He was a carpenter, and he built this two-story limestone house, making it triangular in order to wedge it into the lot bordered by Waller Creek, Red River, and 11th Street. The Austin Symphony Society saved it from destruction, and it serves as a refreshment venue for performances when the symphony performs outdoor musical events here. The other three houses date from 1870 (old Wilson Mercantile), 1880 (Doyle House), and 1887 (Hardeman House).

Woolrich Park, a bright green square with a charming white gazebo, is set in the middle of downtown on Guadalupe between 9th and 10th Streets. One of four parks deeded in the original city plan when Edwin Waller came to survey the city, it has been the scene of countless weddings, political rallies, and the occasional city council swearing-in.

Zilker Park (512-472-4914; austin.citysearch.com Search: Zilker Park; 2100 Barton Springs Rd. on Town Lake) is one of Austin's most popular parks. Originally the site of temporary Franciscan missions in 1730, the 349-acre downtown park along the shores of the lake counts Barton Springs Pool among its attractions. Zilker Gardens in the park includes an oriental garden, a meditation trail, a famous rose garden, a Swedish log cabin from the 1840s, and a fine garden center as well as the Austin Nature and Science Center (www.ci.austin.tx.us/nature-science). Open daily 5am–10pm.

SKATING

Chaparral Ice Center at Northcross Mall (512-451-5102; www.austin360.com Search: Chaparral Ice Center; 2525 W. Anderson Ln., Austin, TX 78757) This may be the only ice-skating rink located inside a shopping mall. You can catch this taste of real winter every day: Sun. noon–6pm; Mon. 12:50pm–5pm, 6:30pm–9pm; Tues. 10am–5pm; Wed. noon–5pm; Thurs. & Fri. 10am–5pm, 7pm–9pm; Sat. 12:15pm–9pm (times subject to change). For a truly professional ice-skating facility, check out Chaparral Ice's new 40,000 square foot rink in North Austin (512-252-8500; 142000 IH-35 N. at Wells Branch Pkwy.).

SWIMMING

Austin's soaring summer temperatures and Austinites' love of outdoor sports makes swimming a popular pastime here.

Barton Springs Pool is open year-round.

Eleanor S. Morris

BARTON SPRINGS POOL
512-867-3080.
austin.citysearch.com Search: Barton Springs Pool.
2100 Barton Springs Rd.
Located in Zilker Park.
Open: 5am–10pm daily, except Thurs., when it closes at 7pm for maintenance.
Admission: Adults $2.50 weekdays, $2.75 weekends; children 12–17 75¢, children 11 and under 50¢.

Barton Springs Pool is a local institution, regardless of the chilliness of the water. The spring-fed water that gushes up from the Edwards Aquifer to fill Austin's favorite swimming pool is said to remain a constant 68 degrees. But although to many it may feel absolutely arctic, water enthusiasts swim all year long in the 944-foot-long, chlorine-free pool. Lifeguards are on duty 9am–8pm.

McKINNEY FALLS STATE PARK
512-243-1643, 800-792-1112.
www.tpwd.state.tx.us/ park/mckinney/htm.
5808 McKinney Falls Pkwy.
Open: Daily year-round.

Two creeks, Onion and Williamson, form quiet pools and waterfalls at the park. There's an excellent visitor center, hiking and interpretive trails, campsites, a playground, and fishing as well as swimming. Historically interesting are the preserved c1850 ruins of the homestead of one of

Admission: $1 per person 13 and over.

STACY POOL
512-476-4521.
800 E. Live Oak.
Open: Year-round,
  Mon.–Fri. 6am–8pm, Sat.
  & Sun. noon–7pm
  (subject to change).
Admission: Free.

Stephen F. Austin's original 300 colonists, Thomas F. McKinney, for whom the park is named. For modern fun, check out the Texas State Park Store.

This is another of the Hill Country's spring-fed swimming holes. Warm, steamy water is the attraction to this outdoor pool during cooler months.

TENNIS

Austin offers more than fifteen tennis facilities totaling 200 courts. For information on public courts all over the city, call the **Austin Parks & Recreation Dept.** at 512-480-3020.

AUSTIN SHOPPING

Austin can boast of a remarkably eclectic shopping scene — you can easily shop till you drop, from the sidewalk arts and crafts market on "The Drag" (Guadalupe Street alongside the University) to major malls like Barton Creek, with its panoramic views of both the Austin skyline and the outlying hills.

ANTIQUES

You can pick up a guide, map included, of twenty-one Austin-area antique shops at the **Austin Convention and Visitors Bureau, Visitor Information Center** (512-478-0098, 800-926-2282; www.austin360.com/acvb; 201 E. 2nd St.; Mon.–Fri. 8:30am–5pm, Sat. 9am–5pm, and Sun. noon– 5pm.

BOOKS

Austin's bookstore sales are the highest per capita of the fifty largest cities in the U.S. Here are several venues for this highly regarded pastime.

Barnes & Noble (512-418-8985; austin.citysearch.com Search: Barnes & Noble; 10000 Research Blvd., Austin, TX 78759; daily 9am–11pm) Not only is there a giant bookstore in the Arboretum, this B&N also has a café (with Starbucks coffee) and a music department.
Book People (512-472-5050, 800-853-9757; www.bookpeople.com; 603 N. Lamar, Austin, TX 78703; daily 9am–11pm) One of America's largest book-

stores is the boast here, with four floors containing more than 300,000 titles, a 2,000-title newsstand, cards and stationery, comfortable chairs and couches, an espresso bar, and even jewelry and arts and crafts from around the world.

Half Price Books (512-454-3664; austin.citysearch.com Search: Half Price Books; 8868 Research Blvd., Austin, TX 78758; Mon.–Sat. 10am–10pm, Sun. noon–9pm) This Texas institution has three locations stocked with new, used, academic, and out-of-print titles, CDs, cassettes, LPs, and videos; most merchandise is half the publisher's price — or less.

Toad Hall (512-323-2665; austin.citysearch.com Search: Toad Hall; 1206 W. 38th St., Austin, TX 78705; Mon.–Sat. 9am–7pm, Sun. noon–4pm) Specialists in children's books (English and bilingual, and various languages), toys, and games.

TravelFest (512-469-7906; 1214 W. 6th St., Austin, TX 78703; and 512-418-1515; Gateway Center, 9503 Research Blvd., Austin, TX 78758; both stores daily 9am–9pm) Largest collection of travel books in Texas, plus a wide assortment of travel gear, travel agents, and other services.

University Co-op Bookstore (512-476-7211; austin.citysearch.com Search: University Co-op Bookstore; 224 Guadalupe St., Austin, TX 78705; Mon.–Fri. 8:30am–7:30pm, Sat. 9:30am–6pm, Sun. 11am–5pm) Across from UT on the Drag, the Co-op has been an Austin landmark for more than 90 years. With a Barnes and Noble bookstore taking up space next door, the Co-op now mainly stocks textbooks, UT clothing and souvenirs, and art supplies, but they have an extensive search service from their Web site and offer discounts on over 500,000 trade books.

CLOTHING AND ACCESSORIES

Visitors looking for authentic Western attire will find the real thing at the following shops, generally open daily:

Allen's Boots (512-447-1413, 1522 S. Congress, Austin, TX 78704) "We know Western wear" is the motto here, with just about every brand of boot made as well as hats, shirts, jeans, and accessories.

Callahan's General Store (512-385-3452; www.general-store.com; 501 Bastrop Hwy., Austin, TX 78741) A little bit east of town out on the Bastrop Highway (Hwy.183) is this picturesque farm and ranch store, with seed and garden tools and baby chicks and ducks amidst the boots and saddles.

Cavender's Boot City (512-892-4747; www.cavenders-boots-city.com/scape; 4435 S. Lamar Blvd., Austin, TX 78741) Another big Western mart, this one claiming to be the "World's #1 Boot Dealer."

Rewards (512-502-9799, 800-292-0195; austin.citysearch.com Search: Rewards; 9722 Great Hills Trail, Austin, TX 78759) Handwork and jewelry of contemporary artists of the Southwest, such as Hopi jewelry and handcrafted belts and buckles.

CRAFTS

Clarksville Pottery & Galleries (512-454-9079; austin.citysearch.com Search: Clarksville Pottery; 4001 N. Lamar, # 200, Austin, TX 78756; Mon.–Sat. 10am–6:30pm, Thurs. until 8pm, Sun. 11am–5pm) A fine crafts gallery representing 300 artists, about a third of them Texans, the rest out of state. "All-American" creations are featured, including pottery, blown glass, gold and silver jewelry, and wooden ware such as boxes and clocks.

Craftown Gallery (512-331-4252; 13945 N. Hwy. 183, Austin, TX 78717 (at Hwy. 620); Mon.–Sat. 10am–6pm, Sun. noon–5pm) An interesting collection of booths offering homier arts and crafts such as stuffed bunnies, hand-painted wall hangings, floral arrangements, T-shirts, hand-sewn vests, country dolls, candles, and ceramics.

ec.lec.tic (512-477-1816; austin.citysearch.com Search: Eclectic Ethnographic Art Gallery; 700 S. Lamar Blvd., Austin, TX 78703 Mon.–Sat. 10am–8pm, Sun. noon–6pm) Primitive and ancient arts, distinctive furnishings, rugs, belts, jewelry, and adornments.

James Avery Craftsman, Inc. (512-327-6342, 2901 S. Capital of Texas Hwy., Austin, TX 78746; daily Mon.–Sat. 10am–9pm, Sun. noon–6pm) Avery handcrafts his work at his studio in the Hill Country in Kerrville, but it's for sale here in Austin at the Barton Creek Square Mall. You'll find unique sterling and 14K gold jewelry, bronze paperweights, and other fine pieces made with the lost wax method and hand finished.

Renaissance Market (512-397-1456; Austin, TX; Mon.–Sun. 10am–sunset; on The Drag at 23rd and Guadalupe Sts.) An outdoor market of sidewalk artisans across from the university.

Tesoros Trading Company (512-479-8377; www.tesoros.com; 209 Congress Ave., Austin, TX 78701; daily 10am–6pm) Folk art and other treasures (*tesoro* is Spanish for treasure) from around the world, although owner Jonathan Williams is especially keen to preserve the crafts of Latin America.

GIFTS

Austin Museum of Art Shop (512-477-0766; www.amoa.org; 823 Congress Ave., Austin, TX 78701; Mon.–Sat. 10am–6pm, Thurs. 10am–8pm, Sun. noon–5pm) You'll find art gifts, jewelry, decorative accessories, books, T-shirts, gift wrap, and cards plus terrific things for children.

El Interior (512-474-8680; austin.citysearch.com Search: El Interior; 1009 West Lynn St., Austin, TX 78703; Mon.–Sat. 10am–6pm, Sun. noon–5pm) Colorful Mexican folk art: hand-painted wooden animals, pottery and rugs from Oaxaca, terra-cotta pieces from Puebla and Jalisco, lacquer work from Guerrero, and traditional Mexican clothing.

Necessities and Temptations (512-473-8334; austin.citysearch.com Search: Necessities and Temptations; 1202 W. 6th St., Austin, TX 78703; Mon.–Sat.

10am–6pm, Sun. 11am–3pm) Austin and Texas souvenirs, T-shirts, bolo ties, postcards and such, all handily downtown just west of Congress Avenue.

Pecan Square Emporium (512-477-4900; austin.citysearch.com Search: Pecan Square Emporium; 1122 W. 6th St., Austin, TX 78703; Mon.–Sat. 10am–6pm, Sun. 11am–4pm) A European-style gift shop with Swiss music boxes and German nutcrackers as well as other gifts and jewelry.

Wild About Music (512-708-1700; www.wildaboutmusic.com; 721 N. Congress Ave., Austin, TX 78701; Mon.–Sat. 11am–7pm, Sun. noon–6pm) Everything with a musical motif: apparel, T-shirts, caps and accessories, stationery, collectibles, even art. Also specializing in items related to the Austin/Texas music scene and contemporary jazz.

SHOPPING MALLS

Austin's shopping malls are generally open daily (although not every shop opens on Sunday).

The Arboretum (512-338-4437; www.austin360.com Search: Arboretum; 10000 Research Blvd., Austin, TX 78759) An outdoor mall with an upscale collections of specialty shops.

Barton Creek Square Mall (512-327-7040; 2901 Capital of Texas Hwy., Austin, TX 78746) Four miles from the center of town, this indoor mall offers a fantastic view of Austin's skyline in addition to Dillard's, Foley's, JC Penney, Montgomery Ward and Sears, and 180 other fine shops.

Highland Mall (512-454-9656; 6001 Airport Blvd., Austin, TX 78752) More than 180 specialty shops plus a food court, cart marketplace, and Foley's, Dillard's, and JC Penney at this indoor mall.

Northcross Mall (512-451-7466; austin.citysearch.com Search: Northcross Mall; 2525 W. Anderson Ln., Austin, TX 78757) Located at Burnet Rd., this indoor mall has sixty specialty shops as well as larger stores like Beall's and Oshman Sporting Goods and the only mall ice-skating rink around, Chaparral Ice.

TRAVIS COUNTY

In 1840, when Austin became the Texas capital, Travis County was created from a portion of Bastrop County, the county to the east. But it wasn't fully organized until 1843, when it was named for Alamo commander and hero Colonel William B. Travis. The main business of the county is government, education, and recreation, along with a little farming and ranching.The rolling hills of Travis County, on the edge of the Hill Country, are the setting for Austin, the Colorado River, and Lake Travis. The city of Austin, its suburbs, and its lake — Lake Austin — take up most of the county. The county's other main attraction is Lake Travis, which offers swimming, boating, camping, picnicking, and otherwise enjoying the sunshine and fresh air. Cedar, oak, live oak, pin oak, and pecan trees abound; flowering trees, such as redbud and crape myrtle, also flourish both in the countryside and in the city.

TRAVIS COUNTY LODGING

Once you leave Austin, most accommodations are on Lake Travis, either a resort or one of the few bed & breakfast inns, all of them generally open year-round.

RESORTS

LAKEWAY INN
Manager: Toby June.
512-261-6600,
    800-LAKEWAY.
www.dolce.com/
    properties/lakeway.
101 Lakeway Dr., Austin,
    TX 78734.
Price: Expensive.
Credit Cards: AE, CB, D,
    DC, MC, V.
Handicap Access: Yes.
Special Features: "A
    concierge who knows
    everything."

The inn's 258 guest rooms and suites — sixteen with fireplaces — all have views of Lake Travis or the marina, so there's water everywhere. The decor is Southwestern and the scenery Hill Country. The resort offers the Travis Room Restaurant for dining, and a pub for more casual fare. Two 18-hole golf courses, tennis, boat rentals, a fitness center and spa, nearby horseback riding, and hiking, biking, and jogging trails.

The inn has just completed a $20-million expansion, adding new rooms and suites.

**RESORT RANCH OF
    LAKE TRAVIS**
Manager: Gary Baker.
512-264-2533, 800-888-5253.
www.resortranch.com.
Rte. 1 Box 27H., Spicewood,
    TX 78669.
Price: Inexpensive (tent
    sites, RV sites, screened
    cabins) to Expensive
    (cottages).
Credit Cards: AE, D, MC, V.
Handicap Access: Yes.

The substantial-looking cottages are built of native Texas stone. Spacious living-dining areas have wood-burning fireplaces and large windows overlooking covered decks and views of the Hill Country. Rustic screened cabins, built of wood, are under the trees, with picnic tables and grills right outside. Swimming is either in the large tree-and-deck-surrounded pool, or in the lake. Wildflowers in the spring and deer all year long make this a pleasant country resort that also offers tennis, BBQ and picnic areas, children's playground, horseback riding, a café, country store, lake cruises, waterfront facilities, softball, horseshoe and washer pits, and basketball, volleyball, and tetherball courts.

BED & BREAKFASTS

COW CREEK LAKESIDE LODGE BED & BREAKFAST

Innkeepers/Managers: Dusty and Janet Hall.
512-267-3652.
www.touringtexas.com/ highlake/cowcreek.
24607 FM 1431, Marble Falls, TX 78654.
On Cow Creek, an arm of Lake Travis.
Price: Moderate to Expensive.
Credit Cards: MC, V.
Handicap Access: Yes.
Special Features: Also motel, RV park, and camping.

Only 30 minutes from Austin, this rural retreat sits on 3,000 feet of Cow Creek, a preferred site for waterskiing and jetskiing. Although the main building's exterior is rustic — set under cedars and oaks amid several campers and RVs, as well as the cabin housing Dusty's real estate office — guest rooms are well furnished, without clutter, and bathrooms are new, spiffy, and decorative. The upstairs common room has a fireplace, slot machine games, and overstuffed sofas strewn with soft pillows. The dining room is almost formal with a cherry Queen Anne table and chairs. "I turn the place over to my guests," Dusty says — but not before filling them with a six-egg omelet each, seasoned potatoes, ham steaks, bacon and sausage, homemade cinnamon apples, biscuits, and French toast. Then they're free to boat or fish — in a rentable canoe, paddleboat, kayak, or motorized fishing boat — swim, hike, or just loll on the decks overlooking Cow Creek and the hills.

Dusty will also provide dinner by reservation — "Whatever they want, but I always suggest lemon chicken, Rock Cornish hen, or beef tenderloin."

TRAIL'S END BED & BREAKFAST

Innkeepers/Managers: JoAnn and Tom Patty.
512-267-2901, 800-850-2901.
austin.citysearch.com
Search: Trail's End.
12223 Trail's End Rd. #7, Leander, TX 78641.
Off Hwy. 183 in Cedar Park.
Price: Moderate to Expensive.
Credit Cards: AE, D, MC, V.
Handicap Access: No.

The Pattys built their dream house way out in the country, so it's aptly named. The large two-story house has two guest rooms with private baths, plus there's a small cottage equipped with full kitchen and all the amenities. Bird-watching, hiking, a gazebo, and swimming pool in the woods, with a view out over the hills, make this a most attractive hideaway. Yet you're not too far from the shops and restaurants of nearby Cedar Park or from the Hill Country Flyer, a renovated steam train that takes to the hills every weekend (see "Family Fun").

LAKE TRAVIS BED & BREAKFAST

Innkeepers: Judy and Vic Dwyer.
512-266-9490,
888-764-LTBB.
www.laketravisbb.com.
4446 Eck Ln., Austin, TX 78734

The smoke-free, adults-only inn has four luxury suites from which you can relax and enjoy views of Lake Travis, with spectacular sunsets over the lake.

The suites — Heart's Delight, Eagle's Nest, Sunset Suite, and Lago Vista Suite — each have a half-canopied king size bed, private bath with tub

Price: Expensive.
Credit Cards: MC, V.
Handicap Access: No.

and shower, private deck, cable TV, refrigerator, hair dryer, CD player, and terry robes. Guests can also enjoy a swim in the pool, a soak in the hot tub, or a game of pool.

You can have breakfast in bed or on your deck, lingering over your coffee and savoring perhaps strawberry soup with apple garnish, homemade rolls, a raspberry chocolate pudding in a heart shape, and coffee and juice. "There's no rush in paradise!" says Judy.

TRAVIS COUNTY RESTAURANTS, NIGHTLIFE, AND CULTURE

Just in case Austin doesn't have enough restaurants, here are several recommendations outside the city limits, along with popular nightspots.

THE BELGIAN RESTAURANT
512-328-0580.
austin.citysearch.com
  Search: Belgian Restaurant.
3520 Bee Cave Rd., Austin, TX 78746.
In the western suburb of West Lake Hills.
Price: Expensive.
Cuisine: Continental.
Serving: L, D.
Credit Cards: AE, D, DC, MC, V.
Reservations: Recommended.
Handicap Access: Yes.

This elegant restaurant brings to the Texas Hill Country fine meats and seafood graced with Continental sauces. "Even Belgians eat steaks," says owner Felix Florez, as he describes one of the restaurant's specialties, Belgian-style Surf and Turf. A 7-ounce tenderloin is topped with a veal sauce brandy demi-glace, accompanied by sautéed Maine lobster in a white wine seafood crème sauce. Another specialty, Dover sole cardinale, presents the whole fish poached in champagne and stuffed with sautéed spinach, smothered in a lobster/ Swiss cheese sauce. The venison au poivre is venison tenderloin flambéed in cognac and topped with a green peppercorn crème sauce.

The menu is topped off with rich desserts such as the Belgian sundae, a concoction of vanilla bean ice cream in an almond tuille. The sauce is a ganache of dark Belgian chocolate, and the whole is covered with whipped cream.

COUNTY LINE ON THE HILL
512-327-1742.
austin.citysearch.com
  Search: County Line on the Hill.

Eat outdoors if the weather's nice (as it is most of the time in the Hill Country!) and enjoy the view from the hill while digging into the big meaty ribs, lean brisket, and the County Line's famous sausage. The atmosphere at this barbecue chain is

6500 W. Bee Cave Rd.,
    Austin, TX 78746.
Located ¼ mile west of
    Loop 360.
Price: Moderate.
Cuisine: American, Barbecue.
Serving: D.
Credit Cards: AE, CB, D,
    DC, MC, V.
Reservations: No.
Handicap Access: Yes.

**HUDSON'S ON THE
    BEND**
512-266-1369.
www.austin360.com Search:
    Hudson's on the Bend.
3509 Hwy. 620, Austin, TX
    78734.
Located 1.5 miles west of
    Mansfield Dam.
Price: Expensive.
Cuisine: Game,
    Contemporary.
Serving: D.
Credit Cards: AE, DC, MC,
    V.
Reservations: Yes.
Handicap Access: No.

THE OASIS
512-266-2442.
austin.citysearch.com
    Search: Oasis.
6550 Comanche Trail,
    Austin, TX 78732.
On Lake Travis.
Price: Moderate to
    Expensive.
Cuisine: Tex-Mex.
Serving: L, D Mon.–Sat., SB.
Credit Cards: AE, D, MC, V.
Reservations: No.
Handicap Access: Yes.

upscale roadhouse, and the view from this site stretches for miles.

Chefs Jeff Blank and Jay Moore didn't plan to specialize in exotic game, but when they featured dishes such as grilled ostrich tenderloin with a porcini mushroom sauce, and medallions of kangaroo with fresh kiwi — even armadillo and rattlesnake — the restaurant got written up in magazines and newspapers. Thus Hudson's acquired a reputation for wild game. But other dishes are delicious, too, such as the pork tenderloin stuffed with homemade chorizo (sausage) and served with a mango-jalapeño sauce. (The restaurant specializes in such sauces, all of which you can find bottled for sale at Austin's Central Market.) But no matter what you order, save room for the corn pudding.

You can't say you've been to Austin if you haven't gone out to the Oasis. It began in 1982 with five outdoor decks over Lake Travis with seating for 300. It's grown to twenty-eight decks and several indoor dining rooms, with seating for 1,500. "Great food, great times — and a terrific view" are what bring the crowds out.

Always a top area attraction because of the view over the lake, especially at sunset, the Oasis is even better these days because the food has greatly improved. We began with crab-stuffed mushrooms — succulent crabmeat topped with Monterey jack cheese in a buttery mushroom cap — then went on to the Oasis super combo of beef enchilada, chile relleno, and a soft chicken taco. Key lime pie and sopapillas (little Mexican puff pastries served with honey to pour inside) were a perfect finish.

And when the sun sets spectacularly over the lake, the music begins. Live entertainment might be anything: blues, jazz, a samba band, or maybe an oldies group. Call to find out who's playing on your night.

... SAM HILL?
WATERFRONT GRILL
512-266-2811; information
hotline 512-266-8534.
austin.citysearch.com
Search: Sam Hill
Waterfront Grill.
16405 Clara Van Trail,
Austin, TX 78734.
Price: Moderate.
Cuisine: Tex-Mex, Korean,
Steak, Seafood.
Serving: L, D daily.
Credit Cards: AE, D, MC, V.
Reservations: No.
Handicap Access: Usually
(depends on level of
lake).

You're sure to ask yourself, "What the Sam Hill?" when you see that there is absolutely nothing left off the menu at this waterfront grill, from oysters and fried green tomatoes to bee bim bop (a Korean dish) and eggs Benedict (for brunch). The certified 12-ounce Angus strip steak was served with roasted red potatoes; the lemon pepper tuna, seasoned with a lemon pepper rub, was char-grilled and served with fresh lemon and herbed wild rice. With our specialty drinks like prickly pear margarita and cowboy colada, we got to take home our ... Sam Hill? mugs as souvenirs.

Upstairs above the restaurant is a bar, poolroom, and a band, with eclectic music playing most nights.

WATERLOO ICE HOUSE
AND BARBECUE
512-263-5400.
13101 W. Hwy. 71, Austin,
TX 789736.
At Hwy. 620 in the town of
Bee Cave.
Price: Moderate.
Cuisine: Hill Country.
Serving: L, D.
Credit Cards: AE, D, MC, V.
Reservations: No.
Handicap Access: Yes,
except for one small step.

The fare here is classic Hill Country, with chicken-fried steak and barbecued meat and shrimp. The decor is in tune with The Backyard next door (see "Nightlife") — tables are laminated with old record jackets, and the walls display autographed posters of the musicians who have performed next door. Hill Country cedar and pine make this a bright and light dining spot, where salads are a specialty: chicken Parmesan, Mexican, or the deliciously different Backyard salad with brisket and horseradish dressing.

WILSON'S TEXAS TEA
ROOM
512-263-1950.
austin.citysearch.com
Search: Wilson's Texas
Tea Room.
12703 W. Hwy. 71, Austin,
TX 78736.
In the town of Bee Cave, in
a shopping center.
Price: Moderate.
Cuisine: American.
Serving: L daily, SB.
Credit Cards: AE, D, MC, V.
Reservations: Yes.
Handicap Access: Yes.
Special Features: High Tea
(24-hour advance
reservations).

This restaurant is a surprise. In addition to the steaks, chicken, and fish for dinner and the Sunday brunch eggs Benedict with chipotle hollandaise, a real treat is "High Tea in the Hill Country." This needs 24-hour notice to prepare the fresh-baked scones with clotted cream and jam plus fresh fruit, canapés, and assorted cakes and cookies. Also, a bountiful plate of finger sandwiches: tomato basil, watercress and cucumber, ham and pineapple. Box lunches, too, can be ordered if you're planning a drive through the Hill Country.

NIGHTLIFE

THE BACKYARD
512-263-4146.
www.thebackyard.net.
13101 W. Hwy. 71 W.,
    Austin, TX 78768
At Hwy. 620 in the town of
    Bee Cave.
Box Office Open: Mon.–Fri.
    10–5, Sat. 10–3.

The Backyard is the bar and outdoor entertainment area next to the Waterloo Ice House and Barbecue (see above). It's an outdoor amphitheater that's the scene of nightly music to every taste ("except symphony"). So for country and country-western, blues and jazz, flamenco guitar, classic rock, and much more, this is the place to come and hear regional and national artists — among them Sheryl Crow, Dwight Yoakam, and Seal — perform in the fresh air of Travis County.

TRAVIS COUNTY FOOD PURVEYORS

Flip's Satellite Café (512-301-1883; 7101 W. Hwy. 71, Austin, TX 78735; Mon.–Sat. 6am–7pm) Although Flip's is technically in the city, it's so close to the city limits at the "Y" at Oak Hill — the crossroads of Hwys. 71 and 290 west to the hills — that it's more in the country than the city. So on the way to Blanco and Gillespie counties, stop here for breakfast or lunch or a snack. You'll find coffee in the form of cappuccino, latte, and breve, and homemade pastries. A deli-full of eat-in or take-out sandwiches, chicken salad, and other foods will send you on your way.

Slaughter Leftwich Winery (512-266-3331; 4301 James Ln., Box 22F, Austin, TX 78734, off Eck Ln. off Hwy. 620; Wed.–Sun. 1pm–5pm, tastings Wed.–Sun., tours Thurs. & Fri. 3pm, Sat. & Sun. 1:30pm & 3:30pm) Not only are the chardonnay vineyards here the oldest in Texas, wine from these grapes is also the most award-winning chardonnay in the state of Texas. The sauvignon blanc is pretty special, too. But judge for yourself at the wine tastings. The vineyards are about 3,000 feet above Lake Travis, which gives the grapes a lovely view.

SEASONAL EVENTS

Lago Vista

In APRIL the **Lago Vista Lions Club Chili Cookoff** includes — in addition to the daytime tastings of the entries of expert chili cooks — a beauty contest, arts and crafts for sale, and a Saturday night barbecue and dance.

MAY is the time for the **Turnback Regatta**, with yachts sailing from the Austin Yacht Club to Bar-K Point on Saturday, then back again on Sunday. Meanwhile, during the 2-day event, the Lago Vista Volunteer Fire Department put on a delicious, and partly fiery, barbecue.

Lakeway

In **APRIL** the **Bluebonnet Bash** celebrates spring with an art exhibit, featuring the works of local artists. Visitors can tour both artists' studios and works hung in galleries at the Oasis Restaurant and the Slaughter Leftwich Winery.

JULY brings **Under A Texas Sky**, a Fourth of July weekend pops concert by the Austin Symphony Orchestra.

DECEMBER, there's more music, a **Carol Concert** at the Lakeway Inn, with songs by the New Texas Festival Singers.

TRAVIS COUNTY RECREATION

Travis County is one huge playground, centered around Lake Travis. During the long summer, Austinites beat the heat by taking to the water here. Weekends on the lake are a central Texas ritual for sailors, swimmers, water-skiers, scuba divers, fishermen (and women), and windsurfers. The latest rage here is the wakeboard, a combination of a surfboard and water ski.

BOATING AND WATER SPORTS

Dutchman's Landing Marina (512-267-4289; austin.citysearch.com Search: Dutchman's Landing; 17900 Easy St., Jonestown, TX 78645) On Lake Travis; has boat slips as well as boat rentals —including a party barge — and fishing.

Wet & Wild Watercraft Rentals can be found at two locations (360 Bridge on Lake Austin and Yacht Harbor Marina on Lake Travis, 512-266-3644). They pride themselves on having the latest equipment, pleasure boats, ski boats (drivers available), pontoon boats, personal watercraft such as Sea Doo, Tiger-shark, and Polaris, as well as kneeboards, waverunners, tubes, and wakeboards. Hourly and daily waterskiing is offered, and although their regular hours are 9am–8pm daily, "if somebody calls us and wants to go skiing at 7am when the water's really nice, we'll go. . . ."

CAMPING

Travis County has a number of campgrounds, set in an assortment of scenery. Two of them don't require reservations — you can just drop in and pitch your tent.

Arkansas Bend Park (512-473-9437, 800-776-LCRA [Lower Colorado River Authority]; www.co.travis.tx.us.tnr/parks/graphic; on Lake Travis) Tent sites, boat ramp. $5 per vehicle day use, $10 camping per night.

Cypress Creek (512-473-4083, 800-776-LCRA; austin.citysearch.com Search: Cypress Creek; on FM 2769 at Lake Travis) Tent sites, boat ramp. $5 per vehicle day use, $10 camping per night. No reservations.

Hudson Bend Camper Resort (512-266-1562; www.hbresort.tripod.com; 17317 W. Beach Rd., Austin, TX 78734; 3 miles from FM 620 near Mansfield Dam on Lake Travis) Hookups, by reservation only.

Mansfield Dam Park (512-473-9437, 800-776-LCRA; www.co.travis.tx.us/tnr/parks/graphic; FM 620 at Mansfield Dam Rd.) Picnic areas, rest rooms, boat ramp, tent sites, swimming. $5 per vehicle day use, $10 camping per night.

Pace Bend Park (512-473-9437, 800-776-LCRA, 512-264-1482 for RV reservations; www.co.travis.tx.us/tnr/parks/graphic; FM 2322, 4.6 miles east of Hwy. 71) Twenty "improved" RV sites, over 200 tent sites, picnic areas, potable water, boat ramp. $5 per vehicle day use, $10 camping per night, $15 improved sites.

Resort Ranch of Lake Travis (512-264-2533, 800-888-5253; 1300 N. Pace Bend Rd., Spicewood, TX 78669) Tent sites, RV sites, cabins.

FAMILY FUN

AUSTIN ZOO
512-288-1490, 800-291-1490.
www.austinzoo.com.
10807 Rawhide Trail,
 Austin, TX 78736.
Open: Daily (except
 Christmas) 10am–6pm.
Admission: Adults $6,
 students $5, seniors and
 children 2–12 $4, children
 under 2 free.

West of Hwy. 71, 20 minutes from downtown Austin, this private zoo offers the whole family a hands-on experience with animals from around the world. The zoo's mission is to foster empathy, understanding, and conservation of nature.

FISHING

Mike Hastings of **Git Bit** is at your service as a fishing guide (512-280-2861), as is Allen Christianson (512-441-6682) and Phillip Walker (512-272-9105), who offer their own fishing guide services. Black and white and stripers (striped bass) and Guadalupe bass abound in Lake Travis. If you're thinking of fishing on your own, please note that access to bank fishing on Lake Travis is limited.

HORSEBACK RIDING

What would any part of Texas be — even as urban an area as Austin and Travis County — without horses and horseback riding? And not just Western cow ponies — you can go English saddle, dressage, hunting, jumping, or just mosey along a trail.

Blue Star Riding Center (512-243-2583; 9513 S. US 183, Austin, TX 78747) Trail rides (weekends only), over 50 acres in Travis County; indoor and outdoor arenas for lessons in Western, English, hunter-jumper, dressage, and cross county.

Resort Ranch of Lake Travis (512-264-2533, 800-888-5253; 1300 N. Pace Bend Rd., Spicewood, TX 78669) Horseback riding.

NATURE

Nature reigns in Travis County, thanks to the average 320 beautiful days you can count on each year. Austinites and visitors alike are drawn to Lake Travis and to the nature areas bordering the city.

WEST CAVE PRESERVE
830-825-3442.
FM 3238, Round Mountain, TX 78663.
Open: Tours only, Sat. & Sun. 10am, noon, 2pm, 4pm, weather permitting, year-round.
Admission: Donations accepted.

Many rare and endangered plants are preserved here in this 30-acre sanctuary for the golden cheeked warbler and other rare birds. Stands of ash juniper and live oak are to be found here, as well as grassland savannas with wildflower meadows. Guided tours of the property only.

SWIMMING

Bob Wentz Park and Windy Point (512-473-9437; www.co.travis.tx.us/tnr/parks/graphic; Comanche Trail off Hwy. 620) This popular Lake Travis beach has a little bit of sand shoreline, which makes it good for windsurfing. There's also some jetskiing and scuba diving. Open: Sept. 10–Oct. 31, 9am–7pm; Nov. 1–Feb. 28, 9am–6pm; Mar. 1–Apr. 30, 9am–7:30pm; May 1–Sept. 9, 8am.–9pm. Admission: $5 per vehicle.

Hamilton Pool Preserve (512-264-2740; www.co.travis.tx.us/tnr/parks/graphic; FM 3238, Hamilton Pool Rd., 30 miles from Austin off Hwy. 71) Hamilton Pool is a unique natural area formed thousands of years ago when the dome of an underground river collapsed. This created a pool and a grotto that not only attracts today's outdoor folk, it also attracted the area's first inhabitants, who left artifacts there 8,000 years ago. The grotto and the downstream area support lush and diverse flora, plus a variety of wildlife. Open: 9am–6pm daily, weather permitting (call for daily updates); no entry after 5:30pm. Admission: $5 per vehicle.

Hippie Hollow Park (512-473-9437; www.co.travis.tx.us/tnr/parks/graphic; Comanche Trail off Hwy. 620) Pick your way carefully down the rocks to reach the water at this Lake Travis beach, the only clothing-optional beach (must be 18 or over to enter). No lifeguards on duty here. Open: Sept. 10–Oct. 31, 9am–7:30pm; Nov. 1–Feb. 28, 9am–6pm; Mar. 1–Apr. 30, 9am–7:30pm; May 1–Sept. 9, 8am–9pm. Admission: $5 per vehicle.

Mansfield Dam (512-473-9437; www.co.travis.tx.us/tnr/parks/graphic; Mansfield Dam Rd., 5 miles south of Hwy. 620 and FM 2222) Sixty-five acres with picnic tables and barbecue grills, a boat launch, and a great little cove for swimmers that's especially favored by SCUBA divers. Sailboats like it, too. (Cars used to be able to drive over the dam, but no more — now the road is open for walkers only.) Open: Year-round sunrise to 9pm. Admission: $5 per vehicle.

TRAVIS COUNTY SHOPPING

In Bee Cave in the mid-1840s, there was a general store, a cotton gin, and a cigar factory by the side of the road. Now there's a small shopping area there, along the west side of Highway 71, next to Wilson's Furniture Store and Tea Room.

House of Harriette and John (512-263-5103, 12719 W. Hwy. 71; Austin, TX 78736; open 10:30–5:30 daily except Mon.) These two small white-trimmed brown cottages are surrounded by greenery with a little patio separating them. John, son of Harriette, is a gemologist, and his shop is a treasure trove of minerals and gems. But be prepared — he'll show you a lovely hunk of blue stone and challenge you to identify it. Here's a clue: it's the Texas state gem. John's specialty in gemstones is the Lone Star Cut, the star of Texas faceted in a gem. The shop holds a fascinating array of gems, mineral specimens, and fossils as well as curios created from natural stones.

Harriette's house across the way is packed with antiques, hand-created apparel, crafts, and toys and "all sorts of oddities." The work of nationally known artists, many signed and dated, are shown here, such as Carolyn Pfleferer's angels, Karen Germany's black dolls, and Linda MacDonald's nativity pieces. "When you shop with us, your friends will remember their gifts," Harriette promises.

Living Desert Cactus Nursery (512-263-2428; 12719 W. Hwy. 71, Austin, TX 78736; daily 10am–5:30pm) This shop is covered inside and out with cacti, succulents, and all sorts of related specialty items — mobiles, gourds, pottery vessels. Cacti are propagated from cuttings or grown from seeds: "We don't go around digging up the Hill Country," says Yvonna Dunten, owner. In addition to indigenous cacti, there are fascinating ones from faraway places like Africa and Brazil. "We're only limited by our imagination," says Darrell Dunten of the wild assortment of things in the nursery.

Serendipity Gifts (512-263-7100; 12705 W. Hwy. 71, Austin, TX 78736; Mon.–Sat. "10ish to 6ish.") This delicious-smelling little shop is full of a medley of things: antiques, jewelry, fine wedding, birthday, and thank-you gifts, original art, fun gifts like puzzles and games, and even edible gifts such as mouthwatering jellies, candies, condiments, and gift baskets full of the same.

CHAPTER FOUR
Out in the Territory
HILL COUNTRY WEST AND
SOUTH OF AUSTIN
Blanco, Burnet, Gillespie, Hays, Kimble, Llano,
& Mason Counties

Eleanor S. Morris

Luckenbach post office/shop/bar under the oaks.

To make such a large territory as the Hill Country manageable, we've divided the fourteen counties around Austin and San Antonio (in every direction except east) into two chapters, this one covering the seven counties closest to Austin: Blanco, Burnet, Gillespie, Hays, Kimble, Llano, and Mason (in alphabetical order). Chapter Six describes the seven counties around San Antonio.

In all of the counties, you'll find a friendly interest in strangers, pride in that specific corner of the land (hostile and wild territory not so very long ago), and much the same cuisine, which features Mexican and Tex-Mex dishes and that all-American favorite, chicken-fried steak. The cedar and pine of the Hill Country landscape, as well as the plentiful supply of rock, have been put to good use in constructing everything from cottages to courthouses, with many of these buildings reflecting the European style of immigrant settlers.

BLANCO COUNTY

Blanco County is hilly, with two rivers, the Blanco and the Pedernales, and lots of cedar and pecan trees. It was named for the river which the Spanish in the 1700s called *blanco,* Spanish for "white," presumably for its pale reflection of the sky. The county was created in 1858 and owes its fame to the late president Lyndon Baines Johnson.

But even before that country boy made good, the Johnson family had put its name on the Blanco County map. LBJ's grandfather, Sam Ealy Johnson Sr., along with his brother Tom, rounded up mavericks, the unbranded longhorn cattle that roamed the open range after the Civil War, and drove them along the Chisholm Trail.

The two main towns in Blanco County are Johnson City (pop. 959) and Blanco (pop. 1,265).

Johnson City

Johnson City, the county seat, is named for the pioneer Johnson family, ancestors of the late president. The town, on the Pedernales River (pronounced "PURD-in-alice") was founded in 1878 and became the county seat in 1891.

Although President Johnson was born in Gillespie County, he spent most of his boyhood years in Johnson City. If you ask a citizen of Johnson City what it's like growing up in a small town that produced a president of the United States, you're apt to get this answer: "I feel like it shows what a person can do. There's no limits. If you work hard, a small town is no handicap."

Blanco

Pioneer stockmen settled Blanco in 1853 and, like most of the settlers in the Hill Country, they had to contend with Indians who naturally wanted to hold on to their land. Blanco was the county seat until 1891, when Johnson City to the north won the honor. But it took three elections for Johnson City to prevail.

The old courthouse building still stands in the center of town. It has been used for a variety of purposes, the most entertaining being a skating rink (on the second floor), but the active Old Courthouse Heritage Society is busy raising funds to restore it to its former glory (see "Seasonal Events"). The town square is joined by a two-block city park, and the square features shops, the town library, its bank, the chamber of commerce, and the little Pecan Street Bakery for sandwiches and coffee on outdoor tables.

Johnson City has joined the trend for bed & breakfast accommodations; here you'll find small two-room cottages. Both Johnson City and Blanco are quiet and relaxing places to spend the night.

The Texas
Hill Country:
West and South
of Austin

BLANCO COUNTY LODGING

Johnson City

There are several two-room houses to stay here, each one offering privacy — you'll have the whole place to yourself — combined with the convenience of being right in the center of things To book one, contact **Bed & Breakfast of Johnson City** (830-868-4548; PO Box 913, Johnson City, TX 78636); descriptions of each follow. Prices are moderate, with continental breakfast included.

Boot Hill Guest House (207 Ranchview Dr., Johnson City, TX 78636) For a true Western experience the atmosphere here is bunkhouse but with comfort included. You'll find cedar bedposts, cowboy-print linens, a woodstove, Louis L'Amour western paperbacks, rocking chairs on the porch, and a barbecue grill — plus a modern kitchen with refrigerator, microwave, toaster, and coffeemaker.

Carolyn's Cottage B&B (103 Live Oak, Johnson City, TX 78636) This stone cottage has lace curtains inside and flower-filled window boxes outside and is furnished with English country antiques.

Gingerbread House (407 W. Pecan Dr., Johnson City, TX 78636) This little house is nestled on a half acre of large oak trees, four blocks from the square. There are wicker rockers on the porch and a white picket fence in front.

Hoppe's Guest House (404 Ave. N, Johnson City, TX 78636) Here, another white picket fence encloses a yard full of century-old oaks. You'll find two bedrooms, one bath, and a wood-burning stove in the parlor; antique furniture adds to the quaintness.

Smith's Tin House (204 Ave. G, Johnson City, TX 78636) In describing this B&B, owner Cynthia Smith says, "Imagine driving up to great-grandmother's house with its pressed-tin sides and front porch swing." The front sitting/sleeping room is furnished in antique wicker and an iron bed. An old iron bed is in the bedroom, too, plus there's a cozy country kitchen.

Motels: Motel accommodations are available at **Charles' Motel** (830-868-7171; 207 Hwy. 281/290 S., Johnson City, TX 78636 — see the "Restaurant" section for *Johnson City*), and the **Save Inn Motel** (830-868-4044;107 Hwy. 281/290 S., PO Box 610, Johnson City, TX 78636). In *Blanco*, there's the **Swiss Lodge** (830-833-5528; 1206 N. Main St., Blanco, TX 78606).

BLANCO COUNTY RESTAURANTS

Hill Country dining is strongly influenced both by life on the range (chuck wagon cooking, fried, and barbecued) and by Texas's neighbor south of the border, which has given rise to Tex-Mex, the style of Mexican food vastly preferred by the majority of Texans. A word of caution: neither "cuisine" (a rather fancy appellation to apply to the food you'll find outside of Austin and San Antonio) is for the fainthearted or cholesterol-conscious.

Johnson City

CASANOVA'S
830-868-2336.
303 Hwy 281/290 S., Johnson City, TX 78636.
Price: Inexpensive.
Cuisine: Country-fried dishes.
Serving: B, L, Sun. buffet.
Credit Cards: Yes, with a $10 minimum.
Handicap Access: Yes.

Next door to the Save-Inn Motel, this restaurant is open only from 6am to 2pm, so if it's dinner you're wanting, the Hill Country Cupboard is right next door. There are daily lunch specials here: When it's liver and onions, "the whole town comes in." Other specialties are pan-fried pork chops, and of course chicken-fried steak. Sunday buffet runs all weekend, Friday, Saturday, and Sunday.

CHARLES' RESTAURANT
830-868-4222.
207 Hwy. 281/290S, PO Box 1513, Johnson City, TX 78636.
Price: Inexpensive.
Cuisine: Home-style.
Serving: B, L daily.
Credit Cards: AE, D, MC, V.
Handicap Access: No.

Owners Duke and Pat Rumpf serve the same tasty down-home cooking that has been Charles' pride for lo these many years. The restaurant, with antlers on the wall and orange booths and stools lined up along the Formica counter, never seems to change, and regulars are greeted as regularly with sincere interest.

Duke takes pride in his chicken-fried steak, "made with certified Angus beef," a 6-ounce cube steak for half an order, 12 ounces for a full. He takes delight in asserting that he must be the only restaurant still serving what in World War II was termed "SOS." Says Duke: "Chipped beef served every weekend, with a biscuit or Texas toast, hashed browns, or grits — and it's not only the old folks who like it; the young'uns order it, too!"

FEED MILL CAFE
830-868-7771.
103 W. Main St., PO Box 1208, Johnson City, TX 78636.
Price: Moderate.
Cuisine: Home Cooking.
Serving: L, D.
Credit Cards: None.
Handicap Access: No.
Special Features: Live weekend entertainment.

Here's the atmosphere of an old roadhouse saloon, in historic Crofts Mill, an 1880s feed mill. Enter via an iron-railed concrete ramp partially covered with scattered red rugs (the red carpet treatment?). Indoors, the cavernous place is filled with tables surrounded by an assortment of old bentwood chairs, and picnic tables, all covered with blue-and-white flowered vinyl cloths. The long wooden front and back walls are completely obscured by a huge collection of old beer signs (Lone Star occupying pride of place) and other roadhouse memorabilia. The scarred wooden floor

Newly renovated exterior of the Feed Mill Cafe.

Eleanor S. Morris

and the raised stage at the end are occupied by an entertainer singing cowboy ballads under the high open beams and rafters.

The Feed Mill burger comes in either quarter- or half-pound size, decked out with all the fixin's, as was the Texas Spud, smothered in cheddar cheese, chopped onion, and large chunks of real bacon, with sour cream and butter on the side. The King Kong burger "serves one hungry cowboy or two city slickers," and if you're there for dinner, the house chicken-fried steak is crusty outside, juicy inside, and served with potatoes and gravy and a mélange of sautéed vegetables. The fried green tomatoes were served with a tangy homemade ranch dressing. The menu also offered a chilled pasta salad with vegetables marinated in balsamic vinegar and extra-virgin olive oil in this friendly family place — like a Texas dance hall without the dancing.

HILL COUNTRY CUPBOARD
830-868-4625.
www.hillcountrycupboard.com.
Hwy. 281/290 S, Johnson City, TX 78636.
Price: Inexpensive.
Cuisine: Contemporary Texan.
Serving: L, D daily 11am–9pm, closed Thanksgiving, Christmas, and New Year's.
Credit Cards: AE, D, MC, V.
Handicap Access: Yes.
Special Features: See "Shopping."

The extensive menu here is pasted on both sides of a paper grocery sack — you can see how pretentious the Hill Country Kitchen is. They claim to serve the "world's best" chicken-fried steak, and we didn't dispute it. While we waited to be seated, we watched Judy Gibson, one of the bakers, fill loaf pan after loaf pan with the most delicious-smelling bread dough. All the baked goods, from bread to hamburger buns to fantastic blackberry and peach cobblers, are made on the premises. Some are health-conscious, too, like the sugar-free apple, peach, coconut, and lemon pies.

PASQUALES' MEXICAN RESTAURANT
830-868-7682.
502 Hwy. 281/290 S,
  Johnson City, TX 78636.
Price: Moderate.
Cuisine: Mexican, Hill
  Country Fare.
Serving: L, D daily except
  Sun.
Credit Cards: Yes.
Handicap Access: Yes.

With more than seventy items on the menu, you won't be limited to Mexican dishes unless you want to be: Special are the chili rellenos, black bean and cheese taquitos, and popcorn shrimp. "We specialize in Mexican food — but with something for everyone," is their motto. Other specialties include Friday night catfish, Saturday night char-broiled steak, all delicious in this family-owned-and-operated eatery.

Blanco

BOWLING CLUB AND CAFE
830-833-4416.
310 4th St., Blanco, TX
  78606.
Price: Inexpensive.
Cuisine: Down-home
  Tex-Mex.
Serving: B, L, D.
Credit Cards: None.
Handicap Access: Yes.

You may have to be a member to bowl here but not to eat at this friendly roadside café fronting on the "exclusive" bowling alley. It's the sort of place where you get up and help yourself to more coffee if the staff is busy elsewhere, and where you can chat with cook Mary Mosby if she surfaces for a moment's respite up at the counter.

The plate lunch is a real bargain, with a choice of two meats (roast beef or chicken) with mashed potatoes, peas, and carrots, and homemade cherry cobbler, tea, or coffee. Fridays and Saturdays it's an all you can eat catfish fry, including salad bar. The pies — coconut, lemon, chocolate — are absolutely smothered in meringue, and Mary's doughnuts, twists, and cinnamon rolls are impossible to resist. So are the carne guisada breakfast tacos, little steaks-in-a-taco with brown gravy.

For some real authentic Hill Country ambiance, drop in early any morning to watch the regulars at their daily domino game.

HARD SCRABBLE CAFÉ
830-833-4350.
www.blancotex.com.
323 Main St., Blanco, TX
  78606.
On the Square, inside the
  Wagner & Chabot
  building.
Price: Inexpensive to
  Moderate.
Cuisine: Eclectic.
Serving: L daily except
  Mon.; D Thurs., Fri. & Sat.
Credit Cards: Yes.
Handicap Access: Yes.

This is a surprise, located inside an antiques and gift shop, with an innovative and imaginative menu. For lunch, a portabella mushroom sandwich with Swiss and Monterey Jack cheese, sautéed onions on grilled rye bread, or confetti sandwiches of cream cheese olive spread, red onions, lettuce and tomato. Weekend meals include steak and quail, Adobe pork loin, and Chicken Blanca on chili pasta. Weekly lunch, 11am–3pm; dinner 5:30pm–8:30pm. Thursday night is Mexican night.

**SUNSET RESTAURANT
    AND BAR**
830-833-5776.
419 W. 3rd St., Blanco, TX
    78606.
Price: Inexpensive to
    Moderate.
Cuisine: Home-style.
Serving: B, L, D; closed
    Tues.
Credit Cards: AE, D, MC, V.
Handicap Access: Yes.

In this indoor/outdoor restaurant on the square the warm family atmosphere and delicious home-cooked meals advertised are a fact, thanks to Chef Steve Becker and his wife, Georgia. The main course — a dinner special of chicken pot pie (a quarter of a whole!) — was preceded by a delicious spicy vegetable soup with rice, and accompanied by steamed broccoli and a baked potato. The bread was homemade, and so were the desserts — creamy cheesecake with a choice of strawberry, blueberry, or chocolate topping and caramel ice-cream pie with a graham crust and Bluebell ice cream (Texas's pride) with a rich caramel center topped with Italian meringue.

A table out on the cool open porch led to a friendly conversation with two French women visiting Houston, who had come to see the Hill Country. The French women were thankful for the friendliness they encountered: "French people don't know how to do this, be like Texans," they said.

BLANCO COUNTY CULTURE

HISTORIC BUILDINGS AND SITES

Johnson City now is the home of the official **Blanco County Courthouse**, on the square at 7th and Nugent. The Greek Revival building was constructed in 1916 to replace the original 1891 courthouse located on the southwest corner. Visit the **Blanco County Jail** there, too, built in 1894. Maps for a walking and/or driving tour of Johnson City's historic structures are available from the **Johnson City Chamber of Commerce** (830-868-7684; www.Instar.com/johnsoncity, 406 W. Main St., Johnson City, TX 78636).

In *Blanco*, The **Old Blanco County Courthouse** is a fine example of Second Empire architecture. Designed by Austin architect Frederick Ernst Ruffini, the limestone building was completed in 1886, and when the county seat moved to Johnson City, this original courthouse was afterward used variously as an office building, opera house, and even a hospital. It's been restored to it's original façade, and there's talk of locating the **Blanco Chamber of Commerce** there (830-833-5101; www.blancotex.com; 315 Main St., Blanco, TX 78606).

**LYNDON B. JOHNSON
    NATIONAL
    HISTORICAL PARK**
830-868-7128.
www.nps.gov/lyjo.

In Johnson City's Lyndon B. Johnson National Historic Park (don't get this mixed up with the LBJ Ranch and state park 14 miles west in Stonewall, Gillespie County), the white frame, white-picket-fenced boyhood home of the presi-

Eleanor S. Morris

The parlor of the LBJ Museum.

100 10th St., PO Box 329, Johnson City, TX 78636.
Visitor Center: 8:45am–5pm; Boyhood Home: 9am–5pm; Johnson Settlement Exhibit Center: 9am–4pm. Daily except Christmas and New Year's.
Admission: Free.

dent is a far cry from his birthplace in Stonewall. A block west is Johnson's Settlement, the old ranch complex owned by the president's grandfather and great-uncle from 1867 to 1872, which was a gathering point for cattle drives from seven counties.

The settlement also served as an aid station for those wounded in the Deer Creek Indian battle. An original "dog-run" cabin, barn, and other buildings are restored and are part of the living-history program offered by the park.

SEASONAL EVENTS

For exact dates, check with the **Johnson City Chamber of Commerce** (830-868-7684), or the **Olde Blanco Merchants & Business Association** (830-833-2201), or check the Blanco Web site, www.blancotex.com and Johnson City Web site, www.Instar.com/johnsoncity.

Johnson City

In **APRIL**, **Johnson City Market Days** offer crafts, antiques, food, and entertainment; also this month the **Riverfest** has demonstrations of pioneer art, spinning, weaving, quilting, etc.

MAY through **OCT**, **Johnson City Market Days** continue on the second or third weekend (see "Shopping"). The third weekend of **AUGUST** offers the **Blanco County Fair & Rodeo**.

Blanco

From **APRIL** through **NOVEMBER**, **Olde Blanco Market Days** are held on the third Saturday.

During **MAY's** Market Day, there's a **Classic Car Show**, too.

In **JULY**, around the Fourth, there's a **Red, White and Blue Celebration.**

In **NOVEMBER** is the annual lighting of Town Square and the **Merchants Open House**, third weekend, as well as the **Parade and Quilt Show** the Friday after Thanksgiving.

NOVEMBER and **DECEMBER** feature the annual **Lighting Tour Spectacular** — 100,000 lights on the Blanco County Courthouse and 500,000 in the community, plus special activities all through late November and December. Call Regional Christmas Headquarters 830-997-8515. On the second Saturday of **DECEMBER**, the **Merry Merchants Market & Christmas Parade**, including a craft show takes place on the second Saturday in December.

BLANCO COUNTY RECREATION

Pedernales Falls State Park east of Johnson City and **Blanco State Park** along the Blanco River Valley are the places in Blanco County for camping, fishing, hiking, and various kinds of fun on the water. Additional ideas for recreation are also noted.

FAMILY FUN

THE EXOTIC RESORT
830-868-4357.
www.zooexotics.com.
HC3, Box 340, Johnson City, TX 78636.
Four miles north of Johnson City on Hwy. 281.

Designed for both wild animals (giraffes, zebras, and springbok antelope, among others) and the people who enjoy their company, this 137-acre zoo provides guided vehicle rides where you can feed the animals, and a petting zoo where both young and old can pet the baby deer, llama, and even a kangaroo. More than half the animals are on, or have been on, the endangered species list.

PARKS

Eleanor S. Morris

Fishing is excellent in the smooth, clear waters of the Blanco River.

BLANCO STATE PARK
830-833-4333.
www.tpwd.st.tx.us/park/
blanco/blanco.htm.
U.S. 281, PO Box 493,
Blanco, TX 78606.
Admission: $1 per person
13 and over day use fee.
Call for camping fees.

The park lies within the city limits along scenic Blanco River Valley. The 110-acre park has twenty-one campsites with water and electricity plus ten others with water, electricity, and sewage for RVs. The park also offers screened shelters, rest rooms and showers, a group pavilion with kitchen, plus fishing, boating, picnicking, hiking, nature study, swimming, seasonal pedal boats and canoe rentals, and a children's play area.

**PEDERNALES FALLS
STATE PARK**
830-868-7304 (ranger
station), 800-792-1112
(state park info).
www.tpwd.state.tx.us/
park/perdenal/perdenal
.htm.
2585 Park Rd. 6026,
Johnson City, TX 78636.
Admission: $1 per person
13 and over day use fee.
Call for camping fees.

On the scenic stretches of the Pedernales River east of Johnson City, strikingly beautiful waterfalls flow over tilted stairs of layered limestone. The 5,212-acre park, with 6 miles of river frontage, offers swimming, tubing, fishing, and 20 miles of hiking and biking trails, plus campsites with water, electricity, picnic tables, barbecue grills, and tent pads. Hike-in primitive campsites are also offered, located a minimum of 2 miles from the trailheads. For birders, over 150 species have been spotted in the park.

Scenic Drive

Two miles south of Blanco take FM 32 off U.S. 281. Portions of the drive toward San Marcos (in Hays County) follow a ridge called "the Devil's Backbone," a wonderful taste of Hill Country landscape. White-tailed deer are often sighted, especially early or late in the day.

Fishing: Single pole or rod and reel only.

Hiking: The 7.5-mile Wolf Mountain Trail leads to primitive camping areas, historic sites, and the river. The primitive trail system is a challenge for adventuresome hikers and includes a short nature trail.

Swimming: The state park swimming area begins 2.5 miles below the falls. There's tubing on the river.

BLANCO COUNTY SHOPPING

Both Johnson City and Blanco offer a small assortment of interesting shops and boutiques featuring antiques, collectibles, and regional products and crafts. And don't forget **Johnson City Market Days** in City Park from April to October on the second or third weekend of the month. You'll find booths and vendors of food, arts and crafts, antiques, and collectibles, including interesting originals like fabric-covered ceramics or a whirling cage around a brilliantly painted parrot or lovebird. In Blanco **Olde Blanco Market Days** are held on the third Saturday of the month, April through November.

ANTIQUES

Johnson City has no lack of antiques shops, including the following:

Bluebonnet Patch: 830-868-7265; 612 E. Main, PO Box 638, Johnson City, TX 78636.

Homespun Country: 830-868-0204; 201 E. Main St., PO Box 736, Johnson City, TX 78636.

Johnson City Antique Emporium: 830-868-7800; 100 N. Nugent, PO Box 913, Johnson City, TX 78636.

Times Ago Collections: 830-868-2072; 110 E. Main St., Johnson City, TX 78636.

Blanco

Cranberry's Antiques (830-833-5596; 400 3rd St., Blanco, TX 78606, at Arts & Collectibles on the Square) Antiques research, repair, and refinishing; items on consignment; pricing guidebooks.

CLOTHING, CRAFTS, AND GIFTS

Johnson City

Hill Country Cupboard (830-868-4625; 101 Hwy. 281/290 S., Johnson City, TX 78636; see "Restaurants") A small boutique here features hand-painted knits labeled "Treasures by Victoria," one of the restaurant's owners. Bright and glittery — and dressy — T-shirts, pants, and other items are for sale, along with jars of Texas salsa, jams, and jellies. (The jalapeño might be hot!)

Blanco

Gandalf's Goldwerks (830-833-4560; 309 Main St., Blanco, TX 78606) Custom-designed fine gold and silver jewelry, as well as diamonds and gemstones. Two cases are filled with silver charms of every description, and there's a wonderful corner of old books. Proprietor Robert J. Cox II is cordial and helpful even if you just want directions around town.

Rainbird Gallery (830-833-4545; 109 Main St., Blanco, TX 78606) This gallery is in an old Baptist church, 400 square feet of art up to the vaulted ceiling. Owner-artist Janet Fisher quotes Thoreau — "Art is nothing more than the meaning of life" — and her gallery is filled with meaning: paintings, Native American and Western art, pottery, and stone and wood sculptures, including a "Texas" totem pole.

On Courthouse Square in Blanco you can also browse in an authentic small-town market, and check out unique gifts in the **Sunflower** (830-833-5344; 317 Main St., Blanco, TX 78606) and antiques, fancy goods and curiosities in **Wagner & Chabot's** (830-833-4350; 323 Main St., Blanco, TX 78606).

BURNET COUNTY

Burnet County — pronounce it "BURN-it" — was created from Bell, Travis, and Williamson Counties in 1852 and named for David G. Burnet, a provisional president of the Texas Republic. Burnet, who was a New Jersey native, came to Texas as early as 1815. He didn't stay, but he must have liked what he saw because he returned in 1826, this time for good.

Like Stephen F. Austin, he also obtained permission from the Mexican government to settle immigrants in southeast Texas. The Convention of 1836, writing the Texas Declaration of Independence at Washington-on-the-Brazos, named him interim president of the Republic, and he served until Sam Houston was elected president. He was an early agitator for independence from Mexico.

The county — full of hills, caves, and cedar trees — has frontage on five of the beautiful Highland Lakes, and is in one of the most ancient geological areas of the world. Every mineral in North and South America can be found in the Burnet County area — even if there's only a little bit of it.

The county's two main towns are Burnet and Marble Falls. In 1848 the Texas Rangers set up a small station about 3 miles south of what is now the town of Burnet. Then, early in 1849, the U.S. Army, which had begun establishing forts across Texas from Fort Worth south to Uvalde to protect early settlements from the Indians, replaced the ranger station with Fort Croghan, and the rangers moved on to other sites.

Burnet

Eleanor S. Morris

The Hill Country Flyer "holdup gang" waiting to "rob the next train.

In 1882 the railroad arrived in Burnet, and not long afterward a block of the regional marble from nearby Holland quarries was shipped from Burnet to Washington, D.C., as Texas's contribution to the building of the Washington Monument.

The Hill Country Flyer, a historic narrow-gauge steam train, arrives in Burnet from Cedar Park (just west of Austin), and the Burnet Gunfighters stage a pretty good performance for the passengers when they arrive. The historic square has some shops, boutiques, and a tearoom, and there's a pleasant walk down along the town's Hamilton Creek, paved and landscaped, with a fountain and picnic areas. Steps lead down from both sides of Hwy. 29 W. just west of the intersection of Hwy. 281.

The Texas Legislature has officially declared Burnet the Bluebonnet Capital of Texas and, of course, there is a big **Bluebonnet Festival** every spring.

Burnet County Chamber of Commerce historic building.

Eleanor S. Morris

For more information, contact the **Burnet Chamber of Commerce** (512-756-4297; 703 Buchanan Dr., Burnet, TX 78611).

Marble Falls

Highway 281 into Marble Falls forms a causeway across the lake on one side and the Colorado River on the other, a pretty sight either entering or leaving on the south side of town. You can see why Adam R. Johnson, Marble Falls's founder, decided the area had potential. Dreaming of a large manufacturing city powered by the "Great Falls," which back then poured over a marble ledge in the Colorado River, he began to buy up property as early as 1850.

But along came the Civil War to interrupt his plans. Johnson rose to the rank of general in the Confederate Army. Although he was blinded in the war, this did not interfere with his inner vision for the town, and by offering some of his land as a right-of-way for a railroad to haul the plentiful granite, he put Marble Falls on the map around 1887.

The waterfall was covered by the development of Max Starke and Wirtz Dams; the "Great Falls" are hidden from view beneath Lake LBJ. But if you're curious to see what they looked like, there's a picture on the wall in the Blue Bonnet Cafe.

For more information, contact the **Marble Falls/Lake LBJ Chamber of Commerce** (830-693-4449, 800-759-8178; www.marblefalls.org; 801 Hwy. 281, Marble Falls, TX 78654.

BURNET COUNTY LODGING

The town of Burnet has several bed & breakfasts, and there is one in Marble Falls. Motels in Burnet include the **Howard Johnson Express Inn** (512-756-4747; 908 Hwy. 29 W., Burnet, TX 78611) and the **Sundown Motor Inn** (512-

756-2171; 205 N. Water St., Burnet, TX 78611). Motels in Marble Falls include a **Best Western** (830-693-5122, 800-578-1234; 1403 Hwy. 281 N., Marble Falls, TX 78654) and a **Ramada** (830-693-7351, 800-1-RAMADA; 1206 Hwy. 281, Marble Falls, TX 78654).

Burnet

1884 AIRY MOUNT INN
Hosts: Charles and
  Rosanne Hayman.
512-756-4149.
Rte. 3, Box 280, PO Box 351,
  Burnet, TX 78611.
Price: Moderate.
Credit Cards: MC, V.
Handicap Access: No.

The Airy Mount Inn is located on 6 acres inside a 150-acre tract of land. In the property's barn, the original hand-hewn rock walls of solid limestone were built by slave hands, brought to Texas by the original owner after the Civil War. Here in Texas, not only were they paid well for their finished work, they were freed and stayed on as caretakers, masons, and farmers.

Accommodations include the Josephine Room, the General's Room, and the Santa Fe Suite, all upstairs, while the living and dining rooms downstairs are filled with fine bronzes, books, and antiques.

Breakfast is a "Texas-size feast" served in the barn's dining room, with huevos rancheros, eggs Benedict, or Alsace quiche.

Additional amenities include use of the full-size kitchen (and outdoor barbecue pit) and the washer-dryer.

MAIN STREET BED &
  BREAKFAST
Hosts: Happy and Mike
  Matthews.
512-756-2861, 512-756-4256.
808 N. Main St., Burnet, TX
  78611.
Price: Moderate, EP.
Credit Cards: None.
Handicap Access: No.

This house dates from the 1930s, when it was built by Dr. Sam Paschall, who practiced dentistry in Burnet for many years. He enlarged his home to include a great room, where guests now enjoy music and games. Happy and Mike Matthews purchased the home in 1994, and Dr. Matthews is following in the footsteps of the original owner: He's a dentist, too. And Happy is as happy as her name.

The three guest rooms, with private baths, are comfortable and uncluttered, furnished in what Happy calls "early traditional." The great room has a player piano, an old-timey jukebox, and slot machine — and a stuffed goose or two.

THUNDERBIRD RESORT
Manager: Charlena Mathis.
512-756-4878, 800-210-7202.
HCR 5, Box 531, Burnet, TX
  78611.

This family-run resort on Lake Buchanan has twenty cottages, large and small, on 30 acres of land facing 1,100 feet of waterfront. There's fishing for bass, crappie, catfish, and perch; canoes for rent at the marina; swimming and sunning in the large

Price: Inexpensive to Very
Expensive, depending on
cottage size.
Credit Cards: None.
Handicap Access: Partial.

**THE VERANDAS GUEST
HOUSE**
Hosts: Wayne and Mary
Brown.
512-715-0190.
www.highlandlakes.com/
verandas.
108 East League St., Burnet,
TX 78611.
Price: Expensive.
Credit Cards: AE, D, MC, V.
Handicap Access: No.

pool with a shaded terrace; and hiking, jogging, and bird-watching, especially in the winter when bald eagles come to nest along the lake.

This handsome historic building was constructed in 1856 as a stagecoach stop. The well on the veranda used to quench the thirst of both travelers and horses; it now supplies water for the inn's handsome water garden and koi pond.

Upstairs, off the veranda that encircles the house, are three guest suites, each with private bath, telephone, and TV/VCR. All have queen-size beds and are decorated with antiques and art.

Breakfast might be huevos poblanos, tomatoes with fresh basil, fresh rosemary-roasted potatoes, a breakfast sundae (yogurt with fresh fruit), and sweet rolls or apple bread.

There's a lovely view of the colorful koi and other goldfish in the water garden, and the Japanese-style bridge over the water, through the large antique painted glass wall in the dining room and common area.

Marble Falls

**LIBERTY HALL GUEST
HAUS**
Host: Wilburn Wall.
830-693-4518, 800-232-4469.
www.marblefallstexas.com
/liberty.htm.
119 Ave. G, Marble Falls,
TX 78654.
Price: Moderate to
Expensive.
Credit Cards: AE, MC, V.
Handicap Access: No.

History buffs enjoy staying in the historic house that was home to Gen. Adam Johnson, founder of Marble Falls, on land awarded to the heirs of Capt. William Baker, hero of the Alamo. From 1919 to 1935 it was the home of George and "Birdie" Harwood; she was America's first woman mayor, one elected by an all-male voting population. Wilburn Wall maintains the inn as his parents did. The Victorian parlor is a shrine to American patriotism. American flags, a table of JFK memorabilia, a DSC (Distinguished Service Cross) Award on the wall, and photos of Wall family members who have served their country fill the room.

White-painted bedrooms have shiny wood floors, Oriental-patterned rugs, and bright brass bedsteads. Some beds are covered in white with lacy dust ruffles, others in colorful quilts. The upstairs porch looks out over the lake and the lovely view beyond.

Each of the seven guest suites is equipped with a coffeemaker, and a continental breakfast is served in your room.

BURNET COUNTY RESTAURANTS AND FOOD PURVEYORS

Burnet

BURNET COUNTY BBQ
512-756-6468.
Hwy. 29 W., Burnet, TX
  78611.
Price: Inexpensive.
Cuisine: Barbecue.
Serving: L, D; closed Tues.
Credit Cards: None.
Handicap Access: Partial.

"You have to go to the country to get country BBQ" is Pat McCall's motto, and it works, since this restaurant has been a Burnet institution for more years than Pat has owned it. Specials include Elgin hot sausage, tender brisket, and meaty ribs.

The real pit-cooked meats tasted even more flavorful in the rustic log-cabin atmosphere. Wood floors, wood walls, and a working wood-burning stove in the corner of the narrow room add to the authenticity. (The only modern note is the air-conditioning in the summer, but who's complaining?) With the barbecue you get the usual fixings: potato salad, coleslaw and beans, and, for dessert, a choice of chocolate, lemon, coconut, or pecan pie.

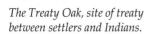
The Treaty Oak, site of treaty between settlers and Indians.

Eleanor S. Morris

**HIGHLANDER
  RESTAURANT AND
  STEAK HOUSE**
512-756-7401.
401 W. Buchanan, Burnet,
  TX 78611.
Price: Moderate.
Cuisine: Steaks, Seafood,
  Pasta.
Serving: B, L, D.
Credit Cards: Yes.
Handicap Access: Yes.

Right next to the historic Treaty Oak — the treaty was between Sam Houston and Mexican General Santa Anna, making Texas a Republic — this restaurant is pretty accommodating. "We offer a variety of hand-cut steaks as well as favorite southern dishes, and if it isn't on the menu, ask and see if we can make it for you!" From rib eye to porterhouse T-bone to sirloin for one or two to southern dishes like grilled chicken seasoned with Cajun blackening or farm-raised catfish, they try to please.

RIVERWALK CAFÉ
512-756-4100.
635 Hwy. 29 W., Burnet, TX
   78611.
Price: Inexpensive.
Cuisine: Country-style.
Serving: B, L, D.
Credit Cards: None.
Handicap Access: Yes.

You'd never guess this pleasantly decorated building once housed a fast-food store with gas pumps out front. Now booths line the wide windows, and there's an attractive salad bar along a wall.

The seafood croquettes are a delicious mix of crab, shrimp, and fish. Try the Riverwalk chicken plate, a grilled chicken breast topped with sautéed mushrooms, onions, and Swiss cheese. The homemade desserts include tasty lemon, coconut cream, and butterscotch pies; apple crisp; and cheesecake.

Marble Falls

BLUE BONNET CAFE
830-693-2344.
www.highlandlakes.com/
   bluebonnet.
211 Hwy. 281, Marble Falls,
   TX 78654.
Price: Inexpensive.
Cuisine: Texas Home-style.
Serving: B, L, D, daily.
Credit Cards: None.
Handicap Access: Yes.

For more than 60 years the Blue Bonnet Cafe has been a haven for both delicious and generous portions of down-home country cooking. Lunchtime brings such old favorites as pot roast, meat loaf, chicken and dumplings, rich cream of cauliflower soup, and a renowned roster of homemade pies — in addition to the more usual apple, peach, and lemon, our favorites are the peanut butter and German chocolate. The restaurant's motto is "Texas friendly spoken here," and you can believe it!

**DOCK'S SEAFOOD,
   STEAKS, & MORE**
830-693-2245.
austin.citysearch.com
   Search: Dock's.
900 FM 1431, Marble Falls,
   TX 78654.
Price: Inexpensive to
   Expensive.
Cuisine: Steak, Seafood.
Serving: L, D daily.
Credit Cards: AE, D, MC, V.
Handicap Access: Yes.

In a friendly atmosphere of polished wood, green vines, and green marbleized tables, and surrounded by such aquatic features as both seascapes and mounted fish, you can have anything from the fresh catch of the day, char-broiled or deep fried, to a rib-eye steak marinated overnight in Dock's special blend of herbs and spices. We began with Bloomers, a huge onion sliced and fried in seasoned batter and served with a delicious sauce. An excellent choice from the comprehensive menu is the seafood grill, a remarkable combination of fish, shrimp, lobster, scallops, and vegetables.

For dessert, the homemade carrot cake, specialty of Belinda Kemper of the Blue Bonnet Cafe (they share), was a tasty choice.

LUIGI'S
830-798-8051.
201 N. Main St., Marble
   Falls, TX 78654.
Price: Expensive.

Dining here along with soft music and candlelight is very pleasant; Luigi Attenasio likens the atmosphere to old-world warmth and friendliness.

The Italian broccoli soup, made fresh daily, is

Cuisine: Italian, Steaks, and Seafood.
Serving: D, closed Sun.
Credit cards: All except Discover.

delicious, as are all the other offerings on the menu. Chicken parmigiana, chicken milenaise, chicken mattia, chicken marsala, eggplant chicken parmigiana are all authentic Italian dishes. Four exotic venison dishes are also offered, along with the more usual steak, lamb chops, and fish. Try one of the sixteen Italian specialties on the menu, too.

MARK'S FAMILY RESTAURANT
830-693-7896.
1125 Hwy. 281 N., Marble Falls, TX 78654.
Price: Inexpensive.
Cuisine: Country.
Serving: B, L, D.
Credit Cards: AE, D, MC, V.
Handicap Access: Yes.

The chicken-fried steak here comes with potatoes and a choice of fried okra, black-eyed peas, or pinto beans (in addition to "regulars" like corn and broccoli). The fajita potato is a delicious novelty — a creamy baked potato covered with broiled chicken strip, brown onion rings, and green peppers, and absolutely smothered in cheddar cheese, sour cream, and guacamole. (We didn't even miss the tortillas, usually de rigueur with fajitas.) The homemade peach and blackberry cobblers were both juicy and delicious.

The dining room is spacious and welcoming, with white tablecloths on the tables, a antlered deer head on the wall, and wagon-wheel chandeliers on the ceiling.

BURNET COUNTY FOOD PURVEYORS

Latta Java Cafe (830-693-7199; 1107 Hwy. 1431 W., Marble Falls, TX 78654; Mon.–Fri. 7am–5pm, Sat. 8am–5pm) Something new for the Hill Country — espresso in the hinterlands! Once considered a mark of urban sophistication, a coffeehouse has popped up in Marble Falls, population just a tad more than 4,000. The owner, Bob Tuteur, greets folks by their first names and what the regulars like as much as the cozy friendly atmosphere are coffee and food as delicious as any you'd find in, say, Austin, but in a place far more personal than those in the big city. This is about the only place for quiche in all of Burnet County; and the crispy Belgian waffle is also recommended. Open for breakfast and lunch. At press time, a move to a new location was planned; double-check the address.

BURNET COUNTY CULTURE

ARCHITECTURE

In *Burnet,* the **Burnet County Courthouse** on the Square is an Art Deco building constructed in 1937. Many of the buildings facing the courthouse date from the 1870s.

Not open to the public but worth a look is the **Adam R. Johnson House** at 404 S. Water, built by the Confederate general who is credited with settling Marble Falls. Its thick walls of hand-hewn stone and logs and the high windows were designed to protect against hostile Indians.

The **Old Burnet County Jail** (Washington and S. Pierce) was designed by the Austin architect F. E. Ruffini, who was responsible for the design of the old Blanco County Courthouse in Blanco. Constructed in 1884 of local limestone, the jail was in use until 1981.

Buildings of architectural interest in *Marble Falls* include the **Roper House**, 707 3rd St. on the east side, built in 1888. This hotel was home to early drummers — traveling salesmen, that is — as well as such Texas politicians as Gov. Stephen Hogg. Completely renovated, with its exterior restored to its original appearance, it's now an office building (not open to the public).

Michel's Drugstore, 216 Main St., dates from 1891 and was rebuilt in 1927. It still has an old-fashioned soda fountain.

The **Brandt Badger House**, S. 4th, is of interest because the two-story house was built from the rubble left from the shaping of the granite blocks used in building the Texas capitol. Brandt Badger was a Confederate veteran, and he formed a partnership with Adam Johnson to found the town.

The **Old Marble Falls Jail** on 2nd St. is not open to the public, but it's one of the oldest structures in town. You can peek through the barred slit-hole windows to see the two cells of the gray concrete blockhouse.

The **Gov. Oral M. Roberts Cottage**, 819 7th, was the home of the governor of Texas from 1879 to 1883. He later taught law at the University of Texas, retiring to this whitewashed cottage in 1893.

Don't miss the **Marble Falls Chamber of Commerce** on Hwy. 281 at Broadway — and not only because of the information potential: It's in a picturesque old railroad depot. Here the 5-mile Granite Mountain and Marble Falls Railroad connected the quarry with the rails in 1889.

LIBRARIES

HERMAN BROWN FREE LIBRARY
512-756-2328.
www.rootsweb.com/
~txburnet/Libraries.html.
On the Square, Burnet, TX 78654.
Open: Mon.–Fri. 10am–6pm.
Fee: None.

The library is a treasure trove of information about Burnet County history and the geology of the area. It also offers a guidebook to the historical markers and cemeteries in Burnet County.

Fort Croghan Museum on the site of a U.S. Army post, 1849–1853.

Eleanor S. Morris

MUSEUMS

FORT CROGHAN MUSEUM
512-756-8281.
703 Buchanan Dr., Burnet, TX 78654.
On Hwy. 29.
Open: Apr.–mid. Oct., Thurs.–Sat. 10am–5pm.
Admission: Free.

The museum is on the site of a U.S. Army post that was in service from 1849 until 1853, the third of four forts established to protect settlements from hostile Indians. It was named for Col. George Croghan, a hero of the War of 1812. Today one of the original fort buildings is still there, along with the "Old Powder House" built during the Civil War and several other 19th-century stone and log buildings that have been moved to the site. The museum depicts local frontier days at the fort in exhibits of restored carriages, guns, furniture, and the like.

HIGHLAND LAKES SQUADRON OF THE CONFEDERATE AIR FORCE MUSEUM
512-756-2226.
www.kdi.com/~caf.
Kate Craddock Field, Burnet Municipal Airport, PO Box 866, Burnet, TX 78611.
On S. Hwy. 281.
Open: Primarily on weekends; call ahead (hours vary).
Admission: Adults $3, seniors $2, children $1.

This museum is operated by the Highland Lakes Squadron of the Confederate Air Force, based in Midland, Texas, whose mission is to preserve, in flying condition, a complete collection of combat aircraft that were flown by all military services in World War II.

The CAF provides museum buildings, of which the Burnet museum is one, for permanent protection and display of these aircraft as a tribute to the thousands of men and women who built, serviced, and flew them.

LCRA NIGHTENGALE ARCHAEOLOGICAL CENTER
830-598-5261, 800-776-5272, ext. 2753.
www.lcra.org/lands.
PO Box 302, Kingsland, TX 78639.
On Burnet County Rd. 126.
Open: 2nd and 4th Sat., 2–5pm; group tours can be arranged at other times.
Admission: Free.

This public archaeological site on the Colorado River is the property of the LCRA (Lower Colorado River Authority) and is operated by the Llano Uplift Archaeological Society. The museum/ educational center displays artifacts from prehistoric times. An outdoor trail reveals the culture of native peoples who inhabited the land for thousands of years; a new exhibit of an "Archaic Camp" shows how people lived 8,000 years ago. (Note: The mailing address is Kingsland, Llano County, but the center is located in Burnet County.)

SEASONAL EVENTS

In APRIL *Burnet* joins in the **Highland Lakes Bluebonnet Trail**, with a parade, arts and crafts fair, street dance, and tours of the fields of bluebonnets, primroses, Indian paintbrush, and many other wildflowers surrounding the Highland Lakes. *Marble Falls* also sponsors the **Bluebonnet Arts and Crafts Trail**.

In MAY, *Marble Falls* offers the **Howdy Roo Chili Cookoff**.

JUNE brings the **Burnet County Fair and Rodeo**, with *Burnet*'s downtown parade, carnival, entertainment, dances, livestock competition, and, of course, a rodeo.

The *Marble Falls* **Rodeo and Parade** is in JULY.

AUGUST brings the **Lakefest Drag Boat Race**.

Fort Croghan Day is in OCTOBER in *Burnet*.

In DECEMBER in *Burnet* **Christmas Lighting** sets the downtown square aglow with a tall tree, deer, smaller animals, a train, and a Hill Country scene. Fort Croghan is decorated as it was for the soldiers' first Christmas in 1849. Carolers and choirs sing, shops are open evenings, and Santa arrives one morning. *Marble Falls* creates the **Walkway of Lights:** thousands of lights reflected in Lake Marble Falls all through the month.

Check with the local chambers of commerce for exact dates: Burnet (512-756-4297; www.burnetchamber.org) and Marble Falls (830-693-4449; www.marble-falls.org).

BURNET COUNTY RECREATION

For camping, swimming, water sports, and other Burnet County outdoor fun, refer to information below on "Parks" and "Lakes."

FISHING

In addition to these sites, good fishing can be found at other Burnet County lakes and parks — refer to those sections below.

Burnet County Park (RR 2341 off Texas 29W) On the east shore of Lake Buchanan, this is an excellent fishing camp. It's open all day, every day; no fee; first come, first served.

LCRA Cottonwood Resource Area (512-473-4083; mailing address: LCRA, PO Box 220, Austin, TX 78767) The LCRA (Lower Colorado River Authority) has reserved this property for a primitive recreation area for fishing and picnicking. The 17-acre site has one public boat ramp on the southeast side of Lake LBJ; no rest rooms and no running water. Camping is permitted, but there are no sites or facilities. No fee.

GOLF

Burnet

Delaware Springs Municipal Golf Course (512-756-8951, golf course; 512-756-8471, pro shop; 127 E. Jackson, Burnet, TX 78611) The 18-hole course is open 7 days a week, from daylight to dark, with a head professional golfer and an assistant professional.

Marble Falls

Blue Lake Golf Club (830-598-5524, 214 W. Bluebonnet Dr., Marble Falls, TX 78654) 9-hole public course, 7:30am–5pm.

Meadowlakes Country Club (830-693-3300, 220 Meadowlake Dr., Marble Falls, TX 78654) 18-hole public course, 6:30am–7pm.

NATURE

Granite Mountain, an 866-foot dome of solid pink granite on the south side of FM 1431, is the largest surface granite quarry in the world. In the late 1880s it furnished pink granite for the Texas State Capitol in Austin. Monday to Friday from 9am–3pm, the public can buy small pieces of granite as souvenirs.

PARKS

INKS LAKE STATE PARK
512-793-2223, 512-389-8900 camping reservations; 800-792-1112 state park info.

Inks Lake is considered one of the most beautiful lakes in Texas. The 1,200-acre park offers camping, hiking (7 miles of trails), swimming, fishing, and water sports — you can rent canoes and pad-

www.tpwd.state.tx.us/
park/inks/inks.htm.
3630 Park Rd. 4 West,
  Burnet, TX 78611.
Off Hwy. 29 on Park Rd. 4
  past Longhorn Caverns.
Open: Year-round;
  reservations necessary
  for camping.
Admission: $1 per person
  13 and over day use fee.
  Call for camping fees.

**LONGHORN CAVERN
STATE PARK**
512-756-4680, business
  office; 512-756-6976, tour
  schedule.
www.tpwd.state.tx.us/
park/longhorn/
longhorn.htm.
RR 2, Box 23, Burnet, TX
78611.
Park Rd. 4 off U.S. 281
  between Burnet and
  Marble Falls.
Open: Year-round
  8am–10pm, except
  Christmas Eve and
  Christmas; cave tours
  start at 10am.
Admission: Adults $8,
  children 5–12, $4.50, 4
  and under free.

dleboats — on the 800-acre Inks Lake. There are RV sites with full hookups, screened shelters, rest rooms with showers, and a dump station (campsite reservations are a must). There's even a 9-hole golf course.

The cavern was once a camp for Indians, a hiding place for outlaws during frontier days, a secret gunpowder factory and storage facility during the Civil War, and a dance hall (and speakeasy) enjoyed by the folks of Burnet during the 1930s — the natural air-conditioning of the large "Council Room" made it very popular during hot Texas summers.

According to geologists, it took a million years of water flowing through to carve out the cave, considered the largest in Texas and the third largest in the world. Although the entire cave is 11 miles long, the tour — taking about an hour and a half — covers 1.25 miles, and it's always 64° down there, so you may want to bring a light sweater or jacket, and flat rubber-soled shoes are highly recommended.

The rest of the 639-acre park offers nature and hiking trails, picnic tables, plus a snack bar and gift shop.

Scenic Drives

Old Lampasas Road–Smithwick is one of the most scenic drives in Burnet County. From Burnet take RR 963 northeast to RR 1174 south to Bertram. There take RR 243 to Oatmeal, the second oldest community in the county (and scene of the annual Oatmeal Festival, Labor Day weekend). Go south and rejoin RR 1174, and continue on south to RR 1431 (or north to Marble Falls and U.S. 281 to return to Burnet).

For a panoramic view of Marble Falls, Lake Marble Falls, and the surrounding Hill Country, stop at the roadside park on U.S. 281 south of the Colorado River. There are picnic tables here, too.

Recreation on Burnet County Lakes

A view of Inks Lake, named for its deep blue color.

Eleanor S. Morris

Lake Buchanan was the first, and is the highest, of the Highland Lakes. It also has the largest surface area: 23,060 acres. Although much of the 192-mile shoreline is privately owned, there are a number of public and commercial places which give access to boating, fishing, swimming, and other water sports, as well as camping. Both Burnet County on the east and Llano County on the west have a park on the lake.

There is excellent fishing for striped bass in Lake Buchanan. Numerous guides on the lake are eager to take visitors out for a fishing adventure. They provide all the bait and tackle you'll need, and they'll even fillet the fish for you on the dock. Call 512-793-2803 for these fishing charters.

Inks Lake, at a constant level, covers 803 acres and is a reservoir used primarily for maintaining heads to produce electric power from the overflow from Lake Buchanan. Inks Lake offers year-round fishing, boating, and water sports; there are lakeside docks and marinas.

Lake LBJ and **Lake Marble Falls** are two constant-level lakes below Buchanan and Inks lakes in the Highland Lakes chain. These two clear lakes offer good fishing, skiing, and water recreation; contact the **Marble Falls Chamber of Commerce,** 830-693-4449; www.marblefalls.org.; 801 Hwy. 281, Marble Falls, TX 78654.

See "Parks" for more information.

BURNET COUNTY SHOPPING

The historic Square in ***Burnet*** is one block east of Hwy. 281 at Jackson St. and is a pleasant place to stroll; there are shops and several historic buildings on or near the Square.

Burnet Antique Mall (512-756-7783; 206 S. Main St., PO Box 838, Burnet, TX 78611, on the Square) Friendly Fannie Shepperd of Rocky Rest Inn is in charge of this enormous collection of everything and anything. The huge mall leads the shopper back and farther back, from one cubbyhole to the next. Furniture, lots of china, glassware, books, light fixtures, collectibles, and who knows what-all are to be had 7 days a week.

Cobblestone Cottage (512-756-7407; www.shopcobblestone.com; 212 E. Jackson St., Burnet, TX 78611) is the place to go for plush bears, aromatherapy candles and oils, garden theme accessories and birdhouses, and Texas souvenirs.

Our Li'l Bit of Texas (512-756-7522; 117 E. Jackson St., Burnet, TX 78611, on the Square) Charlene Miller has a shop chock-full of souvenirs as well as figurines, glassware, china, and bridal gifts. Texas-ware abounds, too: books, placemats, rugs, candleholders, quilt racks, ornaments both Western and Christmas; Texas jam, jellies, and potpourri; and a lovely collection of T-shirts, mailboxes, and baskets hand-painted with Texas wildflowers.

The *Marble Falls* Chamber of Commerce offers a list of local shops selling everything from antiques, clothing, and gifts to pecans (at **Texas Hill Country Pecans,** 1009 N. Main, Marble Falls, TX 78654). Marble Falls favorites include the following:

Antiques Plus (830-693-3301; 1000 W. Hwy. 1431, Marble Falls, TX 78654) has, as the name implies, more than just antiques. They also have new and used furniture, collectibles, and gifts.

The Wood Shed (830-693-2024, 112 Hwy. 281 N., Marble Falls, TX 78654) It would be hard to miss this low rambling building on the west side of the highway — a gift shop that grew over more than 25 years into "the woodshed that was," said owner Carol Collier. The huge interior stocks all sorts of Texas memorabilia, Texana books and jams and jellies, clothing "geared to the Texas look," Indian turquoise and designer silver jewelry, hunting and fishing equipment, and even leather luggage.

Dead Man's Hole

Some 140 years after being part of Texas's sometime violent, colorful past, Dead Man's Hole has been dedicated as a historical site. Some seventeen bodies, forerunners of some of today's Burnet County residents, were dumped here during a violent period of terror between secessionist and unionist sympathizers during the Civil War and the Reconstruction that followed. Located 3 miles southwest of Marble Falls, the site is marked by a historical marker.

GILLESPIE COUNTY

The 180 German immigrants with the sixteen ox-drawn wagons who trekked from New Braunfels to the Pedernales River were either a brave bunch or seriously misinformed, because they ended up in the heart of Comanche country despite the efforts of Prince Carl of Solms-Braunfels to make sure that he was settling his German colonists in safe territory.

It was May of 1846 by the time they arrived on the banks of the Pedernales, and by 1847 stronger measures had to be taken for their protection or else they would have been swept away by the powerful Indians. Thanks to Baron von Meusebach, who, unlike Prince Solms, renounced his title to become plain John O. Meusebach, citizen of Texas, they were saved. Meusebach, evidently a genius at diplomacy, was able to establish lasting peace, making such a successful treaty with the Indians that the tiny town of Fredericksburg was left in peace.

This scenic county of plateaus and hills broken by spring-fed streams was organized in 1848 from Bexar and Travis Counties and named for Texas Ranger captain R. A. Gillespie. And although Blanco County revels in the fact that President Lyndon B. Johnson grew up within its boundaries, Gillespie County can boast that he was born here, in the small town of Stonewall. Gillespie County can also claim another famous American, Fleet Adm. Chester W. Nimitz, born in Fredericksburg.

Fredericksburg

For a taste of still-living Texas history, visit Fredericksburg, where many natives still speak German and live in quaint gingerbread-trimmed houses. Fredericksburg is so friendly even its street signs spell out a welcome. The first letters of the streets running north and south across Main spell out ALL WELCOME and, traveling west from the courthouse square, the first letters spell COME BACK. (All Gillespie County listings are in Fredericksburg, unless otherwise noted.)

Stonewall

Stonewall — named for Confederate general Stonewall Jackson and founded in 1870 — is so small, it doesn't have an organized downtown, just what's along the highway: gas station, motel, restaurant. But it's famed equally for delicious Gillespie County peaches (the Peach Jamboree is usually the middle weekend in June) and the LBJ Ranch, Lyndon B. Johnson's home.

GILLESPIE COUNTY LODGING

Fredericksburg has a dizzying array of bed & breakfast inns and guest houses —over 250! — if you want to spend the night and see even more of this historic spot. Below are three pleasant bed & breakfasts and a motel. **Be My Guest** (830-997-7227) and **Gastehaus Schmidt Reservation Service** (830-997-5612; www.foglodging.com) are reservation services listing many more country inns and bed & breakfasts, historic homes, and secluded guest cottages. (For additional reservation services as well as other area information, log on to the **Fredericksburg Chamber of Commerce** Web site, www.fredericksburg-texas.com/gcedc.htm.)

There are also several motels, among them the **Best Western Sunday House Inn** (830-997-4484, 800-274-3762; 501 E. Main St., Fredericksburg, TX 78624) and other chains such as **Comfort Inn** (830-997-9811; 908 S. Adams St., Fredericksburg, TX 78624), **Days Inn Suites** (830-997-1086, 800-320-1430; 808 S. Adams St., Fredericksburg, TX 78624), **Econo Lodge** (830-997-3437, 888-919-3437; 810 S. Adams St., Fredericksburg, TX 78624), and **Save Inn** (830-997-6568; 514 E. Main St., Fredericksburg, TX 78624), among others.

BED & BREAKFAST INNS

DAS COLLEGE HAUS
Host: Myrna Dennis.
830-997-9047, 800-654-2802.
www.dascollegehaus.com.
106 College St.,
    Fredericksburg, TX
    78624.
Price: Moderate to
    Expensive.
Credit Cards: MC, V.

Built in 1916, this lovely home is a fine example of Greek Revival architecture. Host Myrna has kept the wonderful assortment of old furniture — from auctions in Indiana — that was assembled by the previous owner, a good friend of Myrna's. This makes for an interesting change from the more usual German furniture of Fredericksburg, home of the first group of settlers brought to Texas by the Society for the Protection of German immigrants in Texas.

Downstairs, the Victorian Rose Suite has a paisley and rose-patterned wallpaper in both the king-size bedroom and sitting room (with fireplace and gas log), complementing the pretty flowered quilt and the sheer canopy of lace over the bed. The Arbor Suite has hardwood floors, cedar walls, and beamed ceiling plus a large bathroom with a skylight and stained-glass windows. Upstairs, off the L-shaped porch, the Victorian Green Suite can sleep six, with the sitting room containing a sofa bed. The Country Cream Room, across the hall, features a charming queen-size white-and-brass bed. Breakfast might be apple-pecan pancakes with crisp bacon, maple syrup, and oat-bran muffins. "We're health-conscious," says Myrna. "The pancakes are fat-free. But the amount of syrup is up to you!"

THE DELFORGE PLACE
Hosts: Sandy and Lee Selig.
830-997-6212, 900-997-0462.
www.delforgeplace.com.
710 Ettie St., Fredericks-
    burg, TX 78624.
Price: Moderate, EP.
Credit Cards: AE, D, MC, V.
Handicap Access: No.

Built in 1898, this historic house was moved to its present location in 1975 and considerably enlarged. Now that there are four guest rooms and suites — all with full private baths and mini-refrigerators plus "coffee corners" — in the main house (plus two suites next door in the also-historic Rabke-Weber House), it's hard to believe that this comfortable inn was once a one-room Sunday house. Sandy is following in the footsteps of previous owners, the Delforges, who were famous for breakfasts, and she offers "seven totally different breakfasts" every day. Guests also enjoy privileges at the Baron's Creek Swim & Racquet Club — or they can play horseshoes, croquet, and archery on the inn's own grounds.

MAGNOLIA HOUSE
Hosts: David and Dee
    Lawford.
830-997-0306, 800-880-4374.
www.magnolia-house.com.
101 E. Hackberry,
    Fredericksburg, TX
    78624.
Price: Moderate, EP.
Credit Cards: AE, D, MC, V.
Handicap Access: No.

New owners David and Dee took over this historic home in November 1999, but everything else has remained the same — from the gourmet southern-style breakfasts of fresh fruit, homemade muffins and juice, waffles and crêpes, bacon and sausage, and an egg entrée, sweet rolls, and biscuits and gravy to the antique china and silver the meals are served on. The stately home was built in 1923 for the Stein family: Edward Stein was the architect of the Gillespie County Courthouse. The two suites and three rooms are luxurious, with HBO and Encore premium channels, fresh flowers, and terry robes, and the stone patio and fish pond make the outdoors inviting, too.

ORCHARD INN
Hosts: Annette and Mark
    Wieser.
830-990-0257, 800-439-4320.
13645 S. Hwy. 87, Rt.3, Box
    115, Fredericksburg, TX
    78624.
Price: Expensive.
Credit Cards: All.
Handicap Access: No.

You'll really feel out in the country on these 60 acres, yet the inn is practically right in town. The property has a lake with paddleboats and fish ("and hungry ducks," says Annette), and inside the 1904 Victorian farmhouse has been enlarged into an elegant country inn. There are three suites in the north wing of the house, one of them in the older portion. A fourth room is located nearby in an 1870 log cabin.

Your gourmet breakfast might include Mountain Cherry Frappe, glazed pork tenderloin, a cheddar cheese soufflé, rosemary potatoes, and homemade bread with homemade amaretto peach preserves. So bring a hearty appetite along with your luggage!

GILLESPIE COUNTY RESTAURANTS AND FOOD PURVEYORS

ALTDORF GERMAN BIERGARTEN AND DINING ROOM
830-997-7865.
301 W. Main St., Fredericksburg, TX 78624.
Price: Moderate.
Cuisine: German.
Serving: L, D Wed.–Mon.
Credit Cards: D, MC, V.
Handicap Access: Yes.

Indoors or out in the biergarten behind this restaurant on a sunny corner, the food is delicious. Tourists appreciate good German food, proprietor Cameron Baird says, and local people who eat German food at home come for the restaurant's Tex-Mex fare. From the Hans and Fritz sandwich to the dinners of bratwurst, knackwurst, bockwurst, and schnitzel, or the Tex-Mex *comidas* (dinners) of enchilada, taco, and chalupa plates, everybody enjoys Altdorf — there's often a waiting line.

The oldest part of the restaurant, the indoor dining room, was built in 1846 by German settler Conrad Wissemann. The room has big windows, lace curtains, a pine floor, and paintings and prints of Fredericksburg on the walls. But in good weather (which is almost always the case in the Hill Country) most folks prefer to sit out under the big old trees in the biergarten.

ANDY'S DINER
830-997-3744.
413 S. Washington, Fredericksburg, TX 78624.
Price: Inexpensive.
Cuisine: Central Texas.
Serving: B, L, D.
Credit Cards: All but Discover.
Handicap Access: Yes.

Know that you'll appreciate Andy's brag, that their chicken-fried steaks have been featured in the *Chicago Tribune*, the *Arizona Daily Star*, and the *Philadelphia Enquirer*. In addition, this friendly place is open 7 days a week for three meals a day — and have been since 1957. The large main room has a model train riding on a track around the room, just below the ceiling, which you can watch while enjoying steaks, seafood, Mexican dishes, even German cuisine. Friday night there's an all-you-can-eat seafood buffet.

FRIEDHELM'S BAVARIAN INN AND BAR
830-997-6300.
905 W. Main St., Fredericksburg, TX 78624.
Price: Expensive.
Cuisine: German, Steaks, Seafood.
Serving: L, D Tues.–Sun.
Credit Cards: AE, D, MC, V.
Handicap Access: Yes.

There's often a wait at this bar and restaurant, a huge building with the ambiance of a Black Forest hunting lodge — fallow deer, moose, mule deer, elk, and boar heads are mounted on the wall — or a Bavarian *bierstube* — there are old beer signs decorating the walls, along with a tall mirrored bar with columns, classic beer steins, and friendly if busy service.

Sauerbraten nach bayrischer Art — Bavarian-style roast beef imbued with aromatic spices, herbs, and wine — is a good choice, or the house version of Holstein schnitzel, breaded and topped with jäger mushroom sauce and, surprisingly, two sunny-side-up eggs. The whole-wheat bread is made with molasses and mullet seeds, and apple strudel tops it all off. There's beer from a barrel, premium domestic beer, and imported beers; wines from both German and Hill Country cellars; margaritas, coladas, and daiquiris, and warmth and *Gemütlichkeit* everywhere. Three large dining rooms seat three hundred, and everything runs smoothly in spite of the crowd.

OLD GERMAN BAKERY AND CAFÉ
830-997-9084.
225 W. Main St., Fredericksburg, TX 78624.
Price: Moderate.
Cuisine: German.
Serving: B, L, D Thurs.–Mon.
Credit Cards: None.
Handicap Access: Yes.

For authentic German food, from schnitzels to rouladen, this is a perfect place. And since it's also a bakery, you can choose your dessert right from the display case of fresh-baked goodies. The storefront restaurant is bright and friendly, and you can be sure you're dining in good company, since George's is a popular spot for the locals — including the sheriff and his men.

WHEELER'S
830-990-8180.
204 E. Main St., Fredericksburg, TX 78624.
Price: Inexpensive.
Cuisine: Texan, German.
Serving: L.
Credit Cards: MC, V.
Handicap Access: Yes.

This family owned and operated restaurant has a clean bright look, with its fresh blue-and-white color scheme and white stucco walls. The motif reflects the mix of the menu, with a giant steer hide on one wall and Indian and other Western art on the rest, while outside the restaurant is decorated with flower boxes and scalloped gingerbread trim. The corner room with its wide window walls is great for people-watching while digging into your Texas chili and corn bread and beans, or the German plate of grilled bratwurst or knackwurst, red cabbage, sauerkraut, and hot German potato salad.

GILLESPIE COUNTY FOOD PURVEYORS

BAKERIES

Along with the Old German Bakery and Cafe (see "Restaurants"), try:

Dietz Bakery (830-997-3250; 218 E. Main St., Fredericksburg, TX 78624; 8am until sold out) Fredericksburg's oldest bakery (founded 1876) is famous for its bread — whole wheat, white, rye, and French. They're open only until they're sold out, so don't wait too long, since they're usually emptied out by noon. The pastries and cookies are delicious, too.

Fredericksburg Bakery (830-997-3254; 141 E. Main St., Fredericksburg, TX 78624; Mon.–Sat. 8am–5:30pm, Sun. 8am–5pm) This bakery prides itself on authentic German goods from its German baker — from apple strudel that's "made and tastes just like in Germany" to the popular sweet German pretzels and the breads made from high-fiber grains imported from Germany. Authentic, historic recipes date from 1917.

MARKETS

Das Peach Haus (830-997-7194; Hwy. 87 S., Fredericksburg, TX 78624; open May 15 to August 15) This fresh-fruit stand also stocks jams and jellies in its country store.

WINERIES

Gillespie County is home to three award-winning wineries and a brewery:

Bell Mountain Oberhellmann Vineyards (830-685-3297; Llano St., Box 22, Fredericksburg, TX 78624; off Hwy. 16, 14 miles north of Fredericksburg; tasting room open Mar.–mid-Dec., Sat. only, 10am–5pm; call a day in advance for tour) When winemaking was revived in Texas, Bell Mountain was founded in 1976, establishing the first appellation in the state. Wines are estate bottled: chardonnay, sauvignon blanc, semillon, Johannesburg Riesling, cabernet sauvignon, pinot noir, and Gewürztraminer.

Grape Creek Vineyard (830-644-2710; PO Box 102, Stonewall, TX 78671; Hwy. 290, 10 miles east of Fredericksburg; tours Tues.–Sat. 10am–5pm, Sun. 12–5pm) This Hill Country winery is unique in that it has an underground cellar. In the tasting room sample cabernet sauvignon, chardonnay, and sauvignon blanc under the Texas Hill Country appellation. Gift shop, too.

Fredericksburg Winery (830-990-8747; 247 W. Main St., Fredericksburg, TX 78624) just one block west of the courthouse, boasts fourteen to sixteen winery releases tasted daily, with their wines sold only in the winery. They've won three medals from world wine championships conducted by the Beverage Tasting Institute in Chicago, Illinois, so you might want to taste some of the many offerings.

Fredericksburg Brewing Company (830-997-1646245; www.yourbrewery. com; East Main St., Fredericksburg, TX 78624) offers 7,000 gallons of cold German lagers, ales, and wheat brews. Check out their restaurant — featuring excellent kolaches — and a bar amid a stone fireplace, bright copper vessels, and an enclosed biergarten. You can even spend the night. There are twelve "bed & brew" accommodations above the brewery — it's an adults-only retreat — and in the morning enjoy the Kolache Kafé for fresh baked goods and gourmet coffee.

GILLESPIE COUNTY CULTURE

ARCHITECTURE

Eleanor S. Morris

Two of Fredericksburg's tiny Sunday houses, many of which are now B&Bs.

Special Fredericksburg attractions are the **Sunday houses**, little jewels of homes built in the 1880s by farmers and ranchers to be used on weekends when they came to town to shop, visit, attend Saturday night "oompah" (polka) dances, and church on Sunday.

They would arrive on a Saturday morning to sell their butter and eggs, shop for staples, and that evening they'd go visiting or dancing. Then after church on Sunday it was back to the farm.

Many of the houses have only two rooms, one above the other, with the stairway outside. There are all sorts of entertaining conjectures why. Were the children put upstairs and out of the way? Or were the women and children downstairs so the men could creep upstairs late at night without disturbing them?

Speaking of quaint, the **Vereins Kirche Museum** (www.ktc.net/gchs/tours .htm) is an eight-sided structure that looks just like a giant coffee mill. It was the first public building in the town, serving as a house of worship, school, and meeting hall. Now it holds city archives, a local history collection, and archaeological items. For only $1.50 you can tour the building daily 10am–4pm and Sun. 1–4pm.

The **Fredericksburg Convention and Visitors Bureau**, (830-997-6523; 106 N.

Adams, Fredericksburg, TX 78624) offers a walking-tour map of the historic district, with more than eighty points of interest, including the Sunday houses.

The "Coffee Mill" Vereins Kirche Museum, a replica of the original structure, the community church. To the left is a monument to town founder John Meusebach.

Eleanor S. Morris

MUSEUMS

Fredericksburg

PIONEER MUSEUM COMPLEX
830-997-2835.
www.ktc.net/gchs/tours. htm.
309 W. Main., Fredericksburg, TX 78624.
Open: Mon.–Sat. 10am–5pm, Sun. 1–5pm.
Admission: Adults $3, children 12 and under free.
Handicap Access: No.

The complex consists of a house, store, stone smokehouse, barn, another old home, and a Sunday House. The main building is the Kammlah House, originally the home of the Kammlah family, keepers of the first general store.

ADMIRAL NIMITZ MUSEUM AND HISTORICAL CENTER
830-997-4379.
www.tpwd.state.tx.us/ park/nimitz/nimitz.htm.
340 E. Main St., PO Box 777, Fredericksburg, TX 78624.

The museum building, the Steamboat Hotel, was built by the grandparents of Fleet Adm. Chester M. Nimitz, last of the U.S. five-star admirals and a native son of Fredericksburg. His grandparents were among the first settlers in the community in 1846. The museum's three floors have exhibits about the war in the Pacific and is dedi-

Open: 8am–4pm daily
   except Christmas.
Admission: Adults, $3;
   children and students
   6–12, $1.50.
Handicap Access: Partial.

cated to all who served under the admiral. Behind the hotel, the serene Japanese Garden of Peace is a gift from the people of Japan. The History Walk, one block from the garden, displays guns, boats, and planes from World War II along the pathways.

Also in the rear of the museum, the George Bush Gallery of the Pacific War has been added, in an existing building that has been expanded.

Stonewall

The Steamboat Hotel of Adm. Chester Nimitz's boyhood is now part of the Admiral Nimitz Museum.

Eleanor S. Morris

**LYNDON B. JOHNSON
STATE HISTORIC
PARK**
830-644-2252.
www.tpwd.state.tx.us/
   park/lbj/lbj.htm;
   www.nps.gov/lyjo.
PO Box 238, Stonewall, TX
   78671.
Located 2 miles east of
   Stonewall on Hwy. 290.
Open: Daily 8am–5pm.
Admission: Bus tours ($3,
   children 6 and under
   free) leave from the
   visitor center 10am–4pm
   daily. Abbreviated self-
   guided tours allowed
   from 5pm–dusk.
Handicap Access: Yes.

Laughing crowds listen to recordings of LBJ's jokes before boarding a small bus that tours the ranch to see his birthplace, one-room schoolhouse, and other historic sights. The 700-plus-acre state park includes a visitor center, a "dogtrot" cabin from the 1840s, an outdoor amphitheater, nature trail, and the Sauer Beckmann Living History Farmstead depicting the life of a traditional German family in the early 1900s. The tour includes the Old Junction schoolhouse, the Texas White House, LBJ Ranchlands, LBJ's birthplace, and the Johnson family cemetery.

SEASONAL EVENTS

Check with the **Fredericksburg Chamber of Commerce** (830-997-6523; www. fredericksburg-texas.com/events.htm) for exact dates.

MARCH is the beginning of Fredericksburg's **wildflower season** (which varies with the rainfall, sunshine, and temperature).

APRIL brings more wildflowers, plus the **Easter Fires Pageant**. One of Fredericksburg's biggest celebrations is the Easter Fires, commemorating Meusebach's peace talks. While the Indians and settlers were sitting around fires awaiting the outcome of the peace talks, a pioneer mother quieted her children's fears by telling them a charming tale of the rabbit who lit and tended those hillside fires to boil Easter eggs. Today, hillside fires glow each Easter eve while a pageant retells the story.

On the first or second weekend in MAY is the **Founder's Festival** and **Spring Tour of Homes**.

JUNE brings the **Stonewall Peach Jamboree & Rodeo**; and the **Country Peddler Show** on the second or third weekend.

In JULY: **Fourth of July Race Meet; Night in Old Fredericksburg Festival** midmonth, and the **Pari-Mutuel Horseracing Meet,** which takes place twice a month.

AUGUST is the month for the **Gillespie County Fair,** the oldest continuous county fair in Texas (since 1888). In addition to the fair, the **Pari-Mutuel Horseracing Trials Race Meet** is midmonth, and the **Pari-Mutuel Horseracing Meet** is the fourth weekend.

SEPTEMBER the **Country Peddler Show** comes around again at the beginning of the month. OCTOBER is busy with the **Oktoberfest,** first weekend; **Mesquite Art Festival,** second weekend; **Food & Wine Fest,** fourth weekend.

In NOVEMBER the **Country Peddler Show** is around Thanksgiving, along with the **Turkey Trot,** and the **Christmas Lighting Tour** starts the fourth weekend.

Through DECEMBER the **Christmas Lighting Tour** lights up historic Main Street and residential areas (a map is available at the Convention and Visitors Bureau; 803-997-6523; 106 N. Adams, Fredericksburg, TX 78624). **Kristkindl Market** and **Candlelight Tour of Homes** are on the second weekend.

GILLESPIE COUNTY RECREATION

CAMPING

The "Camping" section below describes park and hiking trails as well as camping facilities. (See also www.fredicksburg-texas.com/camping.htm.)

Enchanted Rock Natural Area (915-247-3903, reservations 512-389-8900; www.
tpwd.state.tx.us/park/enchanted/enchanted.htm; 16710 RR 965, Fredericksburg,
TX 78624; 18 miles north of Fredericksburg) Over 1,600 acres on Big Sandy

Luckenbach, Texas

*There's always music in
this Luckenbach bar, where
"everybody is somebody."*

Eleanor S. Morris

Between Stonewall and Fredericksburg, take a little detour south on FM 1376, 4
miles to Luckenbach, famed in song and story.

The spot was founded in 1849, but it never amounted to anything and was a
ghost town by the 1970s. Nobody would have heard of Luckenbach if the late storyteller of Texas folklore Hondo Crouch hadn't purchased the town in 1970. It was
brought to further notoriety by country-western music stars Willie Nelson and
Waylon Jennings; who sang the song "Luckenbach, Texas." Jerry Jeff Walker got
into the act by recording "Viva Terlingua " there.

The bend in the road is marked, but it's rather easy to miss, so be alert. There's a
post office in downtown Luckenbach, which is a little way down the road on the
north bank of Big Creek, but Fredericksburg has taken over the privilege of post-
marking the town's mail. However, you can buy a Luckenbach postcard here, and
they'll give it an extra postmark.

Under the trees along the creek there's a dance hall. The motto here is
"Everybody's Somebody in Luckenbach," and there's usually a lot of fun and music
going on in the bar at the back of the souvenir shop/post office as well as all sorts of
yearly activities in the dance hall. (For more information, call 830-997-3224 or see
the   Luckenbach   Inn's   Web   site   for   links   to   events   in   the   area:
www.luckenbachtx.com.)

There's usually something musical going on in Luckenbach (except Wednesdays
and Sundays). To find out what, call 830-997-322.

A bed & breakfast inn is just off the road within half a mile of Luckenbach and
just 10 minutes from Fredericksburg.   *Continued on next page*

THE LUCKENBACH INN
Hosts: Capt. Matt and Eva Marie Carinhas.
803-997-2205, 800-997-1124.
www.luckenbachtx.com.
3234 Luckenbach Rd.,
Fredericksburg, TX
78624.
Price: Moderate to Expensive.
Credit Cards: AE, D, MC, V.
Handicap Access: No.

Located on 12 acres along the banks of South Grape Creek, with an abundance of wildlife, you'll feel far from even the business of Fredericksburg. Each of the accommodations are different (with five queen-size beds in all): the two-bedroom 1800s Log Cabin is rustic and filled with antiques, the Coral and Cypress Rooms have a whirlpool tub and a fireplace, the Grape Suite has a full kitchen, and the Old Smokehouse is a charming cottage behind the Log Cabin. A rock fireplace warms the main house, "and we do use our fireplace!" says Eva Marie. Well-behaved children and pets are welcome, but the pets must be "clean and vermin free."

Breakfast might be French toast, pepperwurst sausage, an egg mix of french fried onions, cooking cream and Tabasco sauce, and banana bread. Lacy and Ginger are the two inn dogs, and chickens and roosters run all around the grounds. But the big surprise is the potbellied pink pig — yes, a pig —curled up in a corner. "That's Rooter," says Eva Marie. "So our guests can brag that they slept with a pig!"

Luckenbach also has a famous festival, Willie Nelson's Fourth of July Picnic, of course in July.

Creek features 46 tent sites and 60 primitive campsites, hiking trails, picnic area, barbecue grills, group facilities. (For more information about Enchanted Rock Natural Area, see "Parks" under Llano County Recreation.)

Fredericksburg KOA (830-997-4796; www.touringtexas.com/koa; 5681 Hwy. 290 E., Fredericksburg, TX 78624; 5 miles from Fredericksburg) Facilities here include 90 RV and tent sites. Kamping Kabins (AC/heat), rec room, grocery, laundry facilities, cable TV, pool.

Hill Country RV Park (830-997-5365; 1589 E. Main St., Fredericksburg, TX 78624) The 43 sites here are level pull-through full hookup sites. Cable TV, shower, laundry facilities, rec room.

Lady Bird Johnson Municipal Park (830-997-4202; Hwy. 16 S., Fredericksburg, TX 78624; 3 miles from Fredericksburg) This 340-acre park has 113 sites, all with full hookups, 50 tent sites, sports facilities, an 18-hole championship golf course (see "Golf"), and group facilities at the park.

Oakwood RV Resort (830-997-9817, 800-366-9396; Rt. 21 Box 218-B; Fredericksburg, TX 78624; 2 miles south on Hwy. 16 S. at Tivydale Rd.) 132 sites, full hookups, cable TV, paved roads, pool, laundry facilities.

FAMILY FUN

Scenic carriage rides through Fredericksburg's historic district, with history narration, are offered by the **Fredericksburg Carriage Company** (830-868-4144; W. Main and Orange, Fredericksburg, TX 78624; reservations are recommended).

GOLF

Lady Bird Johnson Municipal Golf Course (830-997-4010, 800-950-8147; Hwy. 16 S., Fredericksburg, TX 78624) 3 miles southeast of town, this par-72 course is considered to be the finest 18-hole championship course in the Hill Country.

HORSE RACING

June, July, and August are racing months for Gillespie County. Since 1888 the folks in Fredericksburg have been enjoying pari-mutuel horse races, first on the abandoned grounds of Fort Martin Scott, where the parade grounds were dragged by logs to make the first racetrack.

The second racetrack was two blocks along East Travis Street. In 1892 a third site was chosen, the 400 block between South Adams and South Lincoln; now the fairgrounds and racetrack are next to the Lady Bird Johnson Municipal Park on Hwy. 16 S., 3 miles from Fredericksburg. The track is 5/8-mile long, with a covered grandstand as well as bleachers, plus ten window ticket offices with full facilities. For racing schedules, contact the Gillespie County Fair Association, 830-997-2359; PO Box 526, Fredericksburg, TX 78624.

NATURE

Visit **Wildseed Farm** (830-990-1393, 800-848-0078; www.wildseedfarms.com; PO Box 3000, 425 Wildflower Hills, Fredericksburg, TX 78624; 9:30am–6pm daily; 7 miles east of Fredericksburg on Hwy. 290) for a tour of the Hill Country's famous wildflowers. While you can see them by the roadside every spring, this is an all-year flowering. It's a 200-acre working wildflower farm, with bluebonnets, poppies, and other colorful Texas wildflowers grown to be harvested for seed. There's a self-guided walking trail, a market center, and the Brew-bonnet Biergarten (with, of course, beer, plus boxed lunches and such snacks as peach sundaes). And be sure to bring your camera.

ROCK CLIMBING

There are no less than forty-five listed climbs in Enchanted Rock State Natural Area, from the hand-crack Raw Hand Climb with a good protection rating to the face-climbing boulder of Sanders Traverse with no protection. The climbs are rated according to the Yosemite Decimal System and range from 5.0 to 5.11, with higher ratings indicating increasing difficulty. Free climbing is permitted, but not the placement of bolts, pitons, or other devices that deface the rock in any way. Needless to say, you climb at your own risk. It's necessary to sign a climbing and rappelling release form before you begin.

TENNIS

FISD Tennis Center (Hwy. 16, Fredericksburg High School, Fredericksburg, TX 78624) The high school campus has eight courts, four lit for night play.

GILLESPIE COUNTY SHOPPING

Fredericksburg's Main Street is lined for blocks with shops, restaurants, and galleries.

Eleanor S. Morris

Fredericksburg is a tourist town, and eight blocks of Fredericksburg's Main Street historic district, from Washington Street east to Bowie west, are lined on both sides with every sort of shop and boutique imaginable. Walking up the south side of the street you'll find the following:

Alley Annex Antiques (830-997-4448; 305 W. Main St., Fredericksburg, TX 78624) Texas and Southwest primitives as well as American oak and "ranch relics."

Ambeance Antiques, Etc. (830-990-8912; 215 W. Main St., Fredericksburg, TX 78624) Tucked behind the Back Porch down a secluded brick walkway are eight rooms where you can browse forever. "Everyone just loves to come here and spend an hour," Betty Bass says. "They say I'm not too touristy!"

The Back Porch (830-997-2757; 211 W. Main, Fredericksburg, TX 78624) A delightful shop full of one-of-a-kind folk art pieces, much of it made by Pam Brunet and proudly displayed by her father Tom. Lamps, clocks, birdhouses, lamp bases, and signs like "God Bless Texas" and "Grow Dammit" — all one of a kind.

Der Kuchen Laden (830-997-4937; www.littlechef.com; 258 E. Main St., Fredericksburg, TX 78624) A complete kitchen shop full of cookware, baskets, spices, coffee beans, teas, and kitchen accessories.

Dodd's Family Tree Nursery (830-997-9571, 800-284-0352; 515 W. Main St., Fredericksburg, TX 78624) A garden and patio shop with native plants for xeriscape gardening. The nursery and flower shop also includes a Christmas store with all sorts of things for the holidays.

Walking up as far as Bowie and crossing over to the north side of Main you'll find:

Der Kuchen Laden (830-997-4937; www.littlechef.com; 258 E. Main St., Fredericksburg, TX 78624) A complete kitchen shop full of cookware, baskets, spices, coffee beans, teas, and kitchen accessories.

The Epicurean Shop (830-997-0124; 315 E. Main St., Fredericksburg, TX 78624) Specializing in self-indulgence, this shop offers jams, jellies, and specialty foods from around the world, combined with bath and body luxuries.

The Grasshopper and Wild Honey (830-997-5012; www.grasshopperfbg.com; 113 E. Main St., Fredericksburg, TX 78624) German nutcrackers and beer steins, Swarovski crystal, Chilmark pewter, and other collectibles.

Jabberwocky (830-997-7071; 105 N. Llano St., Fredericksburg, TX 78624) Quilts, clothing, bed and table linens, a nice selection of Spode Italian ware, and other gift items.

Jeep Collins, Jewelry Maker (830-997-5490; 148A E. Main St., Fredericksburg, TX 78624) Handcrafted jewelry and leather products.

The Main Book Shop (830-997-2375, 800-225-2375; www.main-book-shop.com; 143 E. Main St., Fredericksburg, TX 78624) Lots of Texas guidebooks; Texas cookbooks; Texas gardening, fishing, and nature tomes. They also feature an entire side wall of children's books, along with period paper dolls and such. Souvenirs, too, like Texas dominoes, cards, and Lone Star mugs.

Remember Me, Too (830-997-6444; 203 E. Main St., Fredericksburg, TX 78624) "Antiques and other whimsies," such as unique one of a kind birdhouses, Santas, and Pam and Terry's very own creation, "Prairie Santas," which they carve from wood and clothe in old fabrics.

The Seasons (830-997-9180; 116 E. Main St., Fredericksburg, TX 78624) A shopful of gifts and decorative accessories.

Showcase Antiques (830-997-5505; 119 E. Main, Fredericksburg, TX 78624) A fine selection of cut glass, porcelain, art glass, maps, and prints, as well as furniture.

The Southwest Images Gallery (830-997-8688; 123 E. Main St., Fredericksburg, TX 78624) Antler and horn chandeliers, copper lighting fixtures and furniture, and other Western decorative accessories.

Sweet Annie (830-997-0852; 219 W. Main St., Fredericksburg, TX 78624) The home of American country antiques along with potpourri, books, gifts, and lots of candy: candy sticks and old-fashioned bulk candy (horehound, rock, sour cherry, sour apple) by the pound and weighed on an old-fashioned scale.

Fredericksburg is also attracting art galleries, among them: **Charles Beckendorf** (830-997-5955; 519 E. Main St., Fredericksburg, TX 78624); **Fredericksburg Art Gallery** (830-990-2707; 425 E. Main St., Fredericksburg, TX

78624); **Kowert Art Gallery** (830-997-3311;120 E. Main St., Fredericksburg, TX 78624); **Thomas Kinkade Gallery** (830-990-2335, 131 E. Main St., Fredericksburg, TX 78624); and **Whistle Pik Gallery** (830-990-8151, 800-999-0820; www. whistlepik.com; 425 E. Main St., Fredericksburg, TX 78624).

HAYS COUNTY

The Balcones Escarpment, running right through the center of the town of San Marcos, is what gives Hays County its hills and the canyons, caves, and spring-fed streams are what make Hays County, on the eastern edge of the Hill Country, such an attraction. The Balcones also created the freshwater springs that millions of years ago produced the San Marcos River — springs that are the source of more than 150 million gallons daily of some of the purest water in Texas. This crystalline water flows through 175 miles of the honeycomb lime-stone of the Edwards Aquifer before filling Spring Lake at Aquarena Springs.

The Spanish missions of San Francisco Xavier de los Dolores, San Ildefonso, and Nuestra Señora de la Candelaria remained here only for two years, between 1755 and 1757, before Apache and Comanche raids discouraged them. At the turn of the century several Spanish families arrived from Mexico, establishing a settlement they called San Marcos de Neve. But the Indian raids discouraged them, too, and by 1812 they had returned to Mexico.

Along came Texas Ranger John Coffee (Captain Jack) Hays, one of Stephen F. Austin's rangers. Part of Hays's job was to protect the pioneers who had begun to trickle into the county and into Comanche territory around the end of the decade. However, in the time it took a ranger to reload his single-shot sidearm, a Comanche warrior could charge and shoot half a dozen arrows, which certainly put the rangers at a disadvantage.

Samuel Colt had just invented his new five-shot repeater pistol. The Army scoffed at it, but Hays was clever enough to recognize the gun's potential when pitted against Comanche raiders. The weapon was put to the test in 1840, when a party of seventy Comanches surprised Hays and fourteen other rangers along the Pedernales River. In the past, in order to hold the Indians at bay with their rifles, the rangers had run for cover. Now Hays led his men in a charge, their Colt pistols blazing. Expecting that the rangers' guns would be empty after one round, the Comanches were baffled by these inexhaustible guns and were driven off. After this display, the Comanches soon gave up on this part of Texas.

In 1843 the county was created and named for Hays, for being instrumental in making the land safe for settlers. By the time Texas became a state in 1848, settlers had already established the river crossing. Soon the little town of San Marcos became a regular stopping point on the Old San Antonio Road (also known as the Camino Real) on the 3-day stagecoach trip between Austin and San Antonio.

San Marcos

San Marcos, the county seat, is the home of Southwest Texas State University, opened in 1903 as a teacher's college (and the alma mater of President Lyndon B. Johnson). Now a liberal arts university, it contributes much to the town's cultural and entertainment activities. There's more nightlife here than in other Hill Country towns, thanks to the university — it centers mostly around the town square, with music, billiards, and beer for the college crowd.

With support from the Texas Department of Agriculture, San Marcos has developed a program that established the town as a marketplace for Texas-grown, Texas-produced, and Texas-designed goods. Look for the "Texas Natural" logo in the window of shops and restaurants.

For more information, contact the **San Marcos Convention and Visitors Bureau** (512-393-5900, 888-200-5620; www.sanmarcostexas.com; 202 North C. M. Allen Pkwy, PO Box 2310, San Marcos, TX 78667).

Wimberley

Little Wimberley, on the Blanco River and Cypress Creek, is primarily a summer resort and retirement area. It was settled in 1848 by a miller named William Calvin Winters. He built a mill on the Blanco River that was bought by Pleasant Wimberley in 1872. The town took his name when a post office was established in 1880.

Picturesque Wimberley bustles busily on the Lions' Market Days (first Saturday of the month, April to September), and it's the place to shop for antiques, collectibles, and crafts. The town is quaint, pretty, friendly, and crowded only on market days!

For more information, contact the **Wimberley Chamber of Commerce and Visitor Center** (512-847-2201; www.wimberley.org; PO Box 12, Wimberley, TX 78676).

HAYS COUNTY LODGING

San Marcos has a bed & breakfast, a resort, and a number of motels, as described below. Besides the places listed below, Wimberley has a large number of other overnight lodging places. Call the **Country Innkeepers Reservation Service** at 512-847-1119 or 800-230-0805.

San Marcos

AQUARENA SPRINGS INN
Host: Dave Stewart.

The inn opened in 1929 as the Spring Lake Hotel, which isn't surprising since the inn sits on clear Spring Lake, filled by the famous springs

Wimberley Chamber of Commerce.

Eleanor S. Morris

512-245-7500, 800-893-9466. www.upfss.swt.edu/aqua inn.htm.
951 Aquarena Springs Dr., San Marcos, TX 78666.
Mail: 601 University Dr., San Marcos, TX 78666.
Price: Moderate.
Credit Cards: AE, MC, V.
Handicap Access: Yes.
Special Features: Family fun park and restaurant on the grounds.

formed eons ago by the Balcones Fault. Now owned and operated by the university, the pretty white inn has the lake in the front yard — steps lead down to it —and twenty-four spacious rooms, most with balconies overlooking the lake. The popular Hill Country resort has an Olympic-size swimming pool and a 9-hole golf course. (See "Family Fun" below for more activities here.)

CRYSTAL RIVER INN
Hosts: Cathy and Mike Dillon.
512-396-3739, 888-396-3739.
www.crystalriverinn.com.
326 W. Hopkins, San Marcos, TX 78666.
Price: Moderate.
Credit Cards: AE, D, MC, V.
Handicap Access: No.

There are nine rooms, three suites, and one two-bedroom apartment in this 1883 Victorian bed & breakfast in the historic district. Guest rooms in the Greek Revival home are named for Hill Country rivers, and a full breakfast, including eggs Benedict and raspberry French toast, is served — even in your canopy bed if you wish.

MOTELS

Just about every major motel chain is represented on the Interstate as you enter town, including the **Comfort Inn** (512-396-5665, 800-228-5150; 1611 IH 35 N., San Marcos, TX 78666), **Days Inn** (800-DAYS INN; 1005 IH 35 N., San Marcos, TX 78666), **La Quinta Inn** (800-531-5900; 1619 IH 35 N., San Marcos,

TX 78666), **Motel 6** (512-396-8705; 1321 IH 35 N., San Marcos, TX 78666), **Rodeway Inn** (512-353-1303; 801 IH 35 N., San Marcos, TX 78666), and **Super 8** (512-396-0400; 1429 IH 35 N., San Marcos, TX 78666).

Wimberley

BLAIR HOUSE
Host: Jonnie Stansbury.
512-847-1111, 877-549-5450.
www.blairhouseinn.com.
100 Spoke Hill Rd.,
   Wimberley, TX 78676.
Price: Expensive.
Credit Cards: AE, D, MC, V.
Handicap Access: Yes.

This lovely eight-room inn is nestled on 85 acres of privacy. The guest rooms all have private baths, four with Jacuzzi tubs and all with CD players. The library is stocked with books, videos, CDs, and periodicals, the walls are virtually a gallery of art, and outdoors you can hike in the hills, then go shopping in Wimberley.

And you'll need that exercise, because Jonnie is an excellent chef. A full-scale gourmet breakfast here began with fresh red raspberries, blueberries, and bananas, accompanied by a refreshing frozen orange juice/cranberry slush. Poached eggs were served in a ramekin over broccoli and covered with hollandaise sauce. On the side were tomatoes stuffed with fresh herbed breadcrumbs, and homemade scones with butter and homemade raspberry jam.

Another breakfast to die for is soufflé of French toast with toasted pecans in blueberries and real maple syrup. And Jonnie is generous with recipes: "We feel that food is a gift and an art and, like love, it's no good unless you give it away." (Two-night minimum on weekends.) Each evening a dessert and complimentary tea or coffee are delivered to your room, and Saturday evenings feature five-course dinners.

INN ABOVE ONION
   CREEK
Hosts: Jean and Scott
   Taylor.
512-268-1617; 800-579-7686.
www.bbonline.com/tx/
   onioncreek.
4444 Hwy. 150 W., Kyle, TX
   78640.
Price: Expensive to Very
   Expensive (MAP).
Credit Cards: AE, MC, V.
Handicap Access: Yes.

This lovely rural inn with a total of nine rooms and suites serves guests both breakfast and dinner, and will also provide a lunch basket if requested. Amenities include swimming pool, 5 miles of trails on 500 acres in the Hill Country; and cooking, art, and musical weekends. All rooms have stone fireplaces and sitting areas, balconies with a view, and extra feather mattresses. Six of the rooms have whirlpool tubs.

Breakfast might begin with smoked salmon, continue with quiche and rosemary potatoes, include a fruit medley (bananas in a banana split dish and covered with a mélange of apples, grapes, and pears in a vanilla yogurt sauce) and end with cinnamon coffee cake. Then it's time for a relaxing rock on the porch overlooking a gorgeous view of the hills. Children over 12 are welcome.

The Inn Above Onion Creek, a B&B (and dinner) on 500 Hill Country acres.

Eleanor S. Morris

HAYS COUNTY RESTAURANTS AND FOOD PURVEYORS

In addition to the eateries of San Marcos and Wimberley, we've included the popular Salt Lick in Driftwood, out in the country northwest of Wimberley.

San Marcos

CAFE ON THE SQUARE & BREW PUB
512-353-9289.
126 N. LBJ Dr., San Marcos, TX 78666.
On the Square.
Price: Moderate.
Cuisine: American, Mexican, Game.
Serving: B, L, D; closes early sometimes on Sun. & Mon.
Credit Cards: AE, D, MC, V.
Handicap Access: No.

There's nothing "square" about this lively place, especially on weekends even early in the morn. The loud and lively clientele is all ages, although there are plenty of college students.

The restaurant is in the historic T. A. Talbot Building, built in 1897. On the National Register of Historic Places, the building is charmingly old and worn. Long and narrow, the place still has the original pressed-tin ceiling, wooden floors, and a skylight brightening up the café. Big old fans with huge glass petal globes hang low from the high ceiling. Wooden bar stools are lined up at the black-and-white tile-top bar. Well-scrubbed wooden drop-leaf tables mix with iron-legged ice-cream parlor seats. Art by well-known Southwest artist Amado Pena decorates the walls, along with framed old magazine and sheet music covers.

Eggs Benedict are served on Saturday and Sundays only, but the migas (eggs scrambled with tomatoes, onion, peppers, corn tortillas, and cheddar cheese, served with hashed browns and beans, a choice of pinto or black) are special all week. Also special are the wild game dishes: wild boar chops, fried quail, chicken-fried venison, buffalo burgers, and buffalo fajitas, all served with fries.

The classic Centerpoint Station, San Marcos, has food, drink, and antiques.

Eleanor S. Morris

CENTERPOINT STATION
512-392-1103.
www.cypac.com/mall1/
  centerpoint.
3946 IH-35 S, San Marcos,
  TX 78666.
Price: Inexpensive.
Cuisine: American.
Serving: L, D.
Credit Cards: AE, D, MC, V.
Handicap Access: A ramp
  alongside the rear.

Boasting "the best malts on IH-35," this restaurant offers a wild mix of soda fountain, burgers, and memorabilia all packed into a brand-new building weathered to look as old as the hills. The old-fashioned soda bar and grill doesn't have ice-cream sodas, but there are sundaes, malts, and floats from Texas's own Blue Bell ice cream. Also available are sandwiches, some Mexican food, and homemade fudge filled with Texas-grown pecans — hold out your hand for a free sample. (See "Shopping" for what-all else is crammed into this busy market.)

**GORDO'S BURGERS &
  STUFF**
512-392-1874.
120 E. San Antonio, San
  Marcos, TX 78666.
On the Square
Price: Inexpensive.
Cuisine: Burgers,
  Sandwiches, Steak.
Serving: L, D.
Credit Cards: AE, D, MC, V.
Handicap Access: Yes.

Another San Marcos boast, this time it's "the best burgers in San Marcos." One of these "best burgers" is the Ultimate Gordo Burger with two patties, extra cheese, bacon, chili, mushrooms, and jalapeños. "Does anyone actually eat a whole one?" we asked. The answer was a rousing affirmative.

Gordo's is a treat because it's in the town's old movie theater, with outside marquee and all. The lobby now has a large mirrored bar all along the right side, and the stage in back is all set for the live music Thursday through Saturday nights (see "Nightlife").

Wimberley

CYPRESS CREEK CAFÉ & CLUB
512-847-2515.
PO Box 76, Wimberley, TX 78776.
On the Square.
Price: Inexpensive.
Cuisine: Southwest, Mexican, Vegetarian.
Serving: B, L, D.
Credit Cards: AE, D, MC, V.
Handicap Access: Yes.

Friendly family atmosphere reigns here in this old stone building on the square. Vegetarian dishes like tofu sandwiches, veggie burgers, and vegetable plates vie with old favorites like fried catfish or country-fried steak "just like Mom used to make it." A Cypress Creek Café tradition is the black bean taco: a huge Texas-size flour tortilla filled with beans, sour cream, chunky salsa, and jack cheese garnished with diced tomatoes, onion, and lettuce. We split it in half, it was so big. Pies are from the Wimberley Pie Company down the road, and the choices are legion — such as Dutch cherry pie, brownie pie, coconut, and Kentucky Derby pie, and cheesecake as well. Newest thing on the menu is ostrich (a red-meat ostrich burger has 40 percent less fat than beef, according to Texas A&M University).

There's a bed & breakfast upstairs and a dance hall in the rear (see "Nightlife").

Driftwood

The split-rail fence on the grounds of Driftwood's Salt Lick barbeque restaurant.

Eleanor S. Morris

THE SALT LICK
512-858-4959.
www.saltlickbbq.com.
FM 1826, Driftwood, TX.
Price: Inexpensive.
Cuisine: Barbecue.
Serving: L, D daily 11am–10pm.
Credit Cards: None; cash only.

If you want to be one among a crowd of Texans, visit the Salt Lick on a weekend, where (off-duty) Hays County sheriff's deputies are needed to keep the parking lot in order. This rustic place under the cedar and mesquite is out in the country northwest of Wimberley. The windows of the sprawling cedar and limestone building look out onto hummingbird feeders hanging just outside on the oak trees and, if you have to wait for a table, you'll be entertained by a guitar player.

Take a look at the giant circular open stone barbecue pit as you enter and the clumps of hanging sausages. A typical Saturday night crowd puts away 1,800 pounds of brisket, 800 rings of sausage, 500 racks of pork ribs, and 560 chickens, all smoked over oak, mesquite, and pecan for at least 24 hours — and only the owners know the recipe for the sauce.

You'll dine on bare wooden picnic tables and benches indoors — but you will eat on a plate. Barbecued beef, ribs, and sausage come with beans and coleslaw, and the barbecue sandwiches are delicious, too. Don't be fooled by the menu: Chicken "in season" is something you can order any time.

Absolutely do not miss the daily fresh peach and blackberry cobblers. There's also homemade pecan pie. Notice, too, the sign declaring WE RESERVE THE RIGHT TO SERVE ANYBODY, and you'll know you're deep in the heart of Texas. One note: BYOB; Hays County is dry.

HAYS COUNTY FOOD PURVEYORS

Wimberley

The General Store Coffee Shop (512-847-6128; PO Box 708, Wimberley, TX 78676; on the Square; Sun.–Thurs. 10am–6pm, Fri. & Sat. 10am–8pm) Coffee shop, candy store — delicious odors of both fancy blends and homemade candy assail you as you push open the door. Steve Klepfer's place is down a brick walkway, past a garden, and into a shop made from an old house that was on the site waiting to be pulled down. Now the rare long-leaf pine and square nails have been preserved — even the marble counters were rescued from an old bank building. Plus the fudge is delicious.

Wimberley Pie Company (512-847-9462; www.wimberleypie.com; RR 12, Wimberley, TX 78676 0.25 miles east of the Square, Wimberley, Mon.–Fri. 8am–5:30pm, Sat. 10am–5pm, Sun. noon–4pm.) Twenty-three varieties of pie, freshly baked, are for sale here, and once in a while the baker invents yet another one. Some unusual ones are sour cream peach, peanut butter, Toll House, and chocolate satin (with or without chocolate curls). If you're not a pie person, there's cheesecake — eight different kinds — cakes, muffins, and for your four-legged friends, doggie treats.

Dripping Springs

New Canaan Farms (800-727-JAMS; www.newcanaanfarms.com; PO Box 386, Dripping Springs, TX 78620; 7 miles west of Dripping Springs on Hwy 290) offers forty delicious, unique Hill Country jams, jellies, salsas, dips, and sauces like jalapeño shrimp sauce or garlic onion jelly. But there are traditional flavors as well: to name a few, East Texas blueberry jam, cherry preserve, old-fashioned peach butter.

HAYS COUNTY CULTURE

ARCHITECTURE AND HISTORIC SITES

*The Charles S. Cock Home,
built of hand-hewn native
rock in 1867. A home-cooked
lunch is served here on
Fridays by the Heritage
Association.*

Eleanor S. Morris

The **Heritage Association of San Marcos** (512-393-3735; www.sanmarcos-texas.com/tourism; PO Box 1806, San Marcos, TX 78667) has a *Tours of Old San Marcos* brochure. In the town park you'll find a marker on the site of **Camp Henry McCulloch,** located here during the Mexican-American War. Past the gazebo in the park, the path leads down to the 2-mile scenic **San Marcos River Walkway,** uniting three small parks along the river.

In the 100 block along **Courthouse Square** there are several brick and stone buildings built in the 1880s and 1890s when San Marcos was a busy cotton-raising center. The **Belvin Street Historic District** has several homes along a tranquil, shady street. The **Robert Hixon Belvin** home, **Crookwood,** and the **Herbert Yarbrough** home are open for tours.

Also of interest is the **Charles S. Cock** home, the only stone building of this style remaining in San Marcos. Don't miss the **Merriman Cabin,** built in 1848. Dr. Merriman, along with General Burleson, was responsible for laying out the town. One of the most interesting historic buildings, and possibly the largest log house remaining in Texas, is the **Claiborne Kyle Log House,** on the Old Austin Stagecoach Road. The nearby town of Kyle is named for a son, Fergus Kyle.

NIGHTLIFE

San Marcos is one of only a few exceptions to the dearth of a nightlife scene out in the Hill Country. After all, this *is* a college town, so of course there's life after dark. The following San Marcos venues all have a cover charge, except Nephew's on nights with DJ music.

Like many of the town eateries, **Gordo's** (see "Restaurants") is both a restaurant and a nightclub, catering to the college crowd. Set on the square in the town's old movie theater, the lobby is the spot for a large mirrored bar, and the stage in the back room is all set for the nightly entertainment of live alternative, country, heavy metal, and Tejano music Thursday through Saturday. Not to mention the huge projection TV for those important football games.

Wimberley

Cypress Creek Café & Club (512-847-2515; PO Box 76, Wimberley, TX 78676) comes alive every Friday and Saturday night with music by the likes of Rob Roy Parnell and his brother LeRoy. Everybody's happy, everybody's dancing, and some folks even come down from Austin for the fun. Phone the café for information.

SEASONAL EVENTS

San Marcos

FEBRUARY brings **Carnaval,** a Mexican-style Mardi Gras with music, food, and merriment the weekend before Ash Wednesday.

In APRIL it's bluebonnet time in Texas, and in San Marcos the state flower is celebrated the second weekend by the **Bluebonnet Kite Festival** for food, fun, games, and a serious kite-flying competition.

The focus in MAY is on **Texas Natural and Western Swing Weekend** (512-393-8930), featuring historic downtown San Marcos and merchandise made in Texas by Texans. The festival offers food, music, crafts, cowboy poets, and a mini-chili cook-off. But don't miss the annual **Tours of Distinction,** also held in May, tours of the old homes of San Marcos, sponsored by the Heritage Society.

JUNE is the month for the **Texas Water Safari,** where the world's toughest canoe race takes off from Spring Lake at the headwaters of the San Marcos River. Canoers and kayakers come from all over the nation to see who can race the 260 miles down to the Gulf Coast to the town of Seadrift.

In JULY there's an old-fashioned patriotic **Summerfest** held on the fourth in Sewell Park. Live music, food booths, children's activities, and, of course, fireworks.

The **Gathering of Memories** in AUGUST or SEPTEMBER brings the Confederate Air Force and thousands of followers to San Marcos with an air show, old World War II aircraft, a dinner dance, and an auction.

Republic of Texas Chilympiad, the men's chili cook-off in SEPTEMBER, features chili teams from all over the country, beauty pageants, arts and crafts, food booths, live music, dancing, and lots of fun for the whole family.

The **Sights and Sounds of Christmas** come early in DECEMBER, a community festival on the banks of the San Marcos River. Children's activities, community choirs, arts and crafts booth, and a food court all help to make the season merry.

Check with the San Marcos Convention and Visitors Bureau (512-396-2495, 888-200-5620; www.sanmarcostexas.com/tourism) for exact dates.

Wimberley

Market Day, the first Saturday of every month, from MAY to OCTOBER, draws shoppers to check out work created by local artists and craftsmen along with antiques and flea markets.

Check with the Chamber of Commerce (512-847-2201) for exact dates.

HAYS COUNTY RECREATION

CAMPING

United RV Park (512-353-5959, 800-344-9906; 1610 IH-35 N., San Marcos, TX 78666) Swimming pool, playground, and 100 sites shaded by large trees, each with full hookups 30/50 AMPS. Pets allowed.

FAMILY FUN

AQUARENA CENTER
512-245-75750, 800-999-9767. www.sanmarcostexas.com/tourism Click: Attractions.
One Aquarena Springs Dr., San Marcos, TX 78666.
Open: daily 9:30am–6pm Mar.–May; 9:30am–8pm summer; 9:30am–5pm Sept.–Mar.
Admission: Free; glass-bottom-boat rides $6 adults, $5 seniors, $4 children.

This natural amusement park —now under the auspices of Southwest Texas State University — is built on freshwater springs that created the San Marcos River millions of years ago in the Balcones Fault, a fracture in the earth's crust. The water flows through 175 miles of the honeycomb limestone of the Edwards Aquifer before filling Spring Lake.

Glass-bottom boat rides on Spring Lake view an underwater archaeological site on the bottom and the remains of Clovis Man, who lived on the San Marcos River more than 12,000 years ago. The lake is also the home of more than a hundred varieties of aquatic life, some of them endangered species found nowhere else on earth.

When the university purchased Aquarena Springs in 1994, the focus of the old 90-acre Aquarena Center theme park was changed from entertainment to natural tourism and preservation. Aside from the glass-bottom boat rides, a variety of tours are offered as are educational displays.

WONDER WORLD
512-392-3760.
www.sanmarcostexas.com
/tourism Click: Wonder
World.
Wonder World Dr., San
Marcos, TX 78666.
Off IH-35 at Exit 80.
Open: June–Aug, daily
8am–8pm; Sept.–Oct.,
9am–6pm; Nov.–Feb.,
Mon.–Fri. 9am–5pm, Sat.
& Sun. 9am–6pm;
Mar.–May, Mon.–Fri.
9am–6pm, Sat. & Sun.
9am–7pm.
Admission: Adults $14.95,
children 4–11 $10.95,
under 4 free.

When a huge earthquake rocked this area 30 million years ago, it created an enormous cave underground along the 1,800-mile-long Balcones Fault. You can observe the fault line 160 feet below the earth's surface or above it from the Tejas Observation Tower. Adding to the fun are a wildlife petting zoo, a miniature train ride, and a mysterious Gravity House, where you'll be challenged to keep your balance.

GOLF

SWT Golf Course (512-245-7593; Aquarena Springs Dr., San Marcos, TX 78666) has a 9-hole par 35 course; **Quail Valley Country Club** (512-353-1644; 2701 Airport Hwy. 21, San Marcos, TX 78666) has an 18-hole course. Both are open to the public.

WATER SPORTS

CANOEING: Rapids, twisting channels, and constant flow levels make San Marcos one of Texas's premier canoeing streams. (The **Texas Water Safari,**

Tubing down Cypress Creek in Wimberley.

> **The Devil's Backbone" Scenic Drive**
>
> Take FM 32 just south of Wimberley to the ridge called "The Devil's Backbone" for a trip through classic Hill Country landscape and a glimpse of white-tailed deer on this winding, razor-backed ridge along the 24 miles west to Blanco (Blanco County).

billed as "the toughest boat race in the world," is on the second weekend in June; beginning from City Park it runs nonstop the 267 miles south to Seadrift on the Texas coast.) Canoes are for rent from **TG Canoe Livery** (512-353-3946; 2000 Hwy. 80 #160, San Marcos, TX 78666) and **Spencer Canoes** (512-357-6113; 9515 FM1979, Martindale, TX 78655).

TUBING: About 23.5 miles of the San Marcos River are suitable for tubing, beginning at City Park and ending at the County Road 199 crossing west of Stairtown on Hwy. 80. **Lions Club Tube Rental** (512-396-LION; PO Box 994, San Marcos, TX 78667) rents tubes in City Park for a fun float down the San Marcos River. Tube down the river and then ride the Breakfast Lions River Taxi back to the tube rental building. There you'll find soft drinks, snow cones, and snacks along with San Marcos River souvenirs. Free parking, lockers available.

HAYS COUNTY SHOPPING

San Marcos has a nice assortment of shops around the square and the streets leading off from it. Little Wimberley is a hotbed of shops, most clustered around the small wedge-shaped square.

ANTIQUES AND GIFTS

San Marcos

Centerpoint Station (512-392-1103; www.cypac.com/mall1/centerpoint; 3946 IH-35, San Marcos, TX 787666, at Exit 200) Decorated with old store fixtures and antique advertising signs, Centerpoint Station calls itself "a general mercantile, offering you and your family a nostalgic experience." From the front porch to the old house tacked on at the rear, you'll find all sorts of stuff, old and new — country and Western antiques, hand-dipped candles, old dishpans and baskets, handmade birdhouses, Texas gourmet foods, thousands of old tin signs, even a lamp with a base made of welded horse-shoes. (See also "Restaurants.")

Heartworks Co.–Paper Bear (512-396-2283; 214 N. LBJ Dr., San Marcos, TX 78666, on the Square) A Texas-size 8,000-square-foot former Western Auto store crammed with gifts, toys, candy, games, beads, fake jewels — a wonderful place just to browse and marvel.

Two P's in a Pod (512-392-8967, 306 N. Edward Gary, San Marcos, TX 78666) The two P's in the name of this boutique/gift shop are the owners, Pam and Phyllis. Features the work of Texas artists, including jewelry, tole-painted furniture, and designer clothes, plus antiques and other "heartwarming necessities."

Wimberley

Betsy's Hanger (512-847-3405; 13801 RR 12, Suite 101, Wimberley, TX 78676, half a block south of the Square) "Naturally comfortable" clothing with both a Southwestern and an ethnic flair. Jewelry and other accessories, too.

Woodshed Treasures (512-847-9466; 100 Oak Dr., Wimberley, TX 78676, on the Square) Antiques, crafts, unique jewelry, collectibles. Visit with local craftsmen on site.

ART AND CRAFTS

Wimberley

The Old Mill Store (512-847-3068; PO Box 708, Wimberley, TX 78676, on the Square) Rugs, furniture, wall hangings, hammocks, antiques, jewelry by local artists, and gourmet foods.

Rancho Deluxe (512-847-9570; 14010 RR 12, Wimberley, TX 78676, on the Square) Rustic and eclectic home furnishings. Limestone from deep in the heart of Texas is carved by Hill Country artists into bookends, lamps, candleholders, vases. Also custom furniture and cedar beds, wrought iron lamps and tables. A best-seller is a children's swing made from a small saddle.

Sable V (512-847-8975; PO Box 1772, Wimberley, TX 78676, on the Square) The gallery features special shows throughout the year of original works by artists in ceramics, glass, sculpture, paintings, and jewelry.

Wimberley Glass Works (512-847-9348; www.wimberley.org/index Click on "name"; PO Box 1724, Wimberley, TX 78676, 1.6 miles south of the Square off RR 12; open daily 10am–5pm) Entertaining glass-blowing demonstrations as well as glassware for sale.

SHOPPING MALLS AND OUTLETS

Prime Outlets–San Marcos (512-396-2000, 800-628-9465; www.sanmarcos-texas.com/tourism Click: Your Shopping Outlet; 3939 IH-35 S., San Marcos, TX 78666; Mon.–Sat. 10am–9pm, Sun. 11am–6pm) More than 115 of the top names in merchandising are gathered here in this open-air hacienda-style mall, with ten eateries in the food court, and a children's playground.

Tanger Outlet Center (512-392-7446, 800-408-8424; www.sanmarcostexas.com/tourism/default Click: Your Shopping Outlet; I-35, Exit 200, San Marcos, TX 78666; Mon.–Sat. 9am–9pm, Sun. 11am–6pm) A smaller outlet mall across

Center Point Road from the above mall, with a good but smaller selection of brand-name outlets.

KIMBLE COUNTY

This was Apache land when the Spanish came through here in the 1700s, and they didn't even try to stay. By the time Anglo settlers appeared in the 1850s, some 150 years later, the Apaches had been run off by Comanches, who swooped down from the Great Plains on their fast horses. The legislature went ahead anyway and created Kimble County from Bexar County in 1858, naming it for George C. Kimble (also spelled "Kimbell" and "Kimbel"), who led the "Immortal 32" from Gonzales to the Alamo, coming to the aid of the beleaguered Texans and dying with them on March 6, 1836. Hostilities between the Comanches and the settlers went on for about twenty more years; the last Indian incidents were reported in 1876.

By then outlaws, not Indians, were the settlers' problem. Horse thieves, cattle rustlers, and gunmen needed to be brought to justice, but they threatened to prevent any court meetings in the county. The presiding judge asked the Texas Rangers for help, and three companies of rangers scoured the canyons of the Llano River. When the judge arrived at the oak grove where court was held, he found forty outlaws chained to the trees. He handed out the necessary sentences, thereby considerably reducing the power of the outlaws in the new county.

Kimble County is a leading producer of wool and mohair: Angora goats were brought to Texas in 1849, and since the 1920s Texas has produced the most mohair in the country. Plus there are more flowing streams here than in any other Texas county.

Junction

In the far northwest corner of the Hill Country, Junction (pop. 2,800), the county seat, was originally in the settlement of Kimbleville. It was moved to the junction of the North and South Llano Rivers, which is how it got the name of Junction. The first courthouse was built in 1878, and when it burned, all the county's early records burned with it. The present courthouse was built in 1929.

Although the town admits to being "quite a ways" from most of the Hill Country, Junction calls itself "The Jewel of the Hill Country." (But it also likes to be known as "The Front Porch to the West.") Junction is the place for hunting, fishing, camping, and canoeing on the clear flowing waters of the Llano River. And though all of Texas is friendly, you'll find Junction extra friendly!

KIMBLE COUNTY LODGING

Junction has three bed & breakfasts at this writing, **Broughton Bed & Breakfast** (915-446-2112), **Shady Rest at the Junction** (915-446-4067) and **South Llano River Bed and Breakfast,** which is described below. There is a relatively large selection of motels for such a small town. Two are described below; contact the **Chamber of Commerce of Kimble County** (915-446-3190; www.junctiontexas.net; 402 Main St., Junction, TX 76849) for additional information and a complete list.

DAYS INN
915-446-3730,
   800-325-2525.
I-10 exit 457, 111 Martinez,
   Junction, TX 76849.
Price: Inexpensive.
Credit Cards: AE, CB, D,
   DC, MC, V.
Handicap Access: Two
   rooms.

The motel has fifty comfortable rooms and sits on a rise overlooking the Llano River. Amenities include a pool, hot tub/spa, videos, VCR rental, and a continental breakfast served from 6am–10:30am. It's very popular during the deer and dove hunting season Nov.–Dec.

SLUMBER INN
915-446-4588.
2341 N. Main, Junction, TX
   76849.
On IH-10.
Price: Inexpensive.
Credit Cards: AE, D, MC, V.
Handicap Access: Yes.

This motel has thirty-one nice clean rooms with pastel colors and light modern furniture. Amenities include swimming pool, cable TV, and a family restaurant (see "Restaurants") nearby. The Honeymoon Suite has a king-size bed, refrigerator, microwave, wet bar, and a Jacuzzi.

SOUTH LLANO BED & BREAKFAST
Hosts: Dee and Richard
   Bowen.
915-446-3609.
Hwy. 377 S., Junction, TX
   76849.
Price: Moderate.
Credit Cards: No.
Handicap Access: No.

This rustic bed & breakfast has two cabins overlooking the South Llano River. You can really set up housekeeping in the large cabin: The bedroom has both king-size and single beds, the living room has a queen-size sleeper sofa and two extra sofas, plus there's baby equipment, a fully equipped kitchen, washer and dryer, two bathrooms, telephone, satellite TV with VCR, central heating and air-conditioning, and two wood-burning fireplaces.

The adjacent cabin has a large sleeping area with queen bed, and a single bed on the enclosed porch. Also bath and efficiency kitchen with microwave. Breakfast is coffee, juice and rolls.

KIMBLE COUNTY RESTAURANTS AND FOOD PURVEYORS

Two happy porch sitters at the Come N Git It restaurant, Junction.

Eleanor S. Morris

COME N GIT IT
915-446-4357.
2341 N. Main St., Junction, TX 76849.
Price: Inexpensive.
Cuisine: American, Hill Country.
Serving: B, L, D.
Credit Cards: AE, D, DC, MC, V.
Handicap Access: Yes.

This big wide barn of a room, with high ceilings and wood paneling, soothes and relaxes with soft background music. Tables are spread out in the center of the room, and bushel-basket lampshades shade the blue booths lining the walls that are decorated with beer signs and shining copper pans. Simply delicious here are the chicken quesadillas, one to a serving but huge. A large tortilla, toasted and stuffed with sautéed chicken, green pepper and onion strips, and creamy Monterey Jack cheese, with shredded lettuce and tomato, sour cream, and guacamole, makes a delicious taste treat. The salad bar is fresh, too; especially tasty are the corn bread salad and the corn and black bean salad. You enter the restaurant by way of a convenience store, which seems to be a Junction custom.

ISAACK'S RESTAURANT
915-446-2629.
1606 Main St., Junction, TX 76849.
Price: Inexpensive.
Cuisine: Home-style, Café, Steak.
Serving: B, L, D.

Everything is homemade in this busy restaurant, which sports a classic counter with stools as well as tables and booths, and the daily lunch special might be all-you-can-eat catfish with potato salad, beans, and coleslaw. The huge and tender 12-inch chicken-fried steak is a specialty, as are the mozzarella cheese sticks, fried and served with a red

Credit Cards: AE, DC, MC, V.
Handicap Access: Yes.

horseradish or a white ranch dressing. Homemade vegetable soup and sirloin steak are on the menu daily. "We stick with one soup; we're good at it," says the friendly waitperson. "And we'll substitute anything for anything."

LA FAMILIA RESTAURANT
915-446-2688.
1927 Main St., Junction, TX 76849.
Price: Inexpensive.
Cuisine: Mexican.
Serving: L, D.
Credit Cards: AE, D, DC, MC, V.
Handicap Access: No.

A rtemisa Lozano knows authentic Mexican food — she and her clan in this family restaurant all hail from Chihuahua in northern Mexico. The menu offers steak tampequena, carne asada, and steak à la Mexican, along with such usual Mexican fare as chimichangas. The warm welcoming decor of red walls and wood and the friendly ambiance make this a pleasant dining place.

LUM'S
915-446-3541.
2031 Main St., Junction, TX 76849.
Price: Inexpensive.
Cuisine: Barbecue.
Serving: L, D to 12 midnight.
Credit Cards: MC, V.
Handicap Access: Yes, except for rest rooms.

O ur customers come for our ribs; we're known on the Interstate," Ruth Sepeda says, busy with customers in the family convenience store/self-serve restaurant. Sure enough, a traveling couple — sitting comfortably in the dining room, pleasant with stone walls, a fireplace, and picnic tables said — "We plan our trips from Lubbock to Uvalde so we can stop here." The aroma is mouthwatering the moment you step in the door, and folks were lined up for their platefuls of barbecue ribs, brisket, sausage, and deli food, all where it can be seen and chosen from behind glass counters. There's outdoor patio dining, too.

KIMBLE COUNTY FOOD PURVEYORS

Irma's Donut Shop (915-446-2749, 1907 1/2 Main St., Junction, TX 76489; Tues.–Sat. 4am–2pm) If ever there was a misnomer, this is it. Irma's is a bakery, coffee shop, lunch room, meeting place, and only incidentally a "donut" shop. Oh, she bakes doughnuts: glazed, jellied, twists, chocolate, cheese pockets — even doughnut holes. And they are good. "When I make them, I praise the Lord. I say, 'Lord, let the doughnuts be good' — and they are." Irma and Leroy Loeffler begin before dawn, cheerfully, she with the breakfast pizza and the breakfast tacos, Leroy rolling the tortillas. Customers in the know come from all over — Dallas, Houston, Austin — for the pecan caramel rolls, the apple-raisin strudel, the hamburgers in gigantic light and fluffy homemade buns covering a half a pound of ground chuck. "They're pretty big; sometimes [two] people each eat half," Irma confesses. The small shop is bright with red-checked tablecloths and green ivy.

KIMBLE COUNTY CULTURE

HISTORIC BUILDINGS AND MUSEUMS

The Kimble County Historical Museum, in Junction, has displays of Hill Country pioneer life.

Eleanor S. Morris

Still in use, the stone **Kimble County Jail** (N. 5th St. and Pecan) in Junction was built in 1892. The **old Pepper home,** the first two-story house in Kimble County and the childhood home of the wife of Gov. Coke Stevenson (1941), is about 5 miles south of Junction on U.S. 377. The limestone building was built in 1877.

The **Kimble County Library** (915-446-2342, 208 N. 10th) contains the **O. C. Fisher Museum,** a duplicate of the Washington office of this longtime congressman from the district. Librarian Jerry Fairchild is very helpful.

The **Kimble County Historical Museum** (915-446-4219, 4th and College Sts.) displays pioneer artifacts, documents, clothing, tools, and other relics of early settlers. There is some World War II paraphernalia, too. Longtime resident Frederica Wyatt knows all about it and is happy to share. Open Mon.–Fri. 9:30am–noon, 2–5pm. Weekends by appointment.

SEASONAL EVENTS

Check with the Junction Chamber of Commerce (915-446-3190) for exact dates. Popular in Junction starting in April is the flea market on the courthouse lawn on fifth Saturdays (the months vary from year to year).

APRIL in Junction brings the annual **Easter Pageant,** the Saturday before Easter. In JULY is the **Ole Time Celebration in the Park** on the Fourth of July, with fireworks.

AUGUST offers the **Summer Classic Rodeo & Parade, Goat Sale, and Dance.**

In SEPTEMBER, the annual **Kimble County Kow Kick** (arts and crafts) takes place on Labor Day.

KIMBLE COUNTY RECREATION

CAMPING

Fox Hollow Cabins (915-446-3055; 8315 Box 236, Junction, TX 76849, on the South Llano River) Two cabins with kitchen, dishes, linens are completely furnished.

KOA Kampgrounds (915-446-3138, 800-562-7506; www.gocampingamerica.com /junctionkoa; 2145 N. Main St., Junction, TX 76849; on the North Llano River) Four one-bedroom cabins, forty-eight RV sites (thirty-nine with full hookups), picnic tables, and barbecue pits located on a quarter-mile of river frontage. Hot showers and rest rooms in the main building along with game room, laundry room, convenience store, swimming pool, playground.

CANOE RENTALS

KOA Kampgrounds (915-446-3138, 800-562-7506; N. 2145 Main St., Junction, TX 76849) Rentals for canoeing on the North Llano River.

Sonny's Canoes (915-446-2112; 214 Patricia Dr., Junction, TX 76849; near the South Llano River at Flat Rock Crossing).

South Llano River Canoes (915-446-2220; HC 15, Box 214F, Junction, TX 76849; 6 miles south of Junction off Hwy. 377 on the river) Day trips and weekly rates; drop off and pick up.

GOLF

Junction Golf Association (915-446-2968; FM 2169, Junction, TX 76849) A 9-hole, 2,800-yard course, a challenging one for the size. The irrigated course nestles in the shadows of Lovers Leap and winds along the bottomlands of Cedar Creek and the South Llano River. No reservations needed for individuals.

PARKS

The best places for swimming and other water sports are at Kimble County parks, along with many other activities.

Schreiner Park (915-446-3880; on the South Llano River) Boat ramp, swimming, picnic tables and barbecue grills, and a small covered pavilion.

South Llano River State Park (915-446-3994; www.tpwd.state.tx.us/park/ slano/slano.htm; 5 miles south of Junction off U.S. 377 on Park Rd. 73) The 2,657-acre park lies along the winding South Llano River and is considered one of the best canoeing and tubing rivers in Texas. The wooded park is the home to white-tailed deer, armadillo, fox squirrels, javelina (wild boar), wood ducks, and turkey. (River frontage and bottomlands are closed from

October to April to protect the winter roosting areas of the Rio Grande turkey.) Facilities include campsites with water and electricity, 4 miles of hiking trails, wildlife observation, and picnicking.

Walter Buck Wildlife Management Area (915-446-2986; www.tpwd.state.tx.us/wma/wmarea/walterbuck.htm; PO Box 392, Junction, TX 76849) On the south fork of the Llano River, adjoining the South Llano River State Park, this park has 2,155 acres with several hiking and mountain bike trails. No camping is permitted.

KIMBLE COUNTY SHOPPING

There aren't many shopping spots that would interest the tourist in Junction. **Generations III** (915-446-2663; 911 Main St., Junction, TX 76849) is the only clothing store in town, with attractive and stylish women's clothes and jewelry. The **City Pharmacy** (915-446-2511; 602 Main St., Junction, TX 76849) also carries small gift items, as does **Junction Home Center** (915-446-3394; 310 Main St., Junction, TX 76849).

LLANO COUNTY

The word *llano* is Spanish for plains, and it's hard to understand why such a name was chosen for this spectacularly scenic part of the Hill Country when the county was created from the Bexar District of Gillespie County in 1856.

Originally Llano County was part of the tract purchased by a group of German noblemen, who made a treaty with the Comanche and opened up the Fisher-Miller land for settlement. A hill called Packsaddle Mountain was the scene of a famous 1873 battle between the settlers and the Apaches. A war party of about twenty Apaches had been harassing the settlers, stealing horses, cows, and even clothing. Eight settlers trailed the Indians to their camp on top of the hill and attacked them. Taken by surprise, three Indians were killed, and the others ran away. A granite marker was placed to mark the spot in 1938. There's also a state marker about 14 miles southeast of Llano on Highway 71. Actually, the real Texas Packsaddle Mountain is in Big Bend in West Texas, but this Hill Country hill has been called a mountain ever since the battle.

Today ranching is the main business of the county, with deer hunting in season a good second. The area, part of the Llano Uplift, has also attracted gold and silver prospectors from the Spanish to today's rock hounds. Amethyst, dolomite, garnet, quartz, and tourmaline also abound. The most unusual mineral here, however, is llanite, a rare type of brown granite embedded with

A high-flying deer on Courthouse Square, Llano, symbolizes this "Deer Capital of Texas."

Eleanor S. Morris

crystals of pink and blue feldspar found nowhere else in the world. Rock hounds can enjoy hunting for this and other minerals (see "Rock Hunting" below), but please note that landowners no longer permit rock hunting on their land, due to the threat of lawsuits. Possibly the best place to find llanite is the bar in the Badu House's lounge — one long slab of it.

Llano County has several towns, of which the largest is Llano (pop. 2,990) on the clear waters of spring-fed Llano River. Kingsland, next largest in the county (pop. 2,646) was founded in 1855 as Kingsville and was a popular spot for fishing even before the rivers were dammed to make lakes. Last but not least, Buchanan Dam (pop. 1,109) (pronounced buck-cannon) is the name not only of the dam but also that of this small resort and retirement community, which grew at the construction site of the dam.

For more information, contact the **Llano Chamber of Commerce**, 915-247-5354; www.llanochamber.org; 700 Bessemer Ave., Llano, TX 78643; or see a wonderfully comprehensive Web site: www.llanotexas.com.

Llano

The town was settled around 1855 and became the county seat a year later. By 1860 it was well established, with stores, saloons, and a hotel. When iron was discovered back in the late 1800s, this small town became a boomtown: Llano hoped to become "the Pittsburgh of the West." But there was none of the coal needed to turn the iron into steel, so the boom went bust, and it was back to the granite business as usual. Today the streets named Bessemer and Pittsburgh remain as reminders of Llano's ambitious dream.

A fire destroyed much of the city north of the Llano River where most of the action took place. All that was left was the sturdy First National Bank, now the Badu House Inn, and Bruhl's drugstore, now restored to house the Llano County Museum. Today most of Llano lies south of the river.

Kingsland

Nothing much happened to Kingsland until the railroad — and a general store — came in 1892. Then the railroad began to bring fishermen and vacationers from Austin to the town. In 1951 the construction of the Granite Shoals Dam (now Wirtz Dam) at the junction of the Colorado and Llano Rivers created Inks Lake and Granite Shoals Lake. (The latter was later renamed in honor of Lyndon B. Johnson.) Today Kingsland is both a resort and retirement haven. FM 1431 through Kingsland is lined with cafés, convenience stores, and outlets for fishing and boating supplies.

LLANO COUNTY LODGING

Llano

Three motels are available, a **Best Western** (915-247-4101, 800-346-1578; 901 W. Young, Llano, TX 78643), a **Travelodge** (915-247-4111, 800-578-7878; 700 W. Young, Llano, TX 78643), and the **Hill Country Suites** (915-247-1090, 888-707-4455; www.hillcountrysuites.com; 609 Bessemer Ave., Llano, TX 78643). There are also three hotel/bed and breakfasts:

BADU HOUSE
Host: Sharon Taylor.
915-247-1207.
www.inetport.com/~lakes
/badu.
601 Bessemer Ave., Llano,
TX 78643.
Price: Moderate, EP.
Credit Cards: AE, MC, V.
Handicap Access: No.

Here's a chance to sleep in marble halls that once held a lot of money — the Badu House began life as a bank. Now it's an inn, with a restaurant and lounge. Be sure to check out the latter — called the Llano Badu Club — where the bar is topped with a huge slab of Texas's famous llanite, found nowhere else in the world.

The six guest rooms are not large, but they are filled with antiques, and each has a private bath with Victorian brass fixtures, including pull-chain commodes, pedestal sinks, and claw-foot tubs. There's also a two-bedroom suite with views of Packsaddle Mountain and Sandstone Mountain to the east.

DABBS RAILROAD HOTEL
Host: Gary Smith.

This old hotel has become something of a cult place for the young and adventurous. The

915-247-7905.
www.io.com/~dkb/dabs/
  dabbs.htm.
112 E. Burnet St., Llano, TX
  78643.
Price: Inexpensive, EP.
Credit Cards: None.
Handicap Access: Yes.

hotel has been recreated following the original floor plan, service, and menus as they were in 1907, when the hotel served as overnight lodgings for the men who worked on the railroad. Like those railroad men of long ago, guests can lounge on the front porch in rockers or sit on the throw-covered wooden benches in the small lobby. Don't look for luxury — the railroaders didn't have it back then, and you won't have it now. As stark and sparsely furnished as it was for the railroad men, the bare bones of the place are compensated by the warmth and enthusiasm of the host. Nine rooms contain simple white iron double beds, and guests share two baths, one up and one down. All-you-can-eat breakfasts and Saturday-night dinner are cooked by Gary and are served family style, paper plates and all, on a long picnic table in the kitchen. Campers are permitted to pitch their tents below the rolling lawns down to the river. Guests play games and stroll along the Llano River behind the hotel, in general enjoying the kids-away-at-summer-camp atmosphere of this unusual getaway. (For more information see "Culture" below.)

FORD STREET INN
Hosts: Kris and Bruce
  Rohnstock.
915-247-1127.
1119 Ford St., Llano, TX
  78643.
Price: Moderate.
Credit Cards: None.
Handicap Access: No.

Just three blocks from the downtown square, the inn has two comfortable guest rooms, each with private bath. Built in 1919, the seven-room house was considered one of the finer ones in Llano and is now the setting for the Rohnstocks' European antiques and Oriental rugs. Picnic lunches and candlelight dinners are offered, plus a full breakfast of Scotch eggs baked with cream and yellow cheese and fresh chives, served with bacon, sausage and ham, home-fried potatoes, fruit salad, and muffins. The smokehouse where the first owners kept their winter supply of meat is still in the nice large backyard. The saloon sports a bar from Argentina, made of native quebracho wood, and there is a dartboard and entertainment.

Kingsland

THE ANTLERS HOTEL
915-388-4411, 800-383-0007.
www.theantlers.com.
Hosts: Lori and Anthony
  Mayfield.
1001 King, Kingsland, TX
  78639.
Off Hwy 1431 at the
  railroad crossing.
Price: Expensive.

Accommodations include the historic adults-only Antlers Hotel, one- or two-bedroom cabins and cottages with kitchens in the woods and around the orchard, and the Caboose: imagine spending the night in a real train caboose! Each caboose offers a living and dining area, bath with shower, queen-size bed, and two child-size bunks, efficiency kitchen, and TV/VCR. Enjoy

Credit Cards: All.
Handicap Access: Yes.

morning coffee or watch the sunset up in the cupola.

The Antlers no longer serves breakfast: They have opened the Kingsland Old Town Grill on the property, across the road from the hotel (see "Restaurants").

LLANO COUNTY RESTAURANTS AND FOOD PURVEYORS

Unless you plan to head out to Buchanan Lake, where there are some informal (and not highly recommended) eateries on the shore, expect to dine in town, either in Llano or Kingsland. Llano is known for the exceptional flavor of the local barbecue, and included below are two examples of this Texas specialty, along with the innovative Badu House. Kingsland now has the Kingsland Old Town Grill.

Llano

BADU HOUSE
  RESTAURANT
915-247-4304.
601 Bessemer Ave., Llano,
  TX 78643.
Price: Moderate to
  Expensive.
Cuisine: Continental,
  American, Game.
Serving: L, D.
Credit Cards: AE, MC, V.
Handicap Access: No.

The menu here is innovative and sophisticated for such a small town. To begin with, the surroundings are in marble halls that once were a bank (see "Lodging"). Try the quail, or the New Zealand rack of lamb, marinated in lemon garlic and served with a pesto sauce. The filet of beef is grilled with forest mushrooms, flamed in Scotch, and served with espagnole sauce. For dessert try either the wickedly chocolate Llano river bottom pie with a cream filling or the yellow jacket pie of coconut, lemon custard, and cream, topped with toasted coconut.

COOPER'S OLD TIME
  PIT BAR-B-CUE
915-247-5713.
www.coopersbbq.com.
604 W. Young St., Llano, TX
  78643.
Price: Inexpensive.
Cuisine: Barbecue.
Serving: L, D.
Open: Daily.
Credit Cards: AE, D, MC, V.
Handicap Access: Yes.

Everything is authentic country barbecue here, from the outdoor pits filled with mesquite, which smoke the brisket, ribs, chicken, pork, and goat, to the butcher paper on which your choice is served. Choose your own particular morsels directly from the aromatic pit. It's all priced by the pound, including your potato salad and pinto beans.

INMAN'S KITCHEN
915-247-5257.
809 W. Young St., Llano, TX
  78643.
Hwy. 29 W.
Price: Inexpensive.
Cuisine: Smoked Meats.
Serving: L, D.
Credit Cards: AE, MC, V.
Handicap Access: Yes.

Inman's is famous all over the state for its turkey sausage. Barbecued beef, ham, and turkey are also delicious, along with homemade breads and pies.

Kingsland

**KINGSLAND OLD
  TOWN GRILL**
915-388-2681.
1010 King St., Kingsland,
  TX 78639.
Price: Inexpensive to
  Moderate.
Cuisine: Texas Hill Country
  plus steaks.
Serving: L, D, closed Mon.
  and Tues.
Credit Cards: Yes.
Handicap Access: No.

Steaks are the specialty here, but there's plenty of everyday hamburgers, cheeseburgers, chicken fried steak, etc., with lunch specials Wednesday through Sunday, 11am to 2pm.

**SWEET THINGS DONUT
  AND BAKE SHOP**
915-388-3460.
RR 1431 N., Kingsland, TX
  78639.

Delicious baked treats here for breakfast, lunch, and snacking. Try the crunchy apple cobbler.

LLANO COUNTY FOOD PURVEYORS

Fall Creek Vineyards (512-476-4477; www.fcv.com; 1111 Guadalupe St., Austin, TX 78701; FM 2241 2.2 miles north of Tow on Lake Buchanan; tastings and tours Mon.–Fri. 11am–3pm, Sat. noon–5pm; Mar.–Nov. also Sun. noon–4pm) An interesting detour for wine buffs is a visit to Fall Creek Vineyards, north of Buchanan Dam. Texas is earning a fine reputation as a wine-producing state, and the winery, with European-style buildings on the lake shore, produces chardonnay, chenin blanc, sauvignon blanc, Riesling, and zinfandel. Complimentary tours and tastings, plus in August there's a Grapestomp Celebration, where the public is invited to "Kick off your shoes & stomp some grapes!!!" — along with river cruises and orchard hayrides.

The entrance to award-winning Fall Creek Vineyards in Tow.

Eleanor S. Morris

LLANO COUNTY CULTURE

ARCHITECTURE AND HISTORIC BUILDINGS

In *Llano*, the **Downtown National Historic District** includes many sites of historical interest, such as the **Corner Drug**, 1898, **Buttery's Storage**, 1880, and, more recently, the **Lan-Tex** movie theater. A walking-tour brochure of the district is available from the **Llano Chamber of Commerce** (700 Bessemer Ave.), or you can do so virtually at www.llanochamber.org/walk.htm.

Start with the **County Courthouse**, which was built in 1892; it's the thirty-ninth oldest courthouse in Texas, and one of only three that have had no additions. The forbidding **Old Llano Jail**, of gray granite quarried in the county, still has bars covering the arched entrance and all the windows. The original red metal roof of this Romanesque Revival building gave the jail a nickname — prisoners actually spoke fondly of "staying over at the Red Top." The ground floor was the jailer's office and living quarters; the only jailbirds today are the pigeons who come to roost through the broken upper windows and the gallows opening in the roof.

The **Dabbs Hotel**, a 1907 railroad hotel (see "Lodging"), is the last remaining example of a group of such hotels on the Llano River at the end of the railroad tracks. It was famous for being a "home away from home" for train crews when they parked their locomotive in front of the hotel and stayed the night. The walls are hung with old photographs, and hotelkeeper Gary Smith has many tales to tell of the old days. For example, in the 1930s the hotel was a favorite hideaway for the Barrow gang of Bonnie and Clyde fame.

The **Llano County Museum** (915-247-3026, 310 Bessemer Ave.) is housed in the old Bruhl Drugstore, built in 1922. Displays show Llano's boomtown days,

Historic Lan-Tex Theater, restored for both films and live entertainment.

Eleanor S. Morris

as there are collections of numerous Indian artifacts, and rocks and gems. There's also an exhibit about the days when polo was part of Llano, thanks to "the world's greatest polo player," Llano's own Cecil Smith.

Hill Country Wildlife Museum at 826 Ford Street (915-247-2568) is the repository of the Campbell Collection, the third largest collection of taxidermy mounts in the world.

The **Llano County Library** on Ford Street and the river is in what were three one-story buildings, all built in 1904 and once home to a variety of businesses, from furniture and liquor to a pharmacy and a domino parlor.

In *Kingsland,* the **Antlers Hotel,** built in 1901 by the Austin and Northwestern Railroad as a resort, was once a popular destination, especially for Austinites who came to vacation on the Colorado River. It's now back in business and popular once more (see "Lodging").

SEASONAL EVENTS

In JANUARY, the **Llano County Junior Livestock Show** takes place.

In APRIL the **Bluebonnet Arts and Crafts Trail** is a must stop in both *Llano* and *Kingsland,* the latter town having a juried art show with original works by seventy-five visiting artists and artisans at the Kingsland House of Arts and Crafts. Local artists join with exhibitors from across Texas and neighboring states. Llano also hosts the **Old Time Fiddle Fest,** a **Crawfish Boil,** and a **Golf Open.**

JUNE in *Kingsland,* the annual **Aqua-Boom Festival** begins, offering a scholarship pageant, a golf tournament (at the Packsaddle Country Club), a music fest on grounds of the chamber of commerce, a boat parade, and much more.

In JULY the annual **Aqua-Boom Festival** in Kingsland continues with a pageant, parades, a fish fry, arts and crafts fair, races on the lake, and fireworks. About 10,000 visitors are drawn to this small town of about 3,500.

In JULY in Llano there's the annual **July 4th Party;** for music lovers, in AUGUST, there's the **Grapestomp** out at **Fall Creek Vineyards.**

SEPTEMBER brings the **Llano Chamber Garage Sale.**

OCTOBER offers a **Heritage Day Festival** in Llano, and a **Gem and Mineral Show** in Kingsland, which also sponsors a **Halloween Carnival** on the last weekend.

NOVEMBER brings a **Fall Arts and Crafts Show** on the second weekend to both Llano and Kingsland. In Llano in addition to **Santa's Big Night,** there's both the **Courthouse Lighting** (10 miles of lights!) and the **Hill Country Lighting Trail.**

DECEMBER is busy with more Santa Land and the **Hill Country Christmas Lighting Tour,** plus the **Parade of Lights.** Kingsland celebrates with its **Christmas Tree Lighting** and **Merchants' Christmas Open House.**

Check with the chambers of commerce (Llano: 915-247-5354; Kingsland: 915-388-6211) for exact dates for these events.

LLANO COUNTY RECREATION

A diversity of outdoor recreation can be found in Llano County, be it on land or on water. The county's camping sites and hiking trails are described here under "Parks."

FISHING

There's year-round fishing on the picturesque, spring-fed **Llano River,** which runs through the city, and in **Lake Buchanan,** too, which forms part of the eastern border of Llano County (see below, along with other lakes in the Highland chain). Additional fishing spots are described in "Parks."

GOLF

Llano Municipal Golf Course (915-247-5100; Old Castell Rd., Llano, TX 78643) Two miles west of the Llano courthouse adjacent to Robinson City Park, this challenging 18-hole course is on the banks of the Llano River. A fully equipped pro shop, golf carts. The course has a new clubhouse that serves beer and wine.

Packsaddle Mountain and Other Scenic Routes

Viewed from Highway 71, long, low Packsaddle Mountain is of interest not only to historians, thanks to the famous battle on August 5, 1873, but also to geologists. It consists of 600-million-year-old sandstone in horizontal layers, resting on even more ancient Packsaddle schist. This in turn is exposed in Honey Creek at the foot of the mountain. Tempting traces of gold, silver, and other minerals have been found in the sands of the creek, but most geologists agree that whatever may have been there eroded eons ago.

If you chose to take FM 2241 from Tow (and the Vanishing Texas River Cruise and Fall Creek Vineyards) to Llano, instead of returning to Hwy. 29 west to Llano, you'll find this is another one of the lovely scenic routes in these parts.

HUNTING

The Llano Basin has the highest concentration of deer in the United States, which is why Llano boasts of being the Deer Capital of Texas. It's also considered one of the best in the state for bow hunting. There's the chance of bagging other game, too, such as dove, turkey, and quail. For a license, contact the **Llano Chamber of Commerce** (915-247-5354; www.llanochamber.org; 700 Bessemer Ave., Llano, TX 78643).

PARKS

Robinson City Park (Main St., 2.5 miles west of courthouse) This park on the Llano River offers picnicking, a swimming pool, and a challenging golf course (see "Golf"). Campgrounds are next to the park, and the 100 RV camping sites with electricity and water (call 915-247-5354 for information on camping), the community center, and the rodeo grounds are operated by the Llano County Community Center.

Other camping and RV sites include **Cedar Lodge Resort** (512-793-2820; www.highlandlakes.com/cedar; 1400 RR 261, Buchanan Dam, TX 78609), **Pelican Point Resort** (915-379-2373; PO Box 148, Tow, TX 78672; Hwy. 2241), and **Sunrise Beach Marina & Lodge** (915-388-9393; www.highlandlakes.com/marina; 667 Sandy Mtn. Dr., Llano, TX 78643).

Black Rock Park (512-473-4083, 800-776-5272, ext. 4083; www.lcra.org/lands/blkrock.html; State Hwy. 251 between Hwy. 29 and Bluffton) Black Rock Park on Lake Buchanan is under the aegis of the LCRA, and the 10-acre park on the 23,000-acre lake offers fishing, camping, picnicking, boating, wading, hiking, and water sports. Campers can chose one of thirty designated campsites, equipped with table and grill. Water is available, and there are two rest rooms plus an outdoor wash-off cold shower.

Buchanan Dam and Lake Buchanan

The Falls River Falls, seen along the route of the Vanishing Texas River Cruise, were formed more than 400,000 years ago when volcanic activity created the Llano Uplift.

Eleanor S. Morris

Buchanan (pronounced "buck-an-an") Dam was completed in 1937 and at that time was the longest multiple-arched dam in the United States. It's a popular place for many outdoor and water-related activities around Lake Buchanan. (For more information about the Highland Lakes, see www.highlandlakes.com.)

For BOATING, try **Alexander Boat Dock** (915-379-2721; RR 1, Box 16, Tow, TX 78672) on the lake, a complete marina with boat rentals, fuel, and oil.

A BOAT TOUR can offer a new perspective on sight-seeing and nature observation. **Vanishing Texas River Cruise** (512-756-6986, 800-4-RIVER-4; www.vtrc.com; PO Box 901, Burnet, TX 78611; located on Lake Buchanan, FM 2341, Tow) provides guided nature tours up the Colorado River to see wildlife and waterfalls, towering cliffs, and great birding. In summer there are dinner and sunset cruises; in winter the cruise offers a chance to view American bald eagles nesting on the banks of the river.

When FAMILY FUN is the order of the day, try the **Buchanan Dam Visitor Center** (512-793-2803; Hwy 29, Buchanan Dam, TX 78609). From here there are spectacular views of Buchanan Lake, the largest of the Highland Lakes, and telescopes to view from. The museum tells of the construction of the dam in 1937, one of the largest of its kind in the U.S. Exhibits include photographs, area history, a living history videotape, and a xeriscape garden. It's fun to feed the fish that gather below the observation deck, waiting for handouts.

FISHING enthusiasts will find plenty of opportunities on Lake Buchanan — which covers 23,000 surface acres — with white bass, striped bass, largemouth bass, catfish, spotted bass, crappie, and walleye lurking beneath the surface. Numerous guides on the lake can take visitors out for a fishing adventure, providing tackle and bait, and they'll even fillet the fish for you back on the dock. For fishing charters on Lake Buchanan call 512-793-2803. Two fishing docks on Lake Buchanan are **Cottonwood Cove** (915-379-2641; RR 2241, Tow, TX 78672) and Eagle's Nest Lodge (915-379-3131; 16746 RR 2241, Tow, TX 78672). Additional fishing is at Inks and LBJ lakes, described below.

ON THE LAKES: **Lake Buchanan** was the first created and is the highest of the Highland Lakes, and it also has the largest surface area. Although much of the 124-mile shoreline is privately owned, there are a number of public and commercial access points to boating, fishing, swimming, and other water sports, as well as camping. Both Burnet County, on the east, and Llano County, on the west, have parks on the lake.

Inks Lake, at a constant level, covers 803 acres and is a reservoir used primarily for maintaining heads to produce electric power from the overflow from Lake Buchanan. This lake offers excellent year-round fishing, boating, and water sports; there are lakeside docks and marinas.

Lake LBJ is a constant-level lake below Buchanan and Inks Lakes in the Highland Lakes chain. The clear lakes offer good fishing, skiing, and water recreation. For more information, contact the **Kingsland Chamber of Commerce** (915-388-6211; 1341 Hwy. 1431, Kingsland, TX 78639).

For wading and swimming, be advised that the areas are not designated and lifeguards are not provided. For boating, a single-lane free public boat ramp in neighboring Llano County Park accommodates motorboats and sailboats.

Many anglers consider that the park is a "hot spot" for bank fishing; others enjoy casting from a boat.

Enchanted Rock State Natural Area (915-247-3903; www.tpwd.state.tx.us/park/enchantd/enchantd.htm; 16710 RR 965, Fredericksburg, TX 78624) Even though the mailing address is Fredericksburg (see Gillespie County), this fantastic hunk of rock is located primarily in Llano County, 22 miles south of Llano. One of three exfoliated rock domes in the world (the others are Stone Mountain in Georgia and Ayers Rock in Australia), this massive 500-foot-high mound of solid granite covers almost 650 acres. It's also considered among the oldest (one billion years) exposed rocks in North America, rising like a huge bald pate above the 1,643-acre park.

Myriad tales and legends have contributed to the name "enchanted" — some Indian tribes feared to set foot upon it; they believed it was the site of human sacrifices. Others fancied that ghost fires flickered on the crest on moonlit nights. Others may have used it as a rallying point, but they all held it in awe and reverence.

The diversity of the rock face provides challenging face climbs and numerous crack climbs to those adventurers who make it to the cave on top. And the 4-mile hike around the base can yield great wildlife sightings: One recent hiker reported seeing a big black snake eating a lizard, a large turtle, two armadillos, four cows, twelve deer, and "a lot of rock squirrels" all on one walk. There are several more designated trails in Enchanted Rock Natural Area so visitors can explore the more remote areas of this 1,643-acre park.

ROCK HUNTING

Llano County considers itself the Central Mineral Region of Texas, since the abundance and diversity of minerals here are unequaled anywhere else in the state. Rock hunters can search below Buchanan Dam to find quartz, granite, gneiss, flint, schist, feldspar, and limestone. As for llanite, you might be lucky and find some at the **Llanite Outcropping,** a highway cut on Hwy. 16 at the intersection of Hwy. 29, about 10 miles north of Llano that's a favorite stopping place from rock hunters wanting to get a sample.

LLANO COUNTY SHOPPING

In Llano, the streets around Courthouse Square, Main, Berry, Sandstone, and Ford offer everything from antiques to gifts to clothing and accessories for every occasion and every age. For a real nostalgia trip, the choice is **Acme Dry Goods** (915-247-4457; 109 W. Main St., Llano, TX 78643), an old-fashioned dry goods emporium with the original fittings, including the original polished-brass cash register to ring up sales of today's merchandise. The **Llano Fine Arts Gallery** (915-247-4839; 503 Bessemer Ave., PO Box 8, Llano, TX 78643) is sponsored by the Llano Fine Arts Guild and exhibits more than 200 framed paintings, as well as photographs, prints, sculpture, ceramics, pottery, stained glass, enamels, and an assortment of crafts. Special courtyard exhibitions are organized in the spring and fall.

MASON COUNTY

Mason County, created from Bexar and Gillespie Counties in 1858, is almost an undiscovered secret, placed as it is up at the far northwest edge of the Hill Country. Yet it is only 40 miles north of that popular tourist destination, Fredericksburg; and German settlers, spreading north from Fredericksburg as early as 1848, were some of the county's earliest Anglo residents.

Fort Mason, named for Lt. George T. Mason who lost his life in the war with Mexico, was established to guard against the Comanche and Apache raids on Texas settlements to the east. Both town and county took the name of the fort, the town developing from a trading post alongside the fort. It was designated the county seat in 1861 shortly after U.S. soldiers left when Texas seceded from the Union. This was the year that Col. Robert E. Lee was commanding officer at the fort. Since Virginia had not as yet left the Union, Lee did not shed his U.S. uniform until he arrived home to take over the Army of Northern Virginia.

The vacant fort was irresistible to the people of Mason, and they began to build their town from its stones. Now a replica stands on the site, a hill south of the courthouse.

After the Civil War, Mason became cattle country. In the 1870s cattle rustling led to bloody feuds between ranchers and rustlers — called both the Mason County War and the Hoo Doo War. Texas Rangers soon arrived to restore law and order.

Much of the country was settled before the invention of barbed wire, and so Mason County abounds in rock fences that meander up hillsides, along creek beds, and through live-oak groves, built by Germans settlers who used the most plentiful resource they had to fence in their cattle.

Mason County claims that more deer roam here than any other place in Texas, a claim that Llano — naming itself the "Deer Capital of Texas" — must certainly dispute. Topaz, the state gem of Texas, is found only in Mason County, near the communities of Streeter, Grit, and Katemcy.

Mason (pop. 2,160) is about the only town in the county large enough to have something to offer visitors, but you'll find more here than perhaps you bargained for. For more information, contact the **Mason County Chamber of Commerce** (915-347-5758; www.sig.net/~masoncoc; 108 Ft. McKavitt St., PO Box 156, Mason, TX 76856).

MASON COUNTY LODGING

In Mason there's no mail delivery; everybody picks up mail at the post office. That means that many of the sites have no street address — you have to go by their location. There are two motels, the **Hill Country Inn** (915-347-6317; 454 Ft. McKavitt St., Mason, TX 76856; on Hwy. 87 S.) and **Fort Mason Inn** (915-347-0052; 866 San Antonio, PO Box 1138, Mason, TX 76856; on Hwy. 87 S.), and several small bed & breakfasts. Here are three of the latter, conveniently near all the sights:

BRIDGES HOUSE BED & BREAKFAST
Hosts: Mary and Jamie Hemphill.
915-347-6440.
305 Broad St., PO Box 264, Mason, TX 76856.
Two blocks north of the courthouse on the corner of Broad & Olmos.
Price: Moderate.
Credit Cards: None.
Handicap Access: Yes.

This little house is part of the National Register Historic District. The 1884 stone house is complete with old-fashioned gingerbread trim and 17-inch-thick stone walls. Bright, hand-painted wall and cupboard decorations by Mary, an artist, are everywhere. Colorful birdhouses are painted on the wall of the entry, and grape vines trail along the walls of the bathroom. Both guest rooms share the bath and the sitting room. A Christmas Room has a tree up in a corner all year-round, hung with old-fashioned decorations. There's a small refrigerator and coffeemaker for guests' convenience, and a continental breakfast is served in the sitting room.

MASON SQUARE BED & BREAKFAST
Hosts: Monica and Brent Hinkley.
915-347-6398/6824, 800-369-0405.
134 Ft. McKavitt St., Mason, TX 76856.
North side of the square.
Price: Inexpensive to Moderate.
Credit Cards: MC, V.
Handicap Access: No.

Monica (whose full name is Monica Maria Teresa Veronica Bastidas Valenzuela Hinkley) and Brent totally gutted this upstairs hostelry atop several of the square's businesses. From what was once a rooming house, then apartments, they created three lovely brand-new guest rooms, each with a private bath. A comfortable common room has a dining table and chairs and a TV and VCR. Tall French doors open onto the front balcony, giving a wide view of the courthouse in the center of Mason's town square. A food center is set up along one wall of the wide hall, with refrigerator, dishwasher, microwave, dishes, and whatever is needed for the continental breakfast that is included, or your own provisions. The Hinkleys also run the new Red Door B&B just up the street at #234.

OMA'S & OPA'S HAUS
Hosts: Julia and Merton Pepper.
915-347-6477, 800-508-5101 (in Texas only).
www.sig.net/~masoncoc/ member/omaandopa.
617 El Paso St., PO Box 1158, Mason, TX 76856.
Price: Moderate.
Credit Cards: None (cash and checks only).
Handicap Access: No.

This large Victorian stone house reflects the German pioneer influence — not only in its name, but the home itself looks like a big Sunday House. Painted sparkling white with Dutch blue trim, it's as spic and span inside as out. The four guest rooms are the Green and Pink Room, with a genuine Amish quilt for a coverlet; the Twin Bed Room; the Blue Room with a four-poster bed; and the TV Room, which has a sitting room for its namesake. Bathrooms are shared. Both the Green and Pink Room and the TV Room open onto the large upstairs wraparound porch, but everyone has access to the porch just below. There's a swing downstairs, and a nice side yard with a birdbath, and Julia will feed you pancakes and bacon for breakfast, or just cereal and bananas if you prefer.

MASON COUNTY RESTAURANTS

COOPER'S PIT BARBECUE
915-347-6897.

Like its twin restaurant in Llano, everything is authentic country barbecue here, from the outdoor smoking black pits of mesquite that cook the

Hwy. 87 S., Mason, TX
    76856.
Price: Inexpensive.
Cuisine: Barbecue.
Serving: L, D.
Credit Cards: MC, V.
Handicap Access: Yes.

brisket, ribs, chicken, pork, and goat to the butcher paper on which your choice is served. You pick it out directly from the pit, and it's priced by the pound. Same with potato salad and pinto beans. If you eat it on the premises, on the picnic tables inside, there's an additional small charge for bread, onions, and jalapeño peppers.

Diners enjoying fresh on-the-spot cooking at Santos Tanqueria in Mason.

Eleanor S. Morris

SANTOS TAQUERIA
915-347-6140.
www.sig.net/~masoncoc
    Search Santos Taqueria.
1025 San Antonio, PO Box
    1246, Mason, TX 76856.
On southeast corner of the
    square.
Price: Inexpensive.
Cuisine: Mexican.
Serving: B, L Mon.–Sat.
    6:30am–2pm
Credit Cards: None.
Handicap Access: No.

"From the heart of Mexico to the heart of Texas" is Santos' motto, and you can really believe it when you eat to the sound of hand-patted tortillas in the open kitchen in the center of the restaurant. Gorditas, chalupas, taquitos, quesadillos, all with an authentic south of the border—no Tex-Mex here. And a bonus is that everyone who enters will look a you, a stranger, smile and say "howdy."

WILLOW CREEK CAFE
915-347-6124.
102 Ft. McKavitt St., Mason,
    TX 76856.
North side of the square.

The original thick rock walls from 1904 and high ceilings provide an interesting contrast to the modern wood tables and chairs that furnish this large, light restaurant. Interesting features include the cashier's stand, a tall ledger desk from

Price: Inexpensive to
Moderate.
Cuisine: Sandwiches, Pizza.
Serving: L, D Thurs.–Sun.
Credit Cards: None.
Handicap Access: Yes,
except rest rooms.

an old train station, and a big old table seating six or eight. (The place was once a Ford dealership; it still has a drive-up ramp and bi-fold doors.)

House special pizzas are unusual. The Southwestern is topped with black beans, grilled chicken, onions, and mild green chilies; the Greek Veggie has spinach, sun-dried tomatoes, feta cheese, artichoke hearts, and red onions. A special drink is the prickly pear tea. Or BYOB.

ZAVALA'S CAFE
915-347-5365.
PO Box 1612, Mason, TX
76856.
On Hwy. 87 N.
Price: Inexpensive.
Cuisine: Mexican,
American.
Serving: B, L, D; closed
Christmas.
Credit Cards: MC, V.
Handicap Access: Yes.

Fajitas, huge burritos, cinco cinco, nachos (corn chips topped with refried beans, taco meat, cheese, lettuce, tomato, sour cream, and guacamole), and some of the biggest and best chicken-fried steak is served in this pleasant restaurant with warm wood wainscoting, arched mirrors, a Mexican village mural, and Tiffany-style lamps. Everything is made from scratch and is delicious, from the chicken breast Portuguesa to the chopped steak à la Mexicana. Fresh homemade pies include pecan, coconut, lemon, and chocolate.

MASON COUNTY CULTURE

ARCHITECTURE

The **Mason County Courthouse,** a Classical Revival building from 1909, is made of native sandstone and has been repainted in its original colors. Inside, almost every room has a fireplace trimmed with ornate pressed metal. Newly restored is the small stone building alongside the courthouse, containing a wonderfully welcome old-fashioned convenience: public toilets.

The **Seaquist House,** a large three-story Victorian mansion at 400 Broad St., is one of the most beautiful homes of early Texas. It was built in the 1880s and 1890s for a local banker. He maintained an office in the house, and you can still see his name, E. M. Reynolds, etched into the glass of the door. Now completely restored, the house is the home of the Garner Seaquist family, descendants of Oscar Seaquist, a Swedish boot maker who bought the home in 1919. The house has twenty-two rooms, fifteen fireplaces, and a shower room included in the three-story water tower. It was the first house in Mason to have indoor plumbing, and the third-floor ballroom, 30 by 60 feet, is enlarged by two spacious porches; there's a billiards room, too. The home is open for tours by appointment only (call 915-347-5413 for tour information).

The Reynolds-Seaquist House is still owned by descendants of the original family.

HISTORIC BUILDINGS AND DISTRICTS

Much of Mason has been designated a National Historic District, and you can begin to cover this by taking a walking tour of Mason Courthouse Square. (You can also take a virtual tour: www.sig.net/~masoncoc/walk-tour.htm.) The pecan trees were planted in the 1930s. Other buildings of interest on the square are the **Mason National Bank,** the **Mason County Jail** (still in use!), and the **Bill Martin House.** According to town historians, the occupants of this house once kept Nubian goats out back; it seems that a goat named Opal liked to jump on top of her fence. City crew workers would yell at her to get back in the pen, and she obeyed. She became so well trained that soon anyone driving by who saw her would yell "Opal, get back in your pen," and she would.

City Hall is in a renovated 1923 Mission-style building at 124 Moody St., and next door at 118 Moody is the **Odeon Theater,** in continuous operation since 1928. The theater was the site of the premiere of the Disney film *Old Yeller* — Mason native Fred Gipson was the author of the book. A preservation society has been formed for its renovation and claims that the Odeon is "the oldest continuous running theater in Texas." Nowadays not only new releases but also vintage movies and live theater with local thespians provide the drama.

The Mason County Jail

The Mason County Jail was built in 1894 and is still in use when needed — which is very rarely.

Eleanor S. Morris

Although cattle rustling and general lawlessness took place all over the Texas frontier, the situation came to a head in Mason County in 1875 with the Hoo Doo War. Several rustlers were apprehended and put in the Mason County Jail. But they were soon out on bail, and the sheriff found it impossible to find them to bring them to justice. Other arrests were made, and one man was killed while in the custody of the deputy sheriff. Finally a rancher was shot from ambush and a county official was killed on a street in Mason, a last straw. The county split into three factions, one trying to stay neutral and keep the peace, while the other two continued to fight with each other.

The last act of the Hoo Doo War was the burning of the Mason County Courthouse on January 27, 1877. But by that time the leaders of both factions were either dead, in jail, or had disappeared.

Today Mason invites visitors to "Come see where one of the ten famous Texas feuds took place. Walk the streets that once knew lawmen, outlaws, desperados. . . ."

Fort Mason, about five blocks south of the courthouse, is high on Post Hill above the town, commanding a wide view. Original building materials were used to re-create the one reconstructed building, which rests on the original foundation. The double fireplace foundations are also original. Crumbling foundations of twenty-three buildings include barracks, officers' quarters, and stables. (For the history of the fort, see www.sig.net/~masoncoc/history2.htm.)

LIBRARIES

The Mason County M. Beven Eckert Memorial Library (915-347-5446; 410 Post Hill, Mason, TX 76856) An exhibit here details the career of Fred Gipson, author of *Old Yeller*, the book that became a Walt Disney movie.

MUSEUMS

The Mason County Museum (915-347-6242; 300 Moody St., Mason, TX 76856)
A general collection of Mason County historical items and artifacts. The
museum is housed in an old schoolhouse built in the 1870s of materials gar-
nered from Fort Mason buildings. An old spring that supplied the fort with
water flows just east of the museum. Admission is free, and the museum's
hours are variable, since it is run by volunteers of RSVP (Retired Persons
Volunteer Service) — call for hours.

SEASONAL EVENTS

For information contact the **Mason County Chamber of Commerce** (915-
347-5758; www.sig.net/~masoncoc; 108 Ft. McKavitt St., Mason, TX 76856).

In JANUARY a **Livestock Show** is scheduled.

APRIL and MAY bring riotous fields of **wildflowers,** and the Mason County
Chamber of Commerce offers a map of three spectacular drives through the
county.

In JUNE is a **Catfish Fry** and JULY brings the **Roundup Rodeo** and **Arts and
Crafts Show.**

In NOVEMBER Mason really lights up for the **"Tannenbaum" Arts and Crafts
Show:** the courthouse, historic homes, and churches are all brilliantly aglow
with holiday lights.

Come DECEMBER there's a **Christmas Lighting Tour** through all the lighted
sights, and a **Christmas Home Tour.**

MASON COUNTY RECREATION

CAMPING

You can camp in Mason County at **Garner Seaquist Ranch** (see "Topaz
Hunting") and at **Fort Mason City Park** (915-347-4669), which has shaded
RV spots on the edge of the park's golf course (see "Parks"). For additional
camping choices, contact the **Mason County Chamber of Commerce** (915-347-
5758; www.sig.net/~masoncoc/camp&rec.htm; PO Box 156, Mason, TX 76856).

FISHING

Catfish and bass abound on the Llano River, and you can put into the river
at river crossings where access is made simple by the low-water bridges.
Luther Simon (915-347-6221, HC 60 Box 17, Mason, TX 76856) runs a fishing
camp on the Llano River 8 miles southwest of Mason on RR 1871.

NATURE

The **Eckert James River Bat Preserve** is home to one of the largest (4 to 6 million) free-tailed bat colonies. Wintering in Mexico, the bats arrive in Mason County in the spring, remaining until fall in a "maternity" cave, where female bats bear and rear their young. Each evening the mother bats leave the cave for dinner, each bat consuming perhaps as much as 75 tons of insects each night before returning to the cave to nurse their young.

Both the exodus flight and the returning one are spectacular, with the bats streaking caveward like dive bombers. The preserve, 12 miles from town, is open to the public Thursday through Sunday evenings May through October, 6–9pm. Arrange a tour by calling 915-347-5970 during the season or 915-347-9472 during off-season (www.sig.net/~masoncoc/batcave.htm).

PARKS

Fort Mason City Park (915-347-6449; U.S. 87 1 mile south of town) This 125-acre park has picnicking facilities under large pecan trees, fully equipped RV hookups, primitive campsites, a 9-hole golf course (Comanche Creek Golf Course, 915-347-5798), a rodeo arena, walking trails, and a playscape.

MASON COUNTY SHOPPING

Most shopping in Mason County is around Mason's main square, where you'll find antiques, crafts, gifts, and specialty items.

Antiques abound around the square at these shops: **Antiques and Crafts** (915-347-6440; 201 Westmoreland, Mason, TX 76856; on the south side of the square) was once a combined old lumberyard and funeral parlor. Now it's packed with antiques from early German settlers and later residents, too. Treasures include quilts, pottery, vintage clothes, old sheet music, furniture. **Antique Emporium** (915-347-5330; 106 S. Live Oak, Mason, TX 76856; on the east side of the square) is in the historic C&G Building, built in 1879, with quality antiques, and gifts. **Underwood Antique Mall** (915-347-5258; 100 N. Live Oak, PO Box 752, Mason, TX 76856; on the east side of the square) offers antiques and country treasures; and more antiques are at **P.V. Antiques** (915-347-5496; 1102 El Paso, Mason, TX 76856).

Also (mostly) on the main square:

Market Square (915-347-5516; 105 Ft. McKavitt St., Mason, TX 76856; on the north side of the square) offers all-purpose gifts for all occasions made by area cottage industries and artisans, including iron creations and leather goods. For a bonus, there's a soda fountain in the rear of the shop. **Texas topaz** is available uncut, cut, and mounted at the following locations in Mason: **Benjie's**

Eleanor S. Morris

This typical Hill Country stone building on Mason's Market Square was once a funeral parlor and is now a gift and antiques shop.

Books and Gifts (915-347-6323; 203 Ft. McKavitt St., PO Box 915, Mason TX 76856) and **Market Square** (see above), and at **Country Collectibles** (915-347-5249; 320 Ft. McKavitt St., Mason, TX 76856; out on U.S. Hwy. 87N., 2 blocks from the courthouse square.

Beyond the main square are these two recommended shops:

Glenn Marshall Custom Knives are justly famous. You can order one in your design or his. Visitors are invited to see Glenn at work at his shop, sharpening and honing blades as he has done since he made his first knife in 1930 (915-347-6207; 305 Hoffman St., Mason, TX 76856).

Ramon's Gallery of Arts (915-347-6635; 120 Moody St., Mason, TX 76856) specializes in original art. You'll find paintings, bronzes, oils, pastels, and watercolors plus crafts and art supplies.

CHAPTER FIVE
Along the River
SAN ANTONIO AND BEXAR COUNTY

Eleanor S. Morris

Sight-seers float on a barge on the San Antonio River along the River Walk.

The history of Bexar County is that of its principal city, San Antonio; no written records of the history of the Indian tribes exist before the Spanish came in the 17th century to find Yanaguana, a Payaya-Coahuiltecan Indian village on the San Antonio River. (The story of the coming of the Spanish and the establishment of the missions that formed the nucleus of what is Texas's third largest city can be found in Chapter One.)

Bexar County was created in 1836. Its name derived from the original 17th-century Spanish name for San Antonio: San Antonio de Béjar. The viceroy of New Spain at that time was one Baltazar de Zúñiga, Marqués de Valero, and the town's name honored his brother, the Duque de Béjar, who had died in 1686 defending Budapest against the Turks. San Antonio de Béjar soon became just Béjar — or Bexar, an alternate spelling. Eventually that name was applied

Downtown San Antonio

1. City Hall
2. County Court House
- - - - - - - - - River Walk

to the county, leaving its principal population center to be known simply as San Antonio.

The terrain of Bexar County is hilly, its rich black to thin limestone soil dotted with mesquite and other brush. Deer and wild turkey abound, and, like the rest of the Hill Country, there are spring-fed streams and underground water supplies. The San Antonio River flowing through the center of town is spring-fed.

San Antonio is the county seat and includes several small incorporated towns, such as Castle Hills, Balcones Heights, Alamo Heights, Olmos Park, and Terrell Hills. Outside the city, little Leon Springs, just about the only community in the county outside of San Antonio, has a popular barbecue restaurant and a dance hall.

The city's growth was limited to the central area until after Texas won independence from Mexico in 1836. But even with expansion, the early plan of the city, laid out in 1767, was respected: Alamo Plaza became a major commercial site, and Commerce Street was the main banking and financial district. However, the 20th century brought major changes in the form of skyscrapers and ornate architecture, such as the Smith-Young Tower, built in 1929. The Depression then called a halt to such growth. Not until construction of the Paseo del Rio in the 1940s, the city's great urban project along the San Antonio River, was all of downtown San Antonio brought together as one entity. The river flows twenty feet below street level, right through the heart of downtown. Lined with restaurants and shops and traveled by barges full of sight seers, the River Walk is surely the city's main attraction.

While San Antonio has an abundance of different cultures and cherishes them all, more than half of San Antonio's population is of Hispanic origin, and Spanish is spoken most everywhere. But Native American, Anglo, German, African-American, and Latin American cultures all contribute to the flavor that makes San Antonio such an exciting place to visit. Often called a "party town," San Antonio's many fiestas (at least two a month, usually more) certainly warrant that appellation. Anything and everything is cause for celebration in this happy, friendly town, which even created a Mud Festival to "celebrate" the chore of cleaning out the San Antonio River each spring.

SAN ANTONIO LODGING

Like any large city, San Antonio has its share of large hotels, part of national chains such as the **Hilton Palacio Del Rio** (210-222-1400, 800-445-8667; www.sanantoniocvb.com/visitor/hm-down.htm; 200 S. Alamo St., San Antonio, TX 78205), the **Hyatt Regency** (210-222-1234, 800-233-1234; www. hyatt.com/usa/san_antonio/hotels/hotel_satrs.html; 123 Losoya St., San Antonio, TX 78205), and the **Marriott Rivercenter** (210-223-1000, 800-648-4462; www.marriott.com/marriott/satrc; 101 Bowie St., San Antonio, TX 78205).

New is the **Westin Riverwalk** (210-224-6500, 800-WESTIN-1; 420 W. Market St., San Antonio, TX 78205). Several of the city's historic hotels have become affiliated with national chains, such as the **Camberly Gunter Hotel** (210-227-3241, 800-555-8000; 205 E. Houston St., San Antonio, TX 78205), the **Crown Plaza St. Anthony Hotel** (210-227-4392, 800-227-6963; 300 E. Travis St., San Antonio, TX 78205), and the **Crockett Holiday Inn** (210-225-6500, 800-292-1050; 320 Bonham, San Antonio, TX 78205). But San Antonio also has independent historic hotels such as the **Menger,** the **Fairmount,** and the **Mansion del Rio,** described below. Also well represented, particularly in the historic area of town, are a number of bed & breakfast establishments.

HOTELS

FAIRMOUNT HOTEL
Manager: Tony Rodriguez.
210-224-8800, 800-996-3426.
401 S. Alamo St., San
Antonio, TX 78205.
Price: Very Expensive.
Credit Cards: AE, D, DC,
MC, V.
Handicap Access: Yes.

In 1985 this seventy-nine-year-old hotel was moved halfway across downtown. True to Texas tradition, it was the largest building to have been moved anywhere, and it made the news all over the nation. However, service rather than size is the focus here, as is attention to guests, in the European tradition. Rooms are not large, but such features as 24-hour room service and valet parking, complimentary shoe shines, twice-a-day maid service, and a concierge and a doorman make a stay here very pleasant. Amenities also include a fine restaurant, lounge, and a health club.

LA MANSION DEL RIO
Manager: Michael Bazar.
210-225-2581, 800-292-7300.
www.lamansion.com.
112 College St., San
Antonio, TX 78205.
Price: Expensive.
Credit Cards: AE, D, DC,
MC, V.
Handicap Access: Yes.

La Mansion reflects the Hispanic heritage of San Antonio with its architecture and its atmosphere. Although the hotel is on the River Walk, it's a few blocks away from the traffic both downtown and on the river, so it presents a quiet, relaxed place to stay. Built as a school in the late 1880s by the French-speaking Brothers of St. Mary, the original structure grew from two stories to four. In 1966 the school moved to other quarters, and the rehabilitated building became the luxurious 337-room Mansion del Rio; amenities include room service and a swimming pool. Restaurant Las Canarias (named not after birds but the first civilian settlers, who came from the Canary Islands in 1731) is noted for its fine meals.

MENGER HOTEL
Manager: Hector Venegas.
210-223-4361, 800-345-9285.

The Menger was built in 1859 as a two-story, fifty-room hotel, but it quickly became so popular that a three-story addition was added shortly

Eleanor S. Morris

The lobby of the historic Menger Hotel, on Alamo Square.

www.mengerhotel.com.
204 Alamo Plaza, San
  Antonio, TX 78205.
Price: Expensive to Very
  Expensive.
Credit Cards: AE, D, DC,
  MC, V.
Handicap Access: Yes.

thereafter; "staying at the Menger" is still a byword. There have been many additions and embellishments since; in 1909, marble floors, Corinthian columns, and filigreed balustrades were added to the original lobby by noted architect Alfred Giles, making it an opulent showcase. But just as splendid as the hotel is its colorful history: General Robert E. Lee rode his horse into the lobby; "Teddy" Roosevelt recruited his Rough Riders for the Spanish-American War in the hotel bar; and Sarah Bernhardt, Lilly Langtry, and Mae West called the Menger home when they were in town. The historic rooms in the 19th-century wing have more charm than luxury; the newer rooms are more spacious and up to date. Amenities include a health club, restaurants, room service, swimming pool (in a garden just beyond a large glass wall of the lobby), and some kitchenettes.

BED & BREAKFASTS

In San Antonio, the bed & breakfast scene includes Victorian mansions with either Texas or European accents, and even a log cabin.

BECKMANN INN AND CARRIAGE HOUSE
Innkeepers: Betty Jo and Don Schwartz.
210-229-1449, 800-945-1449.
www.cimarron.net/usa/ tx.beck.html.
222 E. Guenther St., San Antonio, TX 78204.
Five blocks from downtown, in King William Historic District.
Price: Moderate to Expensive.
Credit Cards: AE, D, DC, MC, V.
Handicap Access: No.

On the National Register of Historic Places, as well as within the City of San Antonio's King William Historic District, Beckmann Inn is justifiably proud of its listing: Exceptional. The house was built in 1886 by Alfred Beckmann for his bride, Marie Dorothea, daughter of the San Antonio Guenther flour mill family. Around 1913 the home's Victorian style was converted to Greek Revival, and the porch was extended.

The parquet living room floor has an unusual decorative border, brought all the way from France. The yesteryear ambiance of the inn does not extend to its kitchen, however, where breakfast preparation includes glazed cranberry pear with mint and cranberry bread, and cinnamon-pecan French toast with an apricot glaze topped with strawberries and cream.

THE OGÉ HOUSE
Innkeepers: Sharrie and Patrick Magatagan.
210-223-2353, 800-242-2770.
www.ogeinn.com.
209 Washington St., San Antonio, TX 78204.
Edge of downtown, in King William Historic District.
Price: Expensive to Very Expensive.
Credit Cards: AE, CB, D, DC, MC, V.
Handicap Access: No.

The Ogé House (pronounced oh-jhay), a three-story building squared off by a set of porches top and bottom, is one of the most magnificent homes to be found in San Antonio's King William Historic District of fine houses. Built in 1857 for Louis Ogé, a pioneer cattle rancher and a Texas Ranger, the mansion boasts eleven stairs up to the front door and a central lobby with two guest rooms opening off it. Upstairs, the Giles and Mathis suites both open onto the porch across the front of the house, while Riverview, off the landing by the back stairs, is especially private with its own porch and view of the river. On the main level, the Mitchell Suite has a platform canopy bed and a daybed. The Bluebonnet Room is done in Texas antiques, with a four-poster rolling pin bed and the desk of a Texas judge.

But that's all you'll find of Texas. Sharrie and Patrick prefer to think of their inn as more of a small European hotel. A deluxe continental breakfast begins with poached pears and goes on to such delicacies as pecan log roll, apple torte, cherry cheesecake, and fruit pastries. The library at the rear of the house is relaxing, with soft yellow walls, white woodwork, and satin striped sofas. A brass bucket there is filled with menus from all of the city's many fine eating places.

RIVERWALK INN
Innkeepers: Johnny
  Halpenny and Tammy
  Hill.
210-212-8300.
www.riverwalkinn.com.
329 Old Guilbeau St., San
  Antonio, TX 78204.
On the River Walk at the
  beginning of King
  William Historic District.
Price: Expensive.
Credit Cards: AE, D, MC, V.
Handicap Access: No.

This group of log homes was transported log by log from Tennessee, where the inn's owners, Jan and Tracy Hammer, found them in a state of ruin. Originally built in 1842, the restored cabins represent the inn's philosophy: "We hope that our guests relive the history of old San Antonio through the lifestyles of Texas heroes Davy Crockett and James Bowie, who were from Tennessee," says innkeeper Halpenny. "Of course," he adds, "with all of today's amenities — the feel of the old with the technology of the new." Every Sunday morning at breakfast, a storyteller makes an appearance to entertain guests while they tuck into Johnny's baked French toast with spiced apples, along with ham and cheese kolachkes (a legacy of the ethnic pioneers of central Texas, these are wonderful Czech pastries).

The eleven rooms are named in honor of the heroes of the Alamo; each is decorated with country antique furniture, and nine of them have views of the river from outside porches or balconies. Fireplaces are of stone, and in many of the rooms you can see the cabin's log layers. Tall pine four-poster beds, homey quilts, old chests, and comfy armchairs make each room a relaxing and comfortable haven.

A YELLOW ROSE
Innkeepers: Deb Field-
  Walker and Kit Walker.
210-229-9903, 800-950-9903.
sanantonio.citysearch.com
  Search: Yellow Rose
229 Madison St., San
  Antonio, TX 78204.
Five blocks from
  downtown San Antonio.
Price: Expensive to Very
  Expensive.
Credit Cards: AE, D, MC, V.
Handicap Access: No.

The yellow-painted brick Yellow Rose B&B is a fine example of the many homes that were built in San Antonio's King William Historic District more than a century ago. Built in 1878 by Charles Mueller, a German immigrant house painter, the house, like many in the neighborhood, had been a Victorian beauty. The large entry hall and other rooms still contain some of the English antiques that Deb and Kit purchased along with the inn from the previous owners. It was a turnkey operation, Deb explains, as she serves a breakfast of her famous country French toast, made of French bread oozing with caramel and pecans. The homemade oat bran and pecan muffins are mouthwatering, too.

Both new innkeepers are experienced in making guests happy: They were in charge of food and beverage concessions in the golf industry in their native Albuquerque, New Mexico. Like their predecessors, Deb and Kit believe that innkeeping is all about relaxing and having a good time.

SAN ANTONIO RESTAURANTS AND FOOD PURVEYORS

For such a large and busy city, hosting countless tours, tourists, conventions, meetings, and festivals, many of San Antonio's huge selection of restaurants are surprisingly inexpensive. And the choices are legion — you'll find excellent American, Western, Southwestern, Mexican, French, Italian, Spanish, Chinese, Japanese, Taiwan, Korean, Indian, Greek, Indonesian, Indian, Middle Eastern cuisine, and more. The eateries on the River Walk alone range from innovative Southwestern through Cajun to barbecue and, of course, Mexican.

Clothing is casual chic in most places except along the River Walk, where many visitors are wearing shorts and sandals, and the dining is outdoors; Chez Ardid is an exception, where men are expected to wear jackets.

Following is a representative sample of the many great places to enjoy San Antonio dining.

BIGA ON THE BANKS
210-225-0722.
203 S. St. Mary's, San Antonio, TX 78205.
Price: Moderate to Expensive.
Cuisine: Continental, American.
Serving: D Mon.–Sat.
Credit Cards: AE, D, DC, MC, V.
Handicap Access: Yes.

Biga has recently moved from its original setting in an historic home on Locust Street to the first floor of the International Building on South St. Mary's. The restaurant features such delicacies as antelope and quail with chestnuts and currant sauce, although lamb, veal, scallops, and salmon are also recommended. Such side dishes as sweet potato noodles, served with lamb and rice noodles on Thai salad, add to the flavor.

BOUDRO'S
210-224-8484.
www.sanantonio.citysearch .com Search: Boudro's.
421 E. Commerce St., San Antonio, TX 78205
On the River Walk.
Price: Inexpensive to Moderate.
Cuisine: Texas bistro, Steaks, Seafood.
Serving: L, D.
Credit Cards: AE, CB, D, DC, MC, V.
Handicap Access: Yes, elevator from street level.

The wonderful innovative mixture of Louisiana Cajun and Tex-Mex at Boudro's has won an award from the Texas Hill Country Food and Wine Festival. The herb-cured salmon tacos with marinated cucumbers, red onions, jícama, and slaw on fresh flour tortillas may be a starter, but it's worthy of an entire meal. Other offerings include smoked chicken or crab enchiladas, duck-and-sausage gumbo, blackened fish fillets or prime rib, and mesquite-grilled bobwhite quail. Enjoy your feast under yellow awnings on bright red chairs as the river and the barges float by. Or better yet, with reservations for two or more, dine on a barge.

CASA RIO
210-225-6718.
www.sanantonio.citysearch
  .com Search: Casa Rio.
430 E. Commerce St., San
  Antonio, TX 78205.
On the River Walk.
Price: Inexpensive.
Cuisine: Mexican.
Serving: L, D.
Credit Cards: AE, D, DC,
  MC, V.
Handicap Access: Yes.

Casa Rio celebrated its fiftieth anniversary in 1996. It's the oldest and largest Mexican restaurant on the river, and the very first one to appear on this world-famous waterway. Dine under colorful umbrellas — or barge in (by reservation), enjoying San Antonio–style Mexican food.

COUNTY LINE BARBECUE
210-229-1941.
111 W. Crockett St., San
  Antonio, TX 78205.
On the River Walk.
Price: Inexpensive.
Cuisine: Barbecue.
Serving: L, D.
Credit Cards: AE, CB, D,
  DC, MC, V.
Handicap Access: Yes.

Randy Gross is called the "Rib King" of San Antonio, and for more than ten years the County Line has served up some of the best barbecue in town. And if you don't want barbecue, well, there are grilled steaks, kabobs, chicken, fish, salads, great margaritas, and ice-cold beer.

EARL ABEL'S FAMILY RESTAURANT
210-822-3358.
4200 Broadway, San
  Antonio, TX 78205.
Price: Inexpensive.
Cuisine: American.
Serving: B, L, D.
Credit Cards: AE, D, MC, V.
Handicap Access: Yes.

This San Antonio tradition has been around since 1933. The red-patterned carpet, the captain's chairs, and the wood paneling make a restful atmosphere for enjoying the comfort-food dinner of the day, such as a New England boiled dinner (Monday), flaky turkey turnovers with giblet gravy (Tuesday), and smothered Salisbury steak Swiss-style with mashed potatoes (Wednesday). But of course there are enchiladas, tacos, and chili on the menu as well as other chicken, steak, and seafood choices.

EL MIRADOR
210-225-9444.
www.sanantonio.citysearch
  .com Search: El Mirador.
722 S. St. Mary's St., San
  Antonio, TX 78205.
King William Historic
  District.
Price: Inexpensive.
Cuisine: Mexican.
Serving: B, L, D Wed. and
  Sat.

For more than thirty-five years the Trevino family has been serving delicious food from Mexican family recipes. El Mirador's Mexican cantina decor, with its saltillo tile floor, arches, and hanging baskets, plus the artwork of Frida Kahlo, reflects the adventure of authentic Mexican cuisine, such as sautéed shrimp in mole sauce, fiesta chicken quesadillas, nachos del golfo (sautéed lobster and crab with ancho relish, avocado salsa, and

Eleanor S. Morris

El Mercado, the city's Mexican marketplace, has many shops and restaurants, including El Mirador café.

Credit Cards: AE, MC, V.
Handicap Access: Yes
(restaurant), no
(bathrooms).

FIG TREE RESTAURANT
210-224-1976.
www.figtreerestaurant.com.
515 Villita St., San Antonio,
TX 78205.
At La Villita and the River
Walk.
Price: Very Expensive.
Cuisine: Continental.
Serving: D 6pm–10pm.
Credit Cards: AE, D, DC,
MC, V.
Handicap Access: No.
Special Features:
Reservations
recommended.

GUENTHER HOUSE
210-227-1061.
www.sanantonio.citysearch
.com Search: Guenther
House.

a spinach-radicchio salad), and other unusual dishes. Or try their renowned sopa Azteca, which always draws crowds.

The Fig Tree offers fine continental dining and a romantic atmosphere, with a patio view over the River Walk. The menu lists such long-standing favorites as beef Wellington, chateaubriand, and fresh salmon and lobster.

For an early breakfast in a historic setting, the Guenther House can't be beat. The Guenther name is an old San Antonio one: The restaurant is in the historic Guenther House, surrounded by a

205 E. Guenther St., San
  Antonio, TX 78204.
South of King William
  Historic District.
Price: Inexpensive.
Cuisine: American.
Serving: B, L; open
  Mon.–Sat. 7am–3pm,
  Sun. 8am–2pm.
Credit Cards: AE, D, MC, V.
Handicap Access: No.

garden; next door is the historic Guenther flour mill (now Pioneer Flour Mills). While the place is famed for fluffy biscuits smothered in cream gravy, the breakfast tacos are special, too. Entering the restaurant, cast an eye at the baked goods in the case to your left so you'll know what to order to sweeten your breakfast — or to have for dessert after lunch (soups and salads).

**HOUSTON STREET
  BISTRO**
210-476-8600.
204 E. Houston St., San
  Antonio, TX 78205.
Price: Inexpensive.
Cuisine: European Casual.
Serving: L daily, D when
  there's a performance
  next door in the Majestic
  Theater.
Credit Cards: All.
Handicap Access: Yes.

This storefront café is pretty chic, modeled on European bistros. Fine food in a relaxed, casual atmosphere is the scene, and the only non-French touch is a huge curved American flag covering the ceiling.

International specialties like Tuscan white-bean soup, Greek pasta salad, chicken Gorgonzola, and portabella mushroom sandwich dot the menu. Before you're even served your order, out comes a delicious loaf of fresh bread and olive oil dip to keep you going until the food arrives.

They're now offering lunch boxes to go if you want to eat somewhere al fresco.

IBIZA
210-270-0786.
715 E. River Walk, San
  Antonio, TX 78205.
Price: Moderate.
Cuisine: Mediterranean.
Serving: B, L, D.
Credit Cards: AE, D, DC,
  MC, V.
Handicap Access: Yes.

Dining in the open air along the river, watching the barges float by, is a relaxing way to enjoy a full breakfast, lunch, or dinner at Ibiza, named for one of Spain's Balearic Islands. White chairs, blue-topped tables, and colorful napkins provide a pleasant setting for tapas (Spanish appetizers), specialty coffee drinks, and homemade desserts, too. Live entertainment Friday and Saturday evenings.

LA FOGATA
210-340-1337.
2427 Vance Jackson, San
  Antonio, TX 78205.
Price: Inexpensive to
  Moderate.
Cuisine: Mexican.
Serving: L, D Sun.–Thurs.
  11am–1pm, Fri. & Sat.
  11am–11pm; B Sat. & Sun.
Credit Cards: AE, CB, D,
  DC, MC, V.
Handicap Access: Yes.

Authentic and traditional foods of northern Mexico are on the menu here. Tacos al carbon (charcoal-broiled meat), frijoles borrachos (drunken beans), flour tortillas, quesadillas (melted cheese in corn tortillas), simple but filling, are a treat — so much so that the restaurant is often quite crowded, but the food is worth it.

**LA MARGARITA
MEXICAN
RESTAURANT &
OYSTER BAR**
210-227-7140.
120 Produce Row, San
Antonio, TX 78205.
Market Square (El
Mercado).
Price: Inexpensive.
Cuisine: Mexican, Oyster
Bar.
Serving: L, D, SB.
Credit Cards: AE, CB, D,
DC, MC, V.
Handicap Access: Yes.

La Margarita may be a Mexican restaurant, but it's housed in a two-story building straight out of New Orleans, with lacy balconies and a wrought-iron-fenced patio. With dining both inside and out, La Margarita is the "home of the sizzling fajitas," claiming to be the first to bring that dish to San Antonio. Louisiana oysters and jumbo shrimp served Acapulco style are also on the menu here, and chicken enchiladas topped with tangy green tomatillo sauce and Monterey Jack cheese, served with guacamole, Spanish rice, and beans, keep La Margarita honest as a Mexican restaurant as well as a seafood bar. So does the nightly mariachi music. And the delicious tequila margaritas live up to the restaurant's name.

LIBERTY BAR
210-227-1187.
www.sanantonio.citysearch
.com Search: Liberty Bar.
328 E. Josephine St., San
Antonio, TX 78205.
Price: Inexpensive.
Cuisine: American.
Serving: L, D.
Credit Cards: AE, MC, V.
Handicap Access: Yes.

Don't be put off by the rather rundown exterior here. The decor is aged 19th century, set in what used to be Boehler's Gardens, a venerated San Antonio spot. The menu, printed daily, offers fresh breads, fresh vegetable salads, hearty steaks cooked on a mesquite grill, and specials like linguini, grilled bluefish, and even such a homey thing as a grilled cheese sandwich (but made special with Muenster cheese and chipotle peppers).

**LITTLE RHEIN STEAK
HOUSE**
210-225-2111.
www.littlerheinsteakhouse.
com.
231 S. Alamo St., San
Antonio, TX 78205.
On the River Walk.
Price: Expensive.
Cuisine: Steaks.
Serving: D.
Credit Cards: AE, D, DC,
MC, V.
Handicap Access: Yes.
Special Features:
Reservations
recommended.

Dining here is either in the historic stone building up on the street level or on several levels of the River Walk patio — stairs lead from river to street level. Little Rhein boasts USDA choice steaks as well as fresh seafood, chops, and delicious appetizers and cocktails.

LONE STAR CAFE
210-223-9374.
www.sanantonio.citysearch
.com Search: Lone Star
Cafe.

Here's the only taste of Texas on the River Walk in a restaurant that's on the street level indoors but with a second-story view of the goings-

237 Losoya St., San
  Antonio, TX 78205.
On the River Walk.
Price: Inexpensive to
  Moderate.
Cuisine: Texas.
Serving: L, D.
Credit Cards: AE, MC, V.
Handicap Access: Yes.

on along the river. Although the Texas-sized
steaks, chicken-fried steak, catfish, baked potatoes,
and onion rings served with Texas beer and wine
are delicious inside, they're even tastier if you
climb the stairs from the river up to the porch way
up under the leafy branches of the trees overhanging the river. Live country music Thursday and
Friday nights.

*Mariachi musicians at El
Mercado's famous Mi Tierra
Café & Bakery pose for the
camera.*

Eleanor S. Morris

MI TIERRA CAFE & BAKERY

210-225-1262.
www.pico-de-gallo.com/
  mtc.htm.
218 Produce Row, San
  Antonio, TX 78207.
On Market Square.
Price: Inexpensive to
  Moderate.
Cuisine: Mexican.
Serving: Open 24 hours daily.
Credit Cards: AE, D, DC,
  MC, V.
Handicap Access: Yes.

THE ORIGINAL MEXICAN RESTAURANT

210-224-9951.
www.kangaroocourt.com/
  original.html.
528 River Walk, San
  Antonio, TX 78205.

Mi Tierra is where all visitors go sooner or later
— it's another San Antonio classic. Huge colorful murals cover the walls of the — what else? —
Mural Room, and the lobby boasts the "world-
famous" Mariachi Bar. Mexican dishes, such as
chiles rellenos, cabrito alhorno, and gallina en mole
are relished to the sound of soulful mariachi music
nightly. Take a number and join the lineup in front
of the bakery counters at the entrance to purchase
fresh Mexican pastries: empanadas (fruit turnovers),
pan dulce (sweet rolls), and that creamy Mexican
sweet, dulce de leche (condensed milk candy).

You're certain to get a combination of authentic
Mexican food and authentic San Antonio history here, both paying tribute to the restaurant's
origins in 1899, when it defined Mexican food for
San Antonio. A "new" site overlooking the river
was dug out in 1960 from beneath D. Heye &

Price: Inexpensive to
Moderate.
Cuisine: Mexican.
Serving: L, D.
Credit Cards: AE, D, DC,
MC, V.
Handicap Access: Yes.

**SCHILO'S
DELICATESSEN**
210-223-6692.
424 E. Commerce St., San
Antonio, TX 78205.
Just above the River Walk.
Price: Inexpensive.
Cuisine: German,
Delicatessen.
Serving: B, L, D; closed Sun.
Credit Cards: AE, MC, V.
Handicap Access: Yes.

Company Saddlery (famous for outfitting Teddy Roosevelt's Rough Riders). Wednesday through Sunday evenings from 6 to 9 you'll enjoy strolling mariachi musicians.

Here's another San Antonio classic, from 1917 no less, and consistently voted the best German restaurant for miles around. Not at all fancy, the large storefront restaurant's decor consists of an acrylic tile floor of many colors, old wooden tables and booths, and high ceilings, highlighted by three flags: American, Mexican, and Austrian — and lots of beer signs. The mustard and horseradish is homemade as is the root beer in a barrel in the rear. Split pea soup and potato pancakes are a specialty, along with bratwurst, Wiener schnitzel, and cheesecake. Come Saturday night the place resounds with the tuba and accordion of an oompah band, and everybody has a good ol' time.

**TOMATILLOS CAFE Y
CANTINA**
210-824-3005.
3210 Broadway, San
Antonio, TX 78209.
Price: Inexpensive.
Cuisine: Mexican.
Serving: L, D.
Credit Cards: AE, D, MC, V.
Handicap Access: Yes.

Award-winning margaritas, served with big smiles, and a fiesta party atmosphere characterizes Tomatillos Cafe y Cantina. The food is Tex-Mex and good, beginning with their quesadilla appetizers and on to the enchiladas, tamales, and burritos.

**TOWER OF THE
AMERICAS
RESTAURANT**
210-223-3101.
www.toweroftheamericas.
com.
600 HemisFair Park, Bldg.
222, San Antonio, TX
78205.
Price: Moderate to
Expensive.
Cuisine: American,
Southwestern.
Serving: L, D daily.
Credit Cards: All.
Handicap Access: Yes.

Take an elevator ride into the clouds for some fine dining. Tables for four to six line the wide glass observation windows (with others on a tier above) providing quite a view of San Antonio from 750 feet in the air of the revolving dining room.

Dishes like the Sky-high shrimp and Brie bisque, grilled asparagus, lobster tail and Prime Rib are a treat. (If you make a reservation in advance, a shuttle will pick you up and return you to your downtown hotel.)

Enjoy live jazz piano in the High in the Sky Lounge on Friday and Saturday nights.

ZUNI GRILL
210-227-0864.
www.zunigrill.com.
511 River Walk, San
   Antonio, TX 78205.
Price: Inexpensive.
Cuisine: Southwestern,
   New Mexican.
Serving: B, L, D.
Credit Cards: AE, DC, V,
   TM (Transmedia).
Handicap Access: Yes,
   elevator at Hyatt Hotel
   next door.

Attractive wrought-iron chairs and bright tile-topped tables make this an attractive place to eat and to people watch. The restaurant is opposite one of the high arched bridges that cross the river, and there's a small garden between the river and the restaurant. Zuni's adventurous menu includes fresh anchovy bread, applewood-smoked salmon, blue corn enchiladas, black bean soup with white cheddar cheese, and spinach or duck quesadillas.

SAN ANTONIO FOOD PURVEYORS

This sampling of San Antonio food purveyors focuses on the downtown and River Walk areas.

The Marble Slab Creamery has several locations. Try the one at Rivercenter Mall (849 E. Commerce St., San Antonio, TX 78203) on the river level or the one at North Star Mall (Loop 410 and San Pedro, San Antonio, TX 78212). In both you can enjoy fresh homemade ice cream with a choice of more than thirty mix-ins.

Mi Tierra Cafe & Bakery (210-225-1262; 218 Produce Row, San Antonio, TX 78207, on Market Square) is good for Mexican pastries and other specialties (see "Restaurants" for more information).

Pecan Street Delicatessen (210-227-3226; www.primetimenewspapers.com/sadining/pecan.htm; 152 E. Pecan St., San Antonio, TX 78205, corner of St. Mary's). The name may not match this deli, which calls itself an "Exotic Mediterranean Deli," but the menu does. Try a Greek gyro of beef and lamb on handmade pita bread, or a "Pita the Great," a whole-wheat pita pocket filled with hummus, tabouli, tomatoes, feta cheese, and kalamata olives. Then there's the "Muffaletta," herb-and-cheese-crusted focaccia bread topped with smoked ham, Genoa salami, provolone, and its own olive mix. This is a busy place, packed with small round tables and bentwood chairs all crammed together, and everyone's friendly. Come for breakfast or lunch, Mon.–Fri. 7:30am–3pm, Sat. 10am–3pm.

COFFEEHOUSES

Of coffeehouses there are dozens, all over town. The San Antonio visitor on the River Walk in need of a caffeine (or decaf) lift might try **Starbucks** of the national chain (210-229-4445; 111 W. Crockett St. W., San Antonio, TX

78205) and **Barnie's Coffee & Tea Company** at Rivercenter Mall (849 E. Commerce St., San Antonio, TX 78205).

SAN ANTONIO CULTURE

As a service of the San Antonio's **Office of Cultural Affairs,** recorded information on music and theater performances, literary events, dance, museums, and visual arts is available by calling 210-222-ARTS or 800-894-3819, on their Web site at www.ci.sat.tx.us/daca, or writing them at PO Box 839966, San Antonio, TX 78283.

ARCHITECTURE

San Antonio is variously described as picturesque, charming, even quaint. All of these can be used to describe the city's architecture because the buildings don't reflect any one influence. When the city was founded in 1718 by Spanish soldiers and settlers, they brought with them a strong Baroque style. Next came Anglo, German, and French immigrants, bringing their own architectural styles. Art Deco had its day, too, in the 1920s and '30s.

The climate also exerted an influence so that to many of these various styles were added the thick walls, covered walks, and broad overhangs that provide protection from the heat, creating a style of architecture that became uniquely San Antonio. The Spanish influence is best seen in the missions and the architecture of such buildings as **La Mansion del Rio** (see "Lodging"). The post–Civil War homes of the **King William Historic District** are a mixture of Greek Revival, Romanesque, Palladian, and other styles, and many are the work of English-born architect Albert Giles, who designed numerous other structures in the Hill Country. The **Kress Building** (315 E. Houston) has an Art Deco storefront in shades of pink, yellow, green, and copper terra-cotta; the tall **Casino Club Building** on a triangular lot (102 E. Crockett) crowns its Art Deco style with an eye-catching blue dome.

But it's the **Paseo del Rio**, the **River Walk**, that makes San Antonio unique. The San Antonio River, below street level, winds its way through the downtown and is lined with lush gardens, restaurants, nightclubs, and shops. Arched bridges provide access to each side of the river, and barges float down the center, filled with sight-seers enjoying both the ride and the view.

DANCE

San Antonio is host to a variety of dance events, from ballet to cloggers to ethnic to visiting companies. For information on dance activities, which take place at performance spaces throughout the city, contact **San Antonio Dance Umbrella** (210-212-7775; 825 S. St. Mary's St., San Antonio, TX 78205).

GALLERIES

San Antonio's abundance of ethnic cultures — Native American, Anglo, Spanish, Mexican, German, African-American, and Latin American — all contribute to an array of sophisticated art galleries displaying a wide variety of international and regional art. Here is a sampling:

Blue Star Art Space (210-227-6960; www.bluestar-art.org; 116 Blue Star St., San Antonio, TX 78204) An 11,000-square-foot showcase in the King William Historic District, housing art by regional, national, and international artists. The complex is run by the artists themselves.

Chamade Jewelers (210-224-7753; www.lavillita.com/chamade.html; 504 Villita St., San Antonio, TX 78205) Made-to-order jewelry as well as pieces imported from France and Italy; platinum, silver, and precious stones.

Galeria Ortiz (210-225-0731; 248 Losoya St., San Antonio, TX 78205; also at 102 Concho St., San Antonio, TX 78207) The gallery specializes in contemporary Southwest art. Paintings, sculpture, folk art, silver jewelry, and gift items are collected in two locations: Losoya St. is in the Alamo Historic District downtown, and Concho St. is in Market Square.

Gallery of the Southwest (210-493-3344; 13485 Blanco Rd., San Antonio, TX 78216) Here's a regular trading post of the Old West, with Hopi, Navajo, and Zuni art; jewelry, rugs, pottery, and blankets.

Harry Halff Fine Art (210-822-0713; www.harryhalff.com; 7726 Broadway, San Antonio, TX 78209) European, American, and early Texas paintings and works on paper are the specialty here.

Little Studio Gallery of La Villita (210-227-8893; 103 King Phillip V St., San Antonio, TX 78205) Here you'll find local artists displaying their oil paintings, watercolors, acrylics, and other works, all for sale.

Southwest School of Art and Craft (210-224-1848; www.sanantonio.citysearch.com Search: Southwest School of Art and Craft; 300 Augusta St., San Antonio, TX 78205) This former convent has been put to work as an art center, with galleries, studios, and classrooms. Commissioned in 1848 by the French Catholic order, today within the old walls the Ursuline Gallery sells contemporary crafts from all over the United States in addition to the works of the craft center's teachers, students, and other local artists. You'll find art accessories, ceramics, glass and textiles, jewelry, and other wearable art.

Monte Wade Fine Arts (210-222-8838; 514 Paseo de la Villita St., San Antonio, TX 78205) Spirit warriors, star travelers, raku ceramics, and other diverse styles and flavors of the Southwest are captured here, in both contemporary and classic works.

GUIDED TOURS

A Lone Star Trolley taking visitors to the town's historic sites.

Eleanor S. Morris

Gray Line Tours San Antonio (210-226-1706, 800-472-9546; 217 Alamo Plaza, Suite B, San Antonio, TX 78205) A selection of tours, among them Alamo and the Mission Trail, San Antonio Sampler, and Texas Hill Country Escape.

Lone Star Trolley Tours (210-224-9299; 301 Alamo Plaza, PO Box 2508, San Antonio, TX 78299) Tickets and boarding only at the corner of Crockett and Alamo Sts. across Alamo Plaza from the Alamo.

San Antonio City Tours (210-228-9776, 800-868-7707; 217 Alamo Plaza #400, San Antonio, TX 78205) Professionally narrated tours on air-conditioned buses of the Alamo, the missions, Market Square, King William Historic District, and other local attractions.

The Texas Trolley (210-225-5395; Alamo Visitor Center, 216 E. Crockett St, San Antonio, TX 78205, at the Alamo Plaza) The trolley makes seven stops so passengers can get off and explore at their leisure, hopping back on at their own convenience. Trolley stops include the Alamo, Market Square, Mission Concepcion, IMAX Theater, Lone Star Brewery, HemisFair, and more.

HISTORIC SITES AND DISTRICTS

THE ALAMO
210-225-1391.
www.thealamo.org.
PO Box 2599, San Antonio,
TX 78299.
Alamo Plaza, bet. Houston
and Commerce Sts.

Established in 1716 as the Misión San Antonio de Valero, the building was abandoned as a mission long before the events that earned its place in history: on February 23, 1836, a handful of men, defending the building against the Mexican forces led by Gen. Santa Anna, died to the last one. "Remember the Alamo" became a cry that inspired the final victory that won Texas its independence

Eleanor S. Morris

The Alamo, former Spanish mission and the site of a storied battle for Texas independence.

Open: Mon.–Sat.
9am–5:30pm, Sun.
10am–5:30pm; closed
Christmas Eve and
Christmas Day.
Admission: Free.
Donations accepted.

from Mexico. The Daughters of the Republic of Texas have established both a shrine and exhibits about the battle and the defenders of the fort. The shrine is simple, a dignified memorial to those who are considered the state's first heroes — although they came from many states, even other countries. The atmosphere is hushed and reverential as visitors move through the old stone building.

The Alamo cenotaph on Alamo Plaza in front of the Alamo is a tribute to the Texas heroes who lost their lives defending the Alamo. The sculpture, by Pompeo Coppini, was dedicated during the Texas Centennial of 1936.

SPANISH GOVERNOR'S PALACE
210-224-0601.
105 Plaza De Armas, San Antonio, TX 78205.
Open: Mon.–Sat. 9am–5pm,
Sun. 10am–5pm.
Admission: Adults $1,
children 7–13 50¢,
under 7 free.

Built in 1749 — and dubbed by the National Geographic Society "the most beautiful building in San Antonio" — this national historic landmark housed the officials of what was then the Spanish province of Texas. It's claimed to be the only remaining early aristocratic home in all of Texas.

The Missions

The Mission San José was founded in 1720.

San Antonio has four missions established in the 18th century by Spanish priests: San José, Concepción, Espada, and San Juan. Operated by the San Antonio Missions National Historical Park (210-534-8833), they are still active as parish churches. All are open to the public daily 9–5; admission is free.

Mission San José (210-534-8833; 6701 San José Dr., San Antonio, TX 78214) Called "the Queen of the Missions," San Jose, built in 1720, is noted for its beautiful rose window. The mission is set in a large walled compound and, in addition to the church, a granary and Indian quarters have been restored. It's still a working church: masses are held Mon.–Fri. at 8am; Sat. 5:30pm; Sun. 7:45am (Spanish), 9am, and 10:30am, and at noon there is a mariachi mass. Guided tours are available.

Mission Concepción (210-534-1540; 807 Mission Rd., San Antonio, TX 78210) Built in 1731, this is considered the oldest unrestored stone church in the country. Remaining are the church, sacristy, and several convent rooms.

Mission San Francisco de la Espada (210-627-2021; 10040 Espada Rd., San Antonio, TX 78214) This is the smallest mission, known for its unique archway and nearby stone aqueduct. It was established in 1731, and the Indian quarters are still there, but they have not been restored. Guided tours are available.

Mission San Juan Capistrano (210-534-0749; 9101 Graf Rd., San Antonio, TX 78214) Nested in a rural setting, with rare statues, this, too, is still an active church, with masses Tues.–Fri. at 8am (Spanish); Sat. 6pm; Sun. 9am, 10:30am (Spanish), and noon.

The King William Historic District, a twenty-five-block neighborhood of restored early Texas homes, begins at the corner of King William and South St. Mary's Sts., on the south bank of the San Antonio River. It was the city's most elegant residential neighborhood in the 1800s, and it's once again a fashionable area, with many of the old homes remodeled and restored. The **San Antonio Conservation Society** (210-224-6163; 107 King William St., San Antonio, TX 78204) provides a walking tour brochure, or visit their Web site at www.saconservation.org to take a virtual tour.

1902 Sunset Station is now an urban entertainment complex of indoor venues plus an outdoor pavilion and amphitheater. The historic site mixes the history of the former train depot with live music, concerts, and casual-themed restaurants.

Eleanor S. Morris

Sunset Station (210-222-9481; www.sunset-station.com; 1174 E. Commerce St., San Antonio, TX 78205), set in the 1902 Southern Pacific railroad depot in the heart of the St. Paul Square Historical District, is designed to be an urban entertainment center. Here you'll find all the facets of San Antonio's rich and diverse culture. The complex consists of indoor venues, with an outdoor pavilion and amphitheater.

La Villita means "little village," and this walled square block in the heart of downtown was the original settlement of old San Antonio; it's on the National Register of Historic Places as a historic district. The houses, restored, are now occupied by artists' and artisans' studios, shops, and restaurants open daily (210-207-8610; www.lavillita.com for a virtual tour; 418 Villita, San Antonio, TX 78205, at Presa St.).

MUSEUMS

BUCKHORN SALOON AND MUSEUM
210-2247-4000.

Before you take in this wild place with more than 3,500 specimens of game animals either stuffed in their entirety or mounted on the walls,

www.buckhornsaloon.com.
318 E. Houston Street, San
Antonio, TX 78205.
Open: 10am–5pm daily.
Admission: Adults $9.95,
children 6–11 and seniors
$7.95; with audio tour
$11.95 and $9.95
respectively.

be sure to "belly up to the bar." In this, its new home, the museum has included a virtual recreation of an 118-year-old saloon, where you can step up to the same bar or sit at the same tables where cowboys and cattlemen have enjoyed themselves for ages. And gunfights take place out front at high noon (of course!) every Saturday and Sunday.

HERTZBERG CIRCUS COLLECTION & MUSEUM
210-207-7810, 210-207-7819
(group tour info).
www.sat.lib.tx.us.hertzberg
/prologue.htm.
210 Market St., San
Antonio, TX 78205.
Open: Mon.–Sat
10am–5pm; June–Aug.
Sun. 1–5pm.
Admission: Adults $2.50,
seniors $2, children 3–12
$1.

Everybody loves a circus, and everything about a circus is collected here, from the colorful elephant statues guarding the entrance to the artifacts of P. T. Barnum, Tom Thumb, and Emmett Kelly to the 1903 ticket wagon, 1928 band organ, and a scale model of a 1930s tented circus.

INSTITUTE OF TEXAN CULTURES
210-458-2300.
www.texancultures.utsa.
edu/new.
801 S. Bowie St., San
Antonio, TX 78205.
At Durango Blvd.
Open: Tues.–Sun.
9am–5pm; closed Mon.,
Thanksgiving,
Christmas.
Admission: Adults $4,
seniors $2, children 3–12
$2, under 3 free.

The museum was founded for the interpretation and assimilation of Texas history and folk culture; every ethnic group that helped to form Texas is represented in depth. Much of the entertaining and instructive displays and discussions of Texas history and culture is geared to the younger set.

INSTITUTO CULTURAL MEXICANO
210-227-0123.
600 HemisFair Plaza Way,
San Antonio, TX 78205.
Open: Tues.–Fri.
10am–5pm., Sat. &
Sun. 11am–5pm.
Admission: Free.

Lectures, exhibits, films, and visual and performing arts are presented for an understanding and appreciation of the Hispanic culture so much a part of San Antonio. The gift shop features quality Mexican folk art as well as books and art posters.

McNAY ART MUSEUM
210-824-5368.
www.mcnayart.org.
6000 N. New Braunfels, San
  Antonio, TX 78209.
At U.S. 81 Business Hwy.
Open: Tues.–Sat.
  10am–5pm, Sun.
  noon–5pm.
Admission: Free except for
  some special exhibitions
  and events; donations
  accepted.

The museum is housed in a twenty-four-room mansion once belonging to artist and art collector Marion Koogler McNay, who was "steadfast in her commitment to the advancement and enjoyment of modern art." Here you'll find not only changing exhibits and a fine collection of 19th- and 20th-century art but also collections of post-Impressionist paintings, early New Mexican arts and crafts, and medieval and Gothic art.

**PIONEER TRAIL
DRIVERS AND TEXAS
RANGERS MEMORIAL
MUSEUM**
210-822-9011.
3805 Broadway, San
  Antonio, TX 78205.
Memorial Mall in
  Brackenridge Park, next
  to Witte Museum.
Open: May–Aug., 9am–
  4pm daily; Sept.–Apr.,
  11am–4pm daily.
Admission: Adults $2,
  seniors $1.50, children
  4–12 50¢.

A combined effort of the Texas Trail Drivers Association and the Texas Rangers Association, this museum celebrates the history of "Old Texas," with memorabilia from early cattle ranching and trail drive days.

**SAN ANTONIO
MUSEUM OF ART &
NELSON A.
ROCKEFELLER
CENTER FOR LATIN
AMERICAN ART**
210-978-8100.
www.sa-museum.org.
200 W. Jones Ave., San
  Antonio, TX 78215.
Open: Tues. 10am–9pm,
  Wed.–Sat. 10am–5pm,
  Sun. noon–5pm; closed
  Thanksgiving and
  Christmas.
Admission: Adults $4,
  seniors and students
  with ID $2, children 4–11
  $1.75, under 3 free. Free
  Tues. 3–9pm.

Housed in a restored 1884 brewery, the building has glass elevators, skylights, and a skywalk. The collection of Asian art and Latin American folk art is considered the most comprehensive in the southern United States. There are also exhibits of Greek and Roman antiquities, contemporary art, and in 1998 the museum opened the country's first center for the study and appreciation of Latin American art.

WITTE MUSEUM
210-357-1900.
www.wittemuseum.org.
3801 Broadway, San
　Antonio, TX 78209.
Open: Mon., Wed.–Sat.
　10am–5pm, Tues.
　10am–9pm; Sun.
　noon–5pm; closed
　Thanksgiving, Christmas
　Eve, and Christmas Day.
Admission: Adults $5.95,
　seniors $4.95, children
　4–11 $3.95. Free Tues.
　3–9pm.

In this museum of natural history and science, exhibits include native American and Texas natural and social history, such as "Dinosaurs: Vanished Texas," and natural science. Exhibits include discoveries and hands-on experiences. Don't miss the H-E-B Science Treehouse, a four-level hands-on exhibit space with, yes, a real tree house — plus outdoor water exhibits on the San Antonio River.

MUSIC AND NIGHTLIFE

Most of San Antonio's nightlife centers around the River Walk.

Durty Nelly's Irish Pub (210-222-1400; www.sanantonio.citysearch.com Search: Durty Nelly's; 715 E. River Walk St., San Antonio, TX 78205) is as authentic an Irish pub as you're likely to find this side of Erin. Frosty beer helps the old-time sing-alongs along; professional entertainment nightly as well.

Howl at the Moon Saloon (210-212-4695; www.sanantonio.citysearch.com Search: Howl at the Moon; 111 W. Crockett St., San Antonio, TX 78205, overlooking the River Walk) has been voted the "town's best piano bar" in a local poll. The original Dueling Pianos pound out high-energy, all-request, rock 'n' roll sing-along fun nightly until 2am. Cover charge; entertainment.

Jim Cullum's Landing (210-223-7266; 123 Losoya St., San Antonio, TX 78205) is the place for exciting nonstop jazz from high noon until the wee hours of the morning. Food, too: the lunch and dinner menus feature Southern-style Cajun dishes.

Rivercenter Comedy Club (210-229-1420; www.sanantonio.citysearch.com Search: Rivercenter Comedy Club; 849 E. Commerce St., San Antonio, TX 78205, fourth level of Rivercenter Mall) features stand-up comedy entertainment at the far end of the River Walk. Optional is the dinner-show package.

The **San Antonio Symphony** (210-554-1010; www.sasymphony.org; 222 E. Houston St., San Antonio, TX 78205) performs in the Majestic Performing Arts Center, also the place to see other concerts and touring Broadway shows.

Sunset Station (see "Historic Sites and Districts") is an entertainment complex consisting of five indoor music venues, and outdoor amphitheater and pavilion, with live music and casual theme restaurants.

SEASONAL EVENTS

This happy party town has so many festivals it's impossible to list them all. Contact the **San Antonio Convention & Visitors Bureau** (210-270-8700, 800-447-3372; www.sanantoniocvb.com; Visitor Information Center, 317 Alamo Plaza, San Antonio, TX 78205) for a full list. Meanwhile, here are the highlights:

JANUARY comes in with a bang with a **Cowboy Breakfast**. More than 35,000 cups of coffee, 15,000 breakfast tacos, and 10,000 sausage biscuits are served up free at Central Park Mall along with live entertainment (210-479-3333).

FEBRUARY brings the excitement of the **San Antonio Stock Show and Rodeo**, with sixteen days of livestock judging, rodeo action, carnival fun, and country-western stars at the Joe and Harry Freeman Coliseum (210-225-5851; www.sar-odeo.com). Also in February San Antonio celebrates the **River Walk Mud Festival,** held in honor of the annual river cleanup, when the Parks and Recreation Department dredges the San Antonio River. Events include an **Arts and Crafts Festival** (210-227-4262).

MARCH heralds the annual **Tejano Music Awards**, such a big and important event for the artists and fans of Tejano music that it's held at the Alamodome (210-222-8862, 300-500-8470; www.tejanomusicawards.com). As for St. Patrick's Day, that brings a full weekend of festivities — even the San Antonio River turns green. It's the Irish who do it, begorra, renaming it "The River Shannon," and there's a show of Irish dancing and music at the Arneson River Theater. The **Alamo Irish Festival** (210-497-8435) is usually held at La Villita Historic District, while the annual **St. Patrick's Day Parade** is on the Saturday prior to the holiday, held along the River Walk (210-227-4262). On a more somber note, the Irish gather at the Alamo for the annual **Wreath Laying Ceremony** to honor the fallen heroes of the Alamo (210-497-8435), many of whom were of Irish ancestry.

In APRIL there's an annual **Starving Artist Art Show** (210-226-3593), with about a thousand artists exhibiting and selling their work to support the Little Church of La Villita's program to aid the less fortunate. Later in the month comes the biggest celebration of the year, **Fiesta San Antonio** — 9 days of parades, carnivals, sporting events, band concerts, art shows, and elegant balls are among the more than 100 events to attend (210-227-5191, 877-SA-FIESTA; www.fiesta-sa.org).

MAY has a number of festivals, too. Among them, the **Tejano Conjunto Festival** is a 6-day celebration of the music born in South Texas, a mixture of Mexican and German. It's celebrated, studied, and performed at the Guadalupe Cultural Arts Center (210-271-3151; www.guadalupeculturalarts.org). The Memorial Day weekend is marked by the annual **Return of the Chili Queens** (210-207-8600) to celebrate chili at Market Square. What began as the concoction of the women who set up their stands in the plazas at night in old San Antonio became known as chili.

JUNE celebrates **Juneteenth,** with observances throughout the city (800-447-3372 for details and schedule), including a Freedom Fair and Freedom Parade, honoring the date in 1865 that Texas slaves received word of the Emancipation Proclamation. The annual **Texas Folklife Festival** is a 4-day celebration of some thirty cultures and ethnic groups whose traditions have shaped Texas. Enjoy ethnic entertainment, food, dances, games, and craft demonstrations at the Institute of Texan Cultures (210-458-2300; www.texancultures.utsa.edu).

One of the festivals in JULY lasts the entire month. The annual **Contemporary Art Month** features dozens of events involving scores of artists, performers, and musicians in a celebration of San Antonio's creative community (210-227-6960). Right at the start of the month, of course, comes the **Fourth of July,** which San Antonio celebrates with festivals, concerts, and fireworks all across the city (800-447-3372 for details and schedule).

AUGUST sees the start of Class 1 Thoroughbred horse racing at the **Thoroughbred Meet,** held all month (and through October 29) at Retama Park Racetrack (210-651-7000; ww.retamapark.com). Also this month, watch the **Canoe Challenge** at the SBC/IBC Plaza (210-227-4262; River Walk Association, 213 Broadway St., San Antonio, TX 78205).

Come SEPTEMBER San Antonio helps our neighbors south of the border celebrate Mexican independence during the annual **Diez y Seis de Septiembre.** The Mexican Consul General's office honor's Mexico's independence with an enactment of "El Grito," the cry by Father Hidalgo on September 16, 1810, that launched Mexico's rebellion against Spain. This is the signal for music and dance all over the city: La Villita, the Arneson River Theater, Market Square, Guadalupe Plaza, and Plaza Mexico at HemisFair Park (210-227-9145; 800-447-3372).

Also in September, the annual **Jazz'SAlive** features jazz bands from New Orleans and San Antonio, sponsored by the San Antonio Parks and Recreation Department at Travis Park downtown (210-207-8480; www.ci.sat.tx.us/sapar).

In OCTOBER, **Oktoberfest in San Antonio** takes place on two successive weekends, bringing authentic German food and drink along with brass bands (210-222-1521). Midmonth see the annual **Cojunto Shootout,** a battle of the bands Cojunto style, free in Market Square (210-207-8000). Also this month are **Halloween and Día de los Muertes** celebrations, held in Market Square to celebrate the American and Mexican holidays (210-207-8600).

The beginning of NOVEMBER sees **Día de los Muertos**, the day of the dead, a celebration of life and remembrance. A tradition of the Mexican Amerindians, families decorate graves and make marigold altars, pan de muerto, candles, and food offerings for the dead (210-434-6711, ext. 240 or 254). In late November Santa Claus arrives by river — the San Antonio River, of course — in a floating procession ushering in the **River Parade and Lighting Ceremony.** Some 70,000 Christmas lights on trees and bridges make a fairyland of the Paseo del Rio (210-227-4262).

Following closely in the beginning of DECEMBER is the **Rivercenter Christmas Pageant.** Traditional Christmas stories are portrayed on river barges and on the entertainment island in the Rivercenter Mall Lagoon (210-225-5000; www.shoprivercenter.com). Thousands of candles illuminate the River Walk in the **Fiesta De Las Luminarias**. In the middle of the month, the San Antonio Preservation Society presents their annual recreation of **Las Posadas**, a 16th-century religious pageant. Citizens, choirs, mariachis, and visitors join in a candlelit procession from La Mansion del Rio to the Arneson River Theater, re-enacting the search for shelter by Mary and Joseph (210-224-6163; www.saconservation.org).

THEATER

R ecorded information about theater and other San Antonio performances is provided by the **City of San Antonio Office of Cultural Affairs** at 210-207-8483 or 800-894-3819 or at their Web site at www.ci.sat.tx.us/DACA.

Alamo Street Restaurant and Theater (210-271-7791; 1150 S. Alamo St., San Antonio, TX 78210) Housed in a building listed on the National Register of Historic Places, the restaurant/theater serves home-style cooking seasoned with Texas playwrights.

Arneson River Theater (210-207-8610, 418 La Villita, San Antonio, TX 78205, on the River Walk) A 1939 WPA project, the theater has an open stage on one side of the river with audience seating on the other side. Drama and dance performances are offered here monthly.

Guadalupe Cultural Arts Center (210-271-9070; www.guadalupeculturalart-sorg; 1300 Guadalupe St., San Antonio, TX 78207) With performances fusing theater, music, and dance, this group has become a pacesetter in the country for Hispanic theater. Original plays are performed in both English and Spanish at the beautifully restored Guadalupe Theater, and many have been produced by Hispanic companies in other cities.

Harlequin Dinner Theater (210-222-9694; 2652 Harney Rd., San Antonio, TX 78234) Dinner here, out on the Fort Sam Houston Military Base, is a somewhat formal affair. Cocktails are served in the lounge, there is a salad bar, and a choice of three or four home-style dinner entrées. The shows are on the light side, usually such enduring musicals, mysteries, and comedies as *Arsenic and Old Lace.*

IMAX Theater Rivercenter (210-225-4629; 849 E. Commerce St., San Antonio, TX 78205, Rivercenter Mall, second level) A good way to get into the spirit of Texas and the Alamo is to take in *Alamo . . . The Price of Freedom,* a 45-minute documentary that's larger than life on the six-story screen, with a six-track stereo sound system. *The Alamo* is always on, but in addition there are other offerings; call for titles and show times. Admission is adults $7.50, seniors $6.75, children 3–11 $4.75.

Magik Children's Theatre of San Antonio (210-227-2751; 420 S. Alamo St.,

San Antonio, TX 78205) A daytime and evening series of professional performances for children.

Majestic Theatre (210-226-5700; www.themajestic.com/theatre.htm; 212 E. Houston St., San Antonio, TX 78205) This refurbished 1928 movie house is an attraction on its own, performances or not. This ornate fantasy of design features the towers and arches of a Moorish palace lining the walls and reaching up to the twinkling stars in the sky, and cherubs with musical instruments perched on the proscenium arch. Call for more information about performances, which include film, dance, Broadway shows, and music.

San Pedro Playhouse (210-733-7258; http://members.tripod.com/~San_Pedro_ Playhouse/index.html; 800 E. Ashby Pl., San Antonio, TX 78205, in San Pedro Park) The San Pedro opened in 1929 as the home of the oldest civic company in San Antonio, the San Antonio Little Theater. The Doric columns supporting the imposing Greek edifice come from an older structure known as Old Market House.

SAN ANTONIO RECREATION

THE ALAMODOME
210-207-3663,
800-884-3663.
www.sanantonio.citysearch.
com Search: Alamodome.
100 Montana St., San
Antonio, TX 78205.

Flexibility is the key to the multipurpose Alamodome, with architectural and design elements combined to provide an ideal setting for expositions, trade shows, annual conventions, sports events, and entertainment venues. Past events include NBA All-Star Games, Big 12 Conference Games, Campbell Soups Champions on Ice, and concerts by such performing artists as KISS, George Strait, and Elton John. The NBA San Antonio Spurs also call the Alamodome home. Phone or visit the Alamodome Web site to see what's on when you're in town.

BICYCLING

For bicycling, boating, and other water sports, and for horseback riding, Brackenridge Park (see "Parks") is the place.

CAMPING

Alamo KOA Kampgrounds (210-224-9296; 602 Gembler Rd., San Antonio, TX 78219) Less than 10 minutes from downtown. Complete facilities for campers, tenters, and trailers in a parklike setting with 400 modern spaces, a pool and spa, supplies, and propane — and on a city bus line to boot.

FAMILY FUN

San Antonio offers plenty of activities for children. In addition to those listed below, see the Magik Children's Theatre and the IMAX Theater Rivercenter (under "Theater") and several of the museums listed in "Museums."

SAN ANTONIO CHILDREN'S MUSEUM
210-212-4453.
www.sakids.org.
305 E. Houston St., San Antonio, TX 78205.
Open: Tues.–Fri. 9am–5pm, Sat. 9am–6pm, Sun. noon–5pm.
Admission: $4.

Hands-on and minds-open are the bywords for this museum. More than eighty exhibits are designed for children ages two to ten.

SAN ANTONIO ZOOLOGICAL GARDENS AND AQUARIUM
210-734-7183/7184.
www.sazoo-ag.org
3903 N. St. Mary's St., San Antonio, TX 78212.
Brackenridge Park.
Open: Labor Day– Mem. Day, 9am–5pm daily; Mem. Day– Labor Day until 6pm.
Admission: Adults $7, seniors & kids 3–11 $5, under 3 free.

Widely acclaimed as an outstanding zoo, here are more than 50 acres tucked away in an abandoned rock quarry on the edge of Brackenridge Park, housing one of the largest collection of animals in the country: 3,400 specimens and 700 species. Particularly special is the African animal group, one of the largest and most varied in the world.

SEA WORLD OF TEXAS
210-523-3611.
www.seaworld.com.
10500 Sea World Dr., San Antonio, TX 78251.
Ellison Dr. and Westover Hills Blvd., off Hwy. 151 16 miles northwest of downtown San Antonio.
Open: Mar.–Oct. (weekends and some days in spring, daily in summer, and weekends in fall). Call 210-523-3611 or see their Web site for latest schedules.
Admission: Adults $32.95 + tax, children 3–11 $22.95 + tax; 10 percent off adult price for seniors.

The world's largest marine adventure park, with more than twenty-five shows, exhibits, and rides. The park has the world's largest zoological population of Pacific white-sided dolphin, including the only two born in captivity.

The park kicked off its tenth season in 1997 with the debut of "the Great White," an inverted (upside-down) roller coaster, still going strong. Now there's the "Steel Eel," a hypercoaster with a 15-story drop and speeds of 70 mph. There are also various water rides, a water park (Lost Lagoon), and the Texas Walk sculpture garden.

SIX FLAGS FIESTA TEXAS
210-697-5050,
800-473-4378.
www.sixflags.com/
sanantonio.
PO Box 690290, San
Antonio, TX 78264.
I-10 W. at La Cantera
Pkwy.
Open: Hours vary. Call for
info.
Admission: Adults, $35.50,
guests under 48 inches

Exciting rides and spectacular shows promise fun for the whole family at this Texas park. The wild new rides here are roller coasters Poltergeist and Boomerang, and the Screamin' Skycoaster, a freefall adventure. The latest addition is Superman Krypton Coaster, billed as "the only floorless coaster in the Southwest."

Tower of the Americas, symbol of the 1968 World's Fair, dominates HemisFair Park.

Eleanor S. Morris

TOWER OF THE AMERICAS
210-207-8616.
www.sanantonio.citysearch
.com Search: Tower of
the Americas.
600 HemisFair Park, San
Antonio, TX 78205.
Open: Observation deck
8am–11pm.
Elevator Fees: Adults $3,
seniors $2, children 4–11
$2.

Ride up the elevator inside this 750-foot tower and, if the wind is strong enough, you can feel the tower sway. At the summit, the Observation Deck presents a windy 360-degree view of all of San Antonio, and the restaurant (see "Restaurants") at the summit is a revolving one.

On the River and Around the City

It's fun to take a leisurely clip-clop drive in a horse-drawn carriage along San Antonio's historic streets. **Lone Star Carriage** (210-533-3977; 302 Iowa St., San Antonio, TX 78210), and **Yellow Rose Carriage** (210-225-6490; 1619 Creekview Dr., San Antonio, TX 78219) provide this mode of seeing the city sights.

A river tour along the Paseo de Rio is offered by **Yanaguana Cruise Inc.** (210-244-5700; www.sanantonio.citysearch.com; 315 E. Commerce St., San Antonio, TX 78205). A 35- to 40-minute narrated historic tour is $5.25 for adults, $1 for children 5 and under.

GOLF

San Antonio has ten municipal and public golf courses — plus more than 300 days of sunshine per year. Call each course for green fees and tee times. A *San Antonio Golfing Guide* is also available (call 800-447-3372 to ask for a copy, or log on to www.sanantonio.wb.com/golf/index.htm).

Brackenridge Park (210-226-5612; 2800 N. Broadway, San Antonio, TX 78209) The oldest 18-hole public course in Texas. "Old Brack" opened in 1916 and in 1922 hosted the first Texas Open. With 6,185 yards, it is still a challenge.

Cedar Creek (210-695-5050; 8250 Vista Colina, San Antonio, TX 78255) In northwest San Antonio, this course is set on the picturesque southern border of the Hill Country with steep elevation changes, several waterfalls, and other challenges.

Fair Oaks Ranch Golf & Country Club (830-981-9604; 7900 Fair Oaks Pkwy., San Antonio, TX 78006) Acreage in the hills, with two 18-hole courses in a beautiful Hill Country country-club atmosphere.

La Cantera Golf Club (210-558-4653; 16641 La Cantera Pkwy., San Antonio, TX 78256) Carved from the walls of a limestone quarry, this course includes a tee shot from atop an 80-foot quarry wall, aiming at Fiesta Texas's famous "Rattler" roller coaster.

Mission del Lago Golf Club (210-627-2522; 1250 Mission Grande Rd., San Antonio, TX 78221) Built at the same time as Cedar Creek, but here the land is flatter and golfers contend with a Texas wind.

Olmos Basin Golf Course (210-826-4041; 7022 McCullough, San Antonio, TX 78216) One of the city's most popular courses, having hosted the men's city championship twenty-seven times.

Pecan Valley Golf Course (210-333-9018, 800-336-3418; 4700 Pecan Valley Dr., San Antonio, TX 78223) Only minutes from downtown, this course was the site of the fiftieth PGA championship in 1968. Rated in *Golf Digest*'s "Top 50 Public Courses."

The Quarry Golf Club (210-824-4500; 444 E. Basse Rd., San Antonio, TX 78209; call for directions) Built on the 85-acre site of the former Alamo Cement

Quarry in northeast San Antonio. Rated "#4 Best Course in Texas" by *Golf Digest* in 1995.

Riverside Golf Course (210-533-8371; 203 McDonald, San Antonio, TX 78210) Right on the land where Teddy Roosevelt trained his Rough Riders. Opened in 1929 as a 9-hole course; 11 more were added in 1961, all par 3s. A full-size 18-hole championship course offers "6,729 yards of fun."

Silverhorn Golf Club of Texas (210-545-5300; 1100 W. Bitters Rd., San Antonio, TX 78216) On a 262-acre tract at Blanco and Bitters in North San Antonio; the city's newest course may be one of its finest, with a classic 7,000-yard layout.

Six driving ranges are also located around the city: **Alamo Country Club** (210-696-4000; 9700 Rochelle Rd., San Antonio, TX 78240) is an 18-holer, with discount pro shop, concessions, and PGA professional instructors. **Blossom Golf Center** (210-494-0002; 13800 Jones Maltsberger Rd., San Antonio, TX 78247) is a practice and teaching center, with a full staff of PGA professionals offering clinics and private instruction; club rental available, plus a snack bar. **Panther Springs Gold Practice Center** (210-492-7888; 16900 Blanco Rd., San Antonio, TX 78232) has a putting and chopping green, club repair, and weekly putting contests. The hitting area of **Polo Field Driving and Practice Range** (210-736-9592; 915 E. Mulberry, San Antonio, TX 78212) accommodates sixty people, with a driving range of 450 yards plus separate putting and chipping greens and a sand trap. **Precision Golf Center** (210-822-9412; 450 Ira Lee Rd., San Antonio, TX 78218) offers PGA instruction, club fitting, private lessons, and clinics. **San Pedro Driving Range and Par 3** (210-349-5113; 6102 San Pedro Ave., San Antonio, TX 78216) has accommodations for fifty people in the hitting area and offers lessons and many junior golf activities.

PARKS

Brackenridge Park (210-736-9534; www.sanantoniocbv.com Search: Things to Do–City Parks; 2800 N. Broadway, San Antonio, TX 78209) In the center of town are some 443 acres of wooded parkland, with a playground and picnic area and the nationally recognized San Antonio Zoo; Japanese tea gardens, with outstanding floral displays and ponds; the Witte Museum; a golf course and polo field; plus a miniature railroad, carousel, skyride, paddleboats, and horse and bike trails.

HemisFair Park/Tower of the Americas (210-207-8610; 200 S. Alamo, San Antonio, TX 78205, bounded by S. Alamo and Durango, next to Convention Center) This city park, with cascading water gardens, children's playground, and museums, is on the site of the 1968 World's Fair and includes the Institute of Texas Cultures and the Mexican Cultural Institute.

Paseo del Rio: The River Walk (210-227-4262; Paseo del Rio Association, 213 Broadway St., San Antonio, TX 78205) It may come as a surprise to learn that the famous Paseo del Rio, the River Walk, is operated as a city park. Nestled 20 feet below street level, the cobblestone and flagstone paths border both sides of the San Antonio River as it winds through the very heart of downtown, the center of the business district. Stretching for about 2.5 miles, from the Municipal Auditorium and Conference Center on the north end to the King William Historic District on the south, most of the walkways, arched bridges, and entrance steps were completed between 1939 and 1941. It remained a park until 1968, when San Antonio hosted the HemisFair World's Fair. Now the banks are lined with restaurants and shops, with a few quiet, parklike stretches in between. The area is partially accessible to the handicapped.

SAN ANTONIO BOTANICAL GARDENS
210-207-3263.
www.sabot.org.
555 Funston Pl., San Antonio, TX 78209.
Open: Mar.–Oct., 9am–6pm daily; Nov.–Feb., 8am–5pm; closed Christmas and New Year's Day.
Admission: Adults $4, seniors $2, children 3–13 $1.

Of the garden's 33 acres, about half are dedicated to native Texas vegetation, where there are three gardens, each devoted to a specific ecological region of Texas: the Edwards Plateau (Hill Country), the east Texas Piney Woods, and the south Texas scrub country. Each garden also features a cabin characteristic of its region: a reconstructed stone house from the Hill Country, a log cabin from the Piney Woods, and an adobe structure typical of the scrub country.

The rest of the acreage is devoted to formal gardens, plus a conservatory complex of five buildings displaying plants from various climatic regions around the world. There is also a small Japanese garden donated and built by residents of Kunamoto (San Antonio's Japanese sister city), and a garden for the blind featuring plants of unusual texture and scent, in elevated beds and with signs in Braille.

HORSE RACING

Horse-racing fans can visit **Retama Park Racetrack** (210-651-7000; www.sanantonio.citysearch.com Search: Retama Park; Retama Pkwy., Schertz, TX 78154), a Class 1 thoroughbred and quarter horse track about 15 minutes north of downtown San Antonio. The track is open summer and fall for live racing; open daily year-round for simulcast racing (210-651-7000, I-35 at Loop 1604; admission: general $2.50; clubhouse $3.50).

TENNIS

An additional tennis court is at **Fair Oaks Ranch Golf & Country Club** (see "Golf").

Fairchild Tennis Center (210-226-6912; 1214 E. Crockett St., San Antonio, TX 78202) A municipal center with fourteen lighted courts. Free.

McFarlin Tennis Center (210-732-1223; 1503 San Pedro Ave., San Antonio, TX 78212) A municipal center with twenty-two outdoor lighted courts at $1.50 per hour per person. After 5pm $2.50 per hour per person.

SAN ANTONIO SHOPPING

Eleanor S. Morris

Mexican arts and crafts at El Mercado, San Antonio's popular marketplace.

Uniquely San Antonio is **Market Square,** often referred to by the locals as El Mercado, Spanish for "market" after the large air-conditioned indoor mall within the square (210-207-8600; 514 W. Commerce St., San Antonio, TX 78207). On the square, historic buildings contain dozens of stores, galleries, and gift and fashion stores, and restaurants. As for El Mercado itself, once you enter it's hard to remember that you're not actually south of the border: here you'll find the largest Mexican market outside Mexico. El Mercado houses more than thirty-two specialty shops of Mexican curios, arts and crafts, glassware, ceramics, leather goods, clothing and accessories (such as serapes and sombreros), toys, gifts, and games.

ANTIQUES

Antiques Downtown Mall (210-224-8845; 515 E. Houston St., San Antonio, TX 78205, around the corner from the Alamo) More than thirty dealers offering estate silver and jewelry, glass, pottery, clocks, coins, books, and other collectibles as well as Texana.

River Square Antique, Collectibles & Gifts (210-224-0900; 514 River Walk, San Antonio, TX 78205) Antique and contemporary fine jewelry, art, porcelain, glass, silver, toy soldiers, and smoking and political collectibles.

CLOTHING AND GIFTS

Angelita I (210-224-8362, 208 N. Presa St., San Antonio, TX 78205) Clothing, silver jewelry, and accessories. The shop is housed in one of the historic homes of La Villita; while shopping, take a look at the original fireplace and 200-year-old beams in the adobe house.

The Heritage Gift Shop (210-225-4629; 849 E. Commerce St., San Antonio, TX 78205, at the IMAX in Rivercenter Mall) Texas gifts and souvenirs, with a large collection of Alamo and Texas history books, maps, prints, historical reproductions; clothing and Southwest and Texas jewelry, too.

We Three (210-229-1164; 518 River Walk, San Antonio, TX 78205, Kangaroo Court Shops) The place for souvenirs like T-shirts, Texas teddies, Texas cookbooks, gourmet Texas salsa, road signs, cards, and gifts; they'll caution you: "Don't forget the 'dillos!"

OUTLETS AND SHOPPING MALLS

North Star Mall (210-340-6627; 7400 San Pedro Ave., San Antonio, TX 78216) San Antonio's largest shopping mall has more than 200 specialty stores, such as Saks Fifth Avenue, Marshall Field's, Abercrombie & Fitch. You can pick up a complimentary shopping bag and coupon booklet for shops in the mall at the information booth, or give them a call.

Rivercenter Mall (210-225-0000, 849 E. Commerce St., San Antonio, TX 78205) The San Antonio River was extended so that an arm of it flows into this horseshoe-shaped three-story mall with a view. More than 110 specialty shops, Foley's and Dillard's department stores, restaurants, and the IMAX and other movie theaters have taken root here.

Shoe Warehouse (210-227-3007; 1223 E. Houston St., San Antonio, TX 78205) More than 10,000 pairs of ladies' and men's brand-name shoes.

BEXAR COUNTY

Leon Springs

This small community of about 500 residents on Interstate 10 west of San Antonio began as a stagecoach stop back in the 1840s, and today San Antonians still enjoy stopping here for great barbecue and a lively dance hall.

LEON SPRINGS DANCE HALL
210-698-7072.
24135 IH-10 W., Leon Springs TX 78257.
Open: Thurs.–Sat. evenings, year-round.

Barely 25 minutes from downtown San Antonio, the Leon Springs Dance Hall has had a colorful history, from stagecoach stop to brothel to popular dance hall. There's a cover charge — from $2 to $6, depending on who's playing — but both local South Texas bands like Jay and Eric and nationally known performers like Asleep at the Wheel make it well worthwhile. If you're in town for a holiday, you might catch the likes of the Labor Day Luau, with hula skirts and whole roasted pig, or the St. Patrick's Day party or the New Year's Eve bash. But the hall is open all year (Thursday through Saturday evenings) and there's always a live band and often specialty shows.

RUDY'S COUNTRY STORE AND BAR-B-Q
210-698-2141.
www.rudysbbq.com.
24152 IH-10, Leon Springs, TX 78257.
Cuisine: Barbecue.
Serving: L, D.
Price: Inexpensive.
Handicap Access: Yes.

"I laid the bricks, designed the pits, the recipes — they're all mine," says Doc Holiday, who has been the owner and operator of Rudy's since 1989. The barbecue sales got so great that the groceries got moved back and back again, he says, and now long picnic tables fill the place both inside and out. You order outside and get your barbecue handed to you on butcher paper, and you'll make your own sandwich. The turkey is what Rudy's is most famous for, but the brisket and the ribs — oh, my.

CHAPTER SIX
Old West and Old Country
HILL COUNTRY WEST AND NORTH OF SAN ANTONIO
BANDERA, COMAL, KENDALL, KERR, MEDINA, REAL, & UVALDE COUNTIES

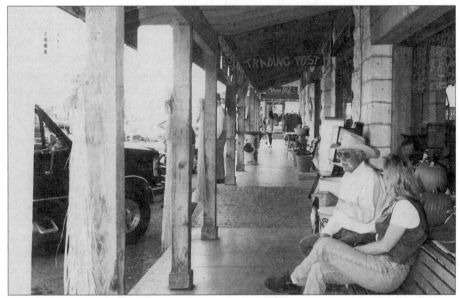

Eleanor S. Morris

View down Main Street of Bandera, the "Cowboy Capital of the World."

Out in the counties west and north of San Antonio, you'll find an interesting mix of cultures. The Old West cowboy atmosphere of Bandera contrasts with European Old Country quaintness in Castroville and Comal County. What doesn't change is the beauty of the Hill Country landscape and the relaxed friendliness of its residents.

BANDERA COUNTY

Bandera, city and county, calls itself "The Cowboy Capital of the World," and with pretty good reason, thanks to the dude and resort ranches (as well as some working ones) concentrated here. It's true horse country, with endless opportunities for horseback riding on supervised trail rides at most dude ranches, and for more independent riding at others. The limestone cliffs towering over the Medina River and the meandering creeks make for spectacular trails. Oaks, walnuts, native cherry, and Uvalde maple grow bounteously among the mesquite and cacti. The Sabinal River, in extreme western Bandera County, also adds to the scenic beauty.

The county was created in 1856 from surrounding Bexar and Uvalde Counties, but nobody is sure how it got the name. In the 1730s there were many Indian battles in what is now called Bandera Pass; a General Bandera was sent to take care of this. The question is: Were Bandera and Bandera Pass named for him, or for the banner (*bandera* is Spanish for "flag") that was raised in 1732 as a reminder of the Spanish/Apache Treaty of that year?

Bandera is the only incorporated town in the county. Tiny Medina calls itself "The Apple Capital of Texas." Tinier Vanderpool's claim to a place on the map is the state natural area of Lost Maples, a surprise in the Hill Country.

For more information about Bandera County, contact the **Bandera Convention and Visitors Bureau,** (830-796-3045, 800-364-3833; www.tourtexas .com/bandera/bandera.html; PO Box 171, Bandera, TX 78003).

Bandera

The town began in 1852 when settlers came to make shingles from the many cypress trees along the river. The town was also the site of a Mormon colony. At last count, Bandera had eleven dude ranches, five motels, seven one- or two-room bed & breakfasts, and nine RV parks, cabins, and campgrounds, in addition to a nice selection of restaurants, shops, and honky-tonks, where Saturday night dances offer popular country-western tunes for Texas two-stepping.

For more information, contact the **Bandera Chamber of Commerce** (830-796-4121; www.banderatexas.com; PO Box 171, Bandera, TX 78003).

BANDERA COUNTY LODGING

Bandera has several motels, such as **Bandera Lodge** (830-796-3191, 800-796-3514; www.texashillcountrymall.com; 1900 Hwy. 16 S., PO Box 2609, Bandera, TX 78003), but most people come here for the dude ranches. Bandera dude ranch prices include either the Full American Plan for meals (breakfast, lunch, and dinner) or the Modified (breakfast and dinner). Price ranges at this writing are listed here, but ask before making reservations in case of change.

BALD EAGLE RANCH
Hosts: Ake and Marcia
    Eriksson.
830-460-3012.
www.baldeagleranch.com.
PO Box 1177, Bandera, TX
    78003.
Off FM 1077, 11 miles west
    of Bandera, next to Hill
    Country State Natural
    Area.
Serving: Full American
    Plan.
Price: Moderate to
    Expensive.
Credit Cards: AE, MC, V.
Handicap Access: No.
Special Features:
    Transportation from San
    Antonio Airport, $180
    round-trip per carload.

The Erikssons are dedicated believers in the Dude Rancher's Association description of a dude ranch: "A unique Western experience in a setting which involves a livestock-oriented way of life and a sincere concern for the visitor's comfort and pleasure." This ranch is serious about riding, beginning with safety. Everyone starts out with a horse orientation session, and children under sixteen are accepted only when the ranch is exclusively reserved by a family or group. These are full-registered quarter horses, available without a set number of trail rides or number of hours in the saddle. The riding arena is always open, and lessons are available at no additional cost.

Other activities include archery, skeet shooting, hiking, bird and wildlife watching, mountain biking, and hay rides. There's a hot tub for soaking after a day in the saddle, and the lodge has a pool table and a variety of card and board games.

**CASAS DE AMIGOS,
    BB&D**
Hosts: J. Pat and Cindy
    Breedlove.
830-460-7479.
446 Live Oak Ridge,
    Bandera, TX 78003.
Price: Moderate.
Credit Cards: No.
Handicap Access: No.

At this BB&D (Bed, Breakfast, and Dinner) you not only get great lodging and breakfast, you also get dinner! You can have breakfast any time, and you might get one of the Breedloves' (they both cook) famous omelets — like one of cream cheese, spinach, and green chilies — served with fresh fruit and homemade bread. As for dinner, J. Pat is great on the grill, with steaks and seafood or chicken cordon bleu or Kiev.

Reservation are required in this hacienda since there are only two guest houses (*casitas*) across the courtyard from the Breedloves' home. But both have living rooms and fully equipped kitchens, Jacuzzis, and sleep four to five people. The courtyard has a cascading fountain, and the rooftop deck, where breakfast is also served, offers spectacular sunset views. All enjoyed with a margarita — "or your choice of beverage," says Cindy. Complimentary beverages await in the fridge, and the cookie jar is always full of homemade cookies

DIXIE DUDE RANCH
Hosts: Clay and Diane
    Conoly.
830-796-4481, 800-375-9255.
www.tourtexas.com/dixie
    duderanch.
PO Box 548, Bandera, TX
    78003.

The Dixie Dude Ranch, a 725-acre working stock ranch breeding longhorn cattle, is the oldest dude ranch in Bandera, dating from 1937. The ranch has nineteen guest rooms in cabins and offers horseback riding, swimming, fishing, and a playground, entertaining families with bonfires,

The Texas
Hill Country:
West and North
of San Antonio

FM 1077 9 miles southwest of Bandera.
Serving: Full American Plan.
Price: Inexpensive.
Credit Cards: AE, D, MC, V.
Handicap Access: Yes.

FLYING L GUEST RANCH
Ranch Manager: John Junker.
830-460-3001, 800-292-5134.
www.flyingl.com.
PO Box 1959, Bandera, TX 78003.
Off Hwy. 173 at Wharton's Dock Rd., 1.5 miles south of Bandera.
Serving: Modified American Plan.
Price: Inexpensive to Moderate.
Credit Cards: AE, D, MC, V.
Handicap Access: Partial.

cookouts, hayrides, rodeos, trick ropers, and other activities. Hike the trails and hunt for fossils and arrowheads, and then come back and chow down on barbecue and fried chicken.

More of a resort than a dude ranch, the Flying L has 542 acres on San Julian Creek, with forty suites, some with fireplaces and Jacuzzis, in twenty-five villas on the property. In addition to the usual dude ranch activities of horseback riding, hayrides, and cookouts, the resort has an 18-hole championship golf course, with some of the villas overlooking the 9th fairway. The course has a driving range and a pro shop. Facilities also include a swimming pool, lighted tennis courts, basketball court, and volleyball. There's a general store, too, and a program of children's activities during holidays, spring break, and summer.

Eleanor S. Morris

Guests at the Mayan Ranch, Bandera, make friends with Norman, the friendly steer.

MAYAN RANCH
Hosts: The Hicks Family.
830-796-3312/460-3036.

Very popular, especially with European visitors, this large dude ranch goes all out, Western-

PO Box 577, Bandera, TX 78003.
0.5 mile from center of Bandera.
Serving: Full American Plan.
Price: Moderate.
Credit Cards: AE, DC, MC, V.
Handicap Access: Yes.

style, for its guests. It's a family affair, with three generations of Hicks making sure that dudes of all ages have a wonderful time. There are sixty-eight guest rooms on this 324-acre spread, some in stone cottages, others in lodges. The Medina River winds around the property, sparkling and cool for swimming, tubing, and fishing. The Hicks family has owned this ranch for more than 40 years, and they put on a real Texas spread: barbecues, steak fries, and cowboy breakfasts cooked on the trail all contribute to a Wild West experience. Trail rides, a Texas-size swimming pool, volleyball, a general store, and saloon are also part of the fun. Children's activities are offered during the summer.

TALLICHET'S SERENDIPITY
Hosts: Jan and Julian Tallichet.
830-460-8343.
PO Box 2069, Bandera, TX 78003.
0.5 mile south of Bandera on Bandera Creek.
Price: Moderate.
Credit Cards: No.
Handicap Access: Yes.

There's a choice here of either a two-room suite consisting of a bedroom with a queen-size bed, a sunroom/library, private bath, and private entry or the "Country Room," furnished with antiques and extra-long twin beds plus a bath with sunken marble tub. The hearty country breakfast is served between 7 am and 10 am. You'll have two of three meats: bacon, ham, or sausage, eggs "any way you want," says Jan, peppy jalapeño cheese grits, hot biscuits, and an assortment of locally made jellies and marmalades.

The hot tub is on a bluff overlooking Bandera Creek, surrounded by shady old oaks, and you can choose either the inn's pond or the Bandera Creek or the Medina River for your fishing, floating, and relaxing.

TWIN ELM GUEST RANCH
Host: Charlsie Browne
830-796-3628, 888-567-3049.
www.twinelm.com.
PO Box 117, Bandera, TX 78003.
On FM 470 off Hwy. 16, 4 miles from downtown Bandera.
Serving: Full American Plan.
Price: Inexpensive.
Credit Cards: AE, MC, V.
Handicap Access: No.

Twin Elm was established in 1939 and, with two hundred beautiful acres on the Medina River, is still going strong. Twenty-one clean rustic rooms, all air-conditioned, are just right for singles, couples, families, and youth groups. Barbecue, country breakfasts with hot biscuits, home-style meals served both indoors and out keep guests fortified for horseback riding, rodeos in the summer, swimming in the pool, or riding the rapids in the Medina River. There are campfires and hayrides, and a game room with TV — but no TV in the guest rooms, or telephone, either, so this is a real getaway.

Vanderpool

TEXAS STAGECOACH INN
Hosts: Karen and David Camp.
830-966-6272, 888-965-6272.
www.bbhost/com/txstage coachinn.
HC 02, Box 166, Vanderpool, TX 78885.
Five miles south of Vanderpool on Hwy. 187.
Price: Moderate.
Credit Cards: None.
Handicap Access: No.

This stately white ranch house with the black shutters and lots of porches stands on the foundations of the original house of 1885. Karen Camp has realized her dream of being the innkeeper of a Texas stagecoach stop where in bygone days horse and wagon drivers tied up at the large iron ring in the massive oak out in front. She and David have remodeled the 6,000-square-foot "mansion" into common rooms, five guest rooms, and a gift shop and gallery (with paintings by David, cowboy turned artist, among the offerings). The two "Christmas" trees in the large common room are always up because they're decorated by season. There are no telephones or television "within reach," says Karen (although, of course, there are phones for emergencies), who encourages guests to take advantage of both contemplating and boating on pretty Sabinal River right down at the bottom of the lawn. (The fishing of bass and catfish is "catch and release.") There's also excellent bird-watching and other nature experiences on these 3 acres along the river, way out in the county, with a lot more to be had at the Lost Maples Natural Area nearby. There's horseback riding nearby at Wagon Wheel Stables in Utopia (Billy Fisher, 830-966-2391, $12 for about a 2-hour ride.)

BANDERA COUNTY RESTAURANTS AND FOOD PURVEYORS

BANDERA ICEHOUSE
830-796-4737.
202 W. Hwy. 16, Bandera, TX 78003.
One block off Main St.
Price: Inexpensive.
Cuisine: Pizza, American.
Serving: B, L, D.
Credit Cards: AE, D, MC, V.
Handicap Access: Yes.

This is the place for quick, light dining, especially if you're hungry, say, at 5am, which is when the Bandera Icehouse opens. The bakery also serves "hot stuff pizza" and fried chicken, as well as made-to-order submarine sandwiches, salads, and ice cream.

BUSBEE'S BAR-B-Q
830-796-3153.
319 Main St., Bandera, TX 78003.
Price: Inexpensive.

This rustic restaurant claims it's the cowboy's choice. They offer delicious barbecued beef, ribs, sausage, ham, and chicken — until they run out. Their specialty salads are delicious, too:

Busbee's Bar-B-Q on Main in Bandera – the cowboys' choice, they claim.

Eleanor S. Morris

Cuisine: Barbecue.
Serving: L, D daily.
Credit Cards: None.
Handicap Access: Yes.

CABARET CAFE & DANCE HALL
830-460-3095.
www.accd.edu/tcmn/
  caberet.htm.
801 Main St., Bandera, TX
  78003.
Price: Moderate.
Cuisine: Fresh Seafood and
  Steaks, Family-style.
Serving: L, D Tues.–Sun.
Credit Cards: AE, MC, V.
Handicap Access: Yes.

HARVEY'S OLD BANK STEAK HOUSE
830-796-8486.
309 Main St., Bandera, TX
  78003.
Price: Moderate.
Cuisine: Steaks, Mexican.
Serving: B, L, D daily.
Credit Cards: AE, D, MC, V.
Handicap Access: Yes.

mesquite-grilled chicken salad, brisket salad, and a combo salad. Draft beer.

Enjoy top regional country-western bands while you dine on steaks, baby back ribs, and other family-style offerings. Desserts include an apple and cranberry cobbler and freshly made puff pastry filled with fruit or cheese fillings. The help is friendly, and the diners are laid back.

The "old bank" was built in 1910 for William J. "Short Bill" Davenport, who operated a private bank until 1920, when with capital of $25,000 it became the First National Bank. In 1921 three bandits tried to blow up the safe with nitroglycerin, but after two explosions alerted citizens armed with shotguns and pistols, the would-be thieves fled empty-handed, only to be caught by a posse in San Antonio. A second robbery in 1932 was more successful — the robbers used an acetylene torch and were never apprehended. The menu makes good use of this history: You can order "Sufficient Funds" appetizers, the "Checking Account" (an 8-ounce sirloin), or the "Simple Interest" (a 10-ounce chopped sirloin). The "First Mortgage" and the "Loan Officer" are chicken dishes, while the "Hot Check" is a pepper steak with spicy jalapeños, cheese, and brown gravy.

O.S.T. RESTAURANT
830-796-3836.
305 Main St., Bandera, TX 78003.
Price: Inexpensive to Moderate.
Cuisine: Mexican, Texan.
Serving: B, L, D.
Credit Cards: D, MC, V.
Handicap Access: Yes.

O.S.T. stands for Old Spanish Trail, which passed through Bandera once upon a time. The restaurant specializes in chicken-fried steak and Mexican dishes like enchiladas in chili as well as down-home food like soup, biscuits, pies, and cakes, all homemade. OST also specializes in "breakfast anytime," and the chuck wagon is ready for the daily buffet.

FOOL MOON CAFE AND COFFEE HOUSE
830-460-8434
204 Main St., Bandera, TX 78003.
Price: Inexpensive.
Cuisine: Southwestern.
Credit Cards: No.
Handicap Access: Yes.

The Southwestern-style food here offers a change from everyone else in town. No chicken-fried steal or barbecue; instead, homemade soup, blue-corn chips, chicken salad, muffins, and carrot cake are on the menu along with espresso, cappucchino, and all the usual favorites offered by a coffeehouse. And you can sit outdoors in the little park alongside if you wish.

FOOD PURVEYORS

The Ice Cream Shoppe (210-796-4925, 306 Main St., Bandera, TX 78003) boasts that it is the best Ice Cream Shoppe, serving Texas's finest, Promised Land Ice Cream, in more than a dozen flavors and in every way: old-fashioned sodas, shakes, floats, malts, cones, banana splits. . .

There's also a gift shop; see "Shopping."

BANDERA COUNTY CULTURE

HISTORIC BUILDINGS AND MUSEUMS

Take a look at the **Bandera County Courthouse** on Main Street between Pecan and Hackberry Streets. The Renaissance Revival structure was built in 1890 of locally quarried limestone with massive cypress trusses; its cupola dominates Bandera's skyline. The bronze monument on the courthouse lawn, dedicated to the champion cowboys of the county, backs up the town's claim as "Cowboy Capital of the World."

Eleanor S. Morris

Discover how the West — and Bandera — were won at the Frontier Times Museum.

FRONTIER TIMES MUSEUM
830-796-3864.
510 Main St., Bandera, TX 78003.
Corner of 13th, one block north of the Bandera County Courthouse.
Hours: Mon.–Sat. 10am–4:30pm, Sun 1–4:30pm.
Admission: Adults $2; under 18 25¢; children under 6 free.

Within the stone walls of the museum you'll find a collection of 33,000 "pieces of history" — everything Bandera considers memorable, from bells and bullets to bottles and branding irons, including a entire room of cowboy lore. Great souvenirs, too. The museum was founded in 1927 by J. Marvin Hunter, who for sixty years collected data and artifacts about Texas (and elsewhere).

LIBRARIES

BANDERA COUNTY LIBRARY
830-796-4213.
515 Main St., Bandera, TX 78003.
Across from the courthouse.
Hours: Mon., Tues., Fri. 8am–5pm; Thurs. 8am–8pm; Sat. 9am–1pm. Closed Wed.

Visitors can obtain temporary check-out privileges for a refundable $20 deposit. The library houses an extensive genealogical research and Texana collection, and there is a paperback book exchange.

NIGHTLIFE

The Blue Cowboys performing in Arkey Blue's Silver Dollar honky-tonk on Main Street, Bandera.

What's a Western cowboy town without a honky-tonk, the whang of a steel guitar, and the wail of a fiddle backing up a forlorn country-western singer? Add a wall full of neon beer signs, a pool table, and the sliding of boots on a sawdust-covered floor and you have pure Texas.

One of the most famous honky-tonks is **Arkey Blue's Silver Dollar Bar** (830-796-8826; www.home.flash.net/~sundanc1/arkeys.htm; 308 Main St., Bandera, TX 78003) where Arkey and the Blue Cowboys set boots to hopping on the sawdust floor. There's a bar, and long tables where you can sip a cool beer in between numbers. So head on down the stairs for some boot-scootin' and listening to Arkey's ballads about cheatin' 'n' heartbreak, fast women, and slow horses.

For more than fifty years the **Cabaret Cafe and Dance Hall** (830-796-8166; www.accd.edu/tcmn/cabaret.htm; 801 Main St., Bandera, TX 78003) has been a big draw, featuring well-known country-western names on weekends like Clay Barker, Johnny Bush, and Kitty Wells when the restaurant/cabaret is open for boot scootin' as well as food, Friday and Saturday until 2am, Thursday, Sunday, and Monday until 11pm (closed Tuesday and Wednesday).

SEASONAL EVENTS

For information on events taking place in Bandera, contact either the **Bandera Chamber of Commerce** (830-796-4121; www.banderatexas.com) or the **Bandera County Convention and Visitors Bureau** (830-796-3045, 800-364-3833; www.tourtexas.com/bandera/bandera/html). Both share the same address: PO Box 171, Bandera, TX 78003.

There are a lot of rodeos here, but it is cowboy country. And there's more, too:

Love's Antique Mall in historic Old Bandera Ranch Store hosts **Market Trade Days** every second weekend of the month.

At the end of **FEBRUARY** the Bandera County Chamber of Commerce puts on an annual **Winter Texas Appreciation Party** for all the Yankees and Canadians who come down to get out of the cold.

There are two rodeos in **MAY**, the **Cowboy Capital Rodeo Association PRCA Rodeo** and the **Cowboy Capital Rodeo**, both toward the end of the month.

In early **JUNE** there's a **Cowboy Capital Chili Cookoff** and three more rodeos, the **County Rodeo** at Twin Elm Guest Ranch, anothe **Cowboy Capital Rodeo** at Mansfield Park, right in Bandera, and the **Oxbow Arena Rodeo** at the Oxbow Arena, all continue on into **JULY** and **AUGUST**.

The Love Creek Orchards Cider Mill & Country Store in Medina, famous for apples.

Eleanor S. Morris

Medina, the "Apple Capital of Texas," hosts the **Texas International Apple Festival** the last Saturday in **JULY**. Love Creek Orchards Cider Mill & Country Store (800-449-0882) on the highway through town stocks everything relating to the apple, even apple trees on dwarfing rootstock suitable for growing in

Texas. There's also a **Fourth of July Pet Parade**, featuring, among others, Best Matched Owner and Pet and Most Talented Pet.

On Labor Day Weekend in SEPTEMBER there's the **All American Cowboy Get-Together** in Mansfield Park, with a chuck wagon cook-off, entertainment and western trade show, among other activities.

OCTOBER brings a **Fall Bar-B-Q** and the **Texas Championship Dutch Oven Cookoff** in Medina.

NOVEMBER celebrates the annual **Hunters Bar-B-Q and Outdoor Expo,** also in Mansfield Park. Call the Bandera Convention and Visitors Bureau (830-796-3055) for information.

The beginning of DECEMBER sees the beginning of a month-long **Cowboy Christmas** in Bandera. Call 830-796-3045 or 800-364-3833 for further information.

BANDERA COUNTY RECREATION

Opportunities for horseback riding are at the ranches described in "Lodging," above. Or contact the **Bandera Convention and Visitors Bureau** at 830-796-3055, or see their Web site: www.tourtexas.com/bandera /bandera 2do.html.

CAMPING

Bandera

Additional camping areas are mentioned under "Parks."

Bandera Beverage Barn and RV Park (830-796-8153; 1503 W. Main St., PO Box 435, Bandera, TX 78003) 5.5 acres on the Medina River; facilities include tent camping, 40 full RV hookups, a full-line convenience store, rest rooms, picnic tables, fishing, and tubing.

Skyline Ranch RV Park (830-796-4958; Hwy. 16, 1.5 miles west of Bandera, PO Box 1990, Bandera, TX 78003) Spacious pull-thru sites and full hookups are

---

On and In the Water

Medina Lake in the southeast corner of the county, created by a dam completed in 1913, is a major reservoir with 254,000 acre-feet storage capacity. The lake is popular for boating, swimming, water skiing, and fishing.

The Medina River is considered one of the most scenic and exciting rivers in Texas. Tubes, canoes, and kayaks can be rented at **Fred Collin's Workshop** (830-796-3553; Hwy. 16 N., Bandera, TX 78003) is half a mile north of Bandera. **Medina Kayaks and River Ranch** (830-589-7215; 761 Haley Ln., Medina, TX 78055; see "Camping — Medina") also rents kayaks.

provided here on 60 acres adjoining the Medina River. There's also a rec hall with full kitchen, showers and rest rooms, laundry facilities, pitch-putt green and shuffleboard, and free cable TV. Pets on leashes are welcome.

Medina

Medina Kayaks and River Ranch (830-589-7215; www.tourtexas.com/bandera/bandera2stay.htm/#camp; 761 Haley Ln., Medina, TX 78055). Private and primitive tent sites, kayak rental. For day use: swimming and picnicking along ½ mile of Medina River frontage. Tent sites are scattered among various species of shade trees and natural vegetation, affording privacy. Campers will also find a canoe awaiting their use.

FISHING

Medina Lake, Medina River, and the Sabinal River are good for fishing. Medina Lake is full of crappie, white bass, and black bass, and it's also the best place to catch huge yellow catfish. The waters of the Medina River, with its canopy of towering cypress trees, provides good fishing for spotted bass, Guadalupe bass, largemouth bass, perch, and catfish. (See "Parks" below for more fishing opportunities.)

GOLF

The Flying L Guest Ranch (800-646-5407; see "Lodging") and **Lost Valley Resort Ranch** (830-460-7958, 800-378-8681; www.golfsatx.com/courses/Lost_Valley_Resort_Ranch) have 18-hole courses open to the public. Both have fully stocked pro shops and offer both individual and group lessons.

PARKS

Bandera County Park (Park Rd. 37 and Medina Lake) The park is open 7 days a week, 8am –10pm. The only public boat ramp on the lake is here, and use of the ramp is free. Amenities include rest rooms, picnic tables, and barbecue pits. Fee: $4 per day per vehicle.

Hill Country State Natural Area (830-796-4413, camping reservations 512-389-8900; www.tpwd.state.tx.us/park/parks.htm; RR 1 Box 601, Bandera, TX 78003, FM 1077, 12 miles from Hwy. 173 intersection) Opened in 1984 primarily for equestrian use, this 5,400-acre park is also popular with hikers, backpackers, and all-terrain bicyclists who enjoy 36 miles of trails, 23 of those miles designated multiuse. Facilities include walk-in tent sites, backpacking camping areas, and fishing and swimming on a spring-fed creek. Mar. 1–Oct. 31, open daily; Nov. 1–Feb. 28, Fri. noon–Sun. 10pm.

Lost Maples State Natural Area (830-966-3413, reservations for camping 512-389-8900; HCR1, Box 156, Vanderpool, TX 78885, 5 miles north of Vanderpool on RR 187) Bigtooth maples, hidden deep in a remote Hill Country canyon, display fall colors that rival any in New England. What are they doing here in a land that has no such flora anywhere else in the big state of Texas? Evidently they are left from a much earlier age, the Pleistocene Ice Age, when the county was much wetter and cooler. Somehow they have survived, protected from high summer temperatures and dry winds by the high canyon walls along the Sabinal River. People come from miles around to marvel at the blaze of red, yellow, and orange in a sea of green Texas live oak. The 2,174-acre park, open all year, has other attractions: steep limestone canyons, nature trails, clear streams, and bubbling springs. Both campsites with water and electricity are available, as are primitive camping areas. At the Interpretive Center exhibits tell about local natural history, and bird-watching is especially rewarding here in the springtime.

Mansfield Park (830-796-3168; PO Box 877, Bandera, TX 78003) is 3 miles from Bandera on Hwy 16 N. The park has thirty RV campsites, water, electricity, dump station, public rest rooms, hot showers, indoor recreaation area, two softball fields, picnic tables, charcoal grills, shady tent sites, and — since this *is* the "Cowboy Capital of the World" — even a rodeo arena.

TENNIS

Tennis courts are at the **Flying L Guest Ranch** and the **Mayan Ranch** (see "Lodging").

BANDERA COUNTY SHOPPING

Folks mostly come to Bandera to enjoy the Old West ranching and cowboy atmosphere, so shopping is not on the fancy side. Here are a few shops, however, if you can't resist:

American Indian Jewelry (830-796-4000; 311-B Main St., Bandera, TX 78003) A large selection of original jewelry designs from the Navajo, Zuni, Hopi, Pawnee, Sioux, and Cherokee tribes, in silver, turquoise, and onyx. Earrings, bolo ties, necklaces, pendants, bracelets, and rings; dreamcatchers, too.

Country Accents (830-535-4979; 8312 Hwy. 16 S., Bandera, TX 78003, bet. Bandera and Pipe Creek) The place for American antiques, furniture, glassware, stoneware, primitives, and quilts; they specialize in Blue Willow china.

Gingerbread House (830-796-3616; 1110 Cedar St., Bandera, TX 78003) Antiques, original craft items, stuffed animal toys, jewelry, homemade candies, stained glass, floral items, beautiful dolls, and T-shirts, all here in abundance.

Fred Collin's Workshop (830-796-3553; Box 1869 Hwy. 16 N., Bandera, TX 78003, 0.5 mile north of Bandera) This fascinating shop features woodcrafting, Western-style, designing and creating rustic furniture to customer specification. Based on your ideas, photographs, or sketches, the workshop supplies the wood, creates the design, and will either complete the project or leave it in any stage of completion for you to finish. Dining tables, benches, fireplace mantels, entertainment centers, freestanding bars, porch swings — just about anything that can be made of wood.

Love's Antique Mall (830-796-3838; 310 Main St., Bandera, TX 78003) in the historic Bandera Ranch Store, not only has antiques, several folks have set up shop there to make furniture. Made out of cedar and old barn wood, this is a growing industry in Bandera.

Old West Imports (830-796-7386; 206 Main St., Bandera, TX 78003) Right on the corner of Main and Hwy. 16, you'll find a great assortment of both Mexican and Indian art. Pottery, rocks, jewelry, serapes, Guadalajara glassware, Mayan figures, and even fountains for indoors and out.

COMAL COUNTY

In the early 1840s, the fledgling Texas government resolved to counter underpopulation in the Hill Country through the *empresario* system, borrowed from the previous Spanish and Mexican governments. Through this arrangement, German-born Henry Fisher had acquired a huge land grant northwest of Austin. Sam Houston, president of the Republic of Texas, commissioned him to represent the republic to the German states of the Rhine, which put Fisher in touch with a group headed by Prince Carl of Solms-Braunfels. This was the Adelsverein, the Society for the Protection of German Immigrants to Texas. The organization proposed to sponsor emigration to Texas and encourage the Germans, once in Texas, to stay together.

Meanwhile, Fisher had discovered that his piece of land was still held by the Comanche. In 1844 he convinced the unsuspecting Prince Carl to buy his 4 million acres, collecting the princely sum of $9,000, his sales pitch being that the land was accessible, fertile, and perfectly suited for coastal commerce — never mind that it was teeming with hostile Comanches.

The first contingent of immigrants was to arrive that December; Prince Carl sailed ahead to the new land to prepare for them. Once there, he learned all too quickly how he had been taken advantage of. But with his immigrants on the way there was nothing to be done but to find another, safer site. He looked to the south of Fisher's land and, 50 miles southeast of Austin, he found 9,000 acres on the Guadalupe River at the foot of the Balcones Escarpment. There, before sailing for home he laid out the town, which he naturally named New Braunfels.

Quiet the rest of the year, New Braunfel's plaza comes alive for November's Wurstfest.

New Braunfels

New Braunfels was established in 1845 on the Comal River, the shortest river in the U.S. It rises from a cluster of springs in the northwest part of town and remains entirely within the city limits until it spills into the much longer Guadalupe River flowing south below Canyon Dam. New Braunfels became the county seat in 1846, and it has grown into a bustling, thriving town with much of historic interest; here you can dine in biergartens and dance to oom-pah music to your heart's content.

Gruene

On the north edge of town is the historic village of Gruene (pronounced "green"), now part of New Braunfels. Gruene began in the 1850s as a German village. Many of the historic buildings there have been restored (though some are still in ruins). You'll find old homes and stores, an inn, a restaurant in an old mill, and, best of all, Gruene Hall, claimed to be the oldest dance hall in Texas (see "Nightlife") and still going strong.

COMAL COUNTY LODGING

Comal County lodging centers around New Braunfels, where the **Greater New Braunfels Chamber of Commerce** (830-625-2385, 800-572-2626; www.nbcham.org; 390 S. Seguin St., PO Box 311417, New Braunfels, TX 78131) maintains a list of additional bed & breakfast establishments, resorts, condominiums, cabins, campgrounds, and motels.

The lobby of the historic Faust Hotel, with a 1929 Model-T Ford.

Eleanor S. Morris

FAUST HOTEL
Managers: Bob and Judy
  Abbey.
830-625-7791.
www.fausthotel.com.
240 S. Seguin St., New
  Braunfels, TX 78130.
Price: Moderate to
  Expensive.
Credit Cards: AE, CB, D,
  DC, MC, V.
Handicap Access: Yes.

The Faust Hotel opened in 1929 (just before the Crash), and it has been restored in the spirit of its times. The spacious lobby sports a bright yellow 1929 Model-T Ford in addition to pillars and posts and wainscoting as a backdrop for the antique sofas and chairs and Oriental rugs. The hotel supposedly has a ghost, that of Walter Faust, original hotel owner, who would be proud of the full-service dining facilities and other amenities. There's even a microbrewery now, producing handcrafted beers.

GRUENE MANSION INN
Hosts: Sharon and Bill
  McCaskill.
830-629-2641.
www.gruene.net/gruene
  mansion.
1275 Gruene Rd., New
  Braunfels, TX 78130.
Price: Expensive.
Credit Cards: No.
Handicap Access: One
  room.

Here's another historic place to spend the night right on the banks of the Guadalupe River. On the National Register of Historic Places, the inn is located in the Historic District on the northern edge of New Braunfels's city limits. The McCaskills treasure the history of the mansion and carry on the tradition of *gemütlich* ("easy-going") begun by Henry Gruene back in the mid 1800s. The cottages along the Guadalupe River have little porches that overhang the riverbank, each furnished with antiques and handmade quilts. The Sunday Haus contains eight rooms decorated in rustic Victoriana: king-size beds, fireplaces, old Victorian bathtubs, and yet more antiques. The inn has a restaurant overlooking the Guadalupe River (see "Restaurants").

THE LAMB'S REST INN
Hosts: George and Judy
  Rothell.

This delightfully restful inn on the Guadalupe River has five guest rooms, one of them a two-room suite. All have private baths and sitting area,

830-609-3932, 888-609-3932.
www.bbhost.com:8008/
  lambsrestbb.
1285 Edwards Blvd., New
  Braunfels, TX 78130.
Price: Moderate to
  Expensive.
Credit Cards: D, MC, V.
Handicap Access: No.

and two also have a Jacuzzi. Sit on the porch or a deck, and listen to the river as it cascades over those Hill Country rocks. Then maybe take a dip either in the clear cool river or the inn's pool.

Breakfast is Judy's delight, beginning perhaps with poached pears in raspberry sauce and topped with almond whipped cream, followed by French toast and homemade sausage, cinnamon-walnut bread, and perhaps a piña colada frappe. And in the afternoon enjoy refreshments reminiscent of high tea.

PRINCE SOLMS INN
Hosts: Bob and Pat Brent.
830-625-9169, 800-625-9169.
www.princesoemsinn.com.
295 E. San Antonio St.
New Braunfels, TX 78130.
Price: Moderate to
  Expensive.
Credit Cards: AE, D, MC, V.
Handicap Access: No.

This famous Texas landmark has been in continuous operation as an inn since it was built in 1898 by immigrant German craftsmen. The eight guest rooms and two suites all have private baths, and all are furnished with lovely antiques. A separate one-bedroom cottage just behind the inn is ideal for honeymooners. The entry doors are 10 feet high, the ceilings are 14 feet high, and there's a courtyard in the rear.

Breakfast will be filling, whether it's quiche, banana pancakes, or scrambled eggs, all always served with either sausage or bacon, homemade breads and banana butter, and English muffins, toast, or bagels. At this writing the fine restaurant in the cellar, Wolfgang's Keller, is closed temporarily, but plans are in progress to reopen it soon.

MOTELS

Among others, New Braunfels has a **Days Inn** (830-608-0004, 800-329-7466; 963 IH-35 N., New Braunfels, TX 78130); a **Holiday Inn** (830-625-8017, 800-465-4329; www.nbtexas.com/holidayinn; 1051 IH-35 E., New Braunfels, TX 78130); the newly renovated **Hill Country Motor Inn** (830-625-7373, 800-982-3609; 210 Hwy. 81 E., New Braunfels, TX 78130); and a **Rodeway Inn** (830-629-6991, 800-967-1168; 1209 IH-35 E., New Braunfels, TX 78130).

COMAL COUNTY RESTAURANTS AND FOOD PURVEYORS

You'd expect — and correctly — to find such culinary specialties as German sausage and German pastry here. Several smokehouses provide such tasty meals; two of them are described below. New Braunfels also has several sophisticated eating spots that are a departure from more traditional fare.

JOHNNY CARINO'S COUNTRY ITALIAN
830-609-1141.
1304 E. Common St.
Price: Moderate.
Cuisine: Country Italian.
Serving: L, D.
Credit Cards: All major.
Handicap Access: Yes.

You almost feel like you're in the countryside of Italy here, what with the open kitchen across the rear of the restaurant, an a open roaring fire (and the delicious dishes that the chef keeps placing on the opening, waiting to be picked up and served), the scarred wooden tables, the dessert trays resting on barrels, the woven baskets hung high on the walls. And there are even little enclosures with tables for two or four in front of lace-curtained "windows."

Specialties are the twelve-layer lasagna, the spicy Roma chicken, and the innovative Italian Nachos: fried pasta chips layered with sausage or chicken, pepperocini peppers, black olives, diced Roma tomatoes, jalapeños, and topped with mozzarella and Parmesan cheeses. And what a plateful, as are all the dishes! "Our patrons are always taking home leftovers," confides the waitperson.

The dining room of the Gristmill Restaurant on the Guadalupe River.

Eleanor S. Morris

GRISTMILL RESTAURANT AND BAR
830-625-0684.
1287 Gruene Rd., New Braunfels, TX 78130.
Price: Inexpensive.
Cuisine: Seafood, Steaks, American.
Serving: L, D.
Credit Cards: AE, D, MC, V.
Handicap Access: Yes.

H. D. Gruene built this mill back in the 1800s to serve the cotton community. The setting, back behind Texas's oldest dance hall (see "Nightlife") and beneath Gruene's water tower, makes for an unusual place to dine. Although there are tables in front beyond the open double doors, try for a table out back overlooking the Guadalupe River or in the pleasant room to the right, with an enclosed view of the river.

Veggie lovers will appreciate the typical "Try These!" menu that includes fresh steamed broccoli, cauliflower, carrots, and green beans. But it's the tortilla soup, the chicken Caesar salad, the pork loin sandwich, the Guadalupe chopped steak, the bronze catfish — and the Jack Daniel's pecan pie, made with chocolate chips and a trace of whiskey — that make folks flock to the Gristmill. Often — especially on weekends — there's a wait, but sitting outdoors under the trees is hardly a hardship.

HUISACHE GRILL
830-620-9001.
www.huisache.com.
303-D W. San Antonio St.,
New Braunfels, TX 78130.
Price: Inexpensive.
Cuisine: New American,
Southwest.
Serving: L, D daily.
Credit Cards: AE, D, DC,
MC, V.
Handicap Access: Yes.

The address notwithstanding, 303 W. San Antonio fronting the street is a deserted storefront, and we had to look way back behind the building to spy this restaurant, which served as a storage shed in the 1930s. But it's well worth the hunt, with innovative dishes like salmon niçoise, grilled spinach with lime garlic butter, Yucatán chicken, pecan-crusted ruby red trout, and grilled mahi mahi, among others.

The restaurant is named for that scrubby tree (pronounced "wee-satch-ee") covering the Hill Country and on down into northern Mexico. Restaurateurs Lynn and Don Forres chose the name because they feel that the native vegetation "provides a thread between the many cultures of our rich regional heritage, just as our cuisine reflects varied influences." That it does — and deliciously, too.

**NEW BRAUNFELS
   SMOKEHOUSE**
830-625-2416.
www.nbsmokehouse.com.
146 Hwy. 46 S., New
   Braunfels, TX 78130.
Corner of Hwy. 46 and U.S.
   81.
Price: Inexpensive.
Cuisine: German, Smoked
   Meats.
Serving: B, L, D.
Credit Cards: AE, D, MC, V.
Handicap Access: Yes.

This family-owned smokehouse is a 50-year-old Central Texas tradition, with delicious meats custom smoked by Rocky Tays according to old German family recipes — with a touch of Mexican influence. Try the special turkey or sausage gumbo with corn bread and coleslaw for a satisfying lunch, or order a dinner plate of baby back ribs, beef brisket, and bratwurst served with German potato salad, pinto beans, and a tossed salad.

OMA'S HAUS
830-625-3280.
541 Hwy. 46 S, PO Box
   310667, New Braunfels,
   TX 78130.
Price: Inexpensive.
Cuisine: German,
   American.
Serving: L, D.
Credit Cards: AE, D, DC,
   MC, V.
Handicap Access: Yes.

Oma is German for "grandma," and the cozy family atmosphere here is planned to be like grandmother's house. The long, low wooden building off the highway has delicious German dishes like jaeger schnitzel and strudel — especially the peach strudel, a departure from the usual apple, and, of all things, a chocolate strudel!

THE RESTAURANT AT GRUENE MANSION INN
830-620-0760.
www.gruene.net/gruene
mansion/food.htm.
1275 Gruene Rd., New
Braunfels, TX 78130.
Price: Moderate.
Cuisine: New American,
Southwest.
Serving: L, D daily.
Credit Cards: AE, D, DC,
MC, V.
Handicap Access: Yes.

Set back under the trees all the way to the Guadalupe River, the restaurant offers dinner and cocktails on the large deck overlooking the river or in a large indoor room with high rafters and colorful paintings adorning the walls.

While Chef Camilo Chavez specializes in steaks and seafood, the menu offers other favorites from schnitzel to the ubiquitous chicken-fried steak. Everything is served with homemade bread and garlic butter, and the wine list encompasses 150 choices.

RUDY'S COUNTRY STORE AND BAR-B-Q
830-609-3337.
www.rudysbbq.com
936 Loop 337, New
Braunfels, TX 78130.
Price: Inexpensive.
Cuisine: Barbecue.
Serving: B, L, D.
Credit Cards: All major.
Handicap Access: Yes.

The Worst BBQ in Texas" is how Rudy's describes its food. Actually, Rudy's is a meat market (sold by the pound) that sells cooked meat either to take home or eat on the spot. The barbecue comes out of the pit, is cut in front of you, and served fresh to your order on white butcher paper, accompanied by slices of fresh bread. There's brisket, turkey breast, pork loin, prime rib, chopped beef, sausage, and pork spare ribs.

Along with the meat you can order side dishes like corn — creamed or on the cob — potato salad, coleslaw, pinto beans, green bean salad, new potatoes, and jumbo smoked potatoes.

COMAL COUNTY FOOD PURVEYORS

Naegelin's Bakery (830-625-5722, 129 S. Seguin St., New Braunfels, TX 78130) The oldest bakery in Texas, baking German, French, and Danish breads and pastries since 1868. Indoors, around the corner from the bakery case crammed with temptation, is a small area with tables and chairs to consume the fresh strudel, bear claws, and pull-aparts on the spot.

New Braunfels Coffee (830-608-9041, 489 Main Plaza, New Braunfels, TX 78130) Sandwiches, ice cream, yogurt, and pastries along with your cup of cappucchino.

Rudy's Country Store and Bar-B-Q (see "Restaurants")

COMAL COUNTY CULTURE

ARCHITECTURE

New Braunfels has fine examples of German *fachwerk* ("framework") construction, adapted to native Texas cedar and limestone, throughout the town. This framework consists of heavy squared timbers with the spaces between the wood filled in with stone and brick. The entire surface is then plastered over.

HISTORIC BUILDINGS

Four of New Braunfel's historic buildings are listed on the National Register of Historic Places. The old **Plaza Hotel** on Main Plaza, built in 1851, is touted as the first hotel in Texas to have running water piped in. Others are the **Stephen Klein** house, built in 1846 (131 S. Seguin St.), and the **First Protestant Church**, established in 1845 (296 S. Seguin St.).

MUSEUMS

BAETGE HOUSE
830-629-2943.
1300 Church Hill Dr., New Braunfels, TX 78130.
Open: Tues.–Fri. 10am–2:30pm, Sat. and Sun. 2–5pm.
Admission: Adults $2, children 6–18 50¢, under 6 free.

This two-story house built in 1852 is a good example of the German *fachwerk* construction then prevalent in New Braunfels. On the second floor you can inspect the construction technique; on the first floor, admire the antique furnishings, which predate 1860.

CHILDREN'S MUSEUM
830-620-0939, 888-928-8326.
www.nbtexas.com/child.
651 N. Business IH-35, #53, New Braunfels, TX 78130.
Located in the New Braunfels Marketplace.
Open Mon.–Sat. 9am–5pm; Sun. 12–5pm.
Admission: Children and adults $3, seniors $2, free under one year.

Five thousand square feet of interactive exhibits, including such favorites as Grandma's Attic; Guadalupe River Wet and Wild, Texas; Schlitterbahn Soft Sculptures; and Dress Up. Explorations in science, art, culture, history, and music to experience, create, imagine, and discover. There's also a gift shop and party area.

HUMMEL MUSEUM
830-625-5636, 800-456-4866.
199 Main Plaza, PO Box

On display are more than three hundred original drawings and paintings of the famous figurines of artist Sister M. I. Hummel. Occasionally

Three-foot-tall Hummel figures in the Hummel Museum.

Eleanor S. Morris

311100, New Braunfels, TX 78130.
Open: Mon.–Sat. 10am–5pm, Sun. noon–5pm.
Admission: Adults $5, seniors $4.50, children up to 18 $3.

MUSEUM OF TEXAS HANDMADE FURNITURE
830-629-6504.
1370 Church Hill Dr., New Braunfels, TX 78130.
Open: Feb. through Nov., Tues.–Sun. 1–4pm; closed Easter and Thanksgiving.
Admission: Adults $5, children 6–12 $1, under 6 free.

SOPHIENBURG MUSEUM
830-629-1572.
www.nbtexas.com/ shophienburg.
401 W. Coll St., New Braunfels, TX 78130.

artisans from the porcelain factory in Germany are on hand to demonstrate the art. There is a gift shop on the premises, with figurines, plates, and calendars for sale.

The historic Andreas Breustedt home is the perfect setting for this collection of handmade furniture — beds, tables, chairs, armoires — crafted during the 1800s. English ironstone and other artifacts from the 1700s are also on display. The one-room log cabin on the property features more furnishings and the tools used to make them.

The museum is on a small hill amid parklike grounds; it's the site where Prince Carl Solms-Braunfels built a log fortress to serve as administrative headquarters for his colony. You'll find many of his personal effects, a model of his castle

Open: Mon.–Sat. 10am–5pm, Sun. 1–5pm. Admission: Adults $5, students free.

back in Braunfels, much historical genealogical information, as well as pioneer items from the colonists' households. There are Indian artifacts as well.

NIGHTLIFE

The **Watering Hole** (830-625-0045; 1390 McQueeney Rd., New Braunfels, TX 78130) is the place for ice-cold beer, after-dinner cocktails, and a night of dancing in air-conditioned comfort. State-of-the-art lighting brightens up the dance hall, where there's dancing to DJ music Thursday, Friday, and Saturday nights, with karaoke on Wednesday evenings.

Take a look at the bar, made with a chainsaw by wood-carver Terry Boguist. He's captured the spirit of New Braunfels with not only cowboys and long-horns, but also tubers floating down the Guadalupe.

Gruene Hall (830-606-1281; 1281 Gruene Rd., New Braunfels, TX 78130) Considered the oldest dance hall in Texas and virtually untouched since 1878, the hall has a large open-air dance floor festooned from the rafters with old advertisements, a huge outdoor garden, and even a wood-burning stove for cold evenings.

This dance hall is featured on the cover of George Strait's first album — he worked as a ticket taker at the hall. And Lyle Lovett launched his career here. The music includes the best in contemporary country, blues, and folk, and "bellying up to the bar" makes you feel like the real thing.

SEASONAL EVENTS

For additional information about events in New Braunfels, contact the Greater New Braunfels Chamber of Commerce (830-625-23895, 800-572-2626; www.newbraunfelschamber.com; 390 S. Seguin St., PO Box 311417, New Braunfels, TX 78131).

Old Gruene Market Days (830-629-6441) take place the third Saturday and Sunday of each month, with more than a hundred vendors featuring craft items (830-629-6441).

MARCH sees **Downtown Alive – Art in New Braunfels** (830-629-8022).

Come APRIL the 2-day annual **Folkfest** celebrates New Braunfels heritage and culture on the grounds of Conservation Plaza and the Texas Museum of Handmade Furniture, with food, furniture-making, demonstrations of old-style crafts, and tours of historic buildings (830-629-6504).

MAY brings more than a hundred artists and craftsmen together for the **New Braunfels Arts League Arts and Crafts Show**, a 2-day event held at the New Braunfels Civic Center (830-629-5959). Another show in July, the Summer Showcase of Arts is at the same venue.

JUNE sees the 2-day **Summer Juried Art Show** at the Hummel Museum & Art Gallery (830-625-5636).

In JULY take in the **Fourth of July Parade.** Enjoy the second 2-day arts and crafts show put on at the New Braunfels Civic Center, the **Summer Showcase of Arts & Crafts.**

SEPTEMBER brings the **Comal County Fair,** one of Texas's oldest and largest fairs, at the fairgrounds (830-625-1505).

In OCTOBER there's the annual **Moving Waters Pow Wow** at Canyon Lake, featuring arts, crafts, intertribal competition dancing, food, and storytelling (830-964-3613).

NOVEMBER is the month for the famous **Wurstfest**, a sausage festival where phenomenal quantities of sausage and beer are consumed each year on the banks of the Comal River. Walk off some of what you've eaten in the 10K walk, and then take in the arts and crafts sale. November also begins **Festtage in New Braunfels,** a half-month-long celebration to showcase New Braunfels as a major holiday mecca for visitors, with something going on every week. For information, contact chamber of commerce, 830-625-2385, 800-572-2626; PO Box 311417, New Braunfels TX 78131.

COMAL COUNTY RECREATION

Much of Comal County's recreation is based on and around the lakes, rivers, and springs; see "On, In, and Along the Water" below for camping, fishing, hiking, swimming, and various water sports.

FAMILY FUN

Children's Museum (see "Museums").

Landa Park Miniature Train (830-625-8285; 2107 Northcrest Dr., New Braunfels, TX 78130) For a mere $1.75 per person you can chug around the park's 196 acres, enjoying both the breeze and the view (summer 10am–8pm).

Natural Bridge Caverns (830-651-6101; www.tourtexas.com/caverns; 26495 Natural Bridge Caverns Rd./FM 3009, Natural Bridge Caverns, TX 78266) The caverns are named for a 60-foot natural limestone bridge that spans the entrance. The caverns were found in 1960 by students from St. Mary's University in San Antonio. The cave's sinkhole, with a tiny passage, had been known for a hundred years, but the students crawled down the 11-inch spiral into what many consider one of the great show caves of the world. In addition to wonderful stalagmites and stalactites and other formations, various minerals create colors compared to melting rainbow sherbet. Open daily at 9am except Thanksgiving, Christmas, and New Year's Day; last tour 6pm. Admission: 13 and over $12, children 4–12 $7, seniors 65 and over $10.

On, In, and Along the Water

Rafting on the Guadalupe River is a popular sport at the Gruene River Crossing.

Eleanor S. Morris

Canyon Lake, about 30 minutes north of town on Hwy. 306, boasts 80 miles of scenic shoreline bordering deep blue water. Seven public parks with picnic areas, swimming beaches, and boat launches are around the lake. Camping, fishing, hiking, cycling, and boating are activities enjoyed here almost year-round. For more information, contact the Canyon Lake Chamber of Commerce, 830-964-2223.

Whitewater Sports (830-964-3800; 11860 FM 306, HC3/Box 22, New Braunfels, TX 78130) offers campgrounds, canoes, rafts and shelter, kayaks, and fishing, all under one facility close to Canyon Lake, where most of those activities take place.

Landa Park is the spot where Comal Springs bubble out of the ground to fill the giant pool with clear, fresh water. There's an Olympic-size pool, too, in the 196 acres right in downtown New Braunfels. The springs were discovered in 9000 B.C. — that's when Native Americans found it, along with roaming buffalo, bears, and panthers. The park has picnic areas, a miniature train (see "Family Fun"), paddleboat and tube rentals, glass-bottom boat tours (830-608-2163), and a golf course (see "Golf"). Hikers enjoy the park's nature trail. The arboretum walking tour has more than ninety-six species of trees.

Prince Solms Park is east of Landa Park, along the Comal River. The tube chute here is popular as a launch pad to a relaxing float down the river.

Rafting the **Guadalupe River** from Canyon Lake through New Braunfels is very popular. There are falls with names like Devil's Playground Rapid, the Chute, and Slumber Falls; your river outfitter can advise you of their varying degrees of difficulty. Outfitters include **Jerry's Rentals** (830-625-2036; 4970 River Rd., New Braunfels, TX 78132), **Roy's Rentals** (830-964-3721; 6350 River Rd., New Braunfels, TX 78130), **Rockin R River Rides** (830-629-9999, 800-55-FLOAT; www.rockinr.com; 1405 Gruene Rd., New Braunfels, TX 78130); **Rio Raft Co.** (830-964-3613; PO Box 2030, New Braunfels, TX 78130), and **Gruene River Raft Co.** (830-625-2800; www.gruene.net/riverraftco; 1404 Gruene Rd., New Braunfels, TX 78130).

A scenic route to drive is FM 306 from New Braunfels to Satler along the Guadalupe River. Another exceptionally beautiful route is along the "Devil's Backbone" on FM 32, northwest of Canyon Reservoir.

Tube

Natural Bridge Wildlife Ranch (830-438-7400; www.nbwildliferanchtx.com; 26515 Natural Bridge Caverns Rd./FM 3009, Natural Bridge Caverns, TX 78266) Take an African safari on two hundred acres of Texas Hill Country to see 500 animals, including giraffes, wallabies, rhinoceros, and zebras. Some of the exotic animals are pretty tame — the African ostrich, the yak, and the sable antelope, among others, will put their heads into your car window, looking for a treat. (Be sure to get a complimentary container of food before you climb aboard.)

There is a petting zoo, snack bar, and picnic area on the grounds. Open Sept.–May, 9am–5pm daily; June–Aug., 9am–6:30pm. Closed Thanksgiving, Christmas, New Year's Day.

Schlitterbahn Waterpark (830-625-2351; www.schlitterbahn.com; 305 W. Austin, New Braunfels, TX 78130) The name translates to "slippery road," and there are slippery spots galore in this exciting water park. Tube shoots, wild slides from a German castle, bumper boats, a giant hot tub, a swimming lagoon and sand beach, and a children's play area make this heaven — especially on a hot Texas summer day. Open weekends in May and Sept., daily Mem. Day–Labor Day. All-day admission: Adults $27.27, children 3–11 $22.72.

GOLF

Landa Park Golf Course (830-608-2174; www.golfsatx.com/courses/Landa_Park_Golf_Course; 340 Landa Park Dr., New Braunfels, TX 78130) An 18-hole municipal course. Green fees weekdays are $14; weekends $16. Call for tee times. Miniature golf, too, for $2 per game per person (830-608-2169; 192 Landa Park Dr., New Braunfels, TX 78130).

Sundance Golf Club (830-629-3817; www.sundancegolf.com; 2294 Common St., New Braunfels, TX 78130) Challenging 18-hole course for the serious golfer. With four lakes on the course, water is a factor on seven of the holes. Signature hole #3 is a 337-yard par 4 dogleg over a large lake named appropriately No Guts, No Glory.

TENNIS

John Newcombe Tennis Ranch (830-625-7105, 800-444-6204; www.newktennis.com; PO Box 310469, New Braunfels, TX 78131) A complete tennis facility with adult programs, junior summer camps, and all sorts of professional tennis training.

Landa Park has tennis courts, over in Prince Solms Park to the east.

COMAL COUNTY SHOPPING

New Braunfels

ANTIQUES

You'll find more than a dozen antiques shops in New Braunfels.

Try **Attic Antiquity** (830-608-0308; 192 Comal Ave., New Braunfels, TX 78130) for fine antique furniture, dolls and doll restoration, toys, and bronze gift items.
The **New Braunfels Emporium** (830-608-9733; 209 W. San Antonio, New Braunfels, TX 78130) holds 10,000 square feet of antiques.
The **Downtowner Antique Mall** (830-629-3947; 223 W. San Antonio, New Braunfels, TX 78130) just down the block has a lot of space, too — more than 7,000 square feet crammed with nostalgia items.
Across the street, the **Furniture & Antique Consignment Shop** (830-609-0004; 236 W. San Antonio, New Braunfels, TX 78130) has "quality gently used furniture and antiques," as well as decorative items and collectibles.

FURNITURE

South of the Plaza down Seguin Street there are several shops specializing in furniture and refinishing. Begin with **Hill Country Trail Antiques** (830-629-1541; 666 S. Seguin St., New Braunfels, TX 78130) with a large selection of hand-made Texas furniture. **Headrick Antiques** (830-625-1624; 697 S. Seguin St., New Braunfels, TX 78130) has early American furniture and vintage quilts; **Hope's Carousel & Poor Richard's** (830-629-8113; 147 E. Faust, New Braunfels, TX 78130) just around the corner does furniture repair, stripping, and refinishing — which might come in handy if you couldn't resist a chair or table discovered on West San Antonio.

SHOPPING MALLS

New Braunfels Marketplace (830-620-6806, 651 Business Loop IH-35 N., New Braunfels, TX 78130) offer about forty shops and outlets, such as Le Creuset and Dress Barn.

Gruene

Visit **Gruene Werks** (830-629-2951; 1720 Hunter Rd., New Braunfels, TX 78130) and **Gruene Antique Corp.** (830-629-7781; 1607 Hunter Rd., New Braunfels, TX 78130), housed in H. D. Gruene's Mercantile Building on the corner of Hunter and Gruene. **Ella's Emporium** (830-629-2059; 1632 Hunter Rd.,

Gruene General Mercantile offers handmade furniture, pottery, and other handcrafts.

Eleanor S. Morris

New Braunfels, TX 78130) is housed in a 1900 historic house. **Texas Home-grown** (830-629-3176; 1641 Hunter Rd., New Braunfels, TX 78130) specializes in denim skirts and jumpers. Try **Cactus Jack's Antiques** (830-620-9602; 1706 Hunter Rd., New Braunfels, TX 78130) and **Buck Pottery** (830-629-78975; 1296 Gruene Rd., New Braunfels, TX 78130), handcrafted wood-fired stoneware.

KENDALL COUNTY

Kendall County was named for a man who was both a pioneer sheepman and an adventurous newspaperman. George Kendall was one of the founders of the *New Orleans Picayune*, in Louisiana, but he also raised sheep and goats in the Hill Country. After a calm spell on the ranch he liked to get out and cover the news himself. In between, he traveled back and forth to New Orleans, keeping an eye on both his newspaper interests and his sheep and goats. When the county was created in 1862 from Blanco and Kerr Counties, they named it after him. The terrain consists of a hilly plateau with spring-fed streams, caves, and scenic drives. Two small towns, Boerne (pronounced "burn-ee") and Comfort, are of interest.

Boerne

In 1851 a town named Tusculum, a commune for a group of German intellectuals, was moved 2 miles east from its original site, and formally declared to be Boerne by a group of German pioneer settlers. Tusculum was renamed after a German political writer and poet of the time, Ludwig Borne, whose criticism of the political order in Germany in the 1840s inspired the immigrants.

Comfort

This little town was established by German settlers from New Braunfels who were so worn out by their journey that when they found this pretty, picturesque site with pure water, they settled right down and called it "Camp Comfort."

KENDALL COUNTY LODGING

A few miles out in the county from the town of Boerne are two resorts: Tapatio Springs and the Guadalupe River Ranch. But fine accommodations can be had in town, as well.

For further information, contact the **Greater Boerne Area Chamber of Commerce** (830-249-8000, 888-842-8080; www.boerne.org; 1 Main Plaza, Boerne, TX 78006).

Boerne

GUADALUPE RIVER RANCH
Hosts: Elisa and Edward McClure and Walter Starcke.
830-537-4837, 800-460-2005.
www.guadaluperiverranch.com.
PO Box 877, Boerne, TX 78006.
Price: Expensive to Very Expensive.
Credit Cards: AE, D, MC, V.
Handicap Access: Yes, two rooms.

Out on FM 474 about 8 miles northwest of Boerne, this beautiful property — forty-six guest rooms, 400 acres along the Guadalupe River — has quite a bit of celebrity status. Once the hideaway of movie star Olivia De Haviland, who wanted relief from her *Gone With the Wind* fame, the resort is now the property of the McClures of San Antonio and Houston hotel management fame along with Walter Starcke, retired producer of such Broadway hits as *The King and I* and *Cabaret*. The ranch offers a "Complete Plan" with breakfast, lunch, and dinner; the "Sightseer Plan" with breakfast and dinner; the "Breakfast Plan"; and a "Family Suite Plan." Or indulge your senses at the ranch's Quail Canyon Spa, which has its own packages.

What's to do here? Tennis, hiking on nature trails, fishing, canoeing, tubing, horseback riding, mountain biking, and enjoying the exercise and game room, swimming pool, hot tub, and sauna — or just plain lazing the day away. The public as well as inn guests may dine, but reservations are necessary.

TAPATIO SPRINGS
Manager: Allen Pierce.
830-537-4611, 800-999-3299.
www.tapatio.com.
PO Box 550, Boerne, TX 78006.

On Deep Hollow Rd. off FM 46 about 4 miles west of Boerne, this resort has been named one of the top ten Texas golf resorts. The 18-hole par 72 course designed by Billy Johnston offers 6,500 yards of challenging play. There are also four

Price: Expensive.
Credit Cards: AE, CB, D, DC, MC, V.
Handicap Access: Yes.
Special Features: Golf packages.

lit tennis courts, a heated swimming pool, Jacuzzi, saunas, and fully equipped exercise rooms. Stay in one of 112 rooms, including seven suites and thirteen junior suites. The Blue Heron Restaurant & Lounge offers gourmet dining in a casual yet elegant setting, or grab a quick bite in the Turn Café.

Eleanor S. Morris

Visitors at Ye Kendall Inn, Boerne

YE KENDALL INN
Host: Shane Schleyer.
830-249-2138, 800-364-2138.
www.yekendallinn.com.
128 W. Blanco, Boerne, TX 78006.
Price: Moderate to Expensive.
Credit Cards: AE, D, MC, V.
Handicap Access: One room.

Here's an old stagecoach stop, built in 1859. The Texas landmark was a gathering place for lawmen, cattle drovers, army officers, and other characters of the frontier. Nowadays the inn's nine rooms and four suites all have private baths. The long, wide building fronts on the downtown plaza and houses both a restaurant and a boutique with very attractive women's apparel. Restored buildings on the property are home to antique and gift shops called The Village. The room rate includes a continental breakfast.

The inn is pretty quiet — "Hill Country quiet," says Shane. "Unless there's something going on the plaza, like the yearly Abendkonzert."

Comfort

THE COMFORT COMMON
Hosts: Jim Lord and Bobby Dent.
830-995-3030.

Six rooms and a suite of this historic hotel are in the original building, the Ingenhuett-Faust Hotel, built in 1880 from plans drawn up by Albert Giles, noted Hill Country architect. The other two,

Eleanor S. Morris

The Comfort Common bed & breakfast is a historic hotel built by a noted Hill Country architect.

717 High St., Box 539, Comfort, TX 78013.
Price: Inexpensive to Moderate.
Credit Cards: AE, D, MC, V.
Handicap Access: No.

one a log cabin, are in the rear of the property, grouped with several picturesque shops and buildings around two large, open, grassy areas. Porches, swings, and a gazebo make this a relaxing spot. Mimi's Cafe just next door shares the green spaces, and it's where Comfort Common guests take their breakfast of scrambled eggs and sausage, biscuits and gravy, sweet breads and fruit (see "Restaurants"). This popular place gets reserved a year in advance for the Christmas holidays.

THE MEYER BED & BREAKFAST ON CYPRESS CREEK
Innkeeper: Kate Barrett; owner: Shane Schleyer.
830-995-2304, 800-364-2138 (reservations are taken by the Kendall Inn in Boerne).
www.ivillage.bbchannel.com/bbc/p211952.asp.
845 High St., Comfort, TX 78013.
Price: Moderate.
Credit Cards: AE, MC, V.
Handicap Access: Yes.

This interesting collection of historic houses is gathered together around a stone-walled courtyard. The oldest building, dating from 1857, was the last stop for the stagecoach before crossing the Guadalupe River. The newest is a four-plex stucco building constructed in 1920 and operated as the Meyer Hotel until 1956. Breakfast is served in the White House Hotel, built in 1887 when the railroad came to Comfort. You might start the day with a mushroom and black olive quiche or scrambled eggs and ham slices rolled into a croissant. Bite-size German potatoes seasoned and stir-fried, sausage in biscuits, rolls and fresh fruit, and lemon poppy seed cake are among the offerings.

KENDALL COUNTY RESTAURANTS AND FOOD PURVEYORS

Boerne

FAMILY KORNER
830-249-3054.
1234 Main St., Boerne, TX 78006.
Price: Inexpensive.
Cuisine: Home-style.
Serving: B, L, lunch buffet, D (closes at 2pm Sun.).
Credit Cards: D, MC, V.
Handicap Access: Yes.

The lunch buffet yielded up fried chicken and roast beef, carrots and green beans, creamed potatoes, cabbage cooked with chunks of ham, fresh pinto beans, fluffy biscuits, and apple cobbler to top it all off, all at bargain prices. Dinners come with potatoes, salad, and dinner rolls.

Restaurant decor is Hill Country German, with signs saying DANKE SCHÖN, AUF WIEDERSEHEN, and DIE KUCHE WILKOM. Wooden booths sport tulip stencils, and there's a birdcage, pictures, and planters. A cocktail lounge, the Dutch Boy Club, is in the rear (closed Sundays), and there's live country music.

PEACH TREE KOUNTRY KITCHEN
830-249-8583.
448 S. Main St., Boerne, TX 78006.
Price: Inexpensive.
Cuisine: American Home-style.
Serving: L Tues.–Sat.
Credit Cards: AE, D, DC, MC, V.
Handicap Access: No.

Daily lunch specials include such old-time favorites as meat loaf, or more gourmet offerings like crispy walnut chicken breast. There's always a delicious homemade soup of the day, plus a quiche of the day. If it should (rarely) happen to be a cold day, you might find Cajun shrimp gumbo on the menu. And you'll want to save room for such desserts as butternut maple or pecan fudge cake. The china is old and fine, the napkins are lace.

Comfort

MIMI'S CAFE
830-995-3470.
814 High St., Comfort, TX 78013.
Price: Inexpensive.
Cuisine: Home-style.
Serving: L Thurs.–Mon.
Credit Cards: MC, V.
Handicap Access: No.

The restaurateurs here aren't fooling when they say they love to cook — and cook whatever strikes their fancy. The bookshelf crammed with cookbooks is testimony to their dedication (the books are not for sale, no matter how much the clientele begs). The tiny stone building was the post office back in 1908, and you can elect to eat inside or on the rear patio, which shares lovely green space with Comfort Common next door. Try the "Monterey Jack Soup," "Magnificent Meat Balls," "Bread Pudding with Bourbon Sauce," and especially the famous German chocolate pie, a remarkable concoction of flaky crust, creamy caramel filling, and a rich and crunchy chocolate, coconut, and pecan topping.

CYPRESS CREEK CAFE
830-995-3977.
408 Hwy. 27 W., Comfort,
TX 78013.
Price: Inexpensive.
Cuisine: American, Home-
style.
Serving: L, D Tues.–Sat.
L Sun.
Credit Cards: AE, CB, D,
DC, MC, V.
Handicap Access: Yes.

Although the Cypress Creek Cafe is no longer on Cypress Creek, it has moved only two and a half blocks away. Delicious liver and onions, chicken and dumplings, and baked meat loaf are popular here. The steaks, fish, seafood, sandwiches, and salads are all prepared from family recipes.

KENDALL COUNTY FOOD PURVEYORS

Bear Moon Bakery (830-816-2327; 401 S. Main, Boerne, TX 78006) Housed in the Joe Voght Building, with a stone marker overhead dating it from 1912. Cinnamon rolls, pigs in a blanket, and assorted cookies, rolls, and cakes fill the bakery case. There is a breakfast buffet of these goodies as well as sandwiches, soups, and salads for lunch.

Sister Creek Vineyards (830-324-6704; www.sistercreekvineyards.com; 1142 Sisterdale Rd., Sisterdale, TX 78006, on FM 1376 12 miles north of Boerne) Chardonnay, pinot noir, and cabernet sauvignon are made here from traditional French techniques in a restored century-old cotton gin. Gracefully aged in French oak casks with a minimum of filtration and fining, the wines can be tasted daily 12–5pm, or by appointment. "Out of the way, but worth the trip," is the winery's boast.

Vic's Farmers Market (830-249-2515; 941 N. Main St., Boerne, TX 78006) Owner Vic Mendez likes to "sell stuff out of baskets and bags." And so bags of Texas pecans and boxes of vine-ripe red tomatoes beckon invitingly outside the wide-open overhead door of what used to be a drive-through convenience store. Small crisp cucumbers, gorgeous green squash, huge broccoli heads, and lush green lettuce all testify to the freshness that is Vic's pride. Also grain-fed Black Angus beef, honey, sorghum, and pecan syrup, and a tableful of fresh baked goods make Vic's a mouth-watering shopping experience.

KENDALL COUNTY CULTURE

ARCHITECTURE

In *Boerne*, almost every structure still standing was built of Hill Country limestone, beginning with the **Kendall County Courthouse**, one of the oldest in the state still in use. It was started in 1870 and finished by 1908. **City Hall**, a two-story limestone building, was originally built to house one of Boerne's first schools.

From 1876 to 1920, Alfred Giles was a prolific architect in South Texas, and *Comfort* boasts having more buildings of his design than anywhere else, with the exception of San Antonio.

HISTORIC SITES AND MUSEUMS

In both Boerne and Comfort, as well as much of the rest of the Hill Country, museums are often housed in historic buildings.

Boerne

AGRICULTURAL HERITAGE CENTER
830-249-8000.
www.boerne.org/agcenter.htm.
PO Box 1076, Boerne, TX 78006.
Next to city park on Hwy. 46 E., Boerne.
Open: Wed. and Sun. 1:30–4:30pm, closed mid-Dec. to mid-Jan.
Admission: Free.

Exhibits tell the tale of pioneer farm life, displaying items used to develop the frontier. A working blacksmith shop here is described as the only one of its kind west of the Mississippi. There's also an 1896 threshing machine plus other antique farm machinery, implements, and equipment.

KUHLMANN-KING HISTORICAL HOUSE AND HENRY J. GRAHAM BUILDING
830-249-2030.
www.boerne.org/graham.htm.
402 E. Blanco St., Boerne, TX 78006.
Open: Sun. 1–4pm, and by appointment.
Admission: Free.

This complex of two historic buildings is staffed by knowledgeable volunteer docents who are well versed in Boerne's history. The changing museum exhibits in the Graham House showcase items donated by community members.

Comfort

All along the 800 block of **High Street** you'll find what may be the most complete 19th-century business district still standing. Many of the buildings were designed by Alfred Giles, and most are still in use today.

Goldbeck-Faltin Cabin (7th St., next to Faltin & Company) is Comfort's oldest building, built in 1854 as the first mercantile establishment. It was bought in 1856 by August Faltin and has been in the Faltin family ever since. Great-grandson August Faltin III is restoring the *fachwerk* cabin. Some of the wood paneling in the house is rare longleaf pine, and August has also collected some fine furniture pieces of the same rare wood.

Eleanor S. Morris

The Goldbeck-Faltin Cabin is Comfort's oldest building, built in 1854 in the fachwerk *style*

Faltin General Store (see "Shopping"), built in 1879, was the first two-story building in town and also the first to be designed by Alfred Giles. It served as a general store and warehouse, with the owners residing on the second floor.

The **Comfort Museum** is in Jacob Gass's blacksmith shop, circa 1891. The present owner has made it available as a museum, but it's open only on special occasions or by appointment. It's on the corner of 8th and High Street.

Comfort has the only **memorial to Union soldiers** in the state of Texas. Many of the German settlers, here only a few years, very naturally were opposed to secession. But being Union sympathizers didn't make them very popular, and when in 1862 sixty-five of them decided to head for Mexico, they were ambushed by a group of ninety-four Confederate cavalrymen. Nineteen of them fell in the battle on the west bank of the Nueces River over in Real County; nine more, wounded, were executed. Grieving friends and relatives erected the monument, with its touching inscription TREUE DER UNION, on High Street.

LIBRARIES

The **Public Library** in *Boerne* (www.boerne.org/bible.htm), in the historic Dienger Building, is recognized as one of the finest for a city of this size.

There's a historic research room and interesting exhibits like the 1614 Low German (Platte-Deutsch) version of Martin Luther's translation of the Bible, one of only ten known in existence today.

SEASONAL EVENTS

Boerne has **Market Days**, usually once a month, on Main Plaza. But some months are skipped, so call ahead.

MARCH has the **Hill Country Optimist Antique Show** at the fairgrounds (830-995-3670).

APRIL hosts the 2-day **Spring Art Walk on Main Street** (830-249-4635).

MAY has the 3-day **Spicy Food & Music Festival** (830-816-1796).

Father's Day in JUNE is the occasion for **Berges Fest**, the **Festival of the Hills** with three days of food, fun, and festivities. The celebration is a rich portrayal of Boerne's German heritage, with lots of lederhosen and oompah music. Also, the 3-day **Berges Fest** is held at Main Plaza (830-249-4635).

JUNE through AUGUST brings **Abendkonzerts**, free summer evening performances by the Boerne Village Band in Main Plaza.

SEPTEMBER brings the **Kendall County Fair** on Labor Day weekend, beginning on Friday night. That's when professional cowboys show off their riding and roping skills at the rodeo. More bronc-busting goes on Saturday and Sunday, while at the Exhibit Hall farmers, ranchers, cooks, and bakers vie for blue ribbons and cash prizes. Saturday morning there is a parade; on the fairgrounds musicians and dancers perform (830-995-4442).

In late OCTOBER visit the Boerne **Key to the Hills Fall Antique Show**, sponsored by the Chamber of Commerce and complementing Boerne's reputation as an antiques destination (830-249-8000).

In NOVEMBER around Thanksgiving enjoy **Dickens on Main**, a Victorian event (830-816-1796).

DECEMBER brings **Lighting of the Town** and **Weihnachts Fest Parade** (830-816-2176).

KENDALL COUNTY RECREATION

Camping enthusiasts should head for **Cascade Caverns** and **Guadalupe River State Park,** described below. For fishing, try **Boerne City Lake,** yielding largemouth bass up to 10 pounds, or **Guadalupe River State Park**. For golfing, **Tapatio Springs,** described in "Lodging," is a good choice.

Places for swimming and other water sports are the parks listed below. Windsurfing is popular on Boerne City Lake since no powerboats are permitted.

NATURE

The Hill Country has several deep, ancient living caverns that offer great hot weather escapes — if only for the moment.

CASCADE CAVERNS
830-755-8080.
226 Cascade Caverns Rd.,
Fair Oaks, TX 78015.
Off I-10, 16 miles southeast
of Boerne.
Open: 9am–6pm daily,
Mem. Day to the week
after Labor Day; off-
season weekdays
10am–4pm, weekends
9am–5pm.
Admission: Adults $8.50,
children 3–11 $5.50,
children under 3 $1.

The caverns here are long and narrow, requiring some stooping under still-dripping ceilings, but this offers an intimate look at many formations not usually seen so closely. The grand finale is the Cathedral Room, with one of the largest waterfalls in Texas, plunging 100 feet down the cavern walls into a 20-foot-deep pool.

A slide presentation before the tour explains the cavern's formation by flowing water, dissolving and absorbing the limestone to carve out the tunnel-like walls. Tours begin every half hour and last about an hour.

The 105-acre park and campground also offers picnic grounds, swimming pool (summers), gift shop, snack bar, dance pavilion, and meeting hall.

CAVE WITHOUT A NAME
830-537-4212.
325 Kreutzberg Rd.,
Boerne, TX 78006.
6 miles north of Boerne on
FM 474, then follow
signs.
Open: Daily (except holidays)
10 am to 4:40 pm.
Admission: Adults $8
children $4; under 5 free.

Deepest, darkest secret in Texas," claims the Cave Without a Name. Why the odd name? When it was discovered, a contest for a name was held at local schools, and this is what won! Guided tours last an hour and a half, and rubber soled shoes are recommended. Maybe even a light wrap: the caverns are 66 degrees year-round.

The **Cibola Wilderness Trail** along Cibola Creek is a great place for hiking, a 65-acre greenbelt divided into various ecosystems: marsh, prairie, cypress creek bottom, and upland woods. Trails vary in length from 0.25 miles to 2.6 miles. The Cibolo Nature Center (830-249-4616; 140 City Park Rd., Boerne, TX 78006) offers environmental awareness programs.

PARKS

Boerne City Park (830-249-9511, Hwy. 46 E.) This park offers an Olympic-size swimming pool, eight lit tennis courts, baseball, soccer and softball fields, and volleyball courts.

Comfort Park (bounded by Main and Broadway, 4th and 5th Sts., Comfort) This city park was dedicated in 1854 by Comfort founder Ernest Altgelt. On the west side of the park there is a bust of Altgelt plus a gazebo.

Guadalupe River State Park (830-438-2656, 512-389-8900 camping reservations; www.tpwd.state.tx.us./park/parks.htm; 3350 Park Rd. 31, Spring Branch, TX 78070, 13 miles east of Boerne on Hwy. 16) Here are over 1,900 acres of scenic Hill Country on the beautiful Guadalupe River. Across from the park, limestone cliffs line the river while cypress trees shade the picnic and camping areas. Natural rapids flow within the park, and all sorts of wildlife may be seen, such as white-tailed deer, coyote, fox, and armadillos. To the delight of birders, the park's juniper thickets provide a resting place for the rare golden-cheeked warbler. The park provides tent and RV camping, rest rooms, showers, picnic sites, fishing, canoeing, swimming, and hiking. There's also a Texas Park Store.

KENDALL COUNTY SHOPPING

Boerne has no less than thirty-three shops full of antiques and other necessities along the seven-block historic downtown district. The street signs say HAUPTSTRASSE (German for "High Street"), but the addresses are listed as on Main Street. In Comfort, the shopping highlight is the town's antiques stores.

Boerne

Alte Stadt Mall (830-249-8192; 265 S. Main St., Boerne, TX 78006) Here's a collection of small shops in a courtyard. **Humdinger's** (830-249-7067; 233 S. Main St., Boerne, TX 78006) has gifts, clothing, and collectibles; **Furniture Plus** (830-249-1821; 233 S. Main St., Boerne, TX 78006) has antiques, handmade furniture, and jewelry. **Boerne Clock Corp.** (830-249-6060; 233 S. Main St., Boerne, TX 78006) is not only the shop for antique and new clocks, they also offer service, repair, and restoration of timepieces. For a break, **Boerne Apple Company** (830-249-4706; 233 S. Main St., Boerne, TX 78006) right in the center of it all offers homemade apple pie, apple crisp, and Cornish pasties.

Antiques 'N Things (830-249-2313; 106 S. Main St., Boerne, TX 78006) Furniture, folk art, and "hard to find items" at this shop on the corner of Main and the Plaza.

Heartland Gifts (830-749-7869; 140 S. Main St., Boerne, TX 78006) has fine gifts, jewelry, and clothing.

HeyDay (830-249-4951; 615 S. Main St., Boerne, TX 78006) There's not only handcrafted furniture, but also primitives, folk art, and decorative accessories.

Traditions at the Depot (830-816-2795; 518 S. Main St., Boerne, TX 78006) On the banks of Boerne's Cibola Creek and housed in a restored 1883 rural Texas railroad depot, you'll find not only women's clothing, but also distressed pine furniture, hooked rugs, lamps, and even Spode china.

<u>Comfort</u>

Antiquities, Etc. (830-995-4190; 702 High St., Comfort, TX 78013, at 7th St.) American primitives, Victoriana, and old pillars, posts, and pediments fill this large shop set back from the corner by a grassy yard. Two sisters, Nancy Billingsley and Jane Braswell, run the establishment from behind a wonderful long wooden seed cabinet whose drawers are filled alternately with seed corn and hard candies. There's a huge, spectacular carved wooden gateway from India.

Faltin & Company (830-995-3279; 7th and Main St., Comfort, TX 78013) You'll find fine collectibles here as well as fine antiques and specialty gifts. August Faltin, whose great-grandfather built the German *fachwerk* cabin next door, prides himself on displaying such fine and unusual items such as Russian filigree jewelry.

KERR COUNTY

Another county named for a member of Stephen F. Austin's Colony is Kerr County. Named for James Kerr, it was created in 1856 from the western part of Bexar (pronounced "bear") County. Hills, spring-fed streams, and Ingram Lake and Dam on the Guadalupe River make Kerr County yet another beautiful Hill Country county, but with a difference.

In 1921 the U.S. Department of Health announced that Kerrville was the healthiest spot in the nation. This brought a regular parade of consumptives here in the early part of the century. Nowadays this healthy reputation probably accounts for the many kids' summer camps up and down the river.

The U.S. Army frontier post Camp Verde was established in 1855 on the banks of Verde Creek, part of a string of forts built to protect pioneers. In 1856 the post had the dubious distinction of being the only camel base on the frontier. Jefferson Davis, secretary of war in 1855, had the bright idea of purchasing a herd of camels to study whether they would make better pack animals in the West than horses and mules. This interesting experiment was interrupted by the Civil War, and reports say that by the time the war was over, the camels were scattered all over. The experiment was not resumed — by then the railroads were beginning to replace pack animals of all kinds.

The Army abandoned the camp in 1869, and the only thing you'll find in Camp Verde is the Camp Verde General Store. But it's a fine old-timey store, and the real friendly folks there enjoy telling the tale of the Texas camels. Most of the action in Kerr County centers around the city of Kerrville, with Ingram and Hunt both centers of summer camping on the river. All three towns are just a few miles apart along the Guadalupe River.

Kerrville

The man behind Kerrville was Charles Schreiner, who came from France in 1852, became a Texas Ranger, went off to the Civil War, and came back broke. He was then backed by a prosperous businessman and opened a department store that is still in business today. A man of many parts, he also believed that sheep raising could be profitable, thus making Kerrville a mohair capital. Additionally, he was instrumental in bringing the railroad to Kerrville, and he established the Schreiner Institute, now Schreiner College.

Hunt

Hunt is on the cypress-laden banks of the Guadalupe River and is the site of many private summer camps for youngsters.

Ingram

Here the Old Spanish Trail crosses the Guadalupe River. Ingram is named for the man who built the first store and post office here.

KERR COUNTY LODGING

Kerrville County lodging offers mainly resorts and motels, the resorts taking advantage of lovely locations on the banks of the Guadalupe River. Bed & breakfast establishments are a smaller-scale alternative.

For more information, contact the **Kerrville Area Chamber of Commerce** (830-896-1155; www.kerrvilletx.com; 1700 Sidney Baker, Suite 100, Kerrville, TX 78028.

Kerrville

DAYS INN OF KERRVILLE
Owner: Arvind Patel.
830-896-1000, 800-329-7466.
2000 Sidney Baker,
  Kerrville, TX 78028.
On Hwy. 16.
Price: Moderate.
Credit Cards: AE, CB, D,
  DC, MC, V.
Handicap Access: Yes.

One of the Hill Country's newest motels, it offers forty rooms, each one with a microwave, refrigerator, coffeemaker, and hair dryer.

FLAGSTAFF INN
Owner: Arvind Patel.

Close to shopping, restaurants, and river recreation areas, this motel has twenty rooms as

830-792-4449.
906 Junction Hwy.,
   Kerrville, TX 78028.
Price: Moderate.
Credit Cards: AE, DC, MC,
   V.
Handicap Access: Yes.
Special Features: Small pets
   allowed.

**INN OF THE HILLS
   RESORT**
Manager: Richard Bill.
830-895-5000, 800-292-5690.
www.innofthehills.com.
1001 Junction Hwy.,
   Kerrville, TX 78028.
Price: Moderate to Very
   Expensive.
Credit Cards: AE, D, DC,
   MC, V.
Handicap Access: Yes.

**RIVER RUN BED &
   BREAKFAST INN**
Hosts: Ron and Jean
   Williamson.
830-896-83353,
   800-460-7170.
120 Francisco Lemos St.,
   Kerrville, TX 78028.
Price: Moderate.
Credit Cards: AE, D, MC, V.
Handicap Access: Yes.

well as nineteen apartments if you're planning to stay for a while. The courtyard has picnic tables and grills, and the motel offers cable TV and some kitchenettes.

The Inn of the Hills is a classic Kerrville resort on the Guadalupe River, where you can lounge by the river or practice your golf on the putting green. Enjoy swimming, fishing, and boating on the river, or work out at the adjacent Family Sports Center, which guests of the resort can enjoy free. There are beautiful gardens, and you can sail a small sailfish or paddle a boat right beneath the window walls of the River View Restaurant, the resort's dining room.

This pretty inn, built of native stone with a sloping tin roof, is a fine example of German-style Hill Country architecture. Containing four guest rooms and two suites furnished in warm country style, with iron bedsteads covered with pretty quilts, the inn is a relaxing spot where bird-watchers get their fill either sitting on a porch or browsing on the property. Check out the turn-of-the-century pharmacy counter in the living room, with a collection of early medicine.

The inn also houses a wonderful cook: "I'm not a chef," protests innkeeper Ron. "I'm a cook, never took formal training."

I think you'll agree he doesn't need it after you down a breakfast of a mild Southwest quiche (with peppy salsa on the side), potatoes Prescott: hashed browns wth ham, Monterey Jack and Colby cheeses, and topped with hollandaise sauce (a la Eggs Benedict), homemade country oat bread, and a fruit bowl of four fruits, perhaps pineapple, peaches, strawberries, and apples.

Ron has one a national award for one of his recipes — there's proof of the pudding!

Y. O. RANCH RESORT
Manager: Virginia Barton.
830-257-4440,
   800-HOLIDAY.

The covered wagon out front gives you a good idea what to expect inside: an interior dedicated to the spirit of the Texas ranch, filled with antiques, artifacts, and other remembrances of a century ago.

2033 Sidney Baker,
Kerrville, TX 78028.
Price: Expensive.
Credit Cards: D, DC, MC,
V.
Handicap Access: Yes.

The stone walls, high-beamed ceiling, mounted animal heads, tile floors, iron chandeliers, and wall sconces all hark back to the days of great ranches when countless cattle roamed endless acres. The Western-theme rooms are grand to stay in, too.

Hunt

RIVER INN RESORT
Manager: Chelsea
Barrington.
830-238-4226, 800-841-0501.
www/riverinnresort.com.
HC 2, Box 269, Hunt, TX
78024.
Price: Moderate to
Expensive.
Credit Cards: MC, V.
Handicap Access: Yes.

This is a real getaway for fun, rest, and relaxation: sixty condominium units are equipped with all the basic necessities — but no telephones or television (though they each do have a cable connection and portable televisions are available if you just can't stand all the nature here). It's much more fun, though, to enjoy all the activities on the beautiful Guadalupe River: a water chute, tubing, canoeing and paddleboating, fishing, playing tennis, volleyball, shuffleboard, and horseshoes, and a game and family room to gather in. A restaurant, Gallops on the River, is also here.

**SUNDOWN CARRIAGE
HOUSE BED &
BREAKFAST**
Host: Sandra Eyster.
830-238-4169.
Rte. 2, Box 263A, Hunt, TX
78024.
Price: Moderate to
Expensive.
Credit Cards: None.
Handicap Access: No.
Special Features: Two-night
minimum.

Accommodations include one comfortable downstairs room with its own entrance, and a two-bedroom, kitchen, and living-room suite upstairs, all furnished in French provincial and antiques. Breakfast is served on a lovely terrace one level down from the house and overlooking the Guadalupe River, very quiet and private. No pets please, Sandy says. "We have enough for anyone!" — a great dane, golden retriever, and three cats.

KERR COUNTY RESTAURANTS AND FOOD PURVEYORS

Kerr County cuisine offers not only the traditional Hill Country menu of chicken-fried steak, tamales, and sauerbrauten, but also some updated fare in Kerrville and Hunt — thanks to the influx of restaurant-goers from Houston and San Antonio, parents of the summer camp kids along the river.

Kerrville

BIGGARDI'S
830-895-1441.
843 Junction Hwy.,
   Kerrville, TX 78028.
Price: Moderate.
Cuisine: American.
Serving: L, D.
Credit Cards: AE, D, MC, V.
Handicap Access: Yes.

Local diners like Biggardi's because the big black-and-white tiled restaurant, with shiny chrome tables and chairs, has the feel of the '50s. Owner Bill True confesses to liking old movies, and the restaurant is full of film-star nostalgia: posters and murals of the likes of Groucho Marx and Laurel and Hardy are interspersed with Walt Disney characters. It's informal, too, with people coming in wearing tuxedos or shorts and sandals. They come in for the no-microwaving, no-rewarming steak and shrimp, burgers and beer, the fresh salad bar, and the crisp and crunchy onion rings and fries piled high. The charbroiled chicken breast is tender, the burgers juicy, and it's all cooked out there right in the open, and you can watch if you want.

Or you might prefer to watch major sporting events on the big-screen TV, while the kids in this family place run up and down the chrome-railed steps leading to the raised dining area. Beers are both domestic and imported, both old faithful and new trends. Of the latter, manager Ron Wynn says, "We try them, and if they stay popular we keep them; otherwise they go."

The juicy sweet/tart peach cobbler is cooked in a cast-iron stove over in a corner, and the chocolate suicide cake is called that because it's to die for. "We're the only Kerrville restaurant listed with the Texas Restaurant Association," Bill and Ron like to brag.

BILL'S BAR-B-CUE
830-895-5733.
1909-A Junction Hwy.,
   Kerrville, TX 78028.
Price: Inexpensive.
Cuisine: Barbecue.
Serving: L Tues.–Sat.;
   closed Sun. &Mon.
Credit Cards: None.
Handicap Access: Yes.

Don't be put off by the rustic look of the place, with its open-woodshed, tin-roof appearance on the edge of the highway to Ingram and Hunt. The locals know what's what, and Bill sells out fast, which sometimes results in even more abbreviated hours. But once you've tasted the succulent ribs, the tender fork-cutting brisket, the well-seasoned sausage, and juicy chicken in Bill's barbecue sauce, you'll understand why this is a Kerrville-Ingram-Hunt classic, a must stop on the road for those in the know. If you think ahead, you can even have *cabrito* (kid) — but you have to order this in advance.

COWBOY STEAK HOUSE
830-896-5688.
416 Main St., Kerrville, TX
   78028.
Price: Moderate to
   Expensive.
Cuisine: Steaks, Seafood.

We're talking serious steak here, in a family-owned-and-operated house considered one of the best places to eat in town. For years they've been cooking over oak and mesquite wood and flavoring everything they put on the open circular stone pit with their own secret seasonings — but not

Serving: D; closed Sun.
Credit Cards: AE, D, MC, V.
Handicap Access: Yes.

before taking care to make sure the patron is not on a special diet (like no salt or pepper). Whether it's a "Super Kicker" top sirloin, a "Cowboy" T-bone, or a "Cowgirl" strip, it's cooked to perfection any way it's ordered — from rare (cool-red center) to well done (cooked dry) or beyond (then you're on your own!). Ours were medium with a perfect hot pink center, the baked potato was soft and creamy, the salad crisp and fresh. It's not all steak, either. Succulent swordfish, catfish, lamb, quail, and buffalo steak are on the menu; Louisiana gumbo, too.

And it was all enjoyed in a mini-museum because we were surrounded by cowboy art. The bronze by Kerrville artist Don Hunt, the etched-glass room divider, the Jack Terry paintings on the walls — it all adds to the Western ambiance of the restaurant. Of the pencil sketches framed on the walls, Linda Ferris, manager, says, "we gave crayons or pencils to artists from the museum [Cowboy Artists of America Museum] and told them to draw whatever they wanted."

There are three dining rooms; in the middle room is an interesting collection of bottles of hot sauce belonging to owner Richard Lorrie Ferris. (His brand RLF is all over the restaurant, too.) "It's still a beginner collection at 250," says daughter Linda. The wine room at the end has floors of mesquite wood; some fine Texas wines are on offer from Llano Estacado, Cap Rock, Slaughter-Leftwich, and Fall Creek vineyards.

This restaurant is so popular you may have to wait, anywhere from five minutes to an hour. "If they're willin' to wait, we're willin' to serve them," Linda says, and it's no hardship in the pleasant Western-motif bar, with a circular open stone fireplace, mesquite floor, and live entertainment on Fridays and Saturdays.

DEL NORTE RESTAURANT
830-257-3337.
710 Junction Hwy.,
  Kerrville, TX 78028.
Price: Inexpensive.
Cuisine: American,
  Mexican.
Serving: B, L.
Credit Cards: AE, D, MC, V.
Handicap Access: Yes.

Being voted the best breakfast in Kerrville has not gone to the heads of owners Carmen and Rudy Rosales; they've been doing this for more than fifteen years. Even though an unending chain of customers pours through the door of this clean, bright roadside café, service remains prompt and cheerful.

The huevos rancheros are just spicy enough, topped with Rudy's special sauce and accompanied by ham, refried beans, and tortillas. Rudy is the main chef, and he serves some mean barbecued spare ribs, with tender meat falling off the bone. This came with mashed potatoes, green beans, and pinto beans. The salad bar was fresh, with crisp greens and fixin's. There are also seafood entrées to be had most days. Dessert choices include homemade buttermilk and pecan pies, and carrot cake.

HILL COUNTRY CAFE
830-257-6665.
806 Main St., Kerrville, TX
    78028.
Price: Inexpensive.
Cuisine: Home-style, Tex-
    Mex.
Serving: Mon.–Fri. 6am–
    2pm, Sat. 6am–11am;
    closed Sun.
Credit Cards: None.
Handicap Access: Yes.

This is where the home folks go for breakfast — and have been doing so for more than 80 years. What with all the meetin' and greetin' it's a wonder any eatin' gets done. Eggs and omelets are served with hash browns or grits, toast, or light and fluffy biscuits; eggs rancheros come with hash browns or beans, flour tortillas, and hot sauce; and the breakfast taco eggs can come with either potato, sausage, bacon, or ham. The daily lunch special is a bargain, with such delectable home-cooked choices as smothered pork chops, stuffed bell peppers, meat loaf, baked chicken, and even a Mexican plate. And of course there's chicken-fried steak and deep-fried catfish.

**JOE'S JEFFERSON
    STREET CAFÉ**
830-257-2929.
1001 Jefferson St., Kerrville,
    TX 78028.
Price: Moderate.
Cuisine: Southern Home-
    style.
Serving: L, D Mon.–Fri., D
    Sat.; closed Sun.
Credit Cards: D, MC, V.
Handicap Access: Yes.

In a lovely old Victorian mansion built in 1890, Joe Sanders, who perfected his culinary art at Threadgill's in Austin, serves Southern-style home-cooked meals, choice steaks, and fresh seafood in the connecting rooms of the oldest home in Kerrville. The house has been virtually unchanged except for closing the open porches on the first and second floors, giving Joe more rooms in which to serve his mouth-watering down-home dishes like chicken-fried steak and chicken-fried chicken, a delicious departure from the classic steak but with the same batter and homemade scratch gravy on the side. Vegetables are country style; there's usually a choice of broccoli and rice casserole, black-eyed peas, mashed and or new potatoes, or carrots glazed with sugar, butter, and cloves.

The grilled filet of sirloin is cut from the heart of the sirloin and served with fresh sautéed mushrooms. Fresh gulf coast shrimp is always available, too, either hand breaded and fried to a golden brown or boiled and served with homemade cocktail sauce. If you like, you can have all one or the other, or half and half. Catfish might be blackened, Cajun style, or hand breaded and deep-fried in pure cholesterol-free vegetable oil (a small concession to health in all this old-fashioned indulgence). Wines are from both California and Texas. "Tourists like Texas wines," Joe says, and he stocks the best from Bell Mountain, Baron Creek, and Pecan Street as well as Shiner and other popular beers.

KATHY'S ON THE RIVER
830-257-7811.
417 Water St., Kerrville, TX
    78028.

Kathy calls her cuisine international because she's from Taiwan, yet learned to cook in America. A good example was the plate of crispy wontons served with salsa, placed in front of us as

Price: Moderate.
Cuisine: International.
Serving: B, L daily, D
Wed.–Sat.
Credit Cards: AE, D, MC, V
(no personal checks).
Handicap Access: Yes.

soon as we sat down on the lovely terrace over-looking the Guadalupe River, high on the edge of the river. The restaurant has an indoor dining room as well as several terrace levels outdoors for viewing the calm river, the greenery of Tranquility Island, the overhanging cypress trees, and the mallard ducks — very relaxing. Wrought-iron chairs, tables covered in bright flower-printed vinyl table-cloths, and the fresh air completed the mood.

The teriyaki-grilled chicken breast was especially tender and tasty — the sauce is one of Kathy's secrets. And the coleslaw was a surprise: crispy and sweet with chunks of pineapple and raisins among the shredded cabbage and carrots. The chicken-fried steak, a Texas standby, was creditable, although perhaps it could have done with a little less generous portion of cream gravy. The wine list includes ones from the Texas's Ste. Genevieve, Llano Estacado, and Fall Creek vineyards. Special drinks from the bar are another of Kathy's fortes. Some she has gathered from different regions while some — like her special frozen margaritas — are her own concoction.

PATRICK'S LODGE
830-895-4111.
2190 Junction Hwy.,
Kerrville, TX 78028.
Price: Inexpensive.
Cuisine: Franco-American.
Serving: L, D.
Credit Cards: All.
Handicap Access: Yes.

Everyone walking in the door is greeted personally by Patrick, a transplanted Frenchman who makes a wonderful friendly Texan. He leads the way (letting you take a look at the delicious lunch buffet as you pass) to the dining area, a square wood-paneled room with large windows overlooking Goat Creek. Specialties are venison, veal, steaks and wild game. On the menu: fried mushrooms and stuffed mussels; filet mignon or chicken au poivre; medallions of venison, Grand Veneur (sauce poivrade, red currant jelly, black pepper, brandy, and wine), as well as seafood and light choices for calorie counters.

Not unexpected is a lengthy wine list; the full bar offers sparkling wines, mixed drinks, import and domestic beer, and nonalcoholic wine and beer.

**THE TORTILLA
FACTORY**
830-257-4646.
228 Jefferson St., Kerrville,
TX 78028.
Corner of Rodriguez.
Price: Inexpensive.
Cuisine: Mexican.
Serving: L, early D Mon.–
Fri. 11am–6:30pm, Sat.
11am–6pm; closed Sun.

This place is such a well-kept secret that it's almost impossible to find. It became a challenge after several people whispered, "Romero's has the best Mexican food in town." Turned out to be in a small white building with the only sign pasted in the window, saying YES WE'RE OPEN. Around to the side along Rodriguez, black paint on the wall announced TORTILLA FACTORY, but there was no Romero anywhere. (As it turns out, Louis Romero is the owner.)

Credit Cards: None.
Handicap Access: No.

Inside, the regulars were all lined up by the window in the small space (with one table in the corner for take-out customers to wait), and their instructions were to get in line at the small counter and place an order. They were all waiting by the window and said, "When it comes you can go in and eat (in a small adjoining room) or take it with you." People kept coming in and doing both, and the place was humming. Tamales are made fresh every day in this mom-and-pop operation, and one happy customer told us they're like home cooking: you never know what to expect, sometimes they were hotter than others.

We tried the chalupa compuesta, a crisp tortilla with a layer of refried beans and cheddar cheese, a mound of lettuce, and all topped with perfectly seasoned guacamole. The Mexican dinner, too, was as good as we've had anywhere, and better than many a Tex-Mex restaurant's offerings of enchilada, tamale, refried beans, rice, and chili, with corn tortillas. The small dining room has two pine-paneled walls and a third decorated with bullfighting murals, and the tables are simple Formica. The food was delicious; the experience, exhilarating.

Hunt

WAGON WHEEL CAFE
830-238-4095, 800-460-4401.
www.moranch.com/dining
  .html.
HC1 Box 158, Hunt, TX
  78024.
Price: Moderate to
  Expensive.
Cuisine: Hill Country
  Contemporary.
Serving: L, D; closed Mon.
  and all of Jan. & Feb.
Credit Cards: D, MC, V.
Handicap Access: Yes.

A touch of California has come to the Hill Country in the form of chef Fred L. Raynaud, whose many credits include a listing in *Palm Springs Life* magazine as one of the "Great Chefs of the Desert" (1986). The restaurant, on the grounds of Mo-Ranch Conference Center, is open to the public, and reservations are definitely in order. The restaurant's western decor of Hill Country stone and redwood decorated with horseshoes, Stetsons, and saddles is elegantly done: tables and chairs are Mexican ranch style, of cedar and pigskin, and tables are covered with long green runners. The glassware is thick-stemmed and handmade, and the china is heavy turquoise pottery.

The food served on those plates is robust and delicious, from the fried green tomato appetizers, crunchy and filled with creamy guacamole and cheese, to the champagne, lime, and herb-poached salmon tossed in a light mascarpone sauce with bow-tie pasta and vegetables. The West Texas rib eye was topped with ancho-chili sauce and Monterey Jack cheese, a tasty blend of flavors. The desserts are fantastic and clever; two must tries are the mango-banana quesadillas — layered flour tortilla with mascarpone cheese and mango coulis — and the chocolate chimichanga, which is filled with melted chocolate, marshmallows, and pecans and served with a Kahlúa chocolate sauce.

KERR COUNTY FOOD PURVEYORS

the greengrocers deli & gourmet shop (sic) (830-257-3354; 225 W. Water St., Kerrville, TX 78028) is open Mon.–Fri. 10am–3pm for delicious sandwiches and desserts, as well as an impressive array of packaged gourmet items for sale. Almost the best part is entering the shop and inhaling the mouthwatering aromas therein. Breads, wheat, onion, rye, sourdough, pumpernickel and white are baked on the premises and make super sandwiches.

KERR COUNTY CULTURE

ARCHITECTURE AND HISTORIC DISTRICTS

The Schreiner Mansion, home of the Hill Country Museum.

Eleanor S. Morris

Architect Albert Giles built Kerrville's **Schreiner Mansion** — now home of the **Hill Country Museum** — and he was the first builder to use the limestone that was everywhere for the taking. Craftsmen from Germany were imported to do the stonework, and the pink granite for the columns was imported from Italy.

Pick up a tour map of Kerrville's **Downtown Historic District** from any one of more than a dozen sponsors. You'll see seventeen historic buildings, including homes, churches, shops, and the courthouse.

MUSEUMS

COWBOY ARTISTS OF AMERICA MUSEUM
830-896-2553.
www.caamuseum.com.
1550 Bandera Hwy. 173.,
Kerrville, TX 78028.
Open:Mon.–Sat. 9am–5pm
Sun. 1–5.
Admission: Adults $5,
seniors $3, children 6–18
$1.

The museum building is a work of art in itself, with a entrance ceiling composed of eighteen domes made of a light brick and positioned without supporting forms. The gallery floors are of mesquite tree trunks cut into squared-off slices and highly polished, and the long galleries and rooms contain a large collection of paintings and sculpture by noted Western artists, many of whom actually lived the cowboy life. (According to the museum, all the artists are cowboys at heart.)

THE HILL COUNTRY MUSEUM
830-896-8633.
226 Earl Garrett St.,
Kerrville, TX 78028.
Open: Mon.–Sat.
10am–noon and
1–4:30pm.
Admission: Adults $3,
children 12 and under
$1.50.

Captain Charles Schreiner's mansion is the home of this museum filled with beautiful things from Schreiner's heyday: parquetry fashioned from ten different woods, Oriental rugs, crystal chandeliers, and lovely furniture. German masons built the stone walls, brass fixtures came from France, and the house contains a collection of both Schreiner family and Kerr County memorabilia.

THEATER AND CINEMA

Smith-Rich Point Theater of the Hill County Arts Foundation (830-367-5122, 800-459-HCAF; www.HCAF.com; PO Box 1169, Ingram, TX 78025) About eight performances take place Feb.–Nov. in an outdoor theater on the Guadalupe River, with the audience sitting under the stars.

The Arcadia Theater (701 Water St., PO Box 1662, Kerrville, TX 78029) in the old opera house building, runs films regularly. A restoration committee, meanwhile, is raising funds for the theater's repair.

SEASONAL EVENTS

APRIL brings the **Kelly Creek Classic Mountain Bike Festival** plus the annual **Easter Hill Country Bike Tour,** the **Easter Festival & Chili Cookoff,** and **5K** and **10K runs** along with other activities for the whole family (830-792-3535).

MAY sees the **Cowboy Artists Museum of America Roundup.** Also, the annual **Kerrville Folk Festival** offers 3 full weeks of musical events beginning the Thursday before Memorial Day. It's held at the outdoor theater of Quiet Valley Ranch, making the quiet valley ring with excellent music all over the scenic campgrounds (830-257-3600; www.kerrville-music.com; admission). On Memorial Day weekend, the **Texas State Arts & Crafts Fair** (designated by the legislature as the official arts and crafts fair of Texas) is sponsored by the Texas Arts & Crafts Educational Foundation, with juried works by two hundred of Texas' finest artists. Paintings, pottery, sculpture, furniture, toys, leatherwork, clothing, and jewelry — it's all both on exhibit and for sale (830-896-5711, 800-221-7958; admission).

In SEPTEMBER, it's the annual 3-day **Kerrville Wine & Music Festival.**

OCTOBER brings the **Kerr County Fair** to the fairgrounds.

In DECEMBER, join townsfolk for **Bethlehem in the Hills,** 3 days of building and reenacting the Christmas story, sponsored by the chamber of commerce.

KERR COUNTY RECREATION

The best places for boating, camping, fishing, hiking, and swimming in Kerr County are the parks described below.

BICYCLING

The **Hill Country Bicycle Works** (830-896-6864;1412 Broadway, Kerrville, TX 78028) has just about everything human powered on wheels: bikes — mountain, road, cruiser, kids, tandems, low riders — in-line skates, and all sorts of accessories. They provide local route maps and sponsor weekly rides. Open Mon.–Fri. 10am–6pm, Sat. 10am–3pm

FAMILY FUN

Take the kids to the **Family Sports Center** (830-895-5555; 1107 Junction Hwy., Kerrville) for swimming, racquetball, and bowling, among other facilities.

Zebras are among the exotic animals on the ground of the Y. O. Ranch in Kerrville.

Eleanor S. Morris

The whole family will enjoy viewing the exotic game on the **Y. O. Ranch,** where zebras, giraffes, and antelope are among the thirty-six species to be spotted on a guided tour of the historic Schreiner Ranch. The 50-square-mile ranch was established in 1880 by Capt. Charles Schreiner, and it's still a family-run working ranch, well-known for registered quarter horses and longhorn cattle (830-640-3222, 800-YO-RANCH; Mountain Home, TX 78058).

GOLF

Scott Schreiner Municipal Golf Course (830-257-4982; Country Club Rd., Kerrville TX 78028, at Sidney Baker) This 18-hole course presents a refreshing challenge among rolling hills with great views — you'll want to take care not to be distracted. Pro shop, electric carts, putting greens, showers, and lockers are on the premises. Open year-round at 7:30am; no reservaions.

Golfland (830-896-4653; 199 Spur 100, Kerrville, TX 78028) A practice facility with night lighting, automatic and grass tees, target green, chipping and putting greens, sand bunkers, and a pro shop. Open Mon.–Fri. 8am–8pm, Sat. 9am–8pm, Sun. 1–6pm.

HORSEBACK RIDING

If you've brought your boots and jeans, you can hit the trail in the Hill Country and feel like a real cowboy or cowgirl. **Lazy Hills Guest Ranch** (830-367-5600; Hwy. 27 W., Henderson Branch, Ingram, TX 78025) offers trail rides and Texas cookouts.

PARKS

Kerrville-Schreiner State Park (830-257-5392, 830-257-CAMP for reservations; www.pewd.state.tx.us/park/parks.htm; 2385 Bandera Hwy., Kerrville, TX 78028, on Hwy. 173) You'll find beautiful hills and the clear waters of the Guadalupe River in this 517-acre park. Wildlife enthusiasts will enjoy spotting white-tailed deer, turkeys, mallard ducks, raccoons, armadillos, and squirrels. There's swimming in the river, but no lifeguard on duty. Canoe and tube rentals are available. Fishing from the lit pier might net perch, bass, catfish, and crappie. Some 8 miles of hiking trails wind amid the live oak, juniper, and Spanish oak. Campsites for tent campers include water; other campsites provide water, electricity, and sanitary dump stations. There's also a Texas State Park Store. The park is open year-round 8am–5pm 7 days a week, with a 2pm checkout for overnight guests. During the busy season, Mar.–Thanksgiving, reservations for camping are recommended (Austin Central Reservations, 512-389-8900).

Louise Hays City Park (830-257-7300; Thompson Dr., Kerrville, TX 78028, west of

Sidney Baker) A lovely park with the Guadalupe River running through it, right in the heart of downtown. There are shaded picnic tables, and a footbridge crosses the river to Tranquility Island, where the grassy riverbanks are shaded by cypress trees. Canoeing, paddleboating, and tubing from 10am to dusk.

TENNIS

H. E. Butt Municipal Tennis Center (830-896-7955; 801 Tennis Dr., Kerrville, TX 78028, south of Tivy High School) Fourteen lit courts open to the public. Pro shop, lessons available. Open Mon.–Thurs. 9am–9pm, Fri.–Sat. 9am–5pm, Sun. 1–5pm.

KERR COUNTY SHOPPING

Browse through **Old Republic Square** (225 Junction Hwy., Kerrville, TX 78028), more of a courtyard than a square, lined with boutiques on either side. Shaded by pecan trees and cooled by fountains, twelve shops offer an assortment of goods and services. For instance, **Lynne's Treasure Chest** (830-257-2800; 225 Junction Hwy., Kerrville, TX 78028) has unique ethnic ladies' apparel, while in **Little Bit of Texas** (830-896-0300; 225 Junction Hwy., Unit D, Kerrville, TX 78028) you'll find gifts, souvenirs, T-shirts, caps, and lots of Texas books. And you can refresh yourself at the **Old Republic Inn** (830-896-7616; 225 Junction Hwy., Kerrville, TX 78028), with great food, homemade desserts, and of course, "friendly service."

Additional shopping places in the county are **James Avery, Craftsman** (830-895-6805; PO Box 290708, Kerrville, TX 78028, off FM 783 north of I-10); **Hill County Arts Foundation** (830-367-5121; PO Box 1169, Ingram, TX 78025, 507 TX Hwy. 39; **Guadalupe Forge** (830-367-4433; PO Box 816, Ingram, TX 78025, TX 27 just off 39); and **Southwestern Elegance** (830-367-4749; Old Ingram Loop, Ingram, TX 78025). At **River Hills Mall** (830-896-0606; 200 Sidney Baker S., Kerrville, TX 78029, on Hwy. 27) you'll find three department stores: **Beall's, J C Penney,** and **Kmart.**

On the outside walls of the **T. J. Moore Lumber Company**, at the intersection of TX 39 and TX 27 between Ingram and Kerrville, are the Kerr County Historical Murals: "History On A Wall."

MEDINA COUNTY

The story of Medina County is a different Hill Country tale. It was settled not by Germans or Spanish but by a small group of Alsatians from Alsace-

Lorraine. Created from Bexar County in 1848, the county is named for the Medina River, which was probably named for Spanish engineer Pedro Medina. There are scenic hills in the north and fertile valleys to the south with both Medina River and Medina Lake within its boundaries.

This land saw a lot of traffic right from the beginning. There was the Old Spanish Trail from Laredo to San Antonio, cutting across the southeast corner. And the stagecoach route from San Antonio to El Paso passed straight through from east to west. Today Hwy. 90 follows the exact same east-west trail.

The county seat is Hondo, without much of interest for the traveler, but the little town of Castroville more than makes up for this as "The Little Alsace of America."

Castroville

St. Louis Catholic Church on the town square in Castroville.

Eleanor S. Morris

Picturesque Castroville, on the banks of the Medina River, has the distinction of being the only Alsatian settlement in the United States. Many of the folks who live here can trace their ancestry back to Alsace-Lorraine, that tiny stretch of Rhineland that has bounced back and forth between France and Germany for years and years.

Castroville was colonized in 1844 by Henri Castro, who wasn't Alsatian, French, or German. He was of Portuguese descent, Jewish faith, and French citizenship, and is considered only second to Stephen F. Austin in the number of colonists that he recruited to Texas.

A banker with a French company when the new Republic of Texas was looking for foreign loans, Castro and Sam Houston, president of the republic, struck up a friendship. Houston appointed Castro as the Texas Consul General in Paris, then awarded him a land grant in the Medina River valley.

Those first 2,134 Alsatians brought by Castro to the land beside the Medina River west of San Antonio were homesick enough to hang on to their heritage in an enduring way — they recreated a European hamlet, with many small whitewashed, peak-roofed stone cottages, small gardens, and old-world food and traditions. A traveler passing through in 1854 remarked: "The cottages are scattered prettily around a square, and there are two churches, the whole aspect being as far from Texas as possible. It might sit for a portrait of one of the poorer villages of the upper Rhône Valley."

As the town grew along the lovely banks of the Medina River west of San Antonio, it blossomed into an intriguing amalgam, derived from the Alsatian, French, German, Spanish, and English heritage of its early and subsequent settlers.

But Castroville has never lost the ambiance created by those first two thousand Alsatians. Architects who made a survey of the city in the 1930s pronounced it to be absolutely unique in the United States. The town is recognized by the Federal Government as a National Historic District and by the state as a Texas Historic District.

For further information, contact the **Castroville Chamber of Commerce** (830-538-3142, 800-778-6775; www.castroville.com; 902 London St., PO Box 572, Castroville, TX 78009).

MEDINA COUNTY LODGING

THE ALSATIAN COUNTRY INN
830-538-2262.
1651 Hwy. 90 W.,
Castroville, TX 78009.
Price: Inexpensive to
Moderate.
Credit Cards: AE, D, DC,
MC, V.
Handicap Access: One room.

This motel up on a hill has forty large, comfortable rooms and a wonderful panoramic view of the town just below, although the desk personnel say, "The best thing about this place is the people."

THE LANDMARK INN
Hosts: Park rangers.
830-931-2133; prior
reservations:
512-389-8900, State Park
Reservation Center.

The Landmark Inn on the Medina River has provided rest for weary travelers for more than a century. Now a State Historic Site, it's owned and operated by the Texas Parks and Wildlife Department (there's a $1 charge to tour the grounds). The inn's

www.tpwd.state.tx.us/
    park/landmark/
    landmark.htm.
402 Florence St.,
    Castroville, TX 78009.
Price: Inexpensive, B.
Credit Cards: D, MC, V (if
    reserved in advance; cash
    or checks on the scene).
Handicap Access: One
    room.
Special Features: Breakfast;
    closed Mon., Tues.

eight rooms (some with private bath) are furnished with authentic period pieces, and if you're lucky, you might get the room Robert E. Lee slept in. Or perhaps the upstairs or downstairs room of the tiny bathhouse: Before the Civil War the Landmark Inn was the only place to take a bath between San Antonio and Eagle Pass. It lost this valuable amenity when the lead lining the upstairs, which served as a cistern for water hauled from the river, was melted down into bullets for Confederate troops. You won't find televisions or telephones in the rooms, though they all have air-conditioning.

The L-shaped lobby of the inn serves as a museum, with artifacts and exhibits depicting the history of both the inn and the town. There's an old gristmill on the property, too.

MEDINA COUNTY RESTAURANTS AND FOOD PURVEYORS

Thanks to the French and Alsatian influence here, the restaurant scene offers some gourmet variations on traditional Hill Country dining.

Guillermo Spinelli presides at the Alsatian Restaurant — with its original beams and stone walls — in Castroville.

Eleanor S. Morris

**ALSATIAN
    RESTAURANT**
830-931-3260.
403 Angelo St., Castroville,
    TX 78009.

Housed in one of the charming Alsatian cottages of Castroville built between 1840 and 1845, the building retains its original look, the restaurant's focus being not on cosmetic updates but on good food.

On Houston Sq.
Price: Moderate.
Cuisine: Alsatian,
   Continental.
Serving: L daily, D
   Thurs.–Sun.
Credit Cards: AE, D, DC,
   MC, V.
Handicap Access: No.

Diners are offered a delectable menu of Alsatian, French, and Italian dishes, all preceded at the table by a cup of rich beef broth and a loaf of homemade whole-wheat bread with a dish of rich green pesto to dip it in.

The comprehensive menu also lists the wines suggested for each dish.

LA NORMANDIE
830-538-3070, 800-261-1731.
1302 Fiorella St.,
   Castroville, TX 78009.
Price: Moderate to
   Expensive.
Cuisine: Traditional
   French.
Serving: L Sat. & Sun., D
   Wed.–Sun.
Credit Cards: No.
Handicap Access: Yes.

Here's another restaurant in a little stone cottage, just down the street from the Henri Castro House. Everything is prepared to order, and since good things take time, diners are invited to relax in the pleasant French country home surroundings "in joyful anticipation of the culinary delights to come." Soupe à l'oignon gratinée, escargots à la bourguignonne, filet mignon béarnaise, entrecôte maitre d'hotel — are all served with sauces on the side if you prefer. The menu continues with frog legs sautéed à la provençal, steak au poivre — seemingly a collection of every French dish you've ever dreamed of. Top off your meal with crêpes Normandie filled with apples flambé, crème anglaise, and crème Chantilly, and you almost believe you're in Paris or a little restaurant in Normandy.

**LARRY'S RESTAURANT
   AND BAKERY**
830-538-2595.
810 Hwy 90 W., Castroville,
   TX 78009.
Price; Inexpensive.
Cuisine: American.
Serving: B, L, D.
Credit Cards: No.
Handicap Access: Yes.

For a casual, relaxed meal, this unpretentious storefront eatery is noted for steak, shrimp, chicken fingers, and old-fashioned hamburgers as well as hand-dipped ice cream — Texas's favorite Blue Bell ice cream.

SAMMY'S RESTAURANT
830-931-2206.
202 Hwy. 90 E., Castroville,
   TX 78009.
Price: Inexpensive.
Cuisine: Home-style.
Serving: B, L, D.
Credit Cards: D, MC, V.
Handicap Access: Yes.

Here's a restaurant with a story as old as Castroville — almost. Sammy Tschirhart's grandfather, August Tschirhart, bought the land in hopes that his sons would start their own business. He lived to see his grandsons Leon and Sammy operate a small icehouse in the 1940s, filling the iceboxes of those days before refrigeration. Soon Sammy began to sell hamburgers, and he eventually took over the business, offering curb service until 1969.

Now Sammy and Yvonne have a full-sized, full-service restaurant, serving steaks, seafood, and homemade pies and biscuits. A specialty is their Alsatian sausage, made with "seasonings that our family brought from Europe," Yvonne says. In Europe they used pork; here they use a mixture of beef, pork, and venison.

MEDINA COUNTY FOOD PURVEYORS

Haby's Alsatian Bakery (830-931-2118; 207 U.S. 290, Castroville, TX 78009) Here the aroma of the honeybuns, apple fritters, fruit stollen, and strudel is irresistible. The bakery is open six days a week — the doors open at 5am (for regulars who come in for coffee and streusel and other goodies on their way to work) and don't close until 7pm.

The bakery is named for Nicklaus Haby, who came to Castroville in 1844 from Oberentzen, France. He was hired by Castro to hunt wild game to feed the colonists. Two years later he returned to France to collect his family and bring them to Texas. He served in the Mexican-American War of 1847 as a captain of the Texas Rangers.

MEDINA COUNTY CULTURE

Castroville was laid out in 1844 around a square, and from the plentiful stones of the Hill Country the Alsatians built sturdy stone houses with sloping roofs like those they had left behind in the Rhineland. The artisans who came over with Castro had to adapt to the material at hand and learned from the Mexicans in Texas to use native materials. Listed on the National Register of Historic Places, ninety-seven of these buildings are still standing; it's interesting to see them scattered in among the contemporary ranch-style homes. Find them with the help of a map from the **Castroville Chamber of Commerce** (830-538-3142, 800-538-3142; www.castroville.com; PO Box 572, Castroville, TX 78009).

HISTORIC BUILDINGS AND SITES

The **Bourquin House**, at the corner of Angelo and Petersburg, behind the Alsatian Restaurant, is considered one of the finest authentic restorations in Texas. It was built in 1849 and remained in the same family until it was sold to the present owners in 1974. It's a perfect little Alsatian cottage, painted a sort of dusty orange, and the stone wall at the rear, abutting the restaurant, is built from an original stone house that had been torn down long ago.

The Tschirhart name is an old Castroville one, too. The family home, known

The historic Cordier-Tschirhart-Seal Home, Castroville, was built of native rock between 1844 and 1847.

Eleanor S. Morris

today as the **Cordier-Tschirhart-Seal Home**, is on Isabella between Paris and London Streets. It was built between 1844 and 1847 of native rock.

The **Henri Castro Homestead** on Fiorella Street, off Hwy. 90 between London and Lafayette, is a small cottage that was recently restored and enlarged. It is now (surprisingly) a business office, but there's a marker out front telling all about it.

Henri Castro left no descendants in Castroville, but his wife, Amelia Castro, is buried here, in the **St. Louis Cemetery** at the foot of Cross Hill. (He's believed to have died in Mexico, date unknown.)

LIBRARIES

Castroville Public Library (830-931-4095, 802 London St., Castroville, TX 78009) Not only are there books and pamphlets about the town, there is also an extensive genealogy section in case you have some Alsatian ancestors to look up. An interesting addition is the Oral History Collection, where visitors can listen to tapes offering an invaluable source of unwritten history.

SEASONAL EVENTS

For specific dates and schedules, check with the Castroville Chamber of Commerce (see "Medina County Culture").

Market Trail Days on the second Saturday of each month from MARCH to DECEMBER are on Houston Square, where booths are packed with ceramics, needlework, wooden toys, painting, jewelry, produce — whatever anybody has to sell. Entertainment, besides shopping, includes music, dancing, an old car show, or whatever is timely, such as an Easter Egg contest or a Santa Claus visit.

The **Castroville Antique Show** is held twice a year, usually in MAY and SEPTEMBER, at Koenig Park on the scenic Medina River. In addition to wares for sale, there's an oompah band, a blacksmith, home tours, baked goods sales, and activities at the historic Landmark Inn. Also in May is **Medina County Trades Day,** which, notwithstanding the name, is a 2-day event held in Castroville Regional Park (830-931-2525).

St. Louis Day in AUGUST is a big event, a day-long celebration and barbecue.

In DECEMBER Castroville has an **Old-Fashioned Christmas** in Houston Square, with 150 vendors, a free train ride and other entertainment, and a visit from Santa and Mrs. Claus (800-778-6775, 830-538-3142).

MEDINA COUNTY RECREATION

For tennis, hiking, fishing, and swimming and other water sports, refer to "Lakes" and "Parks" below.

GOLF

Alsatian Golf Club (830-931-3100; www.golfsatx.com/courses/Alsatian_ Golf_Course; 1339 CR 4516, Ste. 120, Castroville, TX 78009, 2 miles west of downtown Castroville) The 18-hole, 72-par layout is about 6,800 yards in length and has five sets of tees. Fully stocked pro shop and clubhouse. Greens fees $26 weekdays, $35 weekends before noon, cart fee included.

LAKES

Medina Lake, about 20 miles north of Castroville on FM 471 to FM 1283, is 18 miles long and a favorite with water-skiers because of its calm waters both on the lake and in the many coves. Boat ramps are available for launching. Nine miles farther on FM 1283 will bring you to Medina Dam and a spectacular view if you walk across.

PARKS

Castroville Regional Park (830-931-4070; 1209 Fiorella St., Castroville, TX 78009) 126 acres of land on the Medina River. Recreational facilities include an Olympic-size pool; 35 RV camping sites with water, disposal, and electric hookups; two tennis courts and two volleyball courts; and fishing in the river.

(Joe Hoog, who provided the land for the park, used to recall his grandmother's tales of Indians coming down from the hills with wild game and turkey to exchange for sugar, salt, and coffee, and they would let her ride their ponies.)

Landmark Inn State Historic Park (830-931-2133; 402 Florence St., Castroville, TX 78009) In addition to beautiful landscaped grounds and historic structures (see "Lodging"), the park is a setting for many kinds of recreation. Fishing on the Medina River here includes catfish, bass, and panfish (although the locals say it's not the fishing ground it's been in the past). For hikers, there is an interpretive trail and a river ford trail across the river. Swimming and wading in the river here is at your own risk.

MEDINA COUNTY SHOPPING

Castroville Emporium (830-538-3115; 515 Madrid St., Castroville, TX 78009, on Houston Square) A selection of antiques, but Donald Belcher specializes mainly in antique lighting fixtures. The ceiling and walls of what was in 1866 a general store are now hung with fabulous fixtures. One or two are still gas lamps, just for the heck of it, although most have been electrified. "Wasn't so long ago," says Donald, "both gas and electric fixtures were burning in Castroville homes."

Ima's Antiques (830-538-3312/2844; 509 Hwy. 90 W., Castroville, TX 78009) A beautifully preserved rose velvet Victorian settee and chairs are the first things we saw on entering this shop full of quality antiques. A second stunner: the Louis XV suite in the next room. New furniture, reproductions, and collectibles are also offered. (Owners Irma and LeRoy Seal live in the historic Cordier-Tschirhart-Seal Home.)

The Landmark Inn Gift Shop (see "Lodging") Books, homemade soaps, note cards, jellies and preserves, and special handmade pens crafted from local woods.

The Market Place (830-538-3350, 1215 Fiorella St., Castroville, TX 78009) Relax on the patio of this historic building before you browse among the antiques, art, collectibles, crafts, and quilts. Artists and craftspeople are also featured here.

REAL COUNTY

R eal County (pronounced "ree-AL" with accent on the second syllable) may be the most sparsely populated county in the Hill Country, but it is abundant in scenic beauty. Hunting, fishing, camping, and scenic drives are the attractions of this county on the western edge of the Hill Country, where the hills rise up majestically just before the land spreads out toward the plains to the west.

Organized in 1913 from surrounding Bandera, Edwards, and Kerr Counties and named for a legislator-rancher, Julius Real, the county has two small towns, Leakey (pronounced "lay-key"), population 590, and Camp Wood, population 976.

Eleanor S. Morris

Along the picturesque Rio Frio.

The South Llano River wanders across the north edge of the county, but it's the sparkling clear Nueces River, beginning its journey to the Gulf of Mexico from beautiful Nueces Canyon, that gives Real County much of its charm. The hills are dotted with spring-fed streams, and canyons are thick with cedars, pecans, live oak, and walnut trees.

Real County has another claim to canyon beauty. In addition to Nueces Canyon, Rio Frio, a tributary of the Nueces River, forms Frio Canyon. This beautiful stretch of river flows south from Leakey to Concan down in Uvalde County. The river is popular for swimming, tubing, and fishing, and dozens of camps and lodges line its banks.

Leakey

Leakey was founded by early settlers Nancy and John Leakey, early pioneers of Frio Canyon. The main activities for the visitor to Leakey include enjoying the lovely scenery and the outdoor recreation along Rio Frio.

Camp Wood

This town grew around a U.S. Army Post established in 1857 on the site of a Spanish mission, San Lorenzo de la Cruz, which had been founded by

Franciscan missionaries in 1762. Camp Wood is next to the beautiful Nueces Canyon, with the Nueces Lake and Nueces River to enjoy. There's a legend about the Nueces River: Whoever takes three drinks in three minutes from the river is bound to return for another drink before dying.

REAL COUNTY LODGING

There are only two motels in the little town of Leakey and in Camp Wood, but several lodges and lots of cabins and camping areas. A bed & breakfast and a resort are also described below. (For more information, call the **Frio Canyon Chamber of Commerce** (830-232-5222, PO Box 743, Leakey, TX 78773). The town is popular in the summer for family reunions, among other things, and in the fall for hunting, so it's best to make reservations ahead of time.

CLEARWATER RANCH RESORT
Hosts: Ruth Ann and Henry Jones; Lisa and Tom Teske.
830-232-6686.
www.frio.net.
PO Box 1101, RR 1120, Leakey, TX 78873.
Price: Inexpensive (bunkhouse); Moderate (cabins).
Credit Cards: MC, V.
Handicap Access: Yes, one cabin.

Leakey

Imagine owning a mountain! Clearwater Ranch has 400 acres including Cooper Mountain, canyon, and pasturelands along half a mile of sparkling Rio Frio. Here in the great outdoors you can swim, fish, go tubing, hiking, and take in the view — and the sunset — from Cooper Mountain. Cottages are air-conditioned, with king-size beds, microwave ovens, picnic tables on the large front porches, and barbecue pits at the ready. The ranch offers hayless rides (perfect for hay fever sufferers) through the working Brangus cattle ranch up to Cooper Mountain for a beautiful sunset.

FRIO CANYON LODGE
Hosts: Katherine and Elizabeth Ross.
830-232-6800.
www.tricanyonvisitor guide.com.
PO Box 508, Leakey, TX 78833.
Hwys. 83 & 337.
Price: Inexpensive.
Credit Cards: AE, D, MC, V.
Handicap Access: Yes.

The lodge is a wonderful mixture of old and new: The historic stone and cedar buildings were built back in 1941, but the spacious rooms are decidedly up to date, with modern decor, cable TV, and central heat and air-conditioning.

Located in the heart of downtown Leakey, the lodge is only 1/2 mile from the Frio River.

There's a swimming pool, a wooded courtyard, a picnic pavilion, and a restaurant. The restaurant serves lunch daily except Mondays, and dinner Thursday, Friday, and Saturday evenings.

WELCOME INN
Managers: Wade and Kathy
  Martin.
830-232-5246.
PO Box 720, Leakey, TX
  78873.
Hwy. 83 and 7th.
Price: Inexpensive to
  Moderate.
Credit Cards: AE, D, MC, V.
Handicap Access: Yes.

There are twenty rooms in this motel, counting the cabins. The motel rooms are lined up in the usual row, but the cabins are out under the trees.

WHISKEY MOUNTAIN INN
Hosts: Judy and Darrell
  Adams.
830-232-6797, 800-370-6797.
www.whiskeymountaininn
  .com.
HCR 1, Box 555, Leakey, TX
  78873.
Price: Inexpensive.
Credit Cards: D, MC, V.
Handicap Access: Yes.

This German farmhouse just south of town has a cypress plank exterior and a tin roof. The 50-foot porch, held up by huge cedar tree trunks, is the perfect spot to watch deer, rabbits, and raccoons while rocking away in a wicker rocker. "You might even sight an occasional bobcat," says Darrell. And of course there are birds galore. If you stay in one of the inn's two rooms (shared bath) you'll get a breakfast of juice and fruit and some of Judy's baking; if you're in one of the six cabins, you're on your own — but you'll have a kitchenette to cook in.

Camp Wood

HILL COUNTRY MOTEL
Manager: Bernice Hohman.
830-597-3278.
PO Box 103, Camp Wood,
  TX 78833.
One block off Hwy. 55.
Price: Inexpensive.
Credit Cards: MC, V.
Handicap Access: No.

Owner Lana Gildart-Harper and manager Bernice Hohman invite you for a "relaxed, refreshing getaway" at this clean, comfortable motel, with bath/shower combinations and color cable TV. There's a choice of three standard rooms and three with kitchenettes.

WOODBINE INN
Hosts: Judy and Jerry
  Rollison.
830-597-2310.
PO Box 905, Camp Wood,
  TX 78833.
Hwy 55.
Price: Inexpensive.
Credit Cards: AE, D, MC,
  V.
Handicap Access: Yes.

Named for the English word for honeysuckle, this nice new motel has two extra-long full-size beds in each room. The color-coordinated air-conditioned rooms are pretty and clean and have a coffeepot and coffee as well as cable TV.

REAL COUNTY RESTAURANTS AND FOOD PURVEYORS

I nformality is the key to Real County restaurants, as the following descriptions prove.

FRIO CANYON RESTAURANT
830-232-5200.
Hwy. 83, Leakey, TX 78873.
Price: Inexpensive.
Cuisine: American, Tex-Mex.
Serving: B, L, D.
Credit Cards: D, MC, V.
Handicap Access: Yes.

W ood-paneled walls, marbled vinyl tile floor, Formica tables, wooden chairs in a storefront building along Hwy. 83, the town's main street — a typical Hill Country café. But it's mighty friendly. Folks make themselves at home here, like the two men up from San Antonio for the weekend and enjoying a game of cards as they ate their meal.

The Frio Canyon salad was filling, even on the "Lite Side" with either grilled or fried chicken, chopped lettuce, and tomatoes, hard-boiled egg, and cheese. The chef's salad, too, was topped with cheese and a boiled egg. For heartier dining, the pepper steak was spicy with jalapeños and cheese stuffed inside ground beef, with brown gravy on the side and served with baked potato or fries and the vegetable of the day.

Super nachos are topped with refried beans, taco meat, cheese, sliced jalapeños, and chopped tomato, with guacamole on the side, and you can order either eight or sixteen of them. The French silk pie for dessert, among the fruit pies, cinnamon rolls, and doughnuts, was a pleasant surprise.

PAPA'S 83 CAFE
830-232-6112.
Hwy. 83 N., Leakey, TX 78873.
Price: Moderate.
Cuisine: Tex-Mex, American.
Serving: B, L, D.
Credit Cards: AE, D, MC, V.
Handicap Access: Yes.

I f this restaurant looks like a Dairy Queen drive-in to you, you're not far wrong — that's what the building used to be. Now the brick walls and wide windows all around have gotten accustomed to Mexican platters of homemade enchiladas, tacos, and beans. But you'll also find the chicken-fried steak and catfish that is the haute cuisine of the Hill Country.

Camp Wood

CASA FALCON RESTAURANT
830-597-5111.
Hwy. 55, Box 152, Camp Wood, TX 78833.
Price: Inexpensive.
Cuisine: Mexican.

T he Falcon family, Mary, Lupe, and Chano, along with five sisters and four brothers, run this cheery Mexican cantina. Small and cozy under a low ceiling, with the usual pine paneling and Formica tables, the restaurant is made bright with striped Mexican curtains, hanging papier-mâché

Serving: B, L, D; closed Wed.
Handicap Access: Yes.

fruits and vegetables, and mounted game: a formidable set of horns, a beribboned deer head, even a large fish. The beef and chicken fajitas are tender and tasty, the carne guisada (chunks of beef in thick brown sauce) is tender. If you don't find what you want on the menu, "he'll make whatever you want," Mary says of the chef. "But . . . we have everything," she adds.

THE OLD TIMER RESTAURANT
830-597-2112.
Hwy. 55, Camp Wood, TX 78833.
Price: Inexpensive to Moderate.
Cuisine: American, Tex-Mex.
Serving: B, L, D.
Credit Cards: AE, D, MC, V.
Handicap Access: Yes.

Red-checked tablecloths add a cheery note to this pine-paneled restaurant sporting an encouraging sign: SIT LONG, TALK MUCH. The picket-fence decoration along one wall is hung with mugs and pots, fry pans and aprons. The attractive deep-yellow menu offers breakfast egg plates or cowboy-sized pancake stacks; for lunch, deli sandwiches are spiced up out of the ordinary croissant or sub with jalapeños added to the lettuce, tomatoes, onion, green peppers, mustard, and mayonnaise. Dinner steaks range from the ubiquitous chicken-fried to rib eye and T-bone; both fried catfish and whitefish are on offer; chicken and Mexican dishes, too.

REAL COUNTY FOOD PURVEYORS

Manager Harry Florence of the Frio Pecan Farm, Leakey, offers customers samples of pecans.

Eleanor S. Morris

Apple Valley Ranch (830-232-5577; Walter White Rd., Leakey, TX 78873, 3 miles south of town on Hwy. 83) Free orchard tours and apple tastings, and apples for sale whether you pick or they pick for you. Apple jelly, apple butter, and sweet apple cider is for sale too. Open Mon.–Sat. 8am until dark at apple harvesting time beginning the first week of July.

Frio Pecan Farm (830-232-5294; Hwy. 337, PO Box 425, Leakey, TX 78873) Not only can you buy fresh pecans, you can see how they're cracked professionally by taking a tour of the Frio Pecan Farm on Hwy. 337, approximately a mile east of Hwy. 83. Manager Harry Florence (who calls himself a "general flunky") says he'll show people the equipment and answer their questions. And, of course, he'll sell them bags of freshly cracked pecans.

REAL COUNTY CULTURE

HISTORIC BUILDINGS AND SITES

Real County Courthouse, the **First State Bank** building, and **Leakey School**, all on Hwy. 83, are built of hand-cut native stone.

On the courthouse grounds, a marker commemorates the history of Leakey and its founders, Nancy and John Leakey, early settlers of Frio Canyon. Six miles south of Leakey on Hwy. 336, a marker denotes the site of the McLauren Massacres, the last Indian massacre in the Southwest.

MUSEUMS

Room in the Real County Historical Museum, set up just as it was many years ago.

Eleanor S. Morris

REAL COUNTY HISTORICAL MUSEUM
830-232-5330.
Evergreen St., Leakey, TX 78873.

Exhibits here depict the pioneer days in Frio Canyon, with rooms set up just as they were many years ago. Pictures, clippings, and books tell of events in the 1880s plus about the early settlers

At Fourth St.
Open: Fri.– Sat. 10am–4pm.
Admission: Adults $1,
    children 25¢, under 6
    free.

who came from all over the United States to begin new lives in this beautiful canyon.

**WILDLIFE ART
MUSEUM**
830-232-5607.
PO Box 434, Leakey, TX
    78873.
On Hwy. 337 E.
Open: Mon.–Sat. 9am–5pm;
    closed Sun.
Admission: Donations.

This privately owned museum features the art of taxidermy, along with sculpture, paintings, and carvings of wildlife, such as Texas white-tailed deer, buffalo, and birds. The taxidermist combines a knowledge of both zoology and sculpture, often spending years studying animals in their native habitats. The wildlife artist, in turn, captures nature in wood, canvas, and bronze, all displayed in this unique small museum.

On the Rio Frio and in Nueces Canyon

Rio Frio yields catfish, perch, and bass to the anglers casting in its waters. Anywhere along the clear, cold river is also perfect for swimming, snorkeling, and tubing. Snorkelers can clearly see wonderful fish and plant life, and even special underwater rocks for rock hounds.

Campers should contact the **Frio Canyon Chamber of Commerce** (830-232-5222; PO Box 743, Leakey, TX 78873) for a brochure listing the many cabins and campsites along the Frio River.

In **Nueces Canyon** the river and lake offer swimming, fishing, boating, and tubing year-round. (Adventurous snorkelers and scuba divers bring their own gear to plumb the crystal-clear river waters.) The Nueces River yields yellow and blue catfish and largemouth bass all year; Nueces Lake offers African perch and Guadalupe bass, as well. The lake, formed by a dam in the Nueces River, is 3 miles south of Camp Wood. Nueces Canyon is also the home of woodpeckers, hummingbirds, orioles, finches, doves, and many more.

SEASONAL EVENTS

In JULY, the **July Jubilee** in Leakey is a big celebration here, on the weekend of the fourth, beginning with a parade on Hwy. 83 and marching to the corner of Hwy. 337. Floats and horses lead the way to all-day entertainment on the Courthouse Square, where sixty-five booths sell arts and crafts and food and drink. Square dancers, storytellers, cowboy poets, and fiddlers contribute to the merriment. Friday and Saturday there's a rodeo, and afterward on Saturday night there's a street dance (830-232-5222).

In Camp Wood in AUGUST, the **Old Settler's Reunion** is always the first weekend.

For SEPTEMBER, there's all the excitement of a **Rubber Duck Race** in the Frio River over Labor Day.

In **November,** the weekend after Thanksgiving, the **Hunter's Dance** at the American Legion Hall in Leakey swings to country-western music.
December, there's **Christmas on the Square.**

REAL COUNTY RECREATION

Camping, boating, and many other activities that take advantage of Real County's scenic beauty are pursued at Wes Cooksey Park, on the Rio Frio, and in Nueces Canyon.

PARKS

Wes Cooksey Park (830-597-3223; Hwy. 55, Camp Wood, TX 78833) This park is technically in Uvalde County, but is only 3 miles south of Camp Wood (and 37 miles north of Uvalde). Although park managers Mary Lou and Tommy Ward enjoy telling people to "bring your hammock and just rest under the shade of the beautiful oak trees," they're also quick to point out that the park is open year-round for swimming, boating, fishing, hiking, and camping. Campers will find thirty-three tent sites with electricity and water; ten RV sites with full hookups. Facilities include two boat ramps, rest rooms with hot showers, public telephones, a dump station, grills, and campfires.

Scenic Drives

FM 337 between Leakey and Camp Wood is one of the most scenic roads in the Hill Country, passing through a land of massive timbered hills, steep cliffs, and numerous streams in secluded valleys, with roller-coaster dips and winding curves. A close runner-up is the same road from Leakey east to Vanderpool in Bandera County.

If you're interested in seeing the largest Texas live oak tree in the United States, travel 7 miles south of Leakey on Hwy. 1120 to Rio Frio, the county's first settlement, with the same name as the river it's located on.

REAL COUNTY SHOPPING

Leakey isn't exactly the place to shop till you drop, but you may find a treasure or two or pick up some item that you forgot to pack. Camp Wood has just a few shops lining the main street along Hwy. 55, but one or two are well worth checking out.

Leakey

Josh's Landing (830-232-6292; Hwy. 83, Leakey, TX 78873) "Leakey's only bait and tackle headquarters," they say, and this is the place for live bait and fishing tackle as well as camping supplies, swimming gear, river tubes, and hunting supplies. Mon.–Sat. 9:30am–5:30pm, Sun. 9:30am–noon.

Sallie's Antiques (830-232-5588, Hwy. 83 S., Leakey, TX 78873) Browse through six clean (not dusty or musty) rooms of china cabinets, complete with china, jewelry, Oriental chests, an old pump organ, whiskey decanters, and such.

Camp Wood

Campwood Trading Post (830-597-4220, PO Box 549, Camp Wood, TX 78833, on Hwy. 55) "This is the Camp Wood Mall," Billy Joe says as he displays a coffeepot with a steer skull sitting on the top. "Been here for years, wholesale prices." Calling itself an old-fashioned general store, the trading post spreads out along the highway behind a raggedy wooden fence, and inside you go from room to room (three in all), looking at the myriad collection of well, stuff, that Linda June and Billy Joe Wilkinson have collected over what looks to be several lifetimes.

Cluttered and crowded, this is a fascinating place for browsing. Gifts like handmade hummingbirds hang down from the ceiling, suspended on ribbons; Garrett & Winchester farm and ranch supplies are stacked on counters below. There's a jumble of hardware, automotive supplies, giftware, everywhere.

Dolores's Unique Designs (830-597-4152; PO Box 352, Camp Wood, TX 78833, on Hwy. 55) Angora goats produce mohair, a durable, lightweight, soft, and warm natural fiber that Dolores weaves into wonderful articles of clothing. A full-length coat of twenty panels may be black and white, many colors, or a solid color. Eye-catching is her "Texas Flag" jacket, a bomber jacket created originally for former Texas governor Ann Richards. You'll be in good company if you decide upon one of Dolores's creations while here in one of the Hill Country's mohair capitals: Hillary Clinton is a customer, too.

UVALDE COUNTY

U valde County, down in the southwest corner of the Hill Country, was formed in 1850 from part of Bexar (pronounced "bear") County. It was named — more or less — for Gov. Juan de Ugalde of Coahuila, Mexico, a renowned Indian fighter. In 1790 Ugalde united the Comanche, Wichita, and Tawakona Indians and led them against a common enemy, the Mescalero Apache. The successful battle took place in a canyon that became known as

Canon del Ugalde; the county was named for the canyon, with the spelling anglicized to match the way Texans pronounced it.

Since the land is partly on the Edwards Plateau, locals describe Uvalde as having one foot in the Badlands and the other in the Hill Country. But because most of it is below the escarpment and consists of rolling hills, the land also lays claim to being "the back door to the Hill Country." Lots of cool, clear rivers run here, more than 1,100 miles of flowing streams — the spring-fed Sabinal, Frio, Leona, and Nueces Rivers — so Uvalde County is a popular place for water enthusiasts. The land is covered with cypresses, cedars, and, in one unique spot (for Texas), maple groves. It's a major deer and turkey hunting area, too.

Uvalde is the county seat; Concan and Utopia are small communities on the sparkling clear Frio River, with resorts, camps and campgrounds, outfitters, and a restaurant or two.

Uvalde

Both "Cactus Jack" Garner (former Vice President John Nance Garner) and former Texas governor Dolph Briscoe hailed from these parts. Uvalde has a tale of gunslinging days: Though some lawmen in the Old West left the law to become criminals, outlaw John King Fisher did the opposite. Fisher had begun a career of lawlessness in the wild border country, but after being carried off to jail a time or two, he reformed, and ended up as chief deputy sheriff of Uvalde County. Unfortunately his new occupation was short lived. He was ambushed, so the story goes, while he was in San Antonio on "official business." Thirteen bullets felled him — at the age of 26 — and he's buried in Uvalde's Pioneer Cemetery.

Concan

North of Uvalde, the great outdoors beckons along the lovely length of the crystal blue and white waters of the picturesque Frio River. A host of Concan area camps on the Frio offer hiking and water sports.

Utopia

Yes, there really is a Utopia, and it's on the Sabinal River across the Frio River from Concan. Originally the town had several other names, until along came a postmaster who happened to read Sir Thomas More's idea of Utopia: "Perfect climate, happy, healthy people . . ."

This is it, the postmaster decided, and Utopia it became.

UVALDE COUNTY LODGING

Cabins, camps, bed & breakfasts, motels, and combinations of them offer pleasant choices for places to stay in Uvalde, Concan, and Utopia.

For more information, contact the **Uvalde Convention and Visitors Bureau** (830-278-4115, 800-588-2533; www.uvaldecvb.org; 300 E. Main Ave., Uvalde, TX 78801).

Uvalde

On the front porch of Casa de Leona Bed & Breakfast, overlooking the Leona River in Uvalde.

Eleanor S. Morris

CASA DE LEONA BED & BREAKFAST
Host: Carolyn Durr.
830-278-8550.
1149 Pearsall Rd., PO Box 1829, Uvalde, TX 78802.
Price: Moderate to expensive.
Credit Cards: AE, MC, V.
Handicap Access: No.

Casa de Leona is right on the Leona River, and according to Carolyn, the catfish practically jump right out of the river. There's canoeing on the river — you can bring your own — as well as fishing. Breakfast is what Carolyn calls Texican: scrambled eggs with tortillas and refried beans along with fresh fruit, juices, and her homemade cinnamon rolls. Guest rooms line the center patio, and sometimes the fountain is running. Carolyn paints, so there's also her art studio and a gift shop. A sundeck, balcony, and gazebo make for lots of relaxation.

MOTELS

Amber Sky Motel (830-278-5602; 2005 E. Main, Uvalde, TX 78802) 40 units, all on ground floor.

Best Western Continental Inn (830-278-5671; 701 E. Main, Uvalde, TX 78802) 87 units, pool, playground, picnic area, handicap access.

Holiday Inn (830-278-4511; 920 E. Main, Uvalde, TX 78802) 151 units, pool, restaurant, cocktail lounge, handicap access

Inn of Uvalde (830-278-9173; 810 E. Main, Uvalde, TX 78802) 70 units, pool, restaurant, handicap access.

Concan

CAMP RIVERVIEW
Host: Jim Meyer.
830-232-5412.
HCR 70, Box 471, Concan, TX 78838.
Price: Inexpensive.
Credit Cards: MC, V.
Handicap Access: Yes.

Also close to Garner State Park, this is a fine place for family camping on the Frio River, with campsites, shelters, RV sites, cabins, tubing on the river, and lots of picturesque picnicking places. There's a country store here, too.

J & L RIVER CAMP
Host: John Clark.
830-232-5758.
HCR 70, Box 480, Concan, TX 78838.
Price: Inexpensive to Moderate.
Credit Cards: None.
Handicap Access: No.

On the Rio Frio, close to Garner State Park, J & L offers cabins and shelter, full RV hookups, and tent sites with water and electricity. They offer shuttle service, too, to tubers who want to float lazily down the river without worrying about how they're going to get back to camp.

Swimming, tubing, and snorkeling in cool Rio Frio at Neal's Lodges, Concan.

Eleanor S. Morris

NEAL'S LODGES & CAFE
Host: Mary Anna Roosa.
830-232-6118.

This complex includes sixty cabins, a riverside camping area, RV hookups, a dining room, general store, game room, stables, post office, and

Hwy. 127, PO Box 165,
    Concan, TX 78838.
On the Rio Frio.
Price: Inexpensive to
    Expensive.
Credit Cards: D, MC, V.
Handicap Access: Yes.

Utopia

UTOPIA ON THE RIVER
Host: Karyn Jones.
830-966-2444.
www.riverlodge.com.
Hwy. 187, PO Box 847,
    Utopia, TX 78884.
Price: Moderate.
Credit Cards: AE, D, MC, V.
Handicap Access: Yes.

laundromat. Besides camping, swimming, and tubing, there are hayrides, horseback rides, and bird-watching weekends.

Utopia on the River may resemble a motel in that the rooms are all in a row along a common walkway, but it's more like a bed & breakfast because you get full country breakfast every morning, served in the lodge/gift shop. Banana-bran pancakes or scrambled eggs and biscuits will fortify you for the walk down to the river to inspect the old cypress trees that may be anywhere from 750 to 800 years old. There's a hot tub, sauna, volleyball and horseshoes, hiking trails, fishing, and tubing on the Sabinal River, and swimming in the pool.

UVALDE COUNTY RESTAURANTS

This is the country of chicken-fried steak, barbecue, and Mexican, so if you're a vegetarian you'll starve to death," say the friendly folks of the Uvalde Convention & Visitors Bureau.

Uvalde

Bob Gagliardi of Evett's Barbecue, Uvalde, displays a tender brisket.

Eleanor S. Morris

EVETT'S BARBECUE
830-278-6204.
301 E. Main St., Uvalde, TX
　78801.
Price: Inexpensive.
Cuisine: Barbecue.
Serving: L, D Tues.–Sat.
Credit Cards: None.
Handicap Access: No.

The entire 300 block of Main Street is redolent with delicious mouthwatering odors, thanks to the outdoor barbecuing of this longtime Uvalde tradition. Bob Gagliardi is responsible, as he bastes the meat and stokes the fire alongside the small wooden building. Eating is done inside at picnic tables, and the decor is a windowful of paper towels. Evett's specializes in brisket, smoking anywhere from fourteen to twenty a day, and ribs, which are gone by 3pm — so if it's ribs you want, don't dawdle.

HARTS TEXAS GRILL
830-278-4422.
2217 E. Main St., Uvalde,
　TX 78801.
Price: Moderate.
Cuisine: Mexican-
　American.
Serving: L, D.
Credit Cards: AE, D, MC, V.
Handicap Access: Yes.

You can dine indoors or out under the shade in the festive atmosphere of the patio. The large menu is a mix of Mexican specialties, the ubiquitous chicken-fried steak, pizza, steaks, and seafood.

MR C'S RESTAURANT
830-278-6420.
1296 W. Main St., Uvalde,
　TX 78801.
Price: Inexpensive.
Cuisine: Mexican.
Serving: L, D daily.
Credit Cards: Yes.
Handicap Access: Yes.

For real Mexican food, this is the place. As proof, there's menudo (although Sundays only), not to mention cabrito and tatema, as well as your more usual tamales, enchiladas, etc. And if you're not in the mood for Mexican cuisine, there are steaks, seafood, and sandwiches on the menu.

TOWN HOUSE
　RESTAURANT
830-278-2428.
2105 E. Main St., Uvalde,
　TX 78801.
Price: Inexpensive.
Cuisine: Mexican-
　American.
Serving: B, L, D, SB.
Credit Cards: AE, D, MC, V.
Handicap Access: Yes.

The lunch buffet Sunday to Friday is fresh and tasty, as is the breakfast buffet both Friday and Saturday night as well as Sunday morning. The menu, like many in the Hill Country, ranges from enchiladas and chalupas to steaks and seafood. But it also has a few items that are different if you yearn for a change: liver smothered in onions, and ham steak crowned with grilled pineapple. And the chicken breast offers a choice: grilled or breaded and topped with cream gravy. Steaks and seafood are served with the restaurant's signature French toast, and there is a "Healthy Menu" low in fat and seasonings. Though the service was slow, nobody seemed to mind; this popular eatery either sets the town pace or goes along with it.

Concan

NEAL'S CAFE
830-232-6118.
Hwy. 127, PO Box 165,
  Concan, TX 78838.
On the Rio Frio.
Price: Moderate.
Cuisine: Country.
Serving: B, L Fri.–Sun., D
  weekends only.
Credit Cards: D, MC, V.
Handicap Access: Yes.

From the outdoor stone terrace of this restaurant on the grounds of Neal's Lodges (see "Lodging"), you get a gorgeous view of Rio Frio. Indoors, you get generous portions of fried catfish, chicken-fried steak, beef tips, fried chicken — or chalupas to remind you of the locale. "If people don't see what they want on the menu, they order it anyway," said waitperson Mary. "The fried chicken is Mrs. Neal's grandmother's recipe!"

Utopia

LOST MAPLES CAFE
830-966-2221.
Main St., Utopia, TX 78884.
Hwy. 187, 45 miles north of
  Uvalde.
Price: Inexpensive.
Cuisine: Family-style
  American-Mexican.
Serving: B, L, D.
Credit Cards: MC, V.
Handicap Access: Yes.

A surprise in this quaint country place, named for Lost Maples State Park just up the road in Real County, are the antique English church-pew booths. Rustic is the word otherwise, with wood floors, rough beam ceilings — and antiques for sale upstairs! The stools along the tin counter facing the kitchen walls were fully occupied, as was almost all the other seating in this popular place. Appetizers include cheese stixs and nachos. There are burgers and club sandwiches, with side orders including fries, onion rings, or Texas toast with gravy. Dinner choices are Mexican meals, steaks, even a fish or shrimp platter — all in all, a pretty complete menu. Delectable pies, meringues of lemon, coconut creme, chocolate, come from Iva Rae's Bakeshop down the street.

UVALDE COUNTY CULTURE

HISTORIC BUILDINGS AND MUSEUMS

A self-guided driving tour of the town's Heritage Homes starts at the **Grand Opera House,** winds past sixteen old homes, and takes in Pioneer Cemetery, where John Nance Garner and outlaw-turned-lawman John King Fisher are buried. The free tour map, created by the **Uvalde Convention & Visitors Bureau,** is available at the bureau (830-278-4113; 300 E. Main Ave., Uvalde, TX 78801).

**FIRST STATE BANK OF
UVALDE**
830-278-6231.

The extensive $2.5 million art collection of former Gov. and Mrs. Dolph Briscoe is housed in this large local bank. It's an amazing collection,

Eleanor S. Morris

Paintings at the First State Bank of Uvalde, a museum as well as a bank displaying art from the collection of Gov. and Mrs. Dolph Briscoe.

200 E. Nopal St., Uvalde, TX 78801.
Open: Mon.–Fri. 9am–3pm.
Admission: Free.

from Rembrandt etchings of 1633 to works of Gainsborough and Reynolds, plus such western artists as Warren and Salinas.

JOHN NANCE GARNER MUSEUM
830-278-5018.
333 N. Park, Uvalde, TX 78801.
Open: Mon.–Sat 9am–5pm, closed noon–1pm; summer Mon.–Sat. 9am–6pm, Sun. 1–5pm.
Admission: Adults $1, children 50¢.

This museum is in the former home of John Nance "Cactus Jack" Garner, congressman under Theodore Roosevelt and vice president under Franklin D. Roosevelt. He earned the nickname for his Texas plain-speaking: He once said that the office of vice president "isn't worth a bucket of warm spit." When his wife died in 1948, he gave the home to the city as a memorial to her. He died in 1967 a few weeks before his ninety-ninth birthday.

The museum is a treasure house of memorabilia, reflecting the personality of this Texas original. When he broke his gavel during his first day as new Speaker of the House, friends sent more than a hundred gavels as replacement, all now on display.

UVALDE GRAND OPERA HOUSE
830-278-4184.
100 W. North St., Uvalde, TX 78801.
Open: Tues.–Fri. 10am–5pm, Sat. 10am–1pm.

Built in 1891 and fully restored in 1982, this historic opera house offers a variety of dance and theater year-round. When most of Uvalde's buildings were wooden one-story places, this two-story brick edifice was a local marvel. As in many small-town opera houses, the stage is upstairs. The

Admission: Free; donations accepted.

charming peak-roofed bay window looking out over the street was used as an office by John Nance Gardner; although he bought the building in 1916, the show went on. The sculpture draped around the weather vane on the cupola is known as the "drunken dragon" — according to Uvalde folklore, the artist went out drinking with a buddy before getting to work, and this dragon was the result.

Nowadays, about four performances a year showcase area talent in music and drama. A small museum of local history is on the ground floor as well as a gift shop with dragon prints, armadillos, mugs, plaques, and charms.

NIGHTLIFE

Uvalde is surprisingly lively at night. **The Long Horn Club** (830-278-7790; 1131 W. Main, Uvalde, TX 78801) is decorated for Halloween all year long. Open Friday 5pm to midnight, Saturday 5pm to 1am, Thurs. 5pm to midnight, the big old dance hall has a DJ, pool tables, dart games, setups (BYOB), beer, wine, sodas, and juices. The **Purple Sage Dance Hall** (830-278-1006; Hwy 90 W., Uvalde, TX 78801), a big gray metal prefab that offers video and DJ music Thursday nights and a live band on Saturday night.

SEASONAL EVENTS

The year begins with the Uvalde County **Junior Livestock Show** in JANUARY.

In FEBRUARY, catch the **Sahawe Indian Dancers Winter Ceremonials**.

MAY brings the **Cinco de Mayo Festival**.

In JUNE take in **The Dance at Garner State Park** each Friday, Saturday, and Sunday night. Or enjoy the Old-West stories and music of the **Cowboy Serenade at Garner State Park** every Tuesday, Thursday, and Saturday night of the month.

The Sahawe Indian Dancers return in JULY for the **Summer Festival**.

In AUGUST is the Uvalde **Youth Rodeo**, and SEPTEMBER the **Diez y Seis Celebration**.

OCTOBER honors Uvalde's most famous son with the **Cactus Jack Festival** — a parade, horse races, carnival, dance, barbecue cook-off, and more.

In NOVEMBER, there's the **Chamber Arts & Crafts Show & Sale, Downtown Open House**.

DECEMBER, the **"City of Lights"** is turned on, and Santa arrives downtown. DECEMBER is also the time for a **Cowboy Christmas Celebration** and **Night Parade**.

UVALDE COUNTY RECREATION

Many of Uvalde County's recreational activities are based at the camps, lodges, and other places to stay along the Leona, Frio, and Sabinal Rivers (see "Lodging"). For additional places to camp, fish, golf, get out in or on the water, go hiking or bird-watching, and generally relax and enjoy the scenery, visit the county's parks (see below). Another place for a swim is Uvalde's local pool (830-278-7531, Nopal and Wood), open from May to mid-August.

PARKS

Chalk Bluff Park (830-278-5515; www.chalkbluff.com; HC 33 Box 566, Uvalde, TX 78801, 15 miles north of Uvalde on Hwy. 55) This family vacation center on the beautiful Nueces River offers shady camping sites, primitive or with amenities, RV sites, cabins (some with air-conditioning), shelters with picnic tables and barbecue pits, tubing, swimming, scuba diving, fishing, put-put golf, and bird-watching. There's also a children's playground with swings and slides, and games such as volleyball, tetherball, and horseshoes. Rest rooms with shower pavilion, full RV hookups, horseback riding.

Garner State Park (830-232-6132; www.tpwd.state.tx.us/park/parks.htm; HCR #70 Box 599, Concan, TX 78838, 31 miles north of Uvalde on Hwy. 83) The 1,420-acre park was constructed in the 1930s by the WPA and named for John Nance Garner, vice president under FDR. With more than 10 acres of frontage on the Frio River, the beautiful park is pretty popular, so camping reservations are almost a necessity, at least during the summer months. The park has 211 camp-sites with water, 146 with water and electricity, screened shelters, rest rooms, showers, dump stations, cabins, a grocery store, laundromat, and various shops.

A riverside forest, a gallery of bald cypress, and pecan and live oak dominating the main developed area make the park a haven for birds and heaven for bird-watchers. The Texas Parks and Wildlife Department offers a helpful pamphlet, *Birds of Garner State Park*. For a copy, contact them at 800-792-1112; 4200 Smithville Rd., Austin, TX 78744.

Jardin de los Heroes Park (801 W. Main, Uvalde, TX 78801) The "Garden of the Heroes" honors Uvalde Vietnam War veterans. Picnic facilities and play-ground equipment are provided.

Uvalde Memorial Park and Golf Course (830-278-6155; 329 E. Garden, Uvalde, TX 78801) Set on the shady banks of the Leona River, which flows through town, the park has a long jogging and walking trail along the river, a covered pavilion, and the Sahawe Indian Outdoor Theater. Municipal tennis courts and the golf course are open to the public. Golfers can play Tues.–Sun. 8am–8pm; fees are $10 weekdays, $12 weekends for 18 holes, $15 for cart rentals. (The word is that the course is not so easy that it's not fun — but not so hard you wish it were time to go home.)

TENNIS

Uvalde High School has twelve lit courts, no reservations required. There are two more lit courts at **Uvalde Memorial Park** (830-278-6155; 329 E. Garden, Uvalde, TX 78801).

UVALDE COUNTY SHOPPING

U valde is a large center for wool and mohair — angora goats were brought to Texas in 1849, and since the 1920s Texas has been the largest producer of mohair in the country. You'll find Western wear and accessories here, too.

Uvalde

Joe Pena's Saddle Shop (830-278-6531; 2521 E. Main, Uvalde, TX 78801) Leather gear has been hand-tooled here for such celebrities as John Wayne, Joe Namath, and Nick Nolte as well as the Texas Rangers.

Julien the Village Pedlar (830-278-2925; 200 N. Getty, Uvalde, TX 78801) Here you'll find upscale clothing and accessories for men, women, and children.

Just For You (830-278-9571; 250 E. Main, Uvalde, TX 78801) In this nonprofit shop in the Adults Activity Center (Uvalde's senior citizens center), shoppers will find all sorts of handmade items: hand-stitched quilts, shirts, and vests, and crafts as well as some antiques and used books. Open Mon.–Fri. 9:30am–5pm, Sat. 9:30am–1pm.

Market Square Antiques (830-278-1294; 103 N. West St., Uvalde, TX 78801) This multidealer shop in the old Horner's Building on the square in downtown Uvalde displays antiques, classic furniture, jewelry, glassware, accents, collectibles, and gifts. Open Mon.–Sat. 10am–5pm, Sun. "by chance."

Uvalde Producers Wool & Mohair Co. (830-278-5663; Hwy. 90 E., Uvalde, TX 78801) All sorts of wool and luxury fibers are for sale here, both in the wholesale showrooms and the retail shop, which is open Mon.–Fri. 8am–noon, 1–5pm.

The West, Fine Western Wear and Cowboy Furnishings (830-591-2401;120 N. Getty, Uvalde, TX 78801) You can't miss this shop right downtown, what with the sign out front of silhouettes of a bunch of lassoing cowboys galloping toward you. Belt buckles, watches, jewelry, squaw skirts and Western shirts — you'll find everything and anything Western in this Main St. shop, even western cedar furniture with Western linens to match.

Concan

Neal's General Store (830-232-6118; Hwy. 127, PO Box 165, Concan, TX 78838, at Neal's Lodges on the Rio Frio) T-shirts, caps, and scarves among the convenience store items — and used paperbacks, in case you want to loll alongside the river and read.

CHAPTER SEVEN
Hill Country Help
INFORMATION

Eleanor S. Morris

A wall of brochures at the Austin Visitors Center.

Here is a brief compendium of miscellaneous information that may prove valuable for visitors — and perhaps residents as well.

AMBULANCE/FIRE/POLICE

Dial **911** to request an ambulance, to report a fire or any situation requiring immediate police response, or to get help for any and all emergencies in the Hill Country.

AREA CODES

Like other regions of the country, Texas is gaining new area codes. Following a round of changes in 1996–97, there are four area codes for the

Hill Country: **210, 512, 915,** and **830.** Here are codes for each county as of this printing:

County	Area Code
Bandera	830
Bexar (San Antonio)	210
Blanco	830
Burnet	512, 830
Comal	830
Gillespie	830
Hays	512
Kendall	830
Kerr	830
Kimble	915
Llano	915
Mason	915
Medina	830
Real	830
Travis (Austin)	512
Uvalde	830

BANKS

A ustin and San Antonio have dozens of banks and ATM machines, so perhaps the easiest thing to do is obtain whatever cash you might need in either city before heading out to the Hill Country. Two good sources for bank information are a town's visitors guide, which you can usually pick up at the chamber of commerce or visitors center, and the local weekly newspaper. Nowadays, though, convenience stores throughout the Hill Country have ATM machines.

BOOKS ABOUT TEXAS AND THE HILL COUNTRY

H ere are just a few of the many books available about the Texas Hill Country and Texas in general.

Chariton, Wallace O. *One Hundred Days in Texas: The Alamo Letters*. Plano, TX: Wordware Publishing, 1990.

Chipman, Donald E. *Spanish Texas 1519–1821*. Austin: University of Texas Press, 1992.

Crow, Melinda. *The Rockhound's Guide to Texas*. Helena, MT: Falcon Press, 1994.

Douglas, Curran. *Austin Overview*. Austin: Eakin Press, 1995.

Frantz, Joe B. *Texas: A Bicentennial History*. New York: W. W. Norton & Company, 1976.

A Guide to San Antonio Architecture. The San Antonio Chapter of the American Institute of Architects, 1986.

Haley, James L. *Texas: An Album of History*. New York: Doubleday & Company, 1985.

———. *Texas: From the Frontier to Spindletop*. New York: St. Martin's Press, 1985.

Haram, Karen, ed. *San Antonio Cuisine*. Kansas City, MO: Two Lane Press, 1994.

Hill Country Oasis: Barton Springs. Barton Creek. Edwards Aquifer. Austin Parks and Recreation Department, 1992.

Lind, Michael. *The Alamo: An Epic*. Boston: Houghton Mifflin, 1997.

Loughmiller, Campbell, and Lynn Loughmiller. *Texas Wildflowers: A Field Guide*. Foreword by Lady Bird Johnson. Austin: University of Texas Press, 1996.

Michener, James A. *Texas*. New York: Random House, 1985.

Morris, Eleanor S. *Country Roads of Texas*. Oaks, PA: Country Roads Press, 1997

———. *Country Towns of Texas*. Oaks, PA: Country Roads Press, 1999.

———. *Fairs and Festivals of Texas*. Oaks, PA: Country Roads Press, 1996.

———. *Recommended Country Inns of the Southwest: Arizona, New Mexico and Texas*. Old Saybrook, CT: Globe Pequot Press, 1997.

Permenter, Paris, and John Bigley. *Day Trips from San Antonio and Austin*. Kansas City, MO: Two Lane Press, 1995.

———. *Texas Barbecue*. Kansas City, MO: Pig Out Publications, 1994.

———. *Texas Getaways for Two*. Kansas City, MO: Two Lane Press, 1996.

Spearing, Darwin. *Roadside Geology of Texas*. Missoula, MT: Mountain Press Publishing, 1991.

Weems, John Edward. *Dream of Empire: A Human History of the Republic of Texas 1836–1846*. New York: Simon and Schuster, 1971.

Zelade, Richard. *Texas Monthly Guide to the Hill Country*. Houston: Gulf Publishing, 1997.

———. *Texas Monthly Guide to Austin*. Houston: Gulf Publishing, 1996.

CLIMATE AND WEATHER

The Hill Country's location on many rivers and streams ensures a mild climate with an average annual temperature of 70 degrees F. The climate in and around Austin is humid subtropical; but although summer daytime temperatures are hot, summer nights are often more pleasant, with average daily minimums in the lower 70s.

The Hill Country is less humid than either Austin or San Antonio, and it becomes dryer as you head west. The average annual rainfall varies from one location to another (Austin's average is 27.86 inches). The heaviest rain occurs in spring, usually a steady, light rain. Summer rains are usually thundershowers, with large amounts falling in a short time. Snow is very rare and completely insignificant as a source of moisture. When it does fall, it melts soon after reaching the ground.

Prevailing winds are southerly throughout most of the year. The occasional northerly winds, accompanying colder air masses in winter, move over the Gulf of Mexico and soon shift to southerly. Damaging hailstorms and destructive winds are infrequent. Although strong winds, along with sharp drops in temperature, sometimes occur during the winter months as the result of cold fronts, these are of short duration, rarely lasting more than a day or two.

About the only drawback to this temperate climate is the occasional dry spring, during which drought dries up the Hill Country rivers, followed by a season of torrential rains that flood the very same rivers. When this occurs, Hill Country roads can be dangerous to drive. Be sure to heed the cautions in the text (and the signs along the roads); people have drowned trying to drive across low-water crossings during rainy seasons.

But such deluges are infrequent. The Hill Country usually enjoys an average of 300 days of sunshine each year, and winters are truly mild, with below-freezing temperatures rarely occurring more than a few days each year.

COUNTY SHERIFFS

Travelers rarely need the services of county sheriffs, but it's reassuring to know that they're there. Here are numbers to call — "nonemergency" numbers if you have business that doesn't require the use of 911:

Bandera	830-796-3771
Bexar	210-270-6000
Blanco	830-868-7105
Boerne	830-249-9721
Burnet	512-756-8080
Castroville	830-931-4020
Comal	830-620-3400
Gillespie	830-997-7585
Hays	512-393-7896
Kerr	830-896-1216
Kendall	830-249-9721
Kimball	915-446-2766
Llano	915-247-5050
Mason	915-347-5580

Medina	830-741-6150
Real	830-232-5201, or
	911 if no answer
Travis	512-473-9770
Uvalde	830-278-4111

HOSPITALS AND HEALTH CARE

Austin

Brackenridge Hospital (512-476-6461; 601 E. 15 St., Austin, TX 78701)
St. David's Hospital (512-476-7111; 919 E. 32 St., Austin, TX 78705
Seton Medical Center (512-323-1000; 1201 W. 38 St., Austin, TX 78705)
Columbia St. David's South Hospital (512-447-2211; 901 W. Ben White Blvd., Austin, TX 78704)

San Antonio

Methodist Hospital (210-575-4000; 7700 Floyd Curl Dr., San Antonio, TX 78229).
St. Luke's Baptist Hospital (210-617-7000; 7930 Floyd Curl Dr., San Antonio, TX 78229).
San Antonio Community Hospital (210-692-8110; 8026 Floyd Curl Dr., San Antonio, TX 78229).
Southwest General Hospital (210-921-2000; 7400 Barlite Blvd., San Antonio, TX 78224).

Hill Country

Hospitals are located in the major Hill Country towns. Some examples:

Burnet/Marble Falls: Highland Lakes Medical Center (512-756-6000; Hwy. 281 S., Burnet, TX 78611).
Castroville: See San Antonio hospitals.
Fredericksburg/Mason: Hill Country Memorial Hospital (830-997-4353; 1020 Kerrville Hwy., Fredericksburg, TX 78624); serves Gillespie, Mason, Blanco, and other surrounding counties.
Kerrville: Sid Peterson Memorial Hospital (830-896-4200; 710 Water St., Kerrville, TX 78028).
Kimball: Kimble Hospital (915-446-3321; 2101 N. Main, Junction, TX 76849)
Llano: Llano Memorial Hospital (915-247-5040; 200 W. Ollie, Llano, TX 76843)
New Braunfels: McKenna Memorial Hospital (830-606-9111;143 E. Garza, New Braunfels, TX 78130).
San Marcos/Wimberley: Central Texas Medical Center (512-353-8979;1301 Wonder World Dr., San Marcos, TX 78666).

Uvalde: Uvalde Memorial Hospital (830-278-6251; 1025 Garner Field Rd., Uvalde, TX 78801).

LATE-NIGHT FOOD AND FUEL

Out in the Hill Country, folks tend to retire early. But there's still help for those out and about late at night.

If you're benighted in *Bandera*, the **Gas Go Market** at 1001 Main St. is open late at night; In *Burnet* there's **Country Corner** on Hwy. 29 W. In *Castroville* several gas stations stay open until 11pm weekdays, midnight on weekends. In *Comfort* the **Mini Mart #6,** Hwy. 87 and Lindner Ave., 830-995-3232, is open 24 hours and has an ATM machine. **Jek's Pit Stop** in *Fredericksburg* is open 24 hours. In *Kerrville* the **Town & Country** and **Circle K** gas and convenience stores are open late or all night. *Llano* also has a **Circle K**; in *Marble Falls*, the **Circle K** is on Hwy. 1431 W.

Diamond Shamrock in *Leakey* is open until 10 pm. In *Mason* the **Short Stop** is open 24 hours; **Pit Stop Food Mart** is on I-35 in *New Braunfels*. In *San Marcos* both the north and the south **Phillips 66** stations are open late. *Stonewall* has two gas/convenience stores on Hwy. 290, which are open late. In *Uvalde* the **Kettle**, 629 E. Main St., is open 24 hours. In *Wimberley* the **Texaco** and **Diamond Shamrock** gas stations are open late or all night.

NEWSPAPERS AND MAGAZINES

The Hill Country's proximity to its two gateway cities of Austin and San Antonio means that folks in the Hill Country are likely to read the *Austin American-Statesman* or the *San Antonio Express-News* for their daily news fix, while counting on weeklies like Kendall County's *Hill Country Recorder* for local news.

Austin

The Austin American Statesman (512-445-3500; 305 S. Congress Ave., Austin, TX 78704) The only daily newspaper in Austin. The paper publishes a comprehensive entertainment section every Thurs.

The Austin Business Journal (512-494-2500; 1301 Capital of Texas Hwy., Austin, TX 78746) Covers Austin business news; look for it on Fri.

The Austin Chronicle (512-454-5766; 4000 N. IH-35, Austin, TX 78751) Weekly newspaper covering arts, culture, entertainment, politics.

San Antonio

The San Antonio Business Journal (210-341-3202; 70 NE Loop 410, Ste. 350, San Antonio, TX 78216) Weekly business newspaper.

San Antonio Current (210-828-7660; 1500 N. St. Mary's St., San Antonio, TX 78215) A free newsweekly all about the Alamo City.

The San Antonio Express-News (210-225-7411; Ave. E and 3rd St., San Antonio, TX 78205) The only daily newspaper in San Antonio. The paper publishes a comprehensive entertainment section every Fri.

Hill Country

You'll find an array of Hill Country (mostly) weekly newspapers with news and information geared not only to the locals but also to visitors. Here are some:

Bandera Bulletin, Bandera County.
Blanco County News, Blanco County.
Boerne Star, Kendall County.
Burnet Bulletin, Burnet County.
Castroville News Bulletin, Medina County.
Comfort News, Kendall County.
Cowboy Country Express (published monthly in Rio Frio), Real County.
Fredericksburg Standard-Radio Post, Gillespie County.
Hill Country Recorder, Blanco, Hays, Kendall County.
Junction Eagle, Kimble County.
Kerrville Daily Times, Kerr County.
Llano News, Llano County.
Mason County News, Mason County.
Mountain Sun, Kerr County.
New Braunfels Herald-Zeitung, Comal County.
San Marcos Daily Record, Hays County.
Traveler Magazine, Uvalde County.
Uvalde Leader News, Uvalde County.
Wimberley View, Hays County.

RELIGIOUS SERVICES

Hill Country towns have virtually hundreds of churches. You'll find a complete listing of churches and other places of worship in the Saturday edition of the *Austin American Statesman* and the *San Antonio Express-News* as well as in local weeklies like the *Hill Country Recorder* and the *Fredericksburg Standard* (see "Newspapers and Magazines").

Another good source for church information is a town's visitors guide, which you can usually pick up at the local chamber of commerce or visitors center.

For both a religious and historic experience, visit one of the San Antonio missions, all of which still function as parish churches (see the chapter on San Antonio, "Historic Sites and Districts").

ROADSIDE SERVICE

The following is a selected list, by town, of service stations providing emergency towing service.

Bandera: Hill Country Towing, 830-535-4592.

Boerne: Five Star Wrecker, 830-981-9198.

Burnet: Advantage Towing, 512-756-7995; Gary's Wrecker Service, 512-756-6666.

Castroville: McVay's Wrecker Service, 830-538-2207.

Fredericksburg: Behrends Tire and Auto Center, 830-997-2668.

Junction: Loeffler Motor Company, 915-446-2416; Nelson Motor Company, 915-446-4444.

Kerrville: Krauss Wrecker and Road Service, 830-257-3477.

Leakey: Leakey Auto Supply and Wrecker Service, 830-232-6656.

Llano: Harden Garage, 915-247-4956.

New Braunfels: Hernandez Service Center, 830-629-4102.

Stonewall: Eckert & Son Wrecking, 830-644-2388.

Uvalde: Pike's Auto Wrecker, 830-278-2128.

Wimberley: Davis Tire Service, 512-847-2260.

TOURIST INFORMATION

There are numerous public or volunteer agencies ready to serve you with visitor and tourist information:

Austin Convention & Visitors Bureau: 512-474-5171, 800-926-2282; www.austin 360.com/acvb; 201-B E. 2nd, Austin, TX 78701.

Austin Convention & Visitors Bureau Events Line: 800-888-8287.

Bandera County Convention & Visitors Bureau: 830-796-3045, 800-364-3833; www.tourtexas.com/bandera/bandera.html; PO Box 171, Bandera, TX 78003.

Blanco Chamber of Commerce: 830-833-5101; www.blancotex.com; PO Box

626, Blanco, TX 78606.

Boerne Chamber of Commerce: 830-249-8000; www.boerne.org; One Main Plaza, Boerne, TX 78006.

Burnet County Chamber of Commerce: 512-756-4297; www.burnetchamber .org; 703 Buchanan Dr., Burnet, TX 78611.

Castroville Chamber of Commerce: 830-538-3142, 800-778-6775; www.castro ville.com; 802 London St., PO Box 572, Castroville, TX 78009.

Comfort Chamber of Commerce: 830-995-3131; www.comfort-texas.com; PO Box 777, Comfort, TX 78013.

Fredericksburg Convention & Visitors Bureau: 830-997-6523; www.freder icksburgtexas.net/cvb.htm; 106 N. Adams, Fredericksburg, TX 78624.

Frio Canyon Chamber of Commerce: 830-232-5222; PO Box 743, Leakey, TX 78873 (note: as of publication, there is no Web site).

Johnson City Tourism Bureau: 830-868-7684; www.Instar.com/johnsoncity/; PO Box 485, Johnson City, TX 78636.

Kerrville Convention & Visitors Bureau: 830-792-3535, 800-221-7958; 1700 Sidney Baker, Ste. 200, Kerrville, TX 78028.

Kimble County Chamber of Commerce & Tourism Board: 915-446-3190, 800-KIMBLE-4; www.junctiontexas.net; 402 Main St., Junction, TX 76849.

Llano Chamber of Commerce: 915-247-5354; www.llanochamber.org; 700 Bessemer, Llano, TX 78643.

Marble Falls/Lake LBJ Chamber of Commerce: 830-693-4449; www.marble-falls.org; 801 Hwy. 281, Marble Falls, TX 78654.

Greater New Braunfels Chamber of Commerce and Convention & Visitors Bureau: 830-625-2385, 800-572-2626; www.nbtexas.com; PO Box 311417, New Braunfels, TX 78131.

Nueces Canyon Chamber of Commerce: 830-597-6241; www.campwood.com; PO Box 369, Camp Wood, TX 78833.

San Antonio Convention & Visitors Bureau: 210-270-8700, 800-447-3372; www.sanantoniocvb.com; PO Box 2277, San Antonio, TX 78298.

San Marcos Convention & Visitors Bureau: 512-396-2495, 800-782-7653; www.sanmarcostexas.com; PO Box 2310, San Marcos, TX 78667.

Stonewall Chamber of Commerce: 830-644-2735; PO Box 1, Stonewall, TX 78671 (note: as of publication, there is no Web site).

Uvalde Convention & Visitors Bureau: 830-278-4115, 800-588-2533; www.uvaldecvb.org; 300 E. Main St., Uvalde, TX 78801.

Wimberley Chamber of Commerce: 512-847-2201; www.wimberley.org; PO Box 12, Wimberley, TX 78676.

IF TIME IS SHORT

Although we've tried to cover everything that makes the Hill Country special, how do you know what to choose if you have time for only one or two destinations or sights? Here are some highlights for those who have only a short time in the hills.

AUSTIN

In Austin, stay at the *Driskill*, even for only one night, to absorb some of the elegance that was so exceptional when everything else was pretty much raw frontier. Then take a look at that Texas pride, the tall **Texas State Capitol** of native pink limestone with fossils imbedded in the stone. If it's the right time of year, around sunset join the crowd waiting to watch the world's largest colony of Mexican freetail bats come out from under the **Congress Avenue Bridge** for the nightly insect feast. Another special Austin sunset is watching that spectacle over **Lake Travis** from the **Oasis Restaurant**.

WEST AND SOUTH OF AUSTIN

BURNET COUNTY

Longhorn Caverns, in the town of **Burnet**, sheltered everything from cavemen to Confederate gunpowder makers to a subterranean nightclub as an escape from the summer Hill Country heat. Take a light sweater or jacket and wear rubber-soled shoes for the tour. And up the road a piece at **Tow**, the **Vanishing Texas** cruise on **Lake Buchanan** views waterfalls and, in the fall, nesting bald eagles.

GILLESPIE COUNTY

Not to be missed is **Fredericksburg**. With its German-pioneer history, food, and *Gemütlichkeit* (friendliness), it's one of the Hill Country's most popular tourist spots. Check out the **Admiral Chester Nimitz Museum**, an outstanding record of the Pacific theater of World War II. Nimitz was a local boy who made good, and the museum is housed in his grandfather's Steamboat Hotel.

And you wouldn't want to pass up a chance to take a look at — and possibly climb — nearby **Enchanted Rock**, one of three such domes in the world.

Touring nearby **LBJ Ranch** in Johnson country is perfect for history buffs.

HAYS COUNTY

It would be a pity to miss the flavor, both gustatory and atmospheric, of the *Salt Lick*, that quintessential Texas barbecue pit just west of <u>*Wimberley*</u>.

SAN ANTONIO

Of course the *Alamo* in San Antonio is a must, as is the *River Walk*, even for an hour or so. Take some refreshment in the historic *Menger Hotel*'s bar, where Teddy Roosevelt recruited his Rough Riders. And the *Zoological Gardens and Aquarium* are counted among the best in the nation.

WEST AND NORTH OF SAN ANTONIO

BANDERA COUNTY

For a Hill Country Wild West experience, take in a *rodeo* in <u>*Bandera*</u> and follow it with some boot-scootin' across the sawdust at *Arkey Blue's* honky-tonk. And if you have time to spend a night or a weekend at the *Mayan* or the *Dixie Dude Ranch*, all the better.

COMAL COUNTY

In <u>*New Braunfels*</u> feast on goodies from *Naegelin's*, the oldest German bakery in these parts, before taking a look at the model of the German castle of Prince Solms's *Sophienburg Museum*. He's the nobleman who founded the town and fled.

KERR COUNTY

Don't miss the *Cowboy Artists of America Museum* in <u>*Kerrville*</u>, and try to spend a night at *Ye Kendall Inn* in <u>*Boerne*</u>. Maybe you'll see the ghosts that are rumored to roam there.

MEDINA COUNTY

<u>*Castroville*</u>'s *Landmark Inn* was once the only place to take a bath between San Antonio and California — check out the room where Robert E. Lee spent the night.

REAL COUNTY

For the scenic roller-coaster hill ride of your life, drive *FM 337* — slowly — from <u>*Vanderpool*</u> through <u>*Leakey*</u> to <u>*Camp Wood*</u>.

UVALDE COUNTY

In _Uvalde_ the extensive art collection of former Governor and Mrs. Dolph Briscoe is exhibited in the elegant *First State Bank of Uvalde*, an amazing group ranging from Rembrandt etchings of 1633 through works of Gainsborough and Reynolds. And be sure to see the historic *Uvalde Opera House*, crowned with its "Drunken Dragon" weather vane.

Index

LODGING BY PRICE CODE

RESTAURANTS BY PRICE CODE

Price Codes:
Austin & San Antonio:
Inexpensive   Up to $20
Moderate $21 to $30
Expensive $31 to $50
Very Expensive   Over $50

In the Counties:
Inexpensive   Up to $10
Moderate $10 to $20
Expensive $20 to $35
Very Expensive   Over $35

RESTAURANTS BY CUISINE

About the Author

Eleanor S. Morris is a world traveler, author, and photographer based in Austin, Texas. Widely published in national magazines, she has written several books about Texas and the Southwest: *City Smart: Austin; Country Roads of Texas; Country Towns of Texas; Fairs and Festivals of Texas;* and *Recomended Country Inns of the Southwest: Arizona, New Mexico and Texas.*